CHARACTERS...

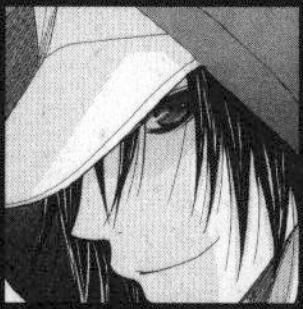

★ Akira ★
Chiharu Mori's partner-in-crime. He continues to stalk Teru and Kurosaki.

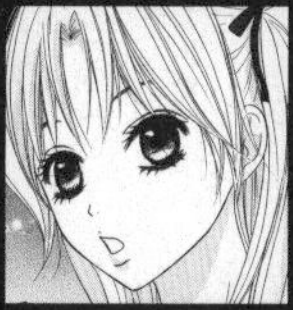

★ Rena ★
Teru's friend. Certainly not the docile type, but she tends to value her friends.

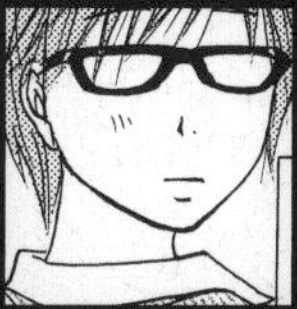

★ Kiyoshi Hasegawa ★
Teru's friend since grade school and Kurosaki's number two servant.

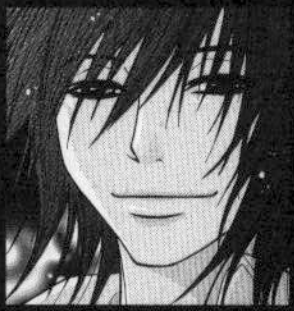

★ Soichiro Kurebayashi ★
Teru's older brother and a genius systems engineer. He died after leaving Teru in Kurosaki's care.

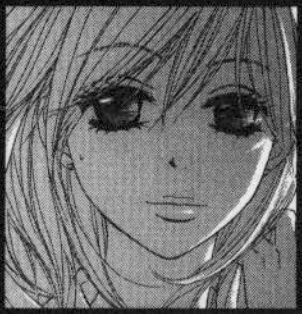

★ Chiharu Mori ★
She used to work at Teru's school. Teaming up with Akira, she continues to target Teru and Kurosaki.

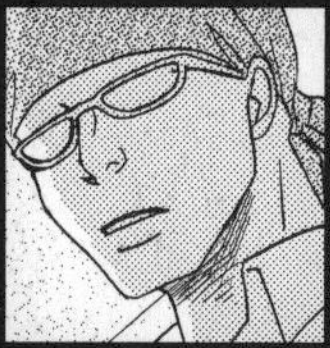

★ Boss (Masuda) ★
Currently runs the snack shop "Flower Garden" but used to work with Soichiro.

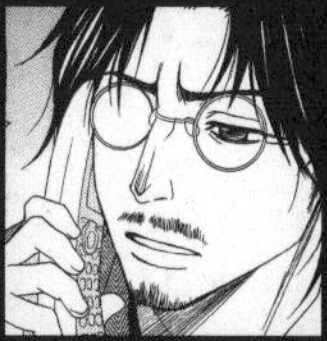

★ Director (Kazumasa Ando) ★
He used to work with Soichiro and is currently the director of Teru's school.

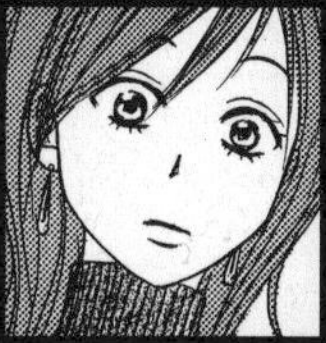

★ Riko Onizuka ★
She was Soichiro's girlfriend and is now a counselor at Teru's school.

STORY...

name and created the code virus known as "Jack Frost." In order to save Kurosaki from being charged with a "Jack Frost"-related murder, Soichiro worked nonstop to decipher the code and died in the process. Teru accepts this newfound knowledge about Kurosaki. She thanks him for all that he has done for her and asks him to stay by her side.

★ One day, Akira suddenly appears before Teru. Although Kurosaki comes to the rescue, Teru can't help but be frustrated with herself and her lingering fear of Akira... Meanwhile, Chiharu Mori meets with Rena's fiancé. Teru and company have no idea that another plot involving "Jack Frost" is about to unfold...!

Dengeki Daisy

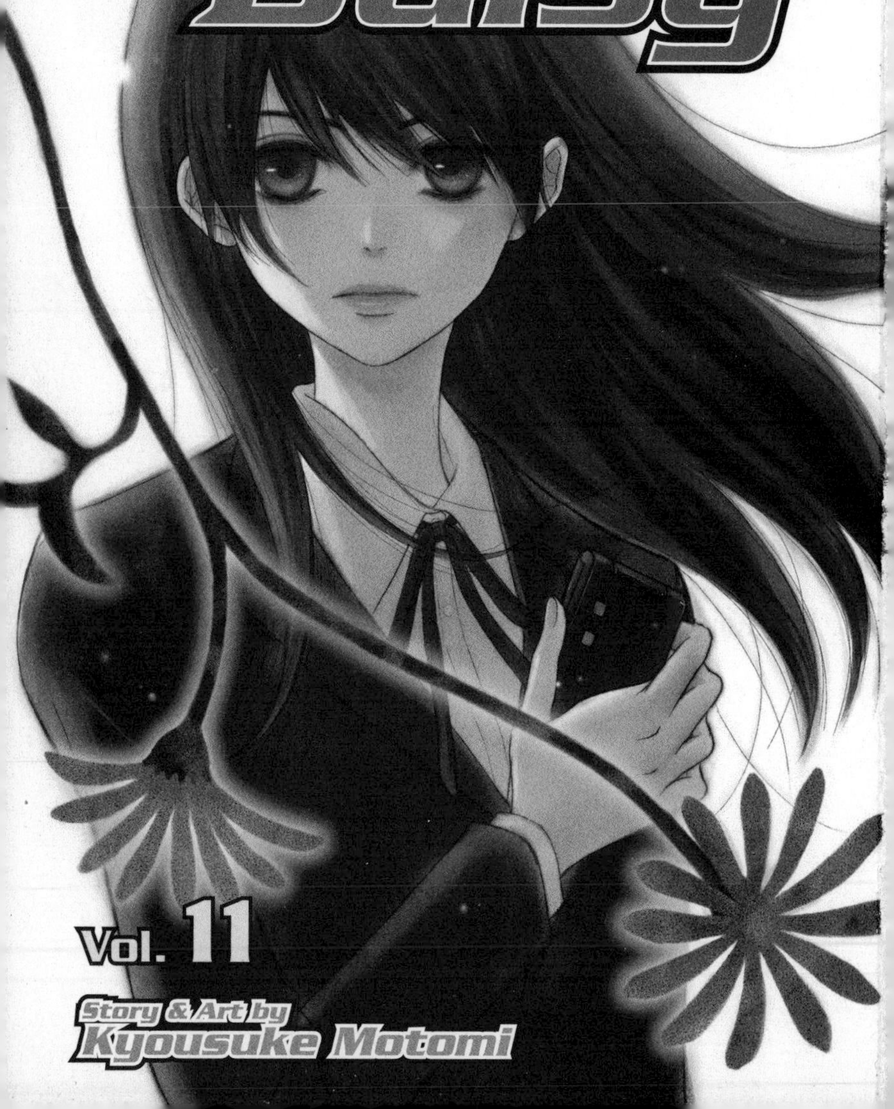

Vol. 11

Story & Art by
Kyousuke Motomi

Dengeki Daisy

Volume 11 CONTENTS

DAISY

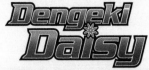

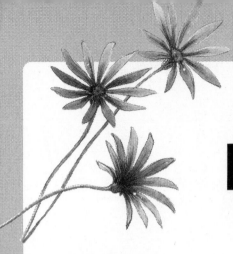

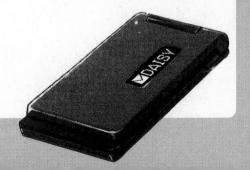

Dengeki Daisy Vol. 11

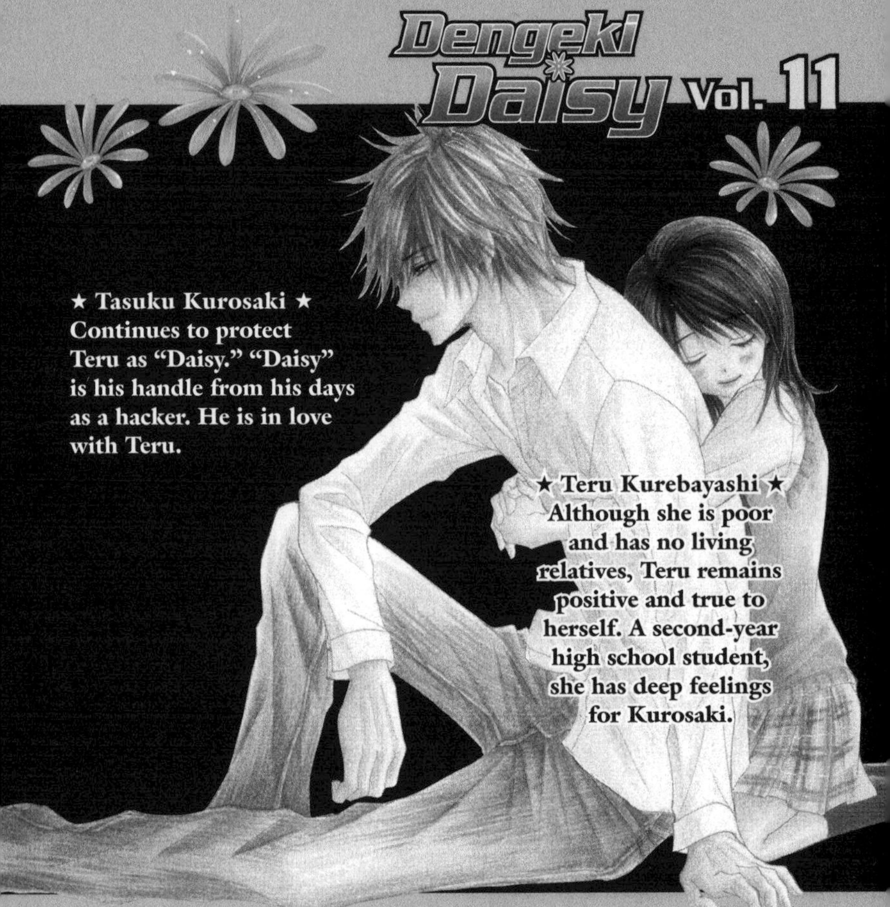

★ Tasuku Kurosaki ★
Continues to protect Teru as "Daisy." "Daisy" is his handle from his days as a hacker. He is in love with Teru.

★ Teru Kurebayashi ★
Although she is poor and has no living relatives, Teru remains positive and true to herself. A second-year high school student, she has deep feelings for Kurosaki.

★ Teru discovers that Kurosaki is Daisy, the mysterious person who supported and encouraged her after her brother's death. Thinking that there must be a reason why Kurosaki has chosen to hide his identity, Teru decides to keep this knowledge to herself.

★ During this time, Teru's life is threatened, and strange incidents involving Teru and Kurosaki occur. Kurosaki decides to disclose the truth to Teru, but Akira beats him to it and tells her about Kurosaki's past "sin." Learning what Akira has done, Kurosaki disappears from sight. Seeing Teru so despondent, the Director and Riko tell her about Kurosaki's past.

★ Teru learns that Kurosaki's father was involved with the development of a top-secret government code, and his death was shrouded in mystery. Kurosaki became a hacker to clear his father's

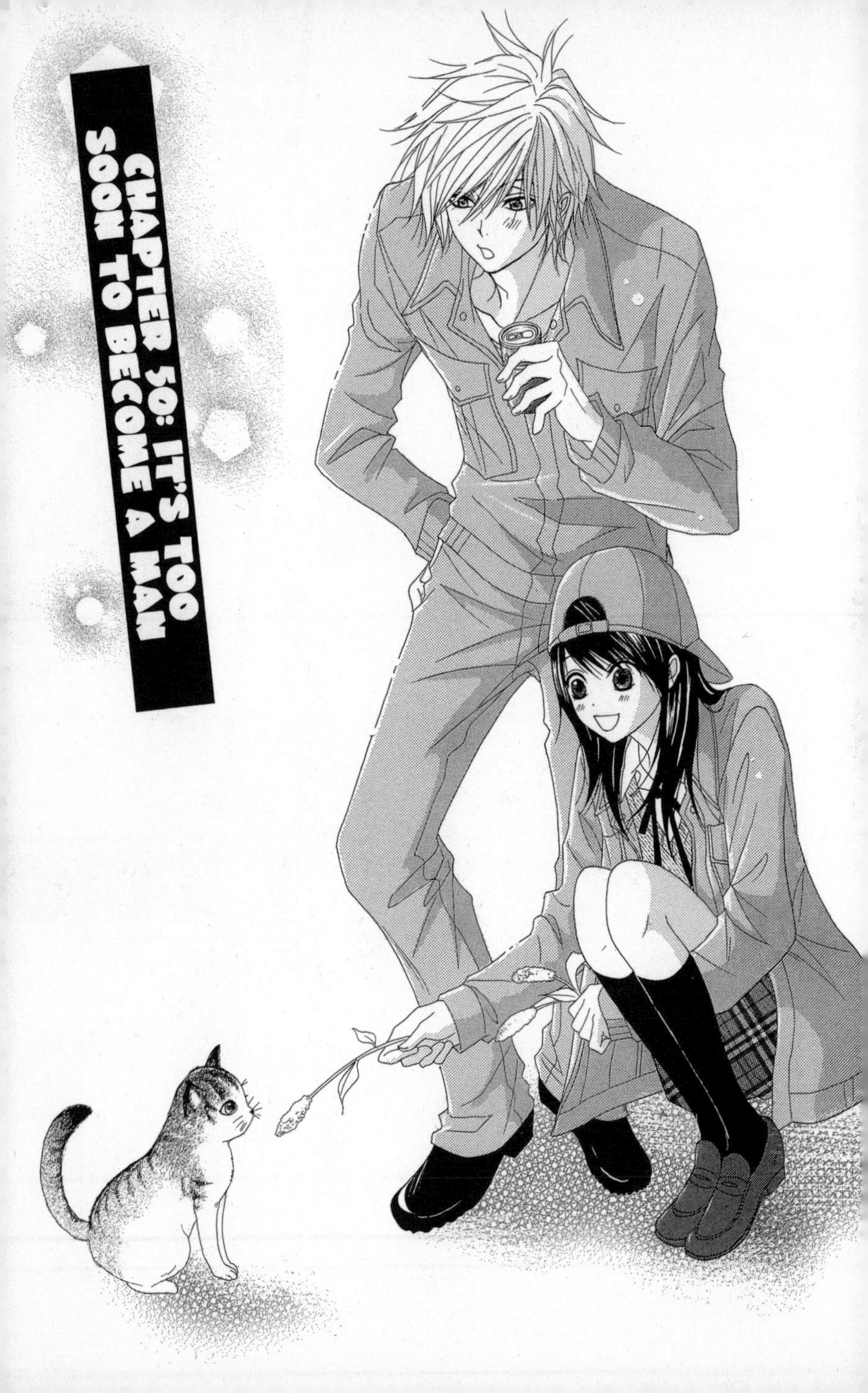
CHAPTER 50: IT'S TOO
SOON TO BECOME A MAN

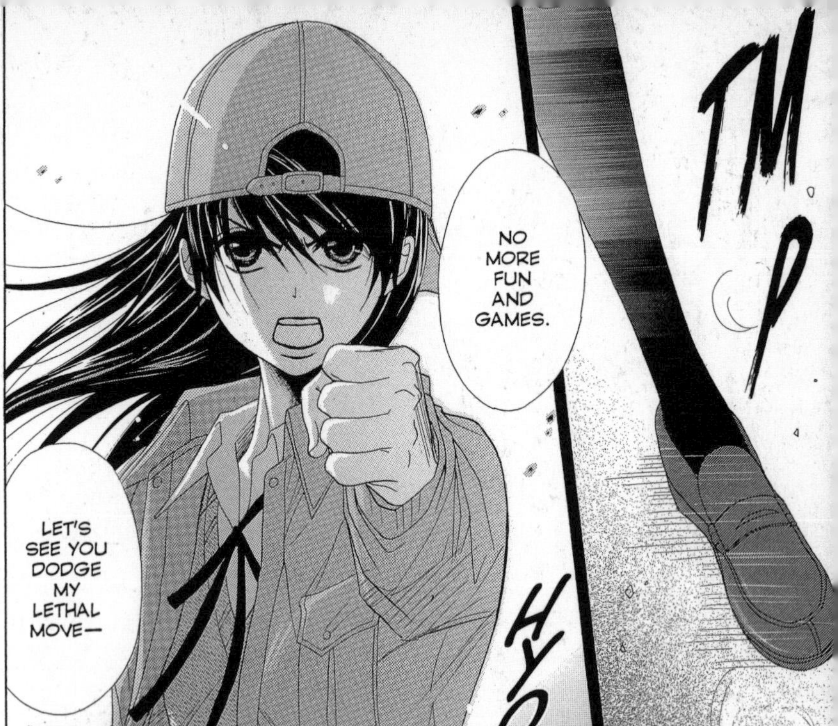
TMP
NO MORE FUN AND GAMES.
LET'S SEE YOU DODGE MY LETHAL MOVE—
HYOOOOO

HELLO, EVERYONE!!
IT'S KYOUSUKE MOTOMI.
THIS IS THE ELEVENTH VOLUME OF
DENGEKI DAISY!!! WOW!! TWO DOUBLE
DIGITS IN A ROW! THERE ARE ENOUGH
DENGEKI DAISIES TO FIELD A SOCCER TEAM!! (?)
IT WOULD MAKE ME HAPPY IF YOU ENJOY
THIS VOLUME TOO. PLEASE STAY WITH IT
UNTIL THE END!!

I'm writing this in the middle of winter, and the blue daisies in the garden are holding on through this cold season. While the perennials around them are flat on the ground, they are toughing it out and refusing to fall. Be strong!!!

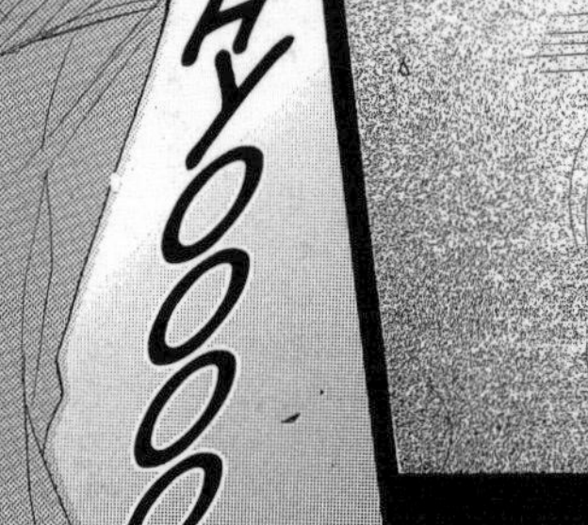

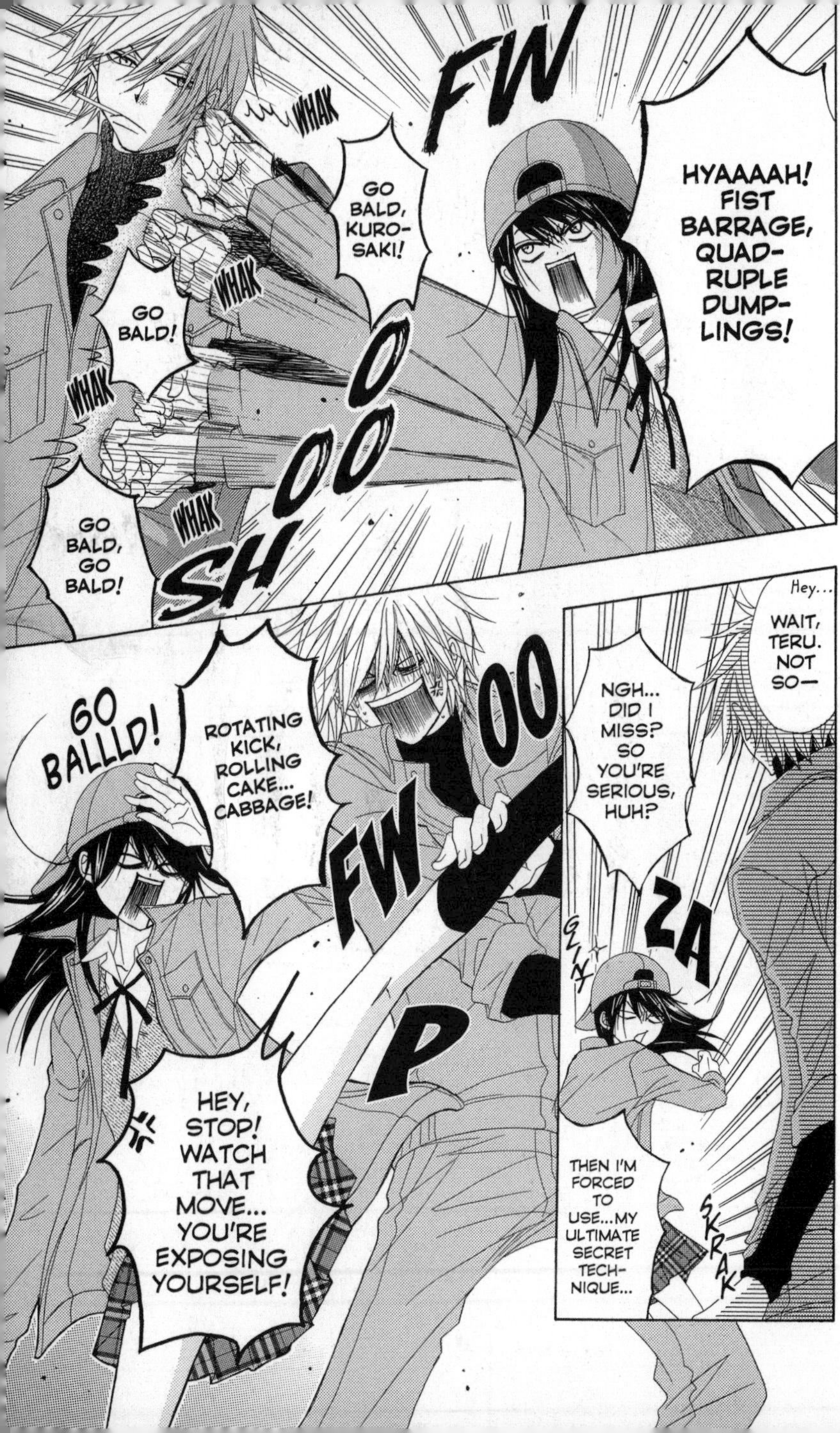
HYAAAAH! FIST BARRAGE, QUAD-RUPLE DUMP-LINGS!
FW
GO BALD, KURO-SAKI!
WHAK
WHAK
GO BALD!
WHAK
SHOOOO
WHAK
GO BALD, GO BALD!
Hey...
WAIT, TERU. NOT SO—
NGH... DID I MISS? SO YOU'RE SERIOUS, HUH?
ZA
GLINT
THEN I'M FORCED TO USE...MY ULTIMATE SECRET TECH-NIQUE...
SKRAK
FWOOP
ROTATING KICK, ROLLING CAKE... CABBAGE!
GO BALLLD!
HEY, STOP! WATCH THAT MOVE... YOU'RE EXPOSING YOURSELF!

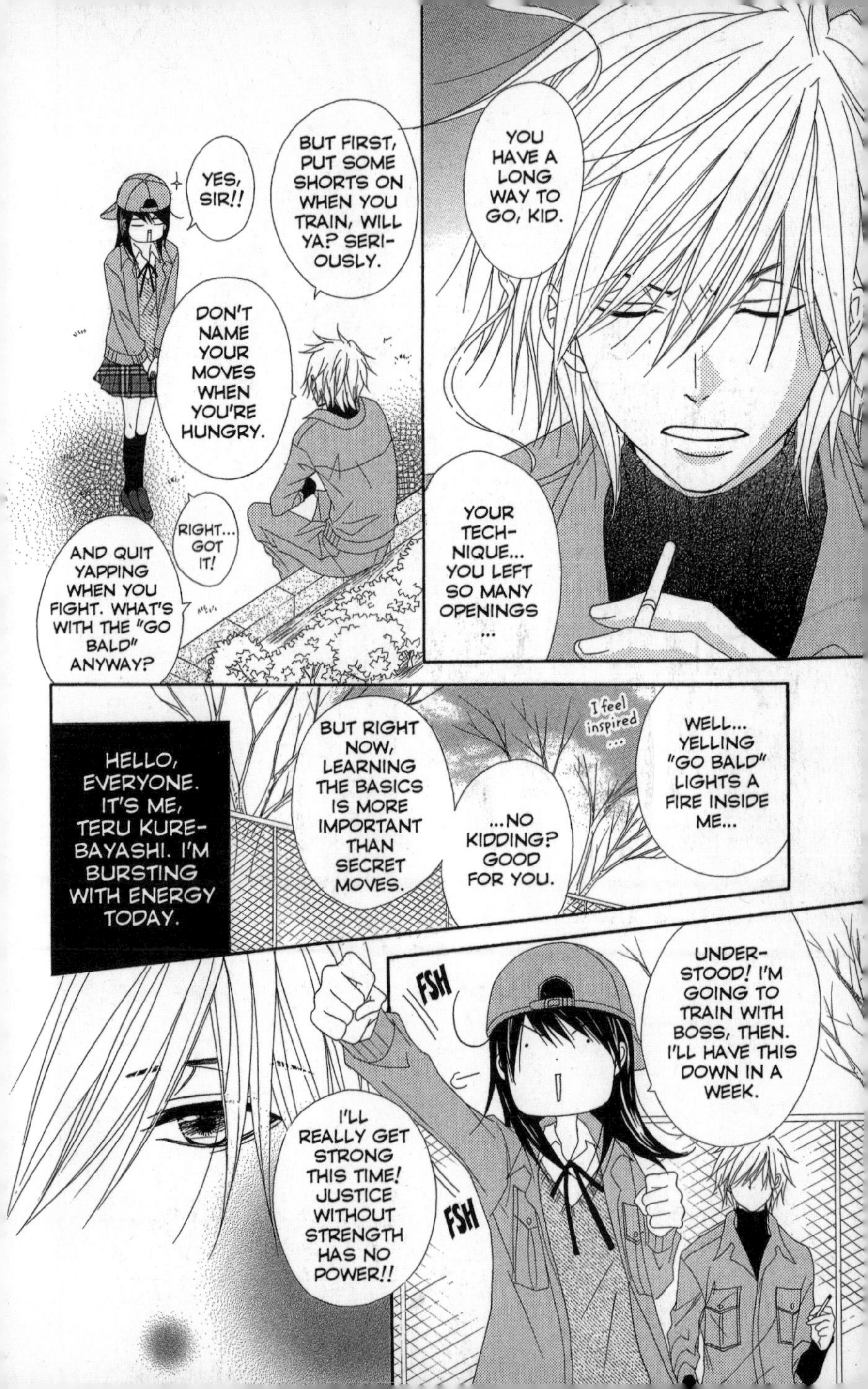
YOU HAVE A LONG WAY TO GO, KID.
YOUR TECHNIQUE... YOU LEFT SO MANY OPENINGS...
BUT FIRST, PUT SOME SHORTS ON WHEN YOU TRAIN, WILL YA? SERIOUSLY.
YES, SIR!!
DON'T NAME YOUR MOVES WHEN YOU'RE HUNGRY.
RIGHT... GOT IT!
AND QUIT YAPPING WHEN YOU FIGHT. WHAT'S WITH THE "GO BALD" ANYWAY?
WELL... YELLING "GO BALD" LIGHTS A FIRE INSIDE ME...
I feel inspired...
...NO KIDDING? GOOD FOR YOU.
BUT RIGHT NOW, LEARNING THE BASICS IS MORE IMPORTANT THAN SECRET MOVES.
HELLO, EVERYONE. IT'S ME, TERU KURE-BAYASHI. I'M BURSTING WITH ENERGY TODAY.
UNDER-STOOD! I'M GOING TO TRAIN WITH BOSS, THEN. I'LL HAVE THIS DOWN IN A WEEK.
FSH
FSH
I'LL REALLY GET STRONG THIS TIME! JUSTICE WITHOUT STRENGTH HAS NO POWER!!

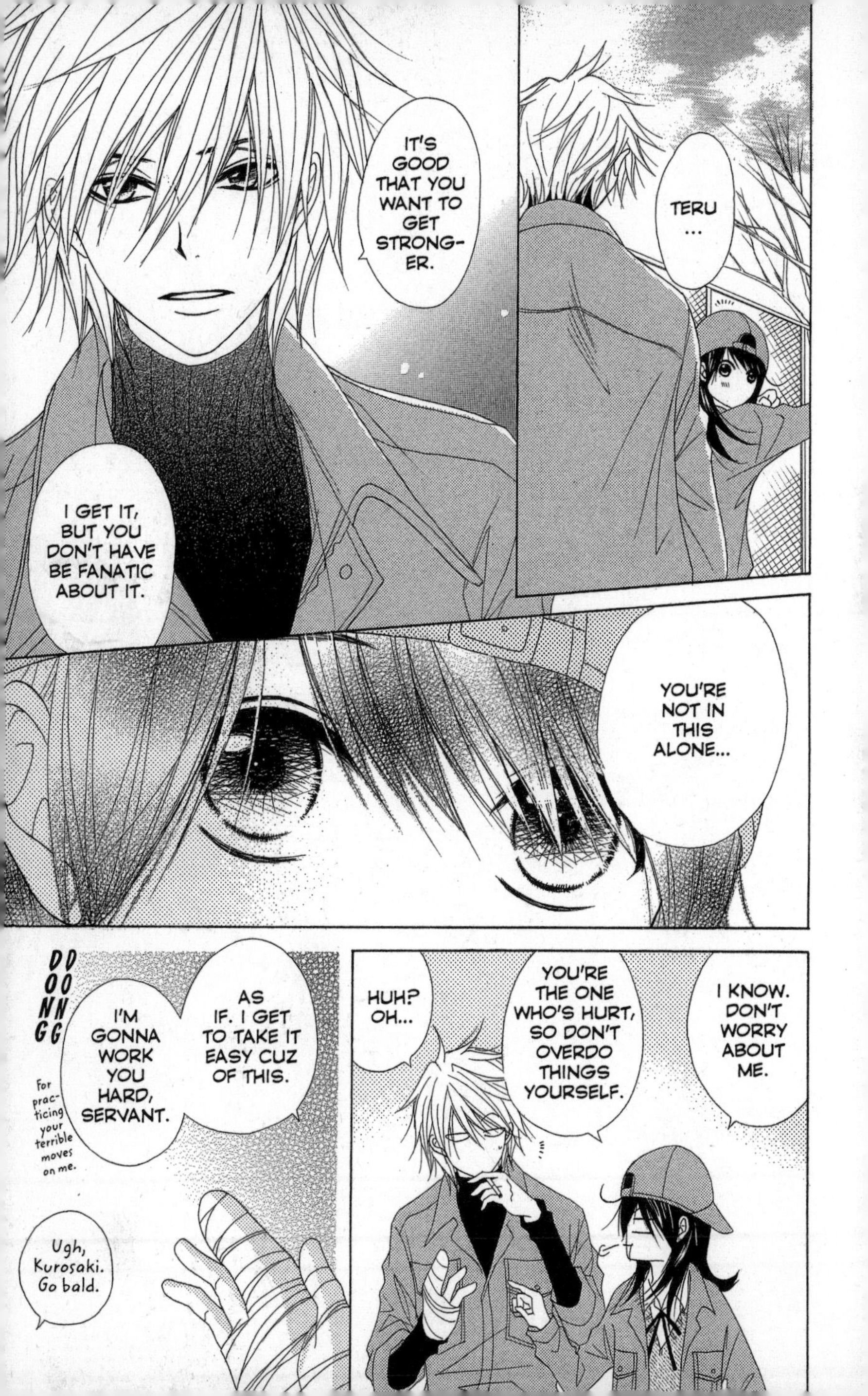
TERU...
IT'S GOOD THAT YOU WANT TO GET STRONGER.
I GET IT, BUT YOU DON'T HAVE BE FANATIC ABOUT IT.
YOU'RE NOT IN THIS ALONE...
I KNOW. DON'T WORRY ABOUT ME.
YOU'RE THE ONE WHO'S HURT, SO DON'T OVERDO THINGS YOURSELF.
HUH? OH...
AS IF. I GET TO TAKE IT EASY CUZ OF THIS.
I'M GONNA WORK YOU HARD, SERVANT.
DOONG
DOONG
For practicing your terrible moves on me.
Ugh, Kurosaki. Go bald.

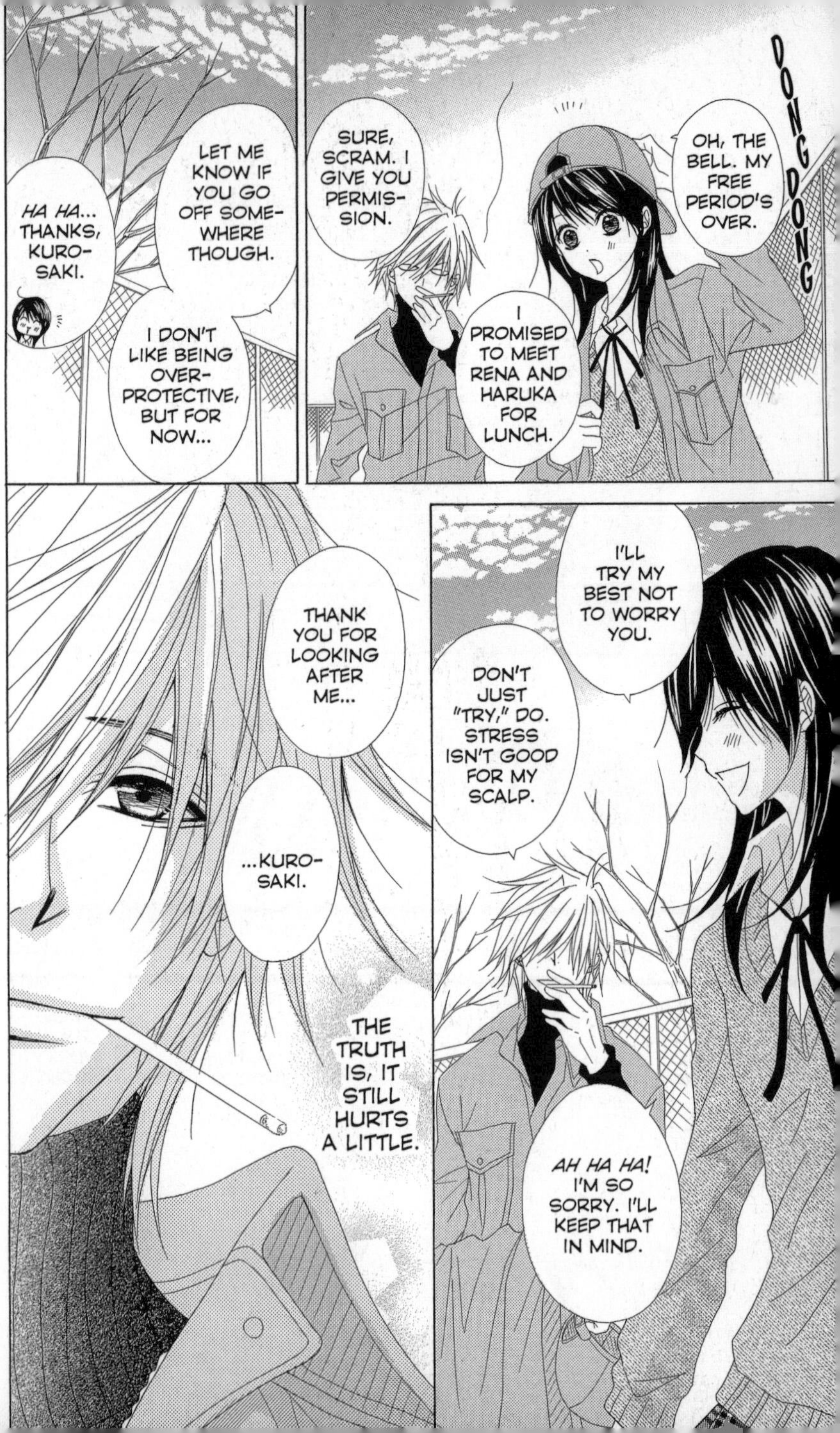
DONG DONG
OH, THE BELL. MY FREE PERIOD'S OVER.
I PROMISED TO MEET RENA AND HARUKA FOR LUNCH.
SURE, SCRAM. I GIVE YOU PERMISSION.
LET ME KNOW IF YOU GO OFF SOMEWHERE THOUGH.
I DON'T LIKE BEING OVERPROTECTIVE, BUT FOR NOW...
HA HA... THANKS, KUROSAKI.
I'LL TRY MY BEST NOT TO WORRY YOU.
DON'T JUST "TRY," DO. STRESS ISN'T GOOD FOR MY SCALP.
AH HA HA! I'M SO SORRY. I'LL KEEP THAT IN MIND.
THANK YOU FOR LOOKING AFTER ME...
...KUROSAKI.
THE TRUTH IS, IT STILL HURTS A LITTLE.

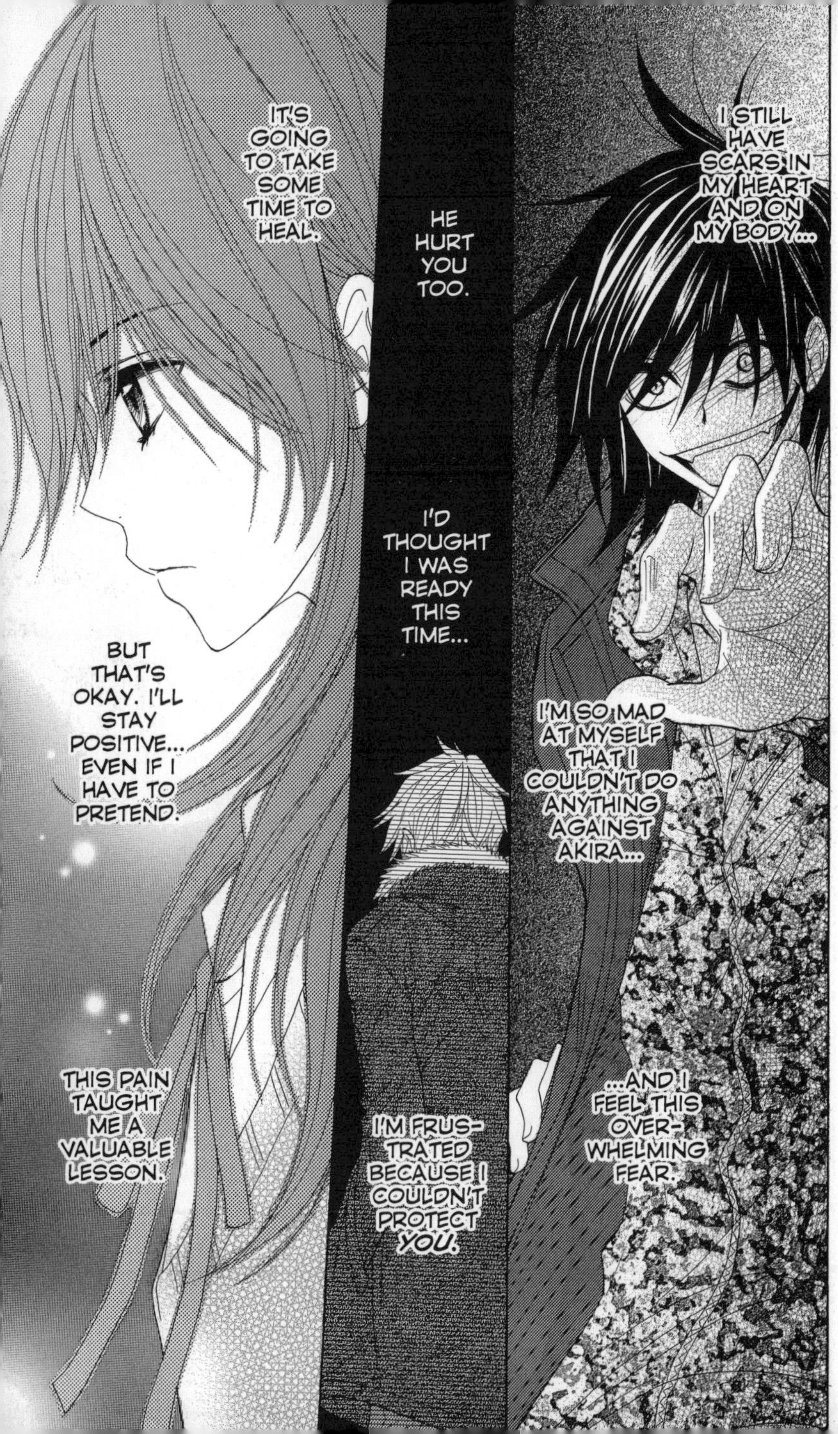
I STILL HAVE SCARS IN MY HEART AND ON MY BODY...
I'M SO MAD AT MYSELF THAT I COULDN'T DO ANYTHING AGAINST AKIRA...
...AND I FEEL THIS OVERWHELMING FEAR.
HE HURT YOU TOO.
I'D THOUGHT I WAS READY THIS TIME...
I'M FRUSTRATED BECAUSE I COULDN'T PROTECT *YOU.*
IT'S GOING TO TAKE SOME TIME TO HEAL.
BUT THAT'S OKAY. I'LL STAY POSITIVE... EVEN IF I HAVE TO PRETEND.
THIS PAIN TAUGHT ME A VALUABLE LESSON.

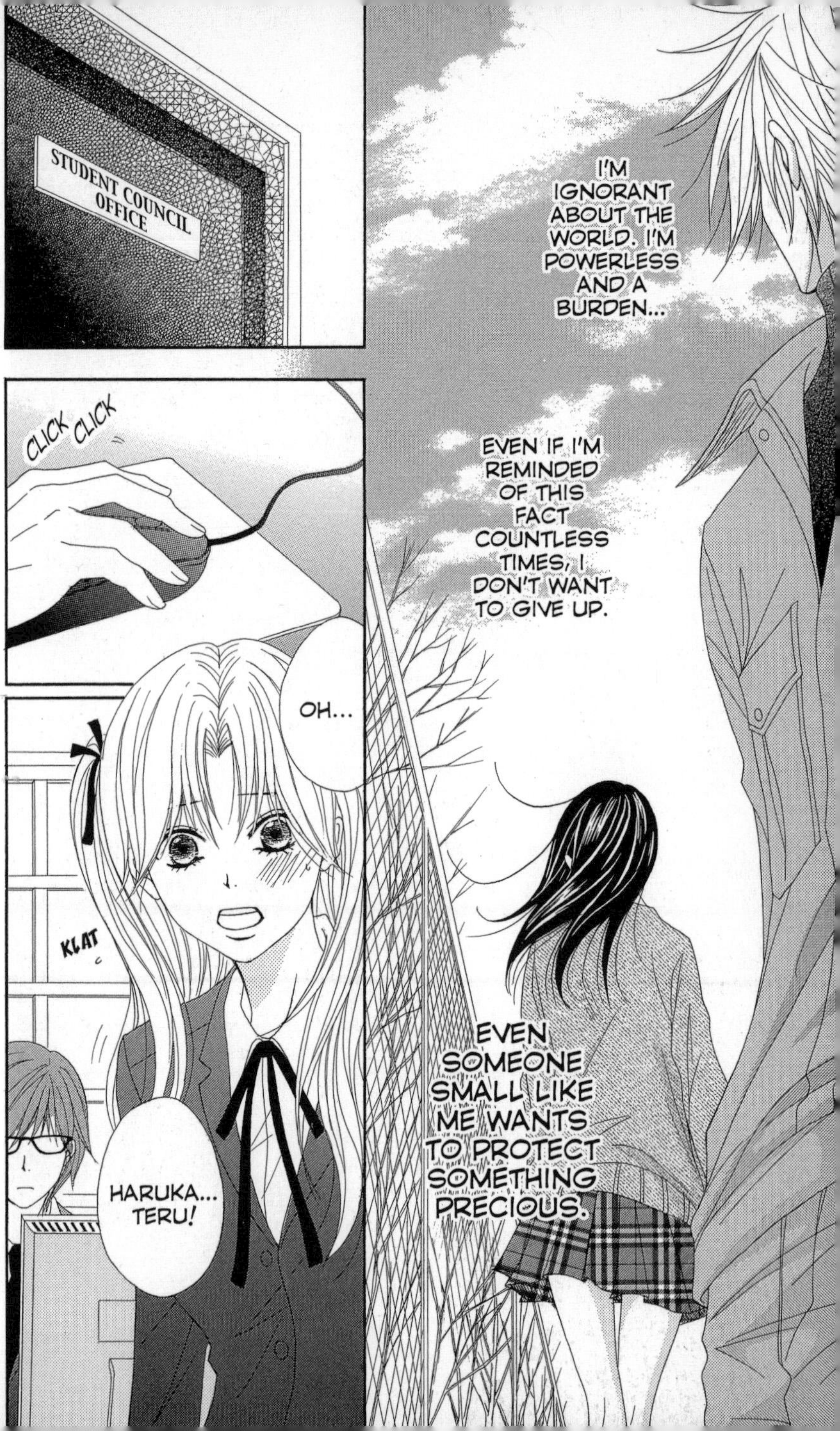
I'M IGNORANT ABOUT THE WORLD. I'M POWERLESS AND A BURDEN...
EVEN IF I'M REMINDED OF THIS FACT COUNTLESS TIMES, I DON'T WANT TO GIVE UP.
EVEN SOMEONE SMALL LIKE ME WANTS TO PROTECT SOMETHING PRECIOUS.
STUDENT COUNCIL OFFICE
CLICK CLICK
OH...
KLAT
HARUKA... TERU!

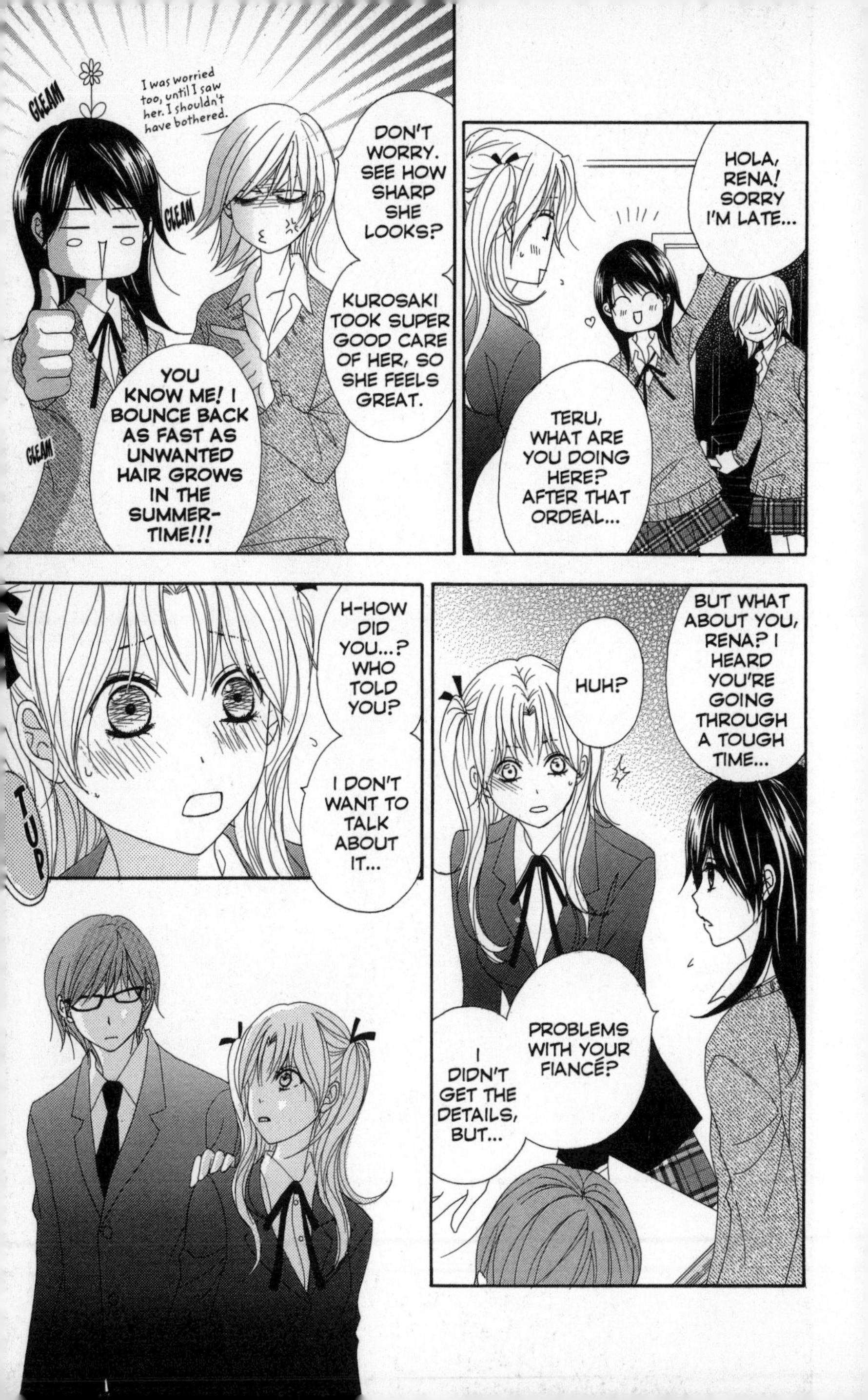
HOLA, RENA! SORRY I'M LATE...
TERU, WHAT ARE YOU DOING HERE? AFTER THAT ORDEAL...
DON'T WORRY. SEE HOW SHARP SHE LOOKS?
KUROSAKI TOOK SUPER GOOD CARE OF HER, SO SHE FEELS GREAT.
I was worried too, until I saw her. I shouldn't have bothered.
YOU KNOW ME! I BOUNCE BACK AS FAST AS UNWANTED HAIR GROWS IN THE SUMMER-TIME!!!
GLEAM
GLEAM
GLEAM
BUT WHAT ABOUT YOU, RENA? I HEARD YOU'RE GOING THROUGH A TOUGH TIME...
HUH?
PROBLEMS WITH YOUR FIANCÉ?
I DIDN'T GET THE DETAILS, BUT...
H-HOW DID YOU...? WHO TOLD YOU?
I DON'T WANT TO TALK ABOUT IT...
TUP

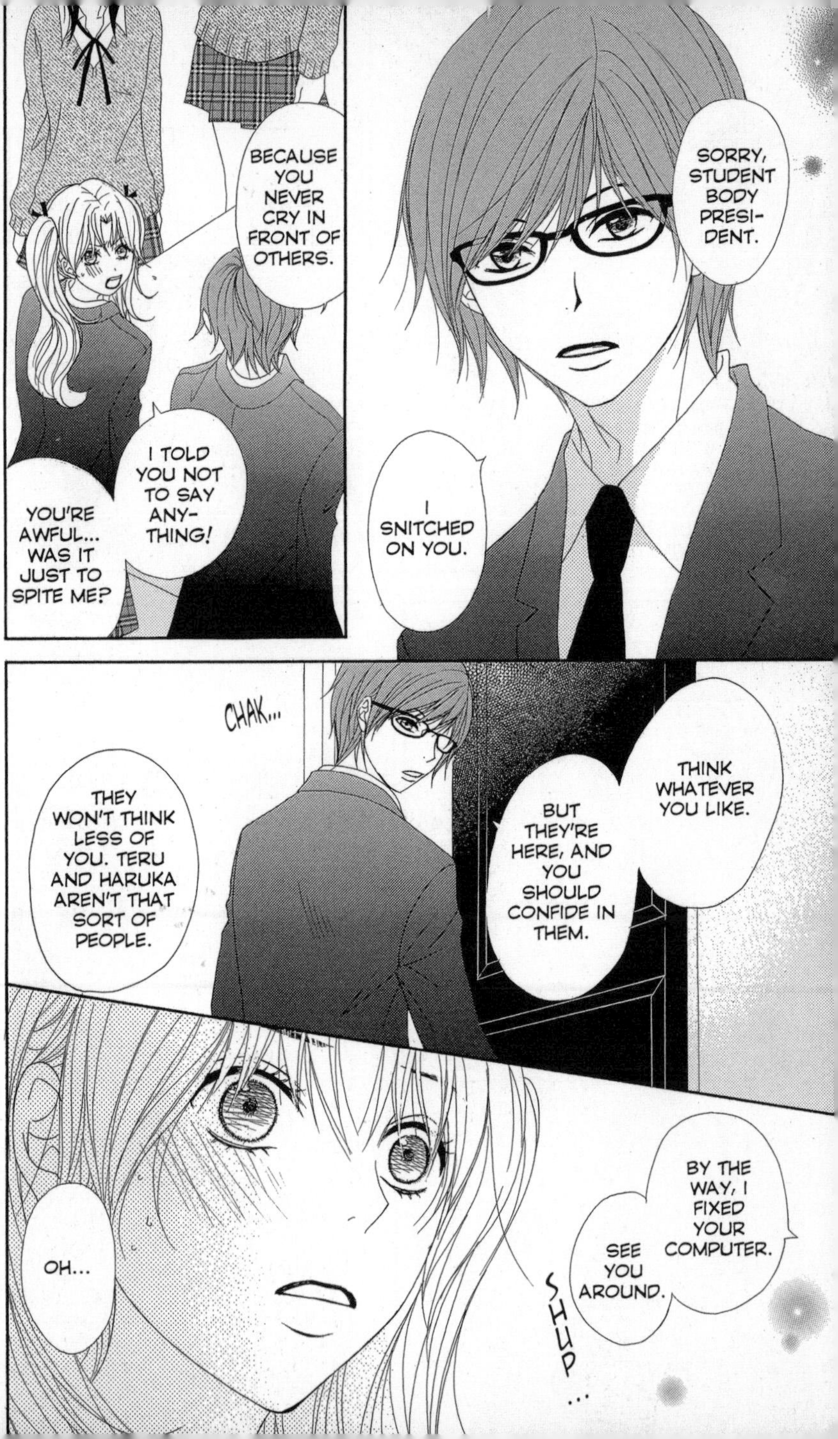
SORRY, STUDENT BODY PRESIDENT.
I SNITCHED ON YOU.
BECAUSE YOU NEVER CRY IN FRONT OF OTHERS.
I TOLD YOU NOT TO SAY ANYTHING!
YOU'RE AWFUL... WAS IT JUST TO SPITE ME?
THINK WHATEVER YOU LIKE.
BUT THEY'RE HERE, AND YOU SHOULD CONFIDE IN THEM.
CHAK...
THEY WON'T THINK LESS OF YOU. TERU AND HARUKA AREN'T THAT SORT OF PEOPLE.
BY THE WAY, I FIXED YOUR COMPUTER.
SEE YOU AROUND.
SHUP...
OH...

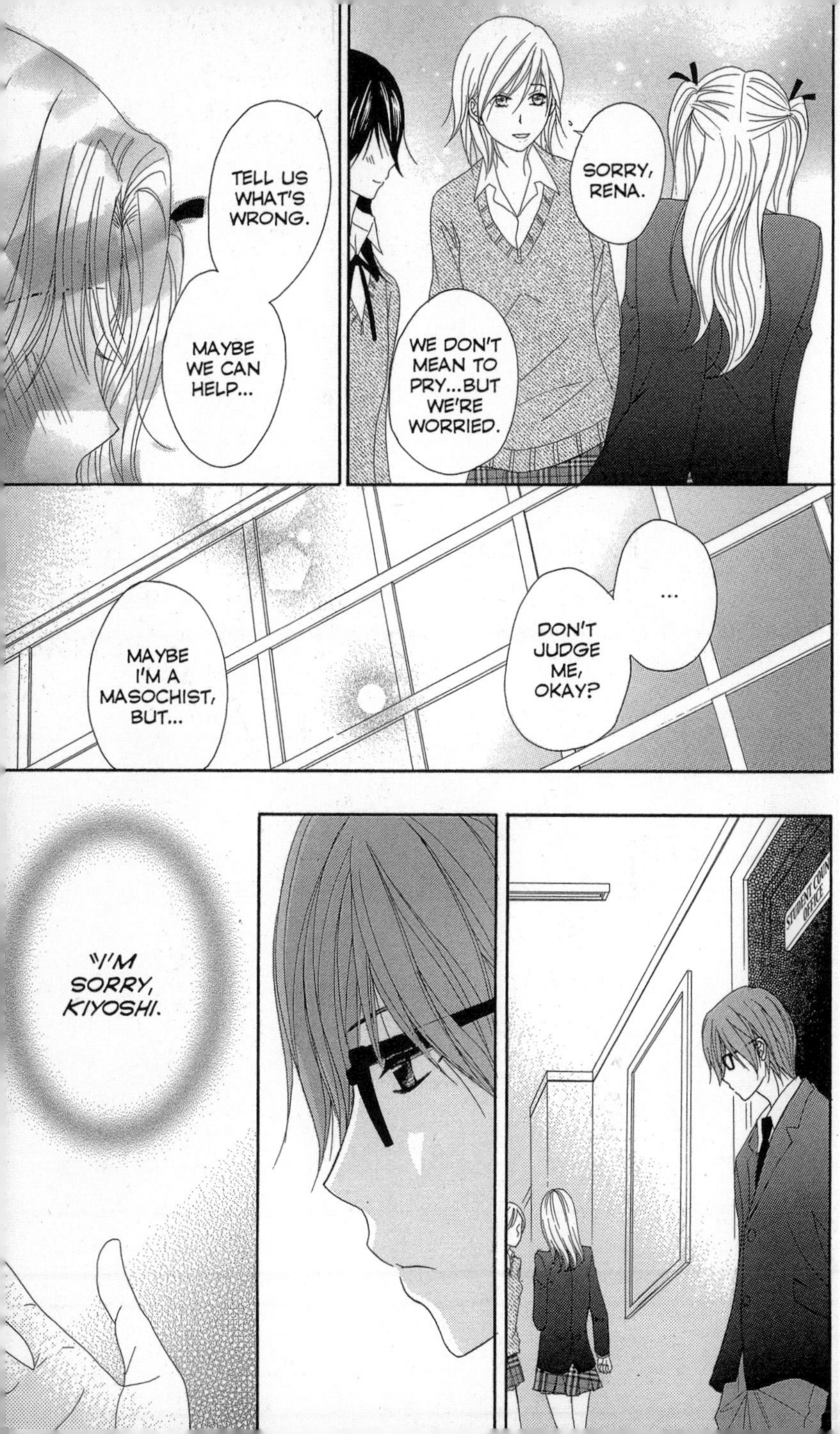
SORRY, RENA.
WE DON'T MEAN TO PRY...BUT WE'RE WORRIED.
TELL US WHAT'S WRONG.
MAYBE WE CAN HELP...
...
DON'T JUDGE ME, OKAY?
MAYBE I'M A MASOCHIST, BUT...
"I'M SORRY, KIYOSHI.

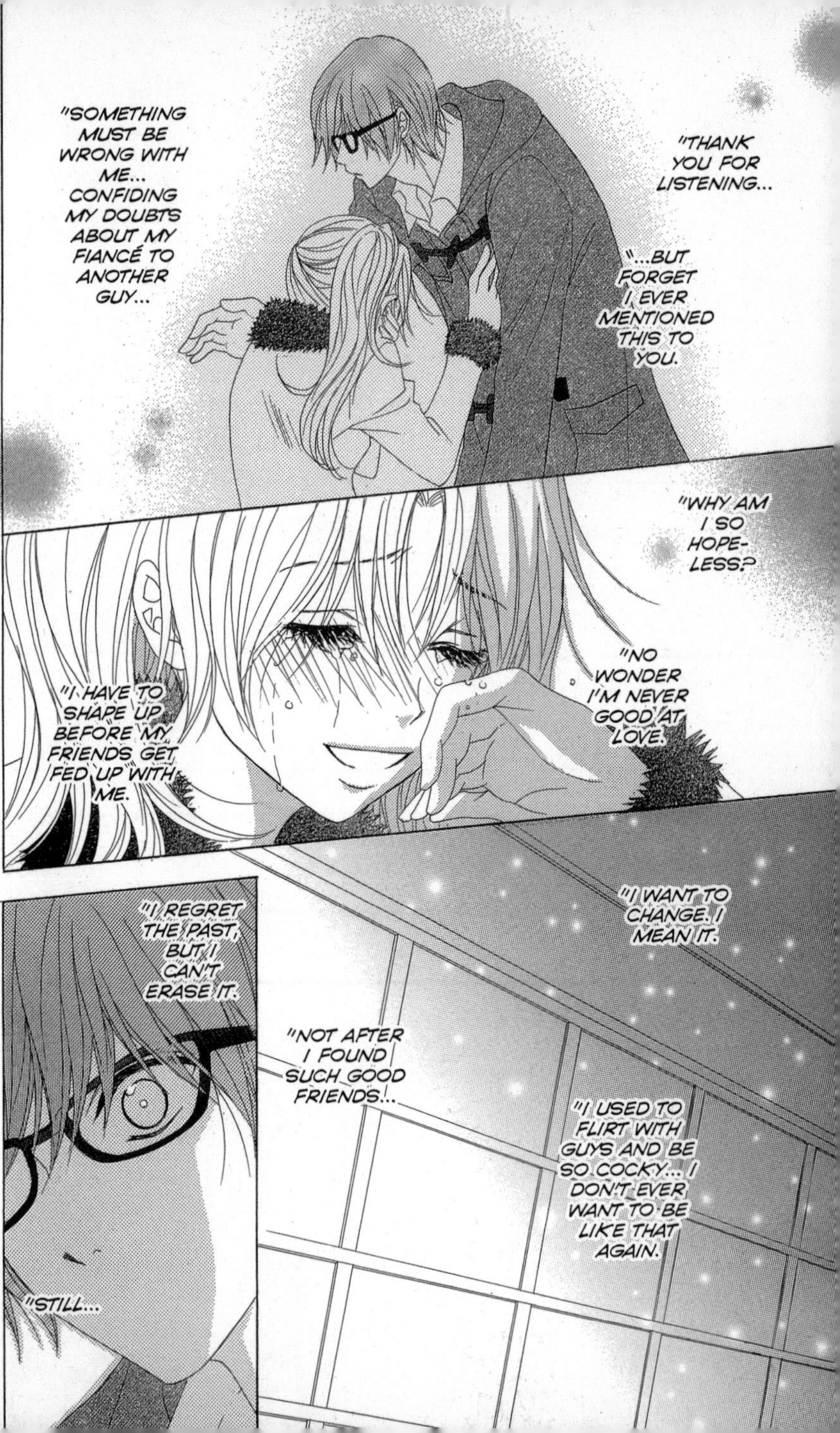
"THANK YOU FOR LISTENING...
"...BUT FORGET I EVER MENTIONED THIS TO YOU.
"SOMETHING MUST BE WRONG WITH ME... CONFIDING MY DOUBTS ABOUT MY FIANCÉ TO ANOTHER GUY...
"WHY AM I SO HOPE-LESS?
"NO WONDER I'M NEVER GOOD AT LOVE.
"I HAVE TO SHAPE UP BEFORE MY FRIENDS GET FED UP WITH ME.
"I WANT TO CHANGE. I MEAN IT.
"NOT AFTER I FOUND SUCH GOOD FRIENDS...
"I USED TO FLIRT WITH GUYS AND BE SO COCKY... I DON'T EVER WANT TO BE LIKE THAT AGAIN.
"I REGRET THE PAST, BUT I CAN'T ERASE IT.
"STILL...

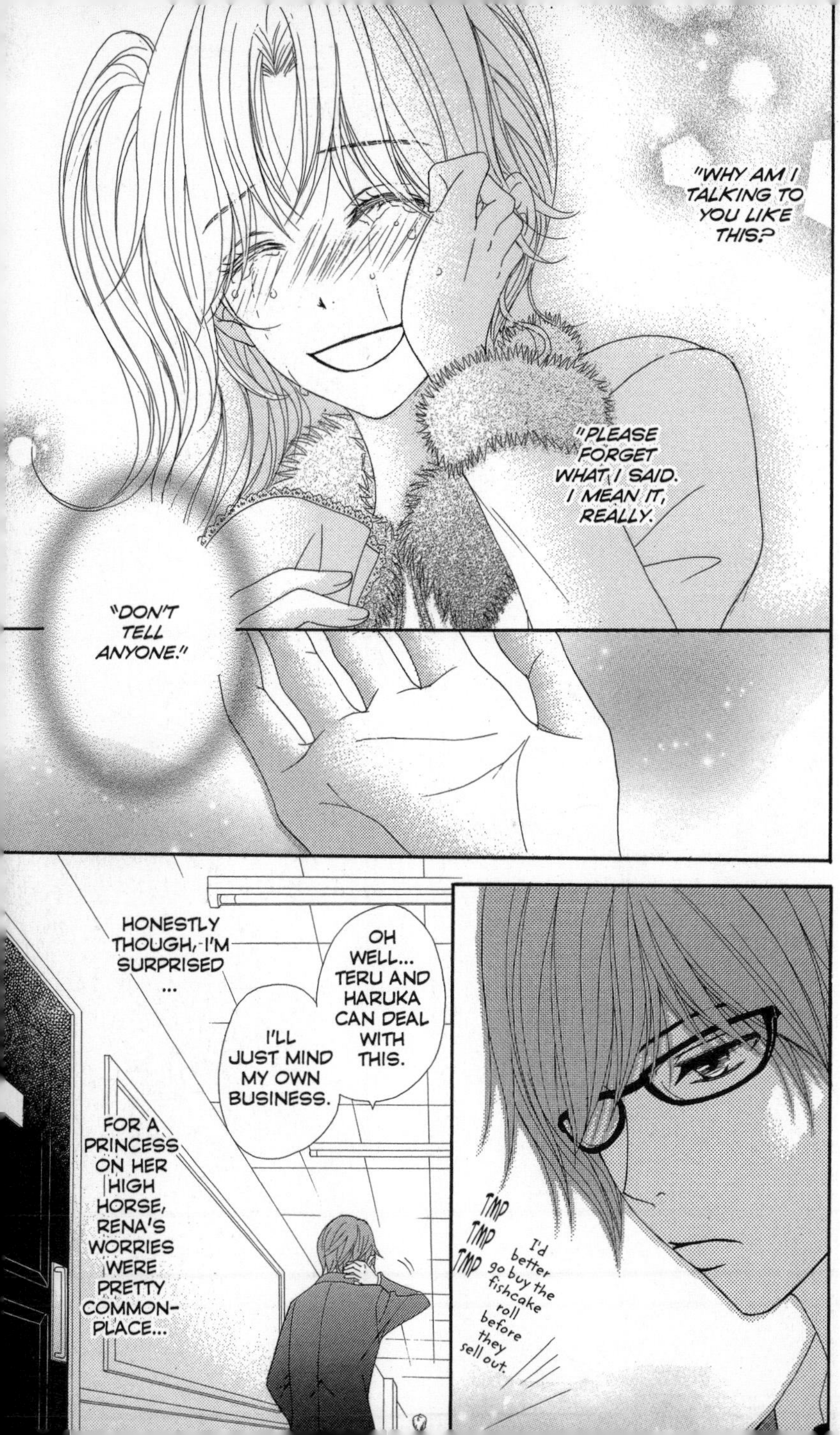
"WHY AM I TALKING TO YOU LIKE THIS?
"PLEASE FORGET WHAT I SAID. I MEAN IT, REALLY.
"DON'T TELL ANYONE."
TMP TMP TMP
I'd better go buy the fishcake roll before they sell out.
OH WELL... TERU AND HARUKA CAN DEAL WITH THIS.
HONESTLY THOUGH, I'M SURPRISED...
I'LL JUST MIND MY OWN BUSINESS.
FOR A PRINCESS ON HER HIGH HORSE, RENA'S WORRIES WERE PRETTY COMMON-PLACE...

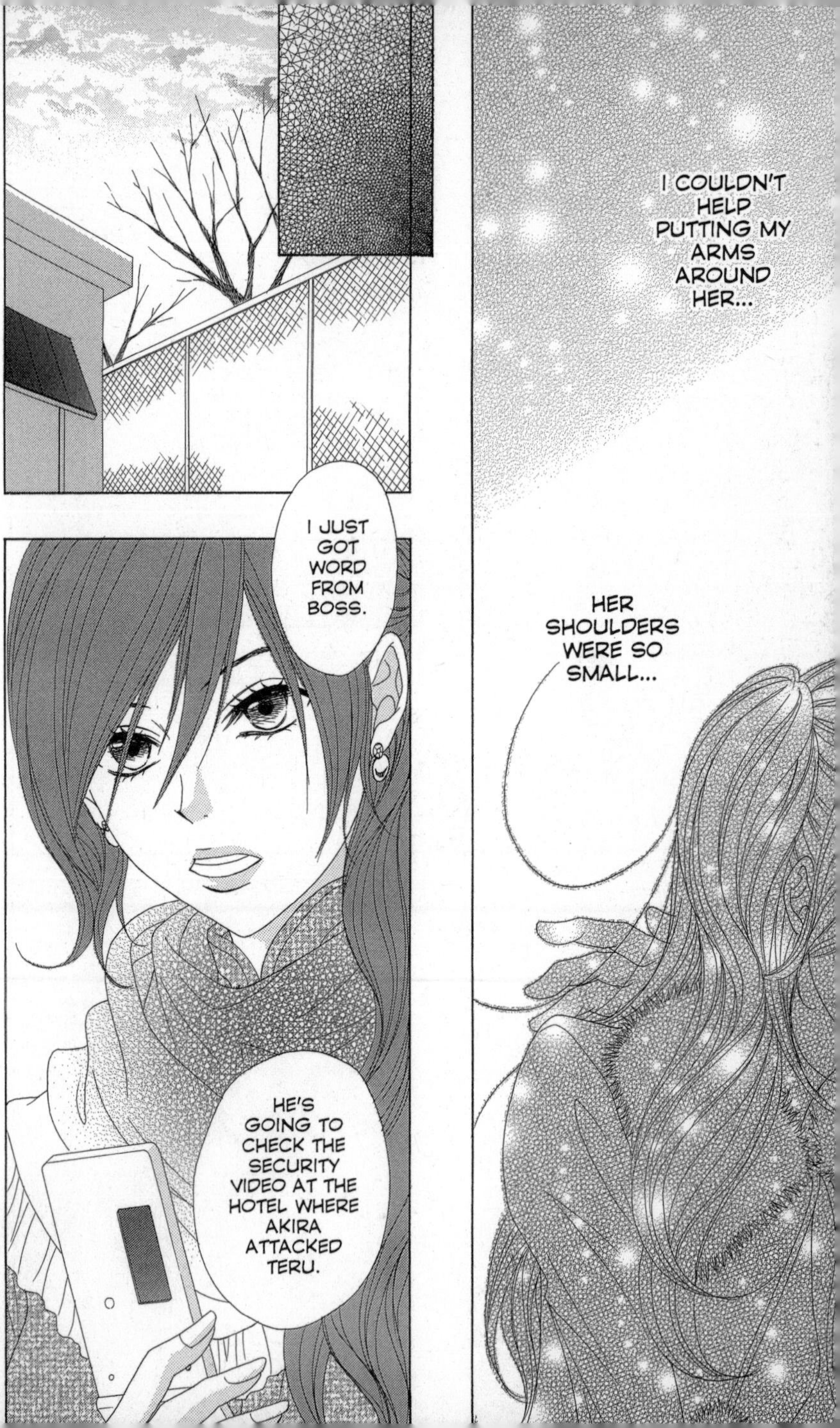
I COULDN'T HELP PUTTING MY ARMS AROUND HER...
HER SHOULDERS WERE SO SMALL...
I JUST GOT WORD FROM BOSS.
HE'S GOING TO CHECK THE SECURITY VIDEO AT THE HOTEL WHERE AKIRA ATTACKED TERU.

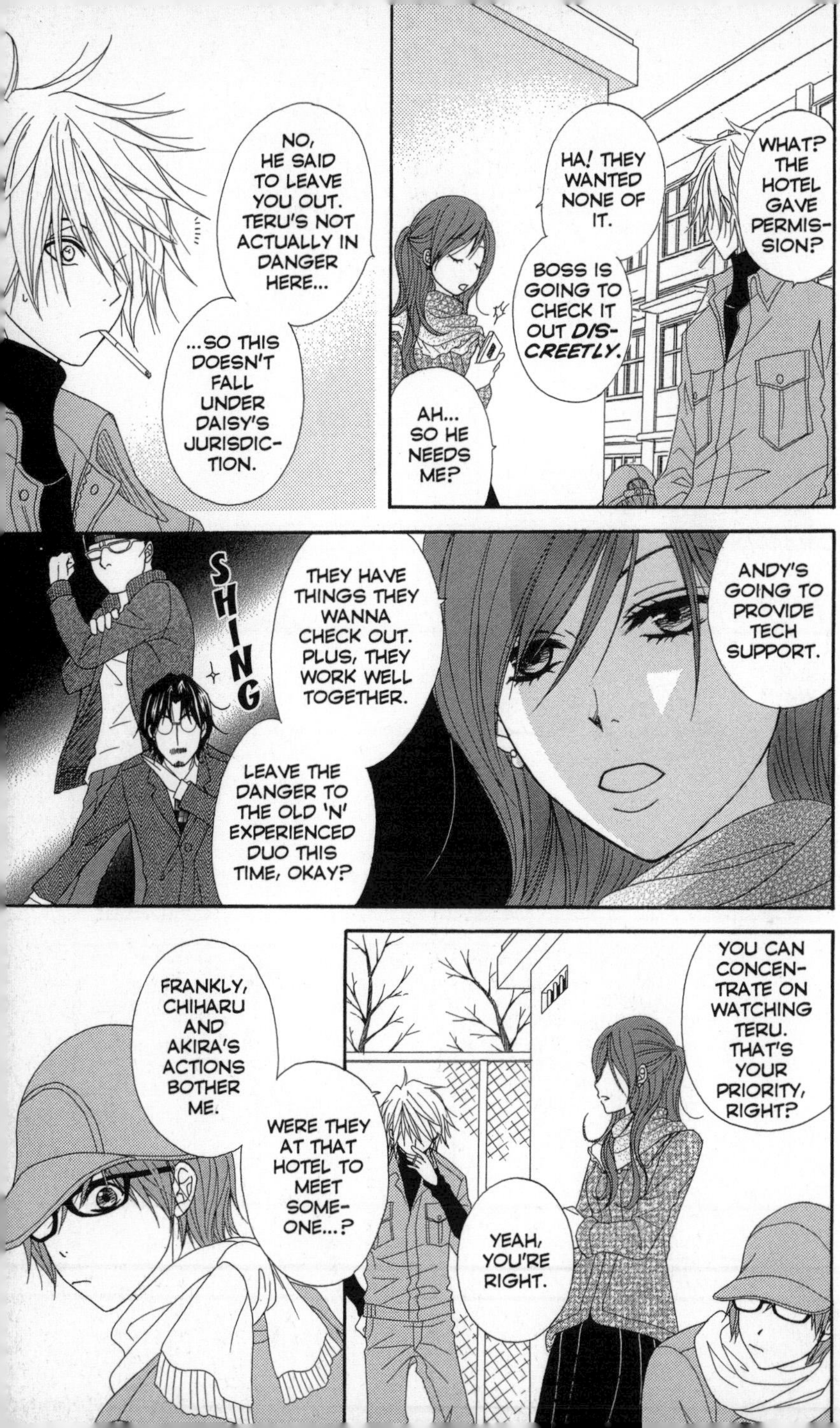
WHAT? THE HOTEL GAVE PERMISSION?
HA! THEY WANTED NONE OF IT.
BOSS IS GOING TO CHECK IT OUT DISCREETLY.
AH... SO HE NEEDS ME?
NO, HE SAID TO LEAVE YOU OUT. TERU'S NOT ACTUALLY IN DANGER HERE...
...SO THIS DOESN'T FALL UNDER DAISY'S JURISDICTION.
ANDY'S GOING TO PROVIDE TECH SUPPORT.
THEY HAVE THINGS THEY WANNA CHECK OUT. PLUS, THEY WORK WELL TOGETHER.
SHING
LEAVE THE DANGER TO THE OLD 'N' EXPERIENCED DUO THIS TIME, OKAY?
YOU CAN CONCENTRATE ON WATCHING TERU. THAT'S YOUR PRIORITY, RIGHT?
YEAH, YOU'RE RIGHT.
FRANKLY, CHIHARU AND AKIRA'S ACTIONS BOTHER ME.
WERE THEY AT THAT HOTEL TO MEET SOMEONE...?

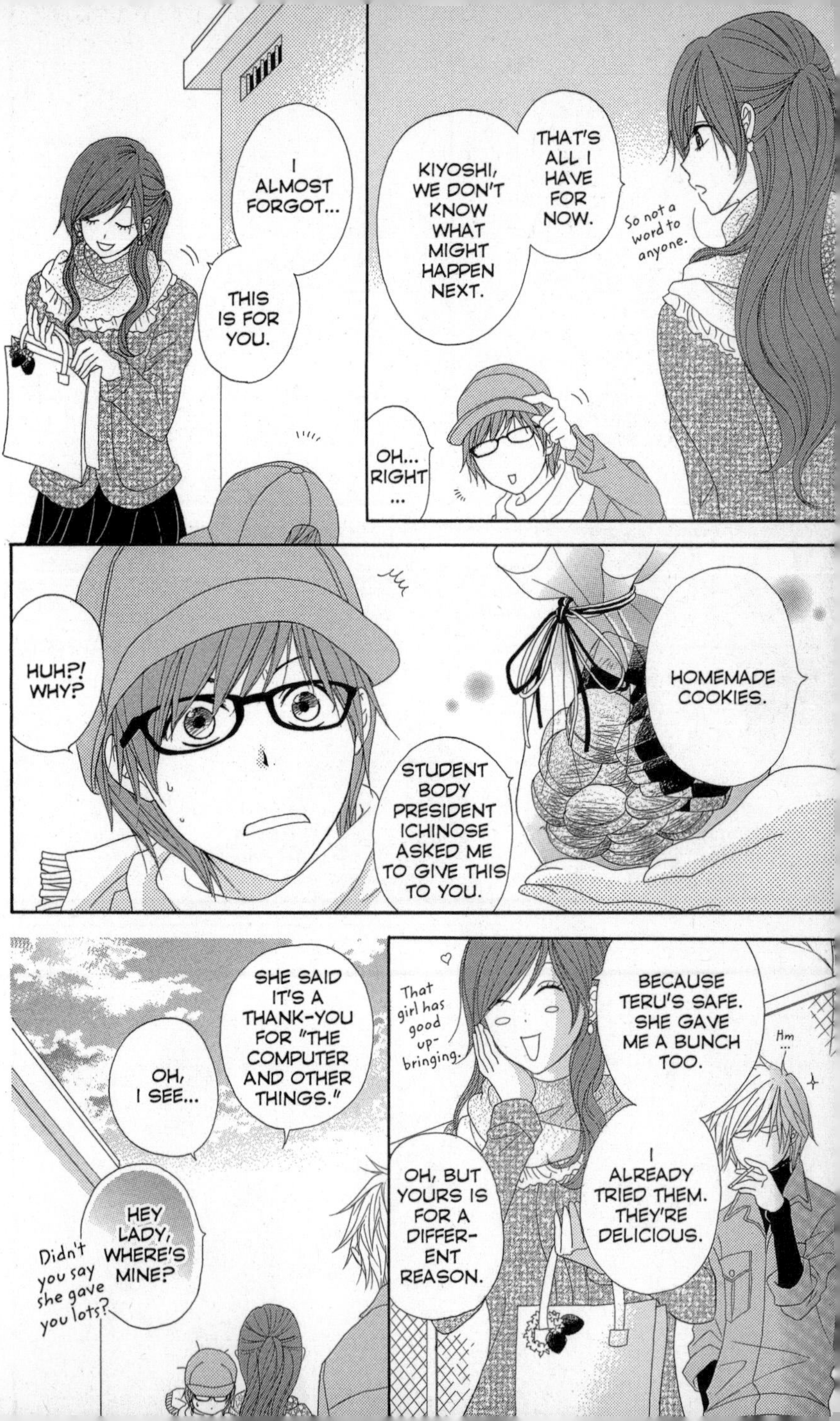
THAT'S ALL I HAVE FOR NOW.
KIYOSHI, WE DON'T KNOW WHAT MIGHT HAPPEN NEXT.
So not a word to anyone.
OH... RIGHT...
I ALMOST FORGOT...
THIS IS FOR YOU.
HOMEMADE COOKIES.
STUDENT BODY PRESIDENT ICHINOSE ASKED ME TO GIVE THIS TO YOU.
HUH?! WHY?
BECAUSE TERU'S SAFE. SHE GAVE ME A BUNCH TOO.
That girl has good up-bringing.
Hm...
I ALREADY TRIED THEM. THEY'RE DELICIOUS.
OH, BUT YOURS IS FOR A DIFFERENT REASON.
SHE SAID IT'S A THANK-YOU FOR "THE COMPUTER AND OTHER THINGS."
OH, I SEE...
HEY LADY, WHERE'S MINE?
Didn't you say she gave you lots?

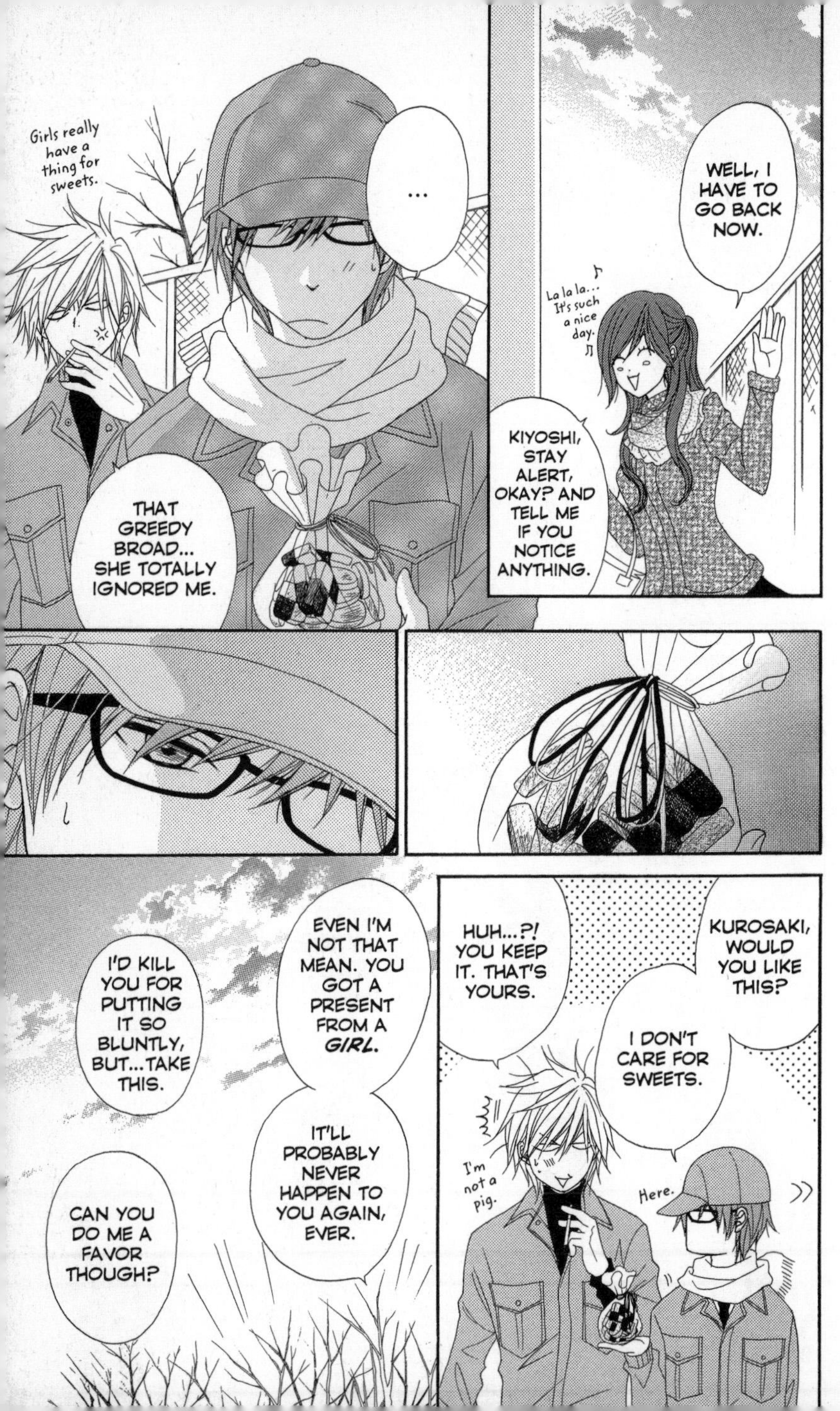
WELL, I HAVE TO GO BACK NOW.
La la la... It's such a nice day.
KIYOSHI, STAY ALERT, OKAY? AND TELL ME IF YOU NOTICE ANYTHING.
...
Girls really have a thing for sweets.
THAT GREEDY BROAD... SHE TOTALLY IGNORED ME.
KUROSAKI, WOULD YOU LIKE THIS?
HUH...?! YOU KEEP IT. THAT'S YOURS.
I DON'T CARE FOR SWEETS.
Here.
I'm not a pig.
EVEN I'M NOT THAT MEAN. YOU GOT A PRESENT FROM A *GIRL*.
I'D KILL YOU FOR PUTTING IT SO BLUNTLY, BUT...TAKE THIS.
IT'LL PROBABLY NEVER HAPPEN TO YOU AGAIN, EVER.
CAN YOU DO ME A FAVOR THOUGH?

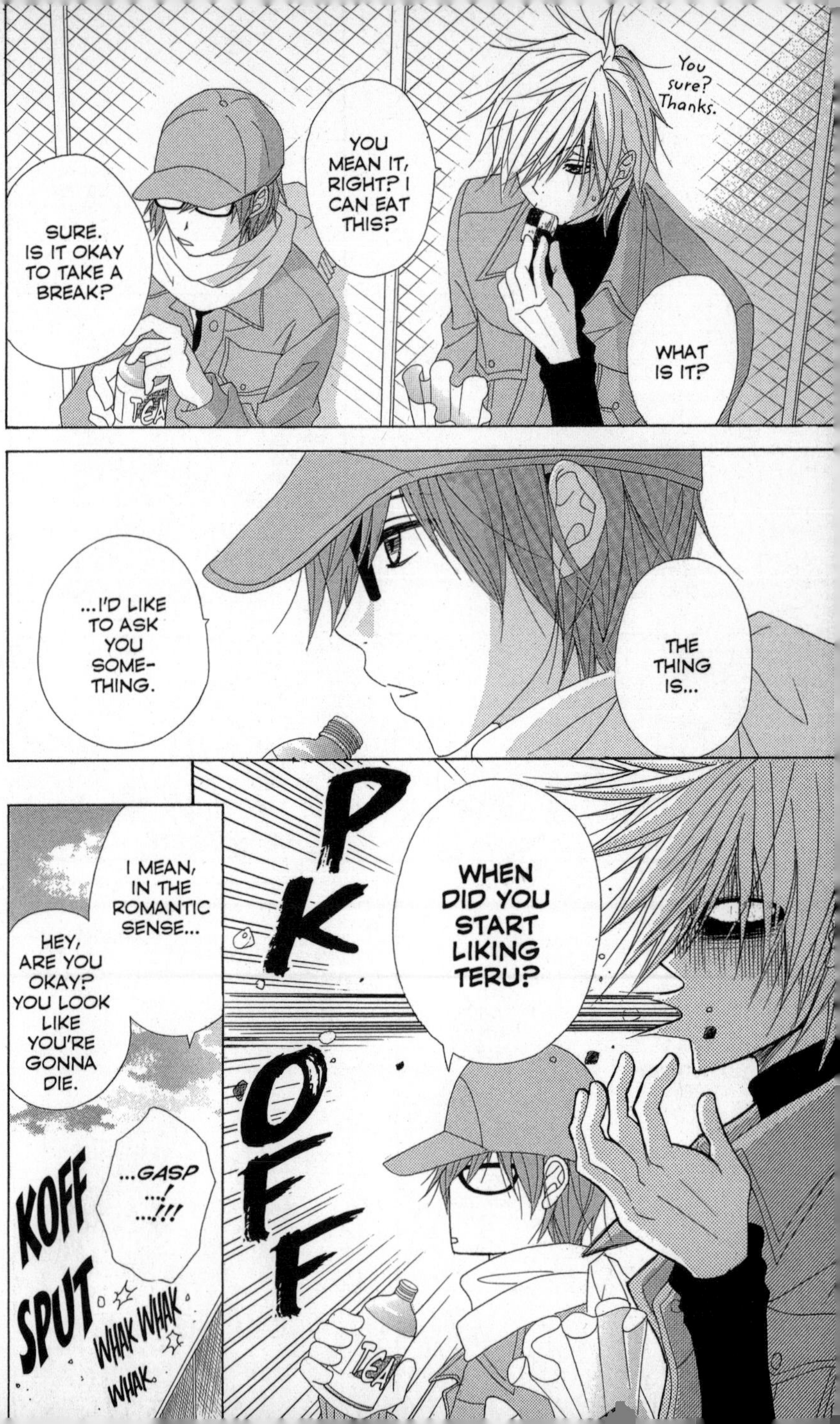
You sure? Thanks.
YOU MEAN IT, RIGHT? I CAN EAT THIS?
WHAT IS IT?
SURE. IS IT OKAY TO TAKE A BREAK?
TEA
THE THING IS...
...I'D LIKE TO ASK YOU SOME-THING.
WHEN DID YOU START LIKING TERU?
PKOFF
I MEAN, IN THE ROMANTIC SENSE...
HEY, ARE YOU OKAY? YOU LOOK LIKE YOU'RE GONNA DIE.
...GASP ...! ...!!!
KOFF SPUT
WHAK WHAK WHAK
TEA

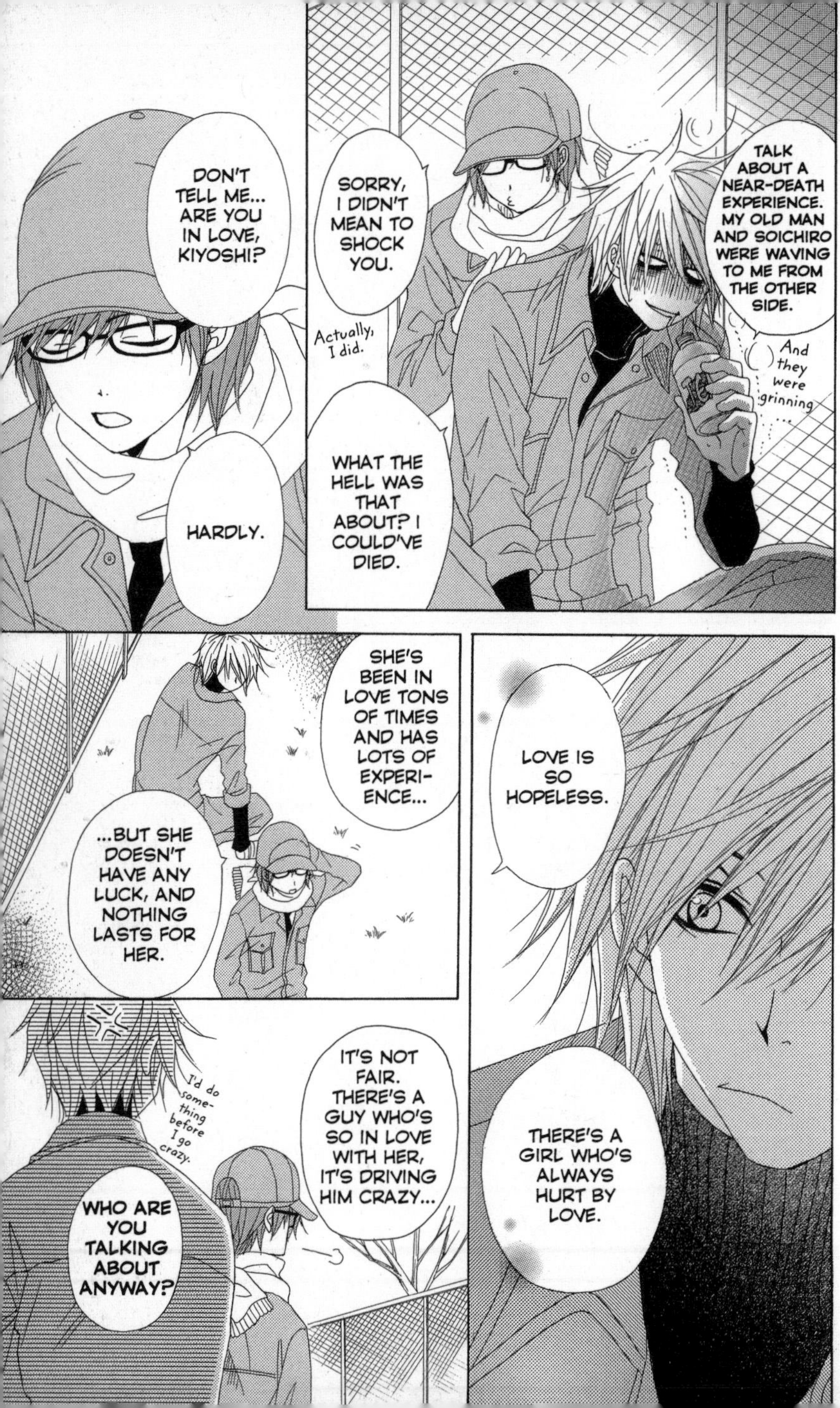
TALK ABOUT A NEAR-DEATH EXPERIENCE. MY OLD MAN AND SOICHIRO WERE WAVING TO ME FROM THE OTHER SIDE.
And they were grinning...
SORRY, I DIDN'T MEAN TO SHOCK YOU.
Actually, I did.
WHAT THE HELL WAS THAT ABOUT? I COULD'VE DIED.
DON'T TELL ME... ARE YOU IN LOVE, KIYOSHI?
HARDLY.
LOVE IS SO HOPELESS.
THERE'S A GIRL WHO'S ALWAYS HURT BY LOVE.
SHE'S BEEN IN LOVE TONS OF TIMES AND HAS LOTS OF EXPERI- ENCE...
...BUT SHE DOESN'T HAVE ANY LUCK, AND NOTHING LASTS FOR HER.
IT'S NOT FAIR. THERE'S A GUY WHO'S SO IN LOVE WITH HER, IT'S DRIVING HIM CRAZY...
I'd do some- thing before I go crazy.
WHO ARE YOU TALKING ABOUT ANYWAY?

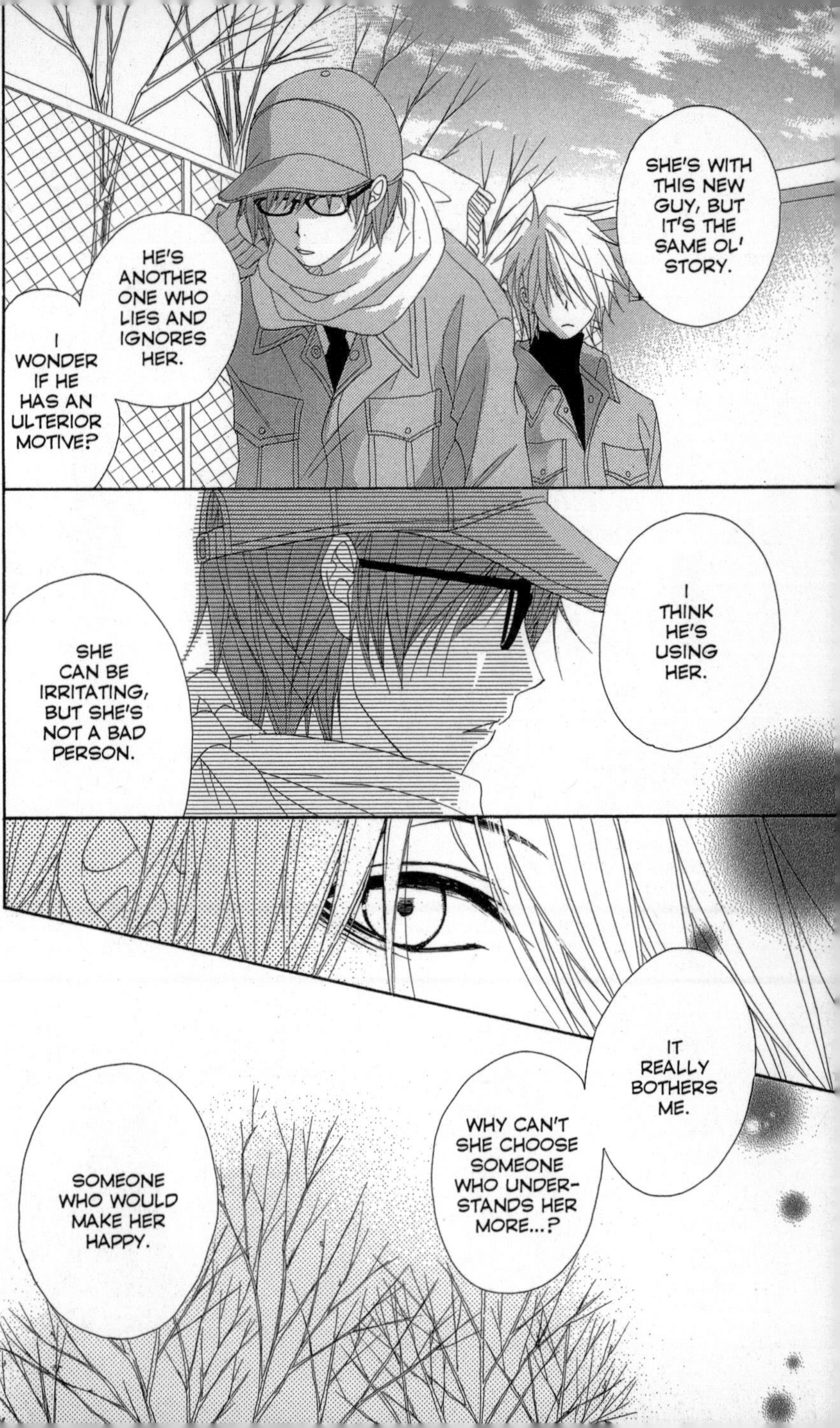
SHE'S WITH THIS NEW GUY, BUT IT'S THE SAME OL' STORY.
HE'S ANOTHER ONE WHO LIES AND IGNORES HER.
I WONDER IF HE HAS AN ULTERIOR MOTIVE?
I THINK HE'S USING HER.
SHE CAN BE IRRITATING, BUT SHE'S NOT A BAD PERSON.
IT REALLY BOTHERS ME.
WHY CAN'T SHE CHOOSE SOMEONE WHO UNDERSTANDS HER MORE...?
SOMEONE WHO WOULD MAKE HER HAPPY.

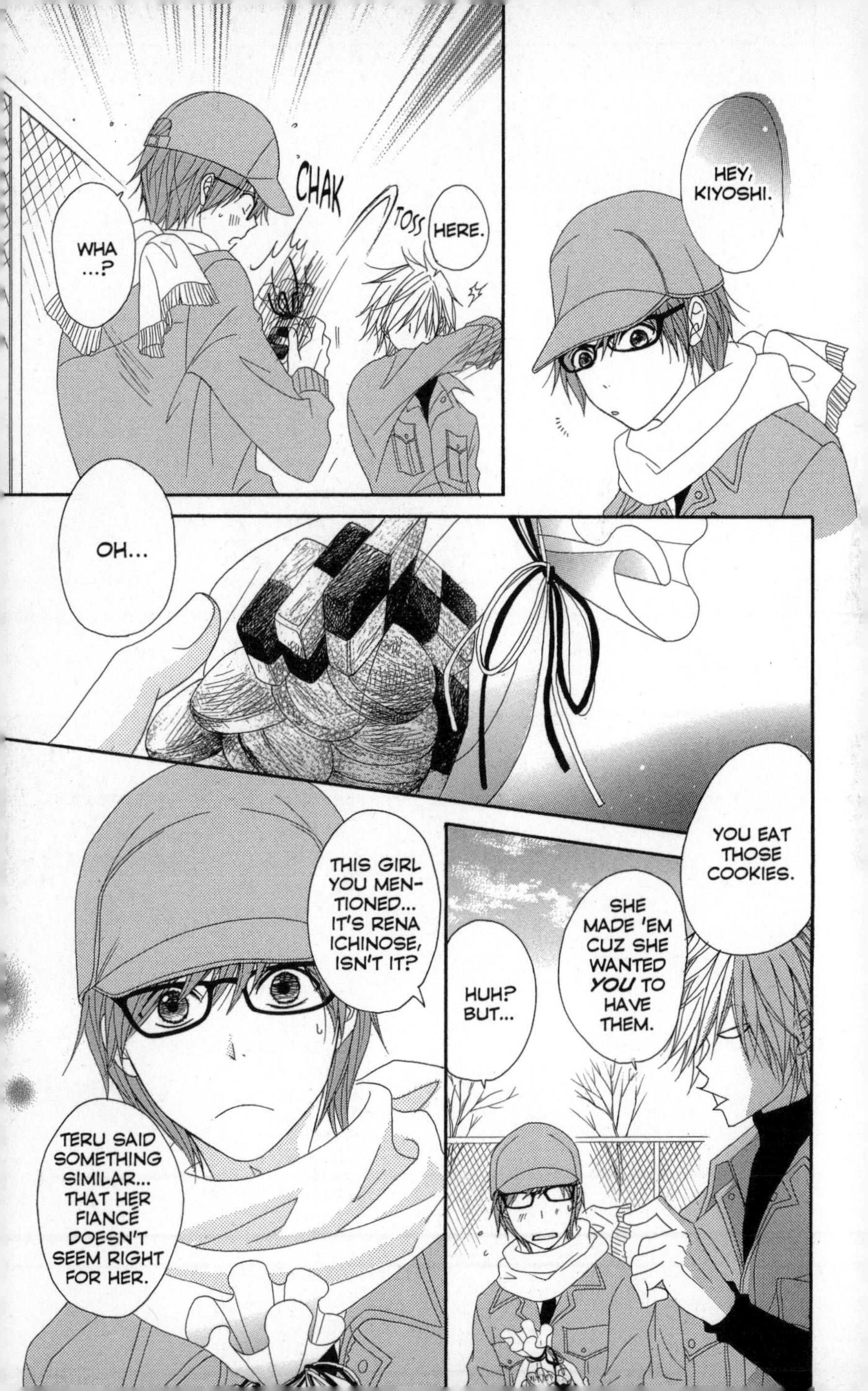
HEY, KIYOSHI.
HERE.
TOSS
CHAK
WHA ...?
OH...
YOU EAT THOSE COOKIES.
SHE MADE 'EM CUZ SHE WANTED *YOU* TO HAVE THEM.
HUH? BUT...
THIS GIRL YOU MENTIONED... IT'S RENA ICHINOSE, ISN'T IT?
TERU SAID SOMETHING SIMILAR... THAT HER FIANCÉ DOESN'T SEEM RIGHT FOR HER.

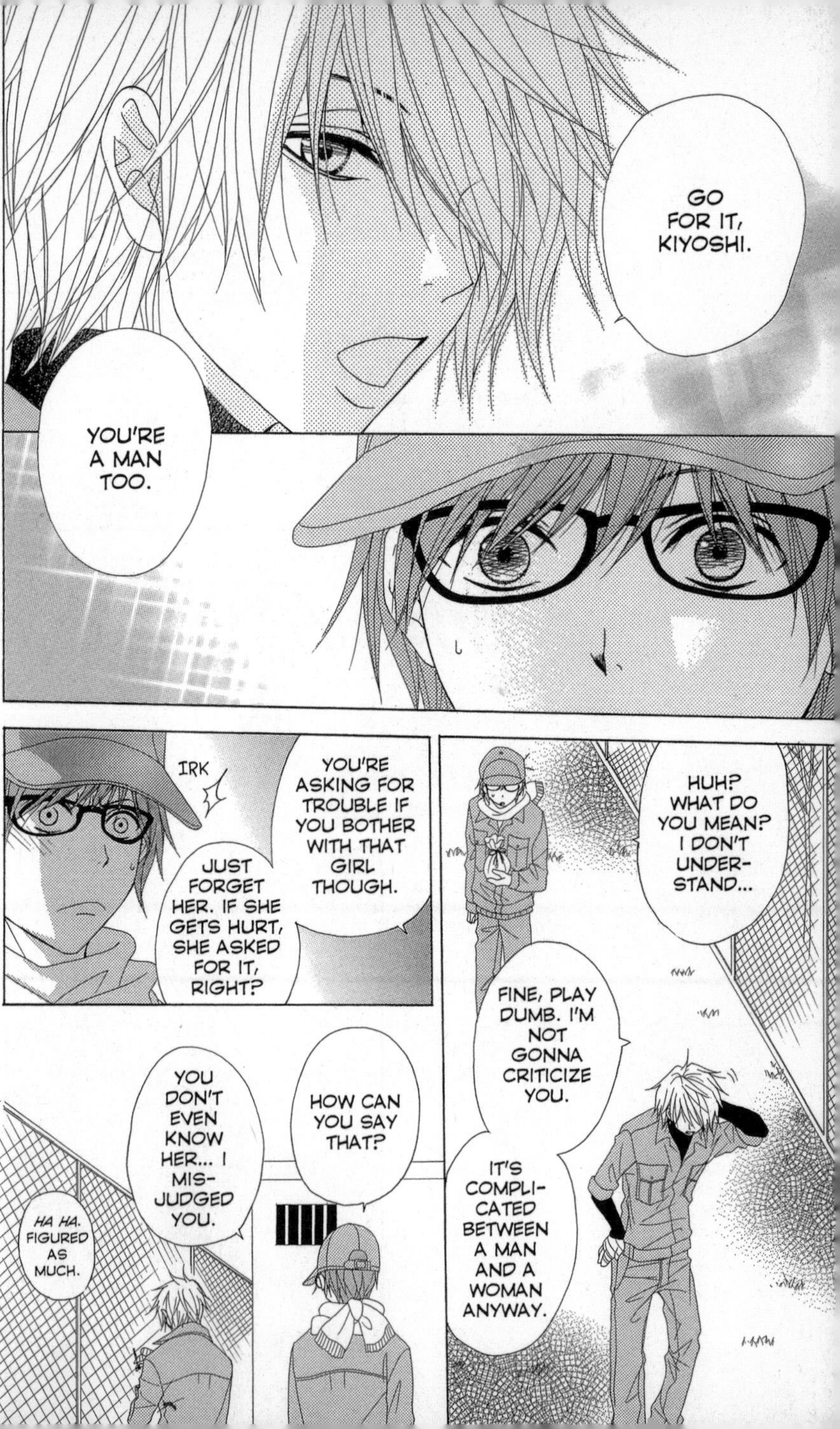
GO FOR IT, KIYOSHI.
YOU'RE A MAN TOO.
HUH? WHAT DO YOU MEAN? I DON'T UNDER-STAND...
FINE, PLAY DUMB. I'M NOT GONNA CRITICIZE YOU.
IT'S COMPLI-CATED BETWEEN A MAN AND A WOMAN ANYWAY.
YOU'RE ASKING FOR TROUBLE IF YOU BOTHER WITH THAT GIRL THOUGH.
IRK
JUST FORGET HER. IF SHE GETS HURT, SHE ASKED FOR IT, RIGHT?
HOW CAN YOU SAY THAT?
YOU DON'T EVEN KNOW HER... I MIS-JUDGED YOU.
HA HA. FIGURED AS MUCH.

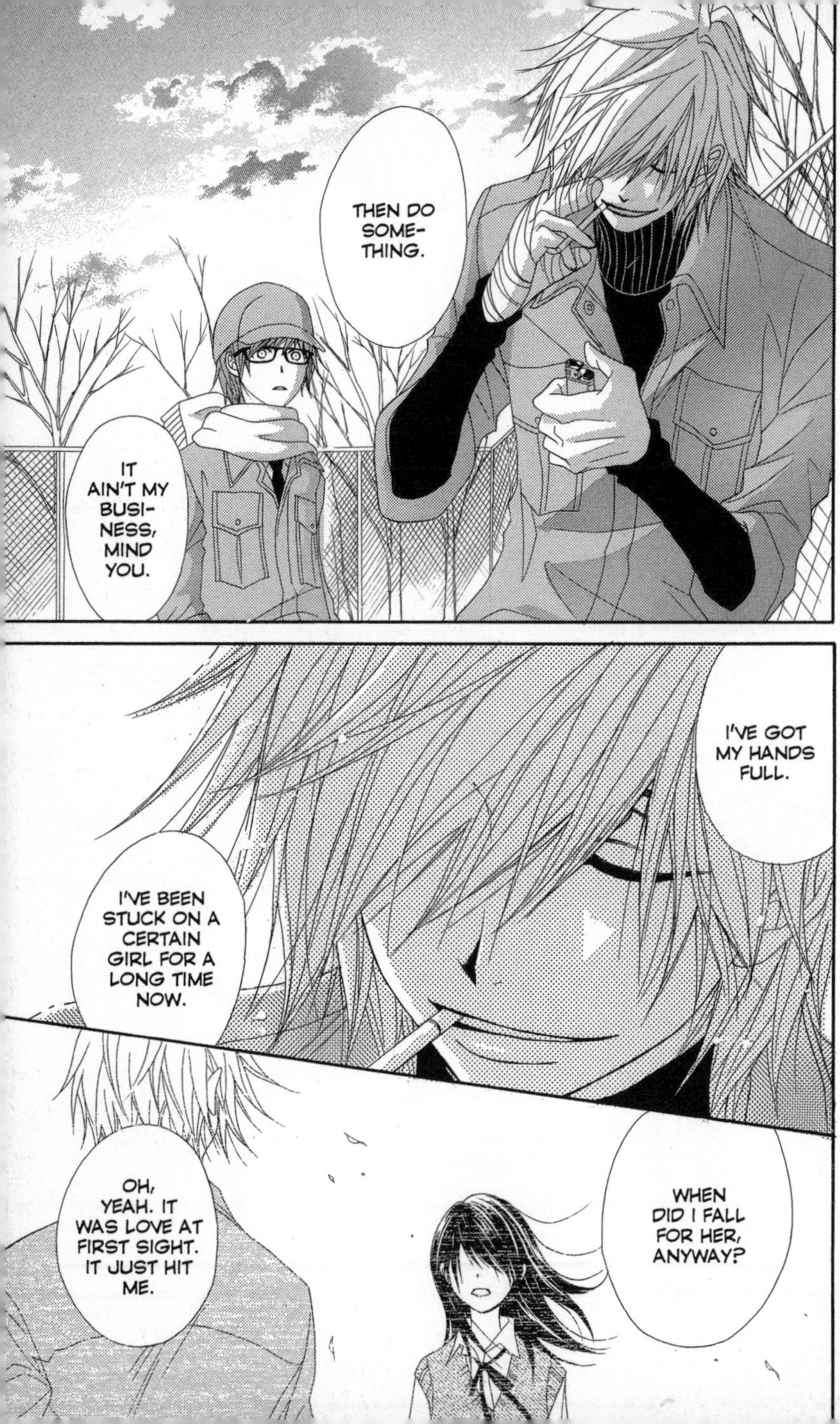
THEN DO SOME-THING.
IT AIN'T MY BUSI-NESS, MIND YOU.
I'VE GOT MY HANDS FULL.
I'VE BEEN STUCK ON A CERTAIN GIRL FOR A LONG TIME NOW.
WHEN DID I FALL FOR HER, ANYWAY?
OH, YEAH. IT WAS LOVE AT FIRST SIGHT. IT JUST HIT ME.

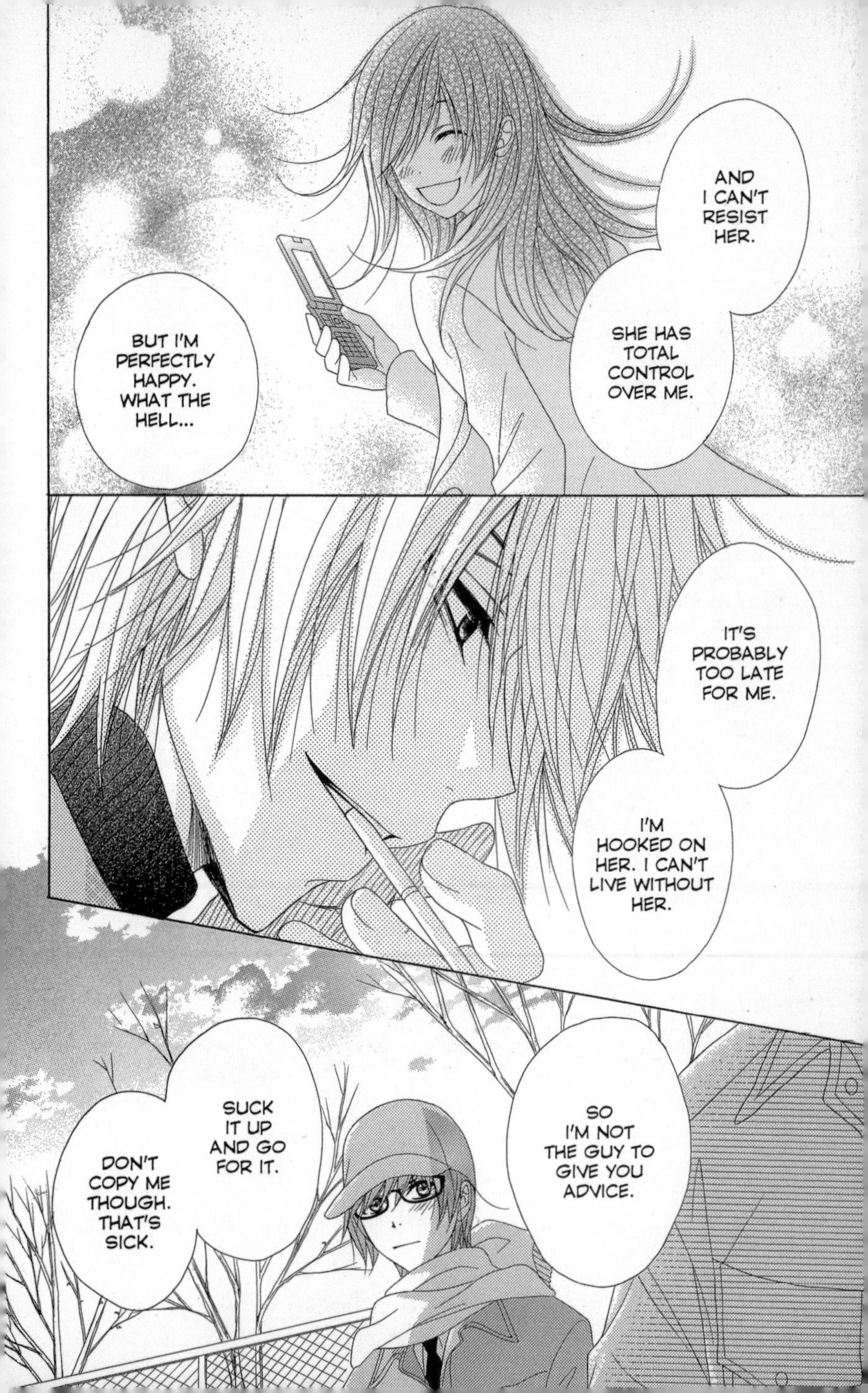
AND I CAN'T RESIST HER.
SHE HAS TOTAL CONTROL OVER ME.
BUT I'M PERFECTLY HAPPY. WHAT THE HELL...
IT'S PROBABLY TOO LATE FOR ME.
I'M HOOKED ON HER. I CAN'T LIVE WITHOUT HER.
SO I'M NOT THE GUY TO GIVE YOU ADVICE.
SUCK IT UP AND GO FOR IT.
DON'T COPY ME THOUGH. THAT'S SICK.

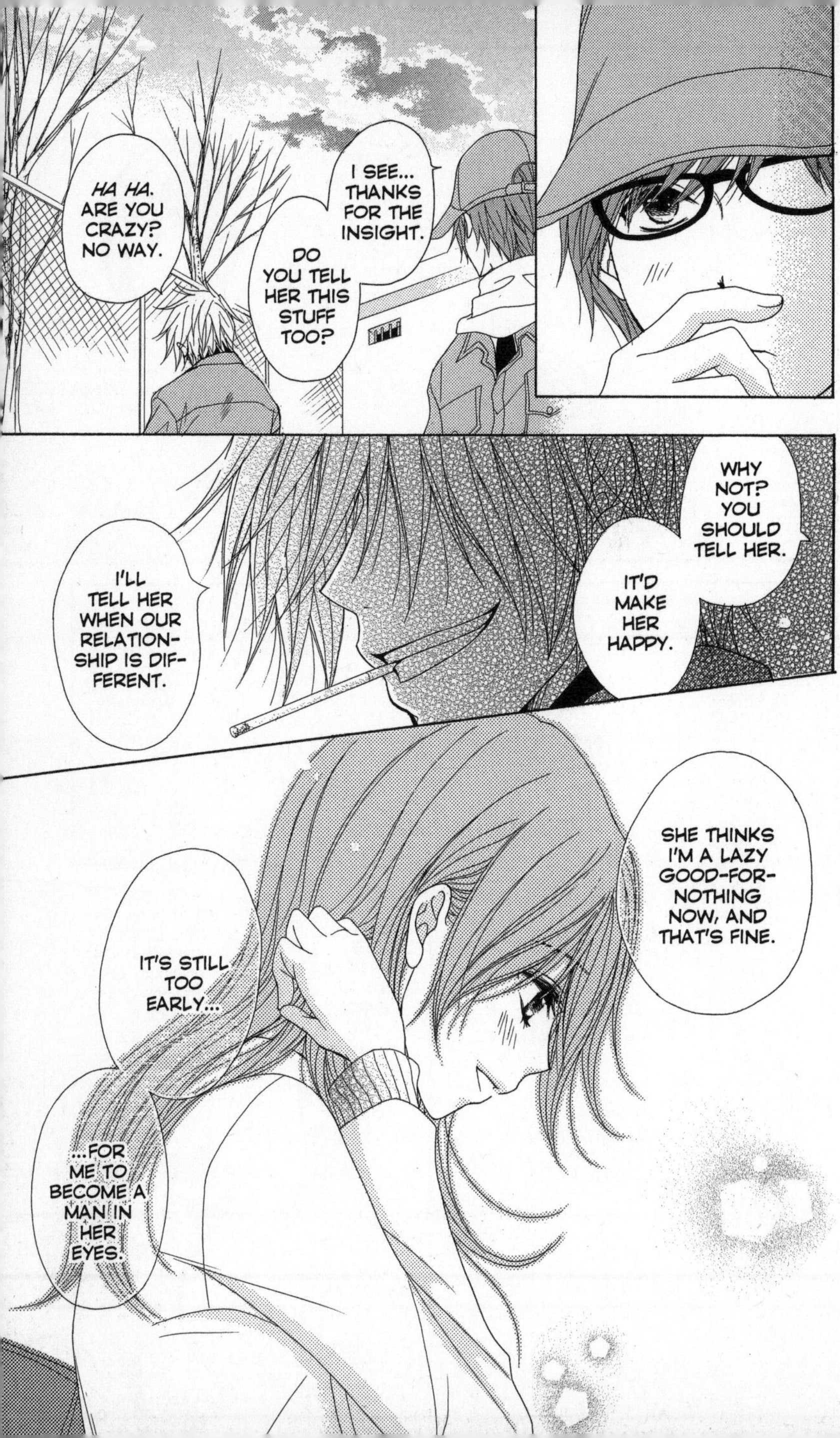
I SEE... THANKS FOR THE INSIGHT.
DO YOU TELL HER THIS STUFF TOO?
HA HA. ARE YOU CRAZY? NO WAY.
WHY NOT? YOU SHOULD TELL HER.
IT'D MAKE HER HAPPY.
I'LL TELL HER WHEN OUR RELATION-SHIP IS DIF-FERENT.
SHE THINKS I'M A LAZY GOOD-FOR-NOTHING NOW, AND THAT'S FINE.
IT'S STILL TOO EARLY...
...FOR ME TO BECOME A MAN IN HER EYES.

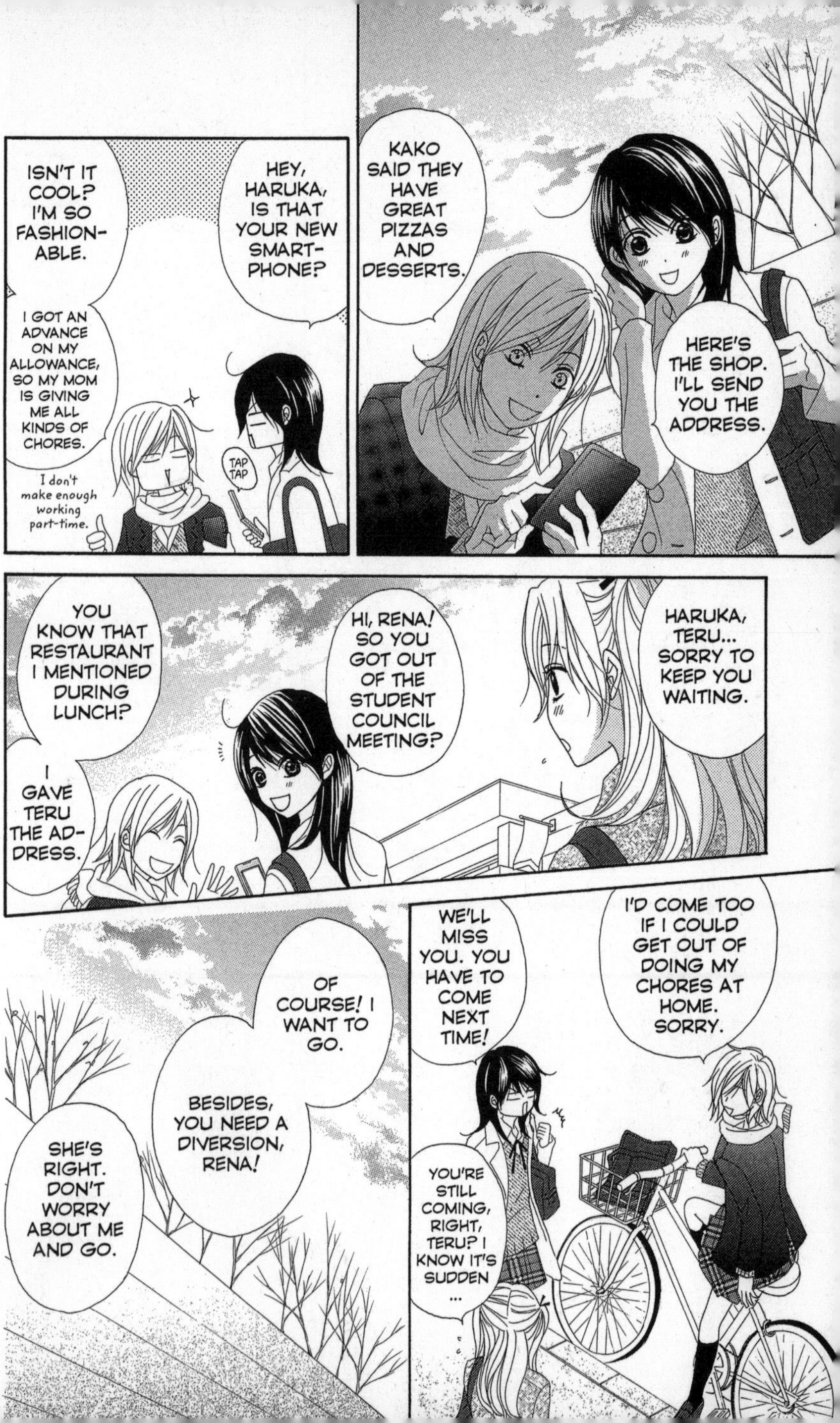
KAKO SAID THEY HAVE GREAT PIZZAS AND DESSERTS.
HERE'S THE SHOP. I'LL SEND YOU THE ADDRESS.
HEY, HARUKA, IS THAT YOUR NEW SMART-PHONE?
ISN'T IT COOL? I'M SO FASHION-ABLE.
TAP TAP
I GOT AN ADVANCE ON MY ALLOWANCE, SO MY MOM IS GIVING ME ALL KINDS OF CHORES.
I don't make enough working part-time.
HARUKA, TERU... SORRY TO KEEP YOU WAITING.
HI, RENA! SO YOU GOT OUT OF THE STUDENT COUNCIL MEETING?
YOU KNOW THAT RESTAURANT I MENTIONED DURING LUNCH?
I GAVE TERU THE AD-DRESS.
I'D COME TOO IF I COULD GET OUT OF DOING MY CHORES AT HOME. SORRY.
WE'LL MISS YOU. YOU HAVE TO COME NEXT TIME!
YOU'RE STILL COMING, RIGHT, TERU? I KNOW IT'S SUDDEN...
OF COURSE! I WANT TO GO.
BESIDES, YOU NEED A DIVERSION, RENA!
SHE'S RIGHT. DON'T WORRY ABOUT ME AND GO.

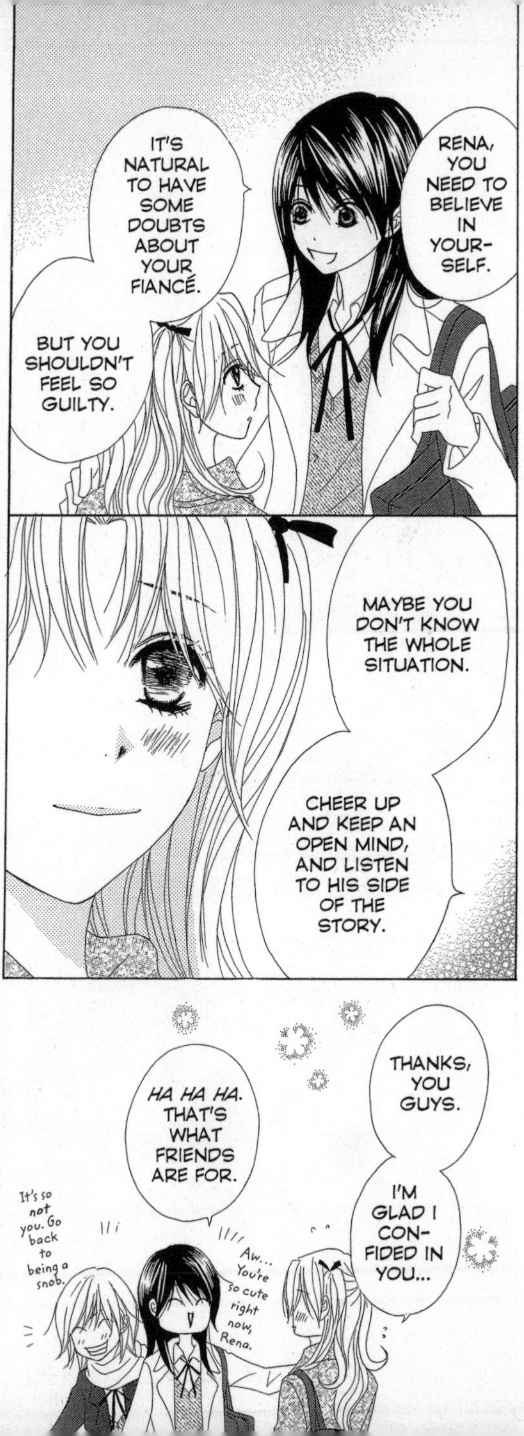
RENA, YOU NEED TO BELIEVE IN YOURSELF.
IT'S NATURAL TO HAVE SOME DOUBTS ABOUT YOUR FIANCÉ.
BUT YOU SHOULDN'T FEEL SO GUILTY.
MAYBE YOU DON'T KNOW THE WHOLE SITUATION.
CHEER UP AND KEEP AN OPEN MIND, AND LISTEN TO HIS SIDE OF THE STORY.
THANKS, YOU GUYS.
I'M GLAD I CONFIDED IN YOU...
HA HA HA. THAT'S WHAT FRIENDS ARE FOR.
Aw... You're so cute right now, Rena.
It's so not you. Go back to being a snob.

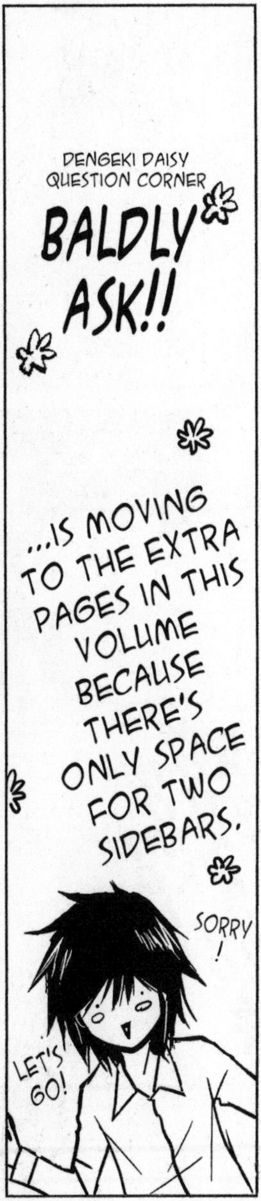
DENGEKI DAISY QUESTION CORNER
BALDLY ASK!!
...IS MOVING TO THE EXTRA PAGES IN THIS VOLUME BECAUSE THERE'S ONLY SPACE FOR TWO SIDEBARS.
SORRY!
LET'S GO!

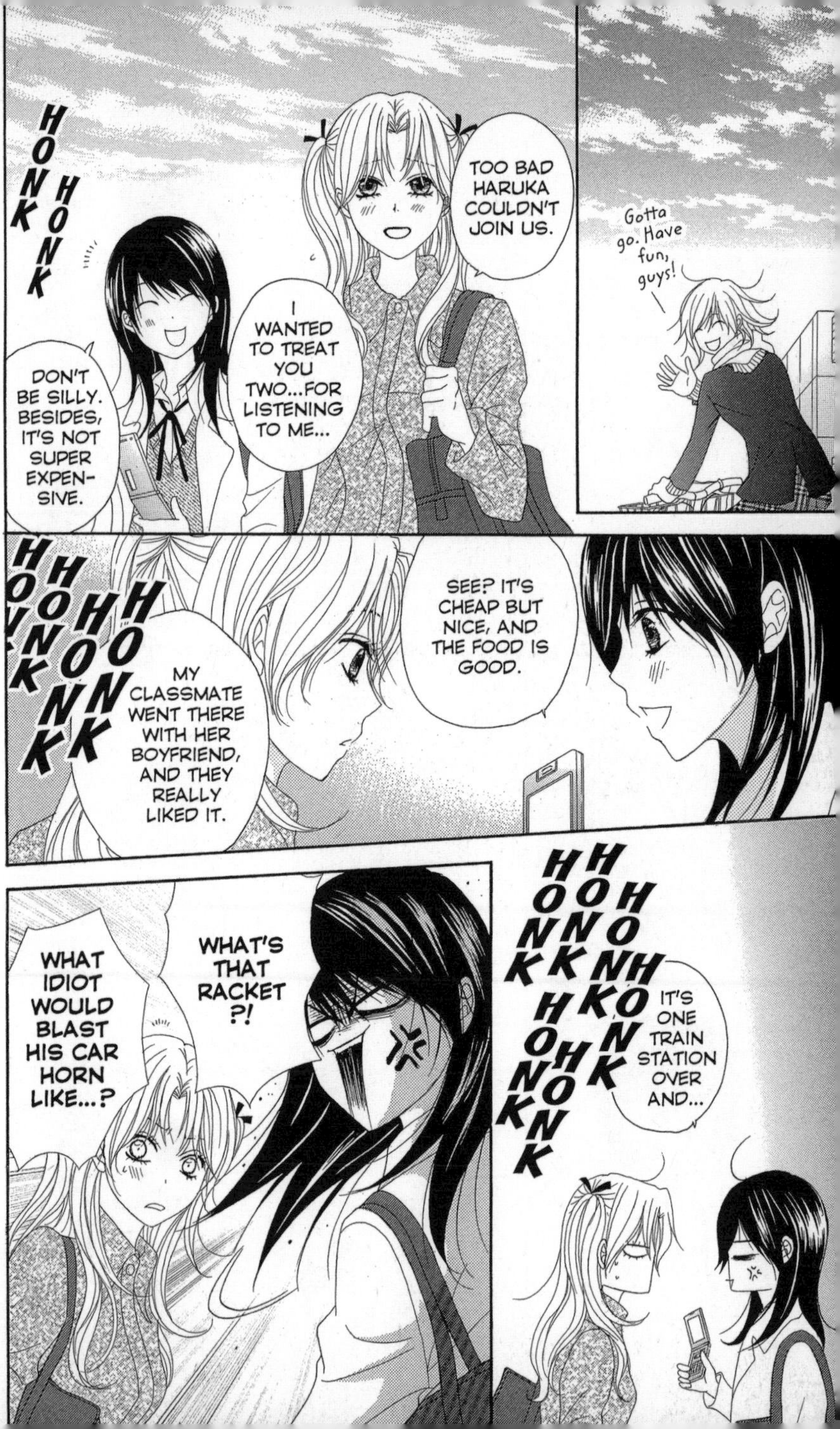
Gotta go. Have fun, guys!
TOO BAD HARUKA COULDN'T JOIN US.
I WANTED TO TREAT YOU TWO...FOR LISTENING TO ME...
HONK HONK
DON'T BE SILLY. BESIDES, IT'S NOT SUPER EXPEN-SIVE.
SEE? IT'S CHEAP BUT NICE, AND THE FOOD IS GOOD.
MY CLASSMATE WENT THERE WITH HER BOYFRIEND, AND THEY REALLY LIKED IT.
HONK HONK HONK HONK
HONK HONK HONK HONK HONK HONK HONK
IT'S ONE TRAIN STATION OVER AND...
WHAT'S THAT RACKET?!
WHAT IDIOT WOULD BLAST HIS CAR HORN LIKE...?

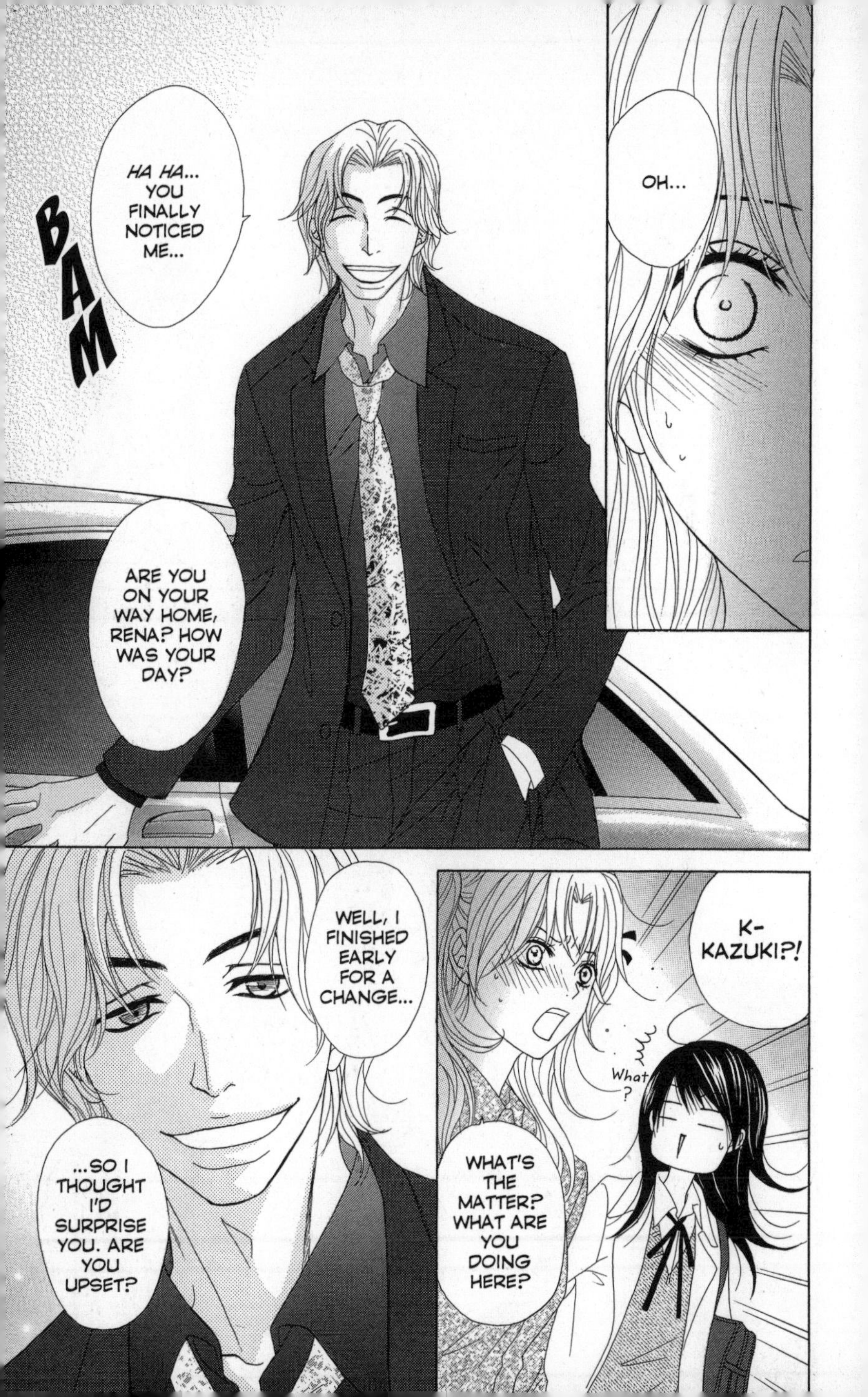
OH...
HA HA... YOU FINALLY NOTICED ME...
BAM
ARE YOU ON YOUR WAY HOME, RENA? HOW WAS YOUR DAY?
K-KAZUKI?!
What?
WHAT'S THE MATTER? WHAT ARE YOU DOING HERE?
WELL, I FINISHED EARLY FOR A CHANGE...
...SO I THOUGHT I'D SURPRISE YOU. ARE YOU UPSET?

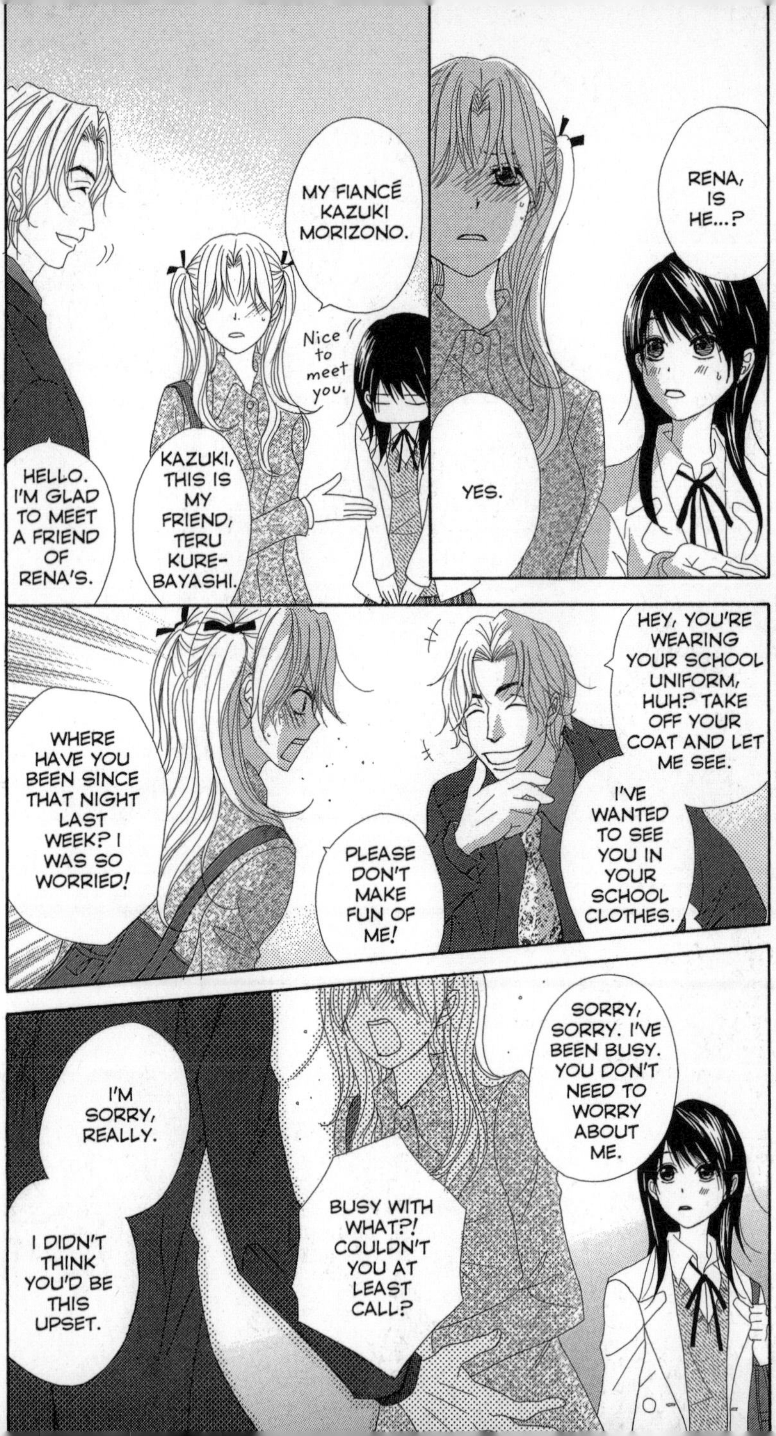
RENA, IS HE...?
YES.
MY FIANCÉ KAZUKI MORIZONO.
Nice to meet you.
KAZUKI, THIS IS MY FRIEND, TERU KURE-BAYASHI.
HELLO. I'M GLAD TO MEET A FRIEND OF RENA'S.
HEY, YOU'RE WEARING YOUR SCHOOL UNIFORM, HUH? TAKE OFF YOUR COAT AND LET ME SEE.
I'VE WANTED TO SEE YOU IN YOUR SCHOOL CLOTHES.
PLEASE DON'T MAKE FUN OF ME!
WHERE HAVE YOU BEEN SINCE THAT NIGHT LAST WEEK? I WAS SO WORRIED!
SORRY, SORRY. I'VE BEEN BUSY. YOU DON'T NEED TO WORRY ABOUT ME.
BUSY WITH WHAT?! COULDN'T YOU AT LEAST CALL?
I'M SORRY, REALLY.
I DIDN'T THINK YOU'D BE THIS UPSET.

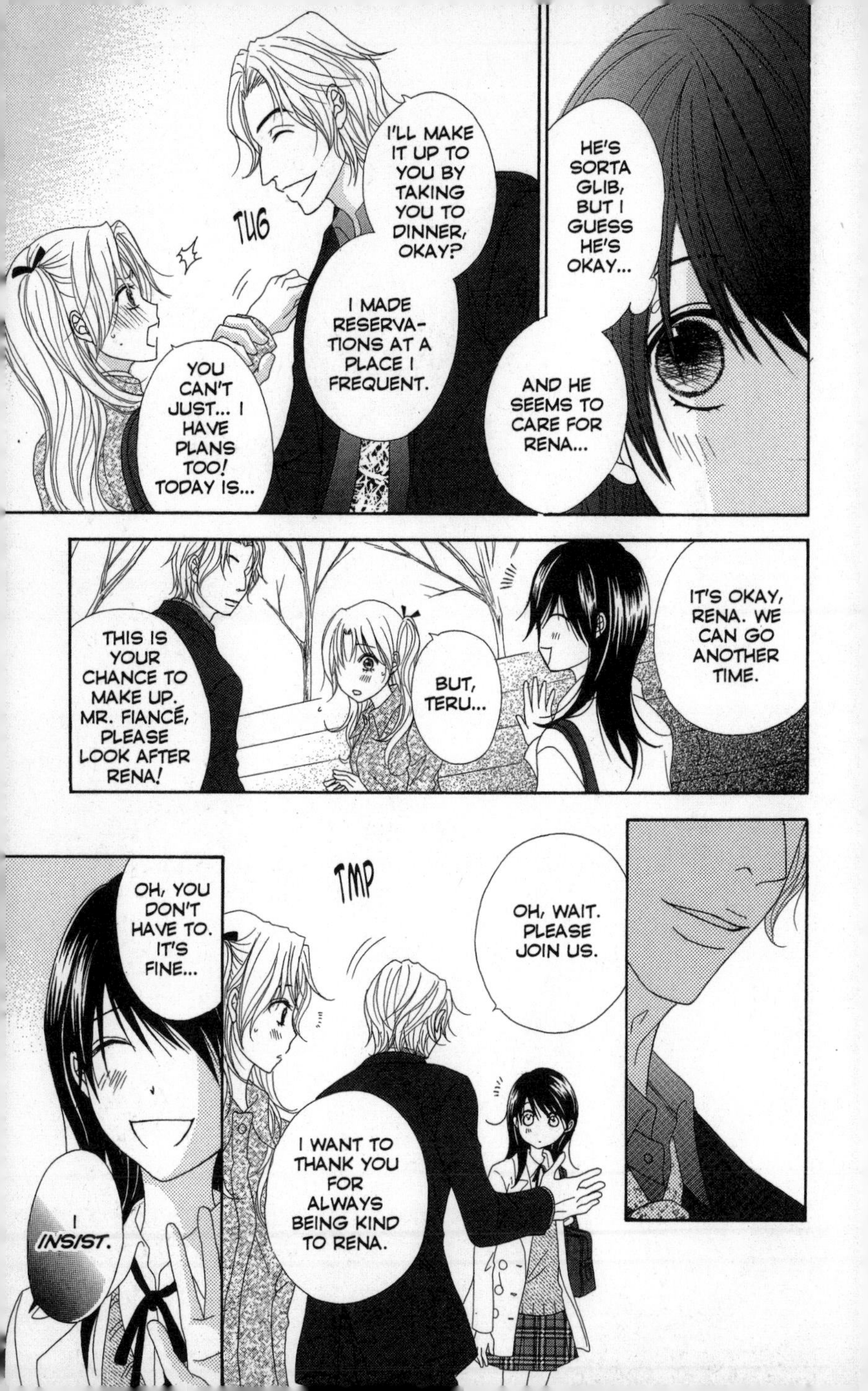
HE'S SORTA GLIB, BUT I GUESS HE'S OKAY...
AND HE SEEMS TO CARE FOR RENA...
I'LL MAKE IT UP TO YOU BY TAKING YOU TO DINNER, OKAY?
I MADE RESERVATIONS AT A PLACE I FREQUENT.
TUG
YOU CAN'T JUST... I HAVE PLANS TOO! TODAY IS...
IT'S OKAY, RENA. WE CAN GO ANOTHER TIME.
BUT, TERU...
THIS IS YOUR CHANCE TO MAKE UP. MR. FIANCÉ, PLEASE LOOK AFTER RENA!
OH, WAIT. PLEASE JOIN US.
TMP
I WANT TO THANK YOU FOR ALWAYS BEING KIND TO RENA.
OH, YOU DON'T HAVE TO. IT'S FINE...
I *INSIST*.

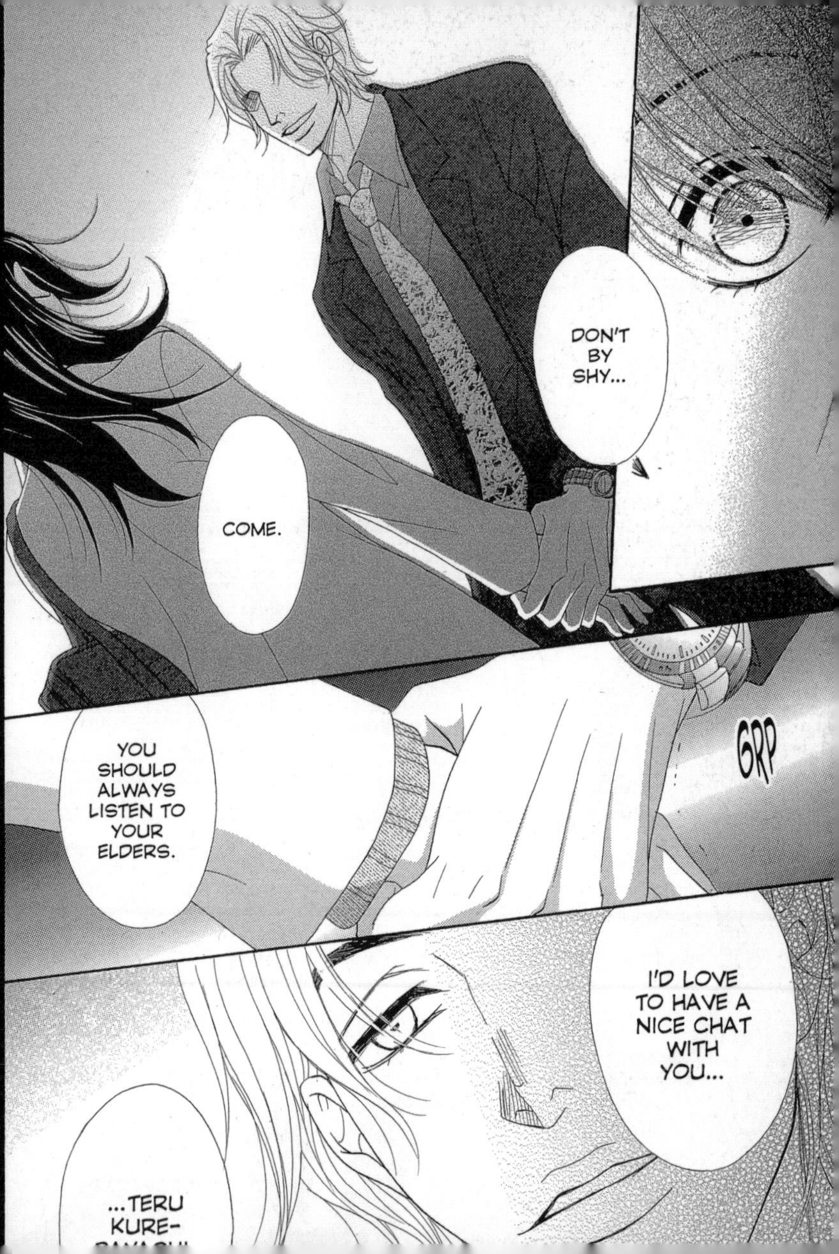
DON'T BY SHY...
COME.
GRP
YOU SHOULD ALWAYS LISTEN TO YOUR ELDERS.
I'D LOVE TO HAVE A NICE CHAT WITH YOU...
...TERU KURE-

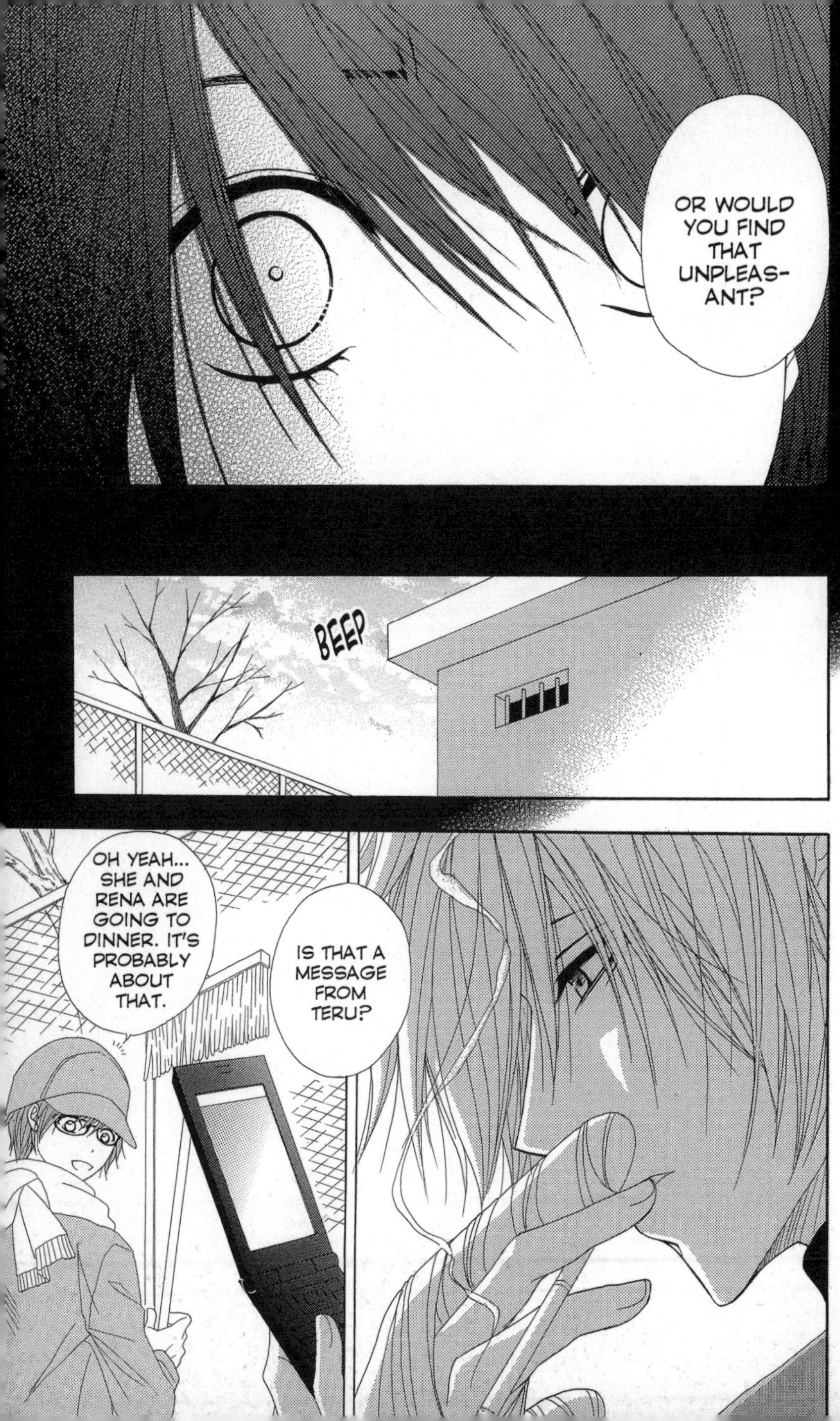
OR WOULD YOU FIND THAT UNPLEAS-ANT?
BEEP
IS THAT A MESSAGE FROM TERU?
OH YEAH... SHE AND RENA ARE GOING TO DINNER. IT'S PROBABLY ABOUT THAT.

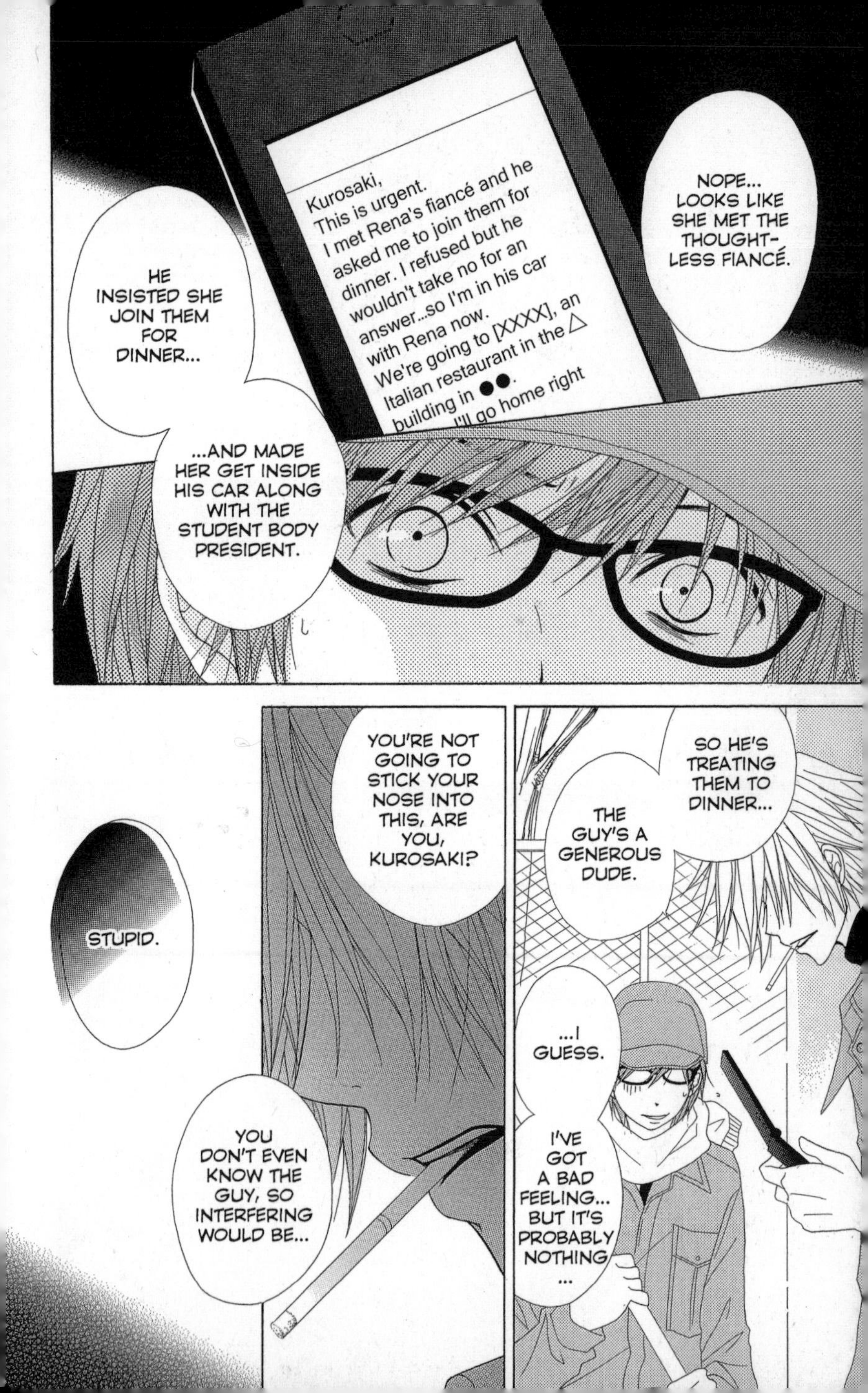
NOPE... LOOKS LIKE SHE MET THE THOUGHT-LESS FIANCÉ.
Kurosaki, This is urgent. I met Rena's fiancé and he asked me to join them for dinner. I refused but he wouldn't take no for an answer...so I'm in his car with Rena now. We're going to [XXXX], an Italian restaurant in the △ building in ●●. I'll go home right
HE INSISTED SHE JOIN THEM FOR DINNER...
...AND MADE HER GET INSIDE HIS CAR ALONG WITH THE STUDENT BODY PRESIDENT.
SO HE'S TREATING THEM TO DINNER...
THE GUY'S A GENEROUS DUDE.
...I GUESS.
I'VE GOT A BAD FEELING... BUT IT'S PROBABLY NOTHING...
YOU'RE NOT GOING TO STICK YOUR NOSE INTO THIS, ARE YOU, KUROSAKI?
YOU DON'T EVEN KNOW THE GUY, SO INTERFERING WOULD BE...
STUPID.

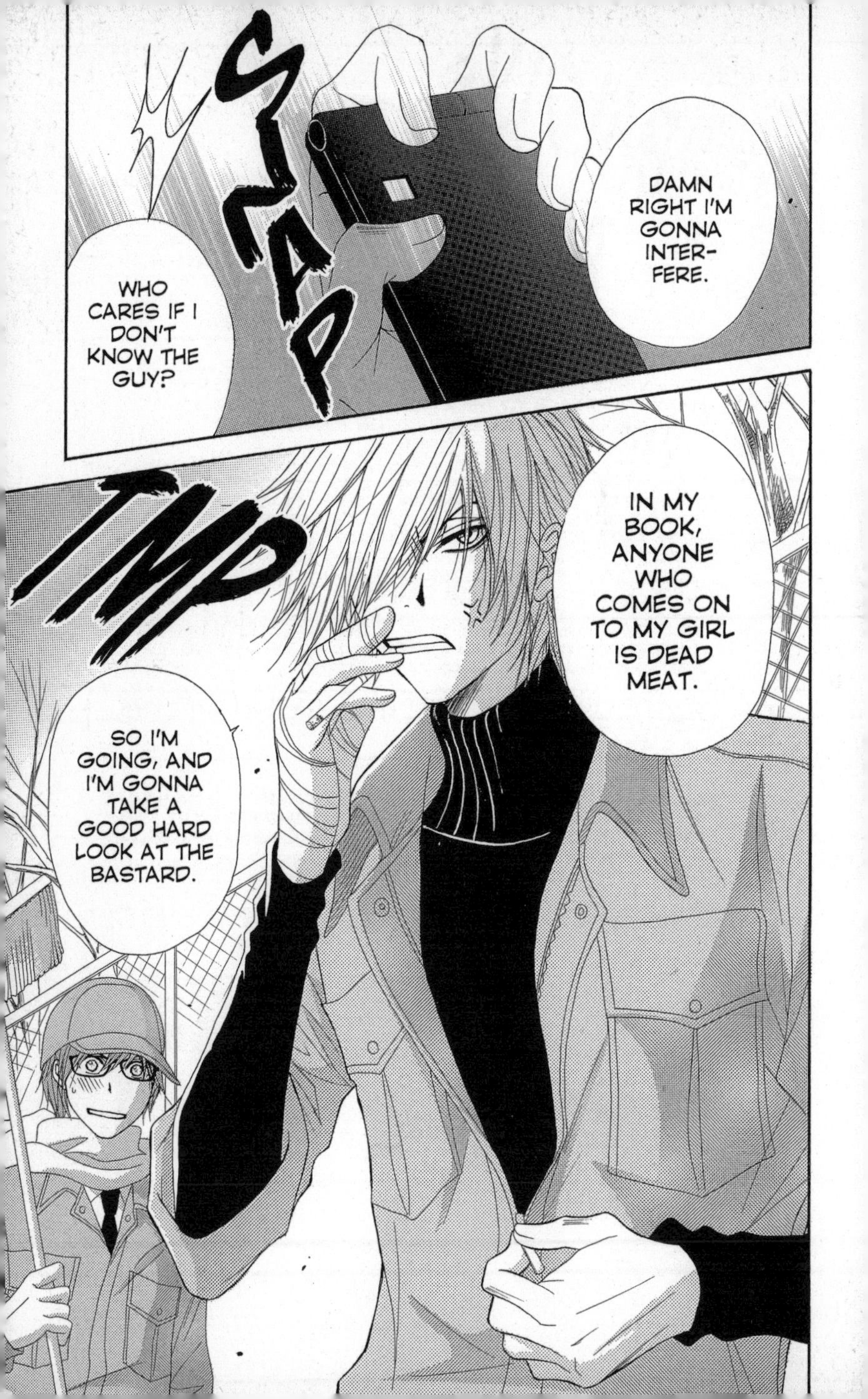
DAMN RIGHT I'M GONNA INTER-FERE.
SNAP
WHO CARES IF I DON'T KNOW THE GUY?
IN MY BOOK, ANYONE WHO COMES ON TO MY GIRL IS DEAD MEAT.
TMP
SO I'M GOING, AND I'M GONNA TAKE A GOOD HARD LOOK AT THE BASTARD.

DENGEKI DAISY QUESTION CORNER

RELOCATED

BALDLY ASK!!! ①

OKAY. THERE WASN'T EXTRA SPACE IN THIS VOLUME, SO WE TRIED RELOCATING "BALDLY ASK!!" I'M SORRY THIS SECTION ISN'T HANDWRITTEN. WE THOUGHT THIS WOULD BE EASIER TO READ THAN THE USUAL SCRIBBLE. ANYWAY, HERE WE GO!!

Q. IN CHAPTER 42, BOSS SAID IT WOULD BE BETTER TO LAY LOW FOR A WHILE AND NOT RETURN HOME. BUT IN CHAPTER 43, EVERYONE IS BACK TO THEIR NORMAL DAILY LIVES. DID KUROSAKI JUST SPEND A SHORT TIME AWAY?

(I.M., OSAKA)

A. IT WASN'T OBVIOUS, WAS IT? MY APOLOGIES. LET ME EXPLAIN IN GREATER DETAIL. IN CHAPTER 42, KUROSAKI AND TERU STAYED AT THAT HOTEL WHILE BOSS AND HIS BACK-UP FROM THE MINISTRY ACTED IMMEDIATELY TO MAKE SURE THAT KUROSAKI WOULD BE SAFE. AS A RESULT, TERU WAS ABLE TO RETURN HOME IN A FEW DAYS, AND KUROSAKI FOLLOWED ABOUT A WEEK LATER.

STILL, THE COUPLE WERE TOGETHER IN THAT HOTEL FOR SEVERAL DAYS. I UNDERSTAND THAT KUROSAKI WASTED NO TIME IN LOOKING FOR A SLEEPING BAG AND A BOOK ON ZEN MEDITATION.

Q. MS. MORI CHANGES HER HAIRSTYLE A LOT, DOESN'T SHE? HOW DOES HER REAL HAIR LOOK?

(A.C., OKAYAMA PREFECTURE)

A. CHIHARU ALMOST ALWAYS WEARS WIGS. MY CONCEPT OF CHIHARU IS THAT EVERY TIME SHE APPEARS, PEOPLE ASK, "WHO ARE YOU?" BY THE WAY, THAT SHORT HAIRSTYLE AT THE START OF CHAPTER 48 (VOLUME 10) IS HER OWN HAIR.

Q. IS TERU PRO FE●REZE OR PRO ●ESESH? WHAT SCENT DOES SHE LIKE?

(H.M., TOKYO)

A.

TERU IS FAN OF FE ●REZE, WHICH HAS BEEN AROUND A BIT LONGER. LATELY, SHE'S TAKEN A LIKING TO THE SUN-SCENTED ONE. IN ADDITION, SHE LIKES SPRAYS OF DEHYDRATED ETHANOL AND PURIFIED WATER, SCENTED WITH AROMA OILS (RIKO MIXES THEM HERSELF). RIKO'S "PEPPERMINT-TEA TREE-LEMONGRASS" SPRAY IS THE BOMB.

You can use it for cleaning too. It's so convenient. ♡

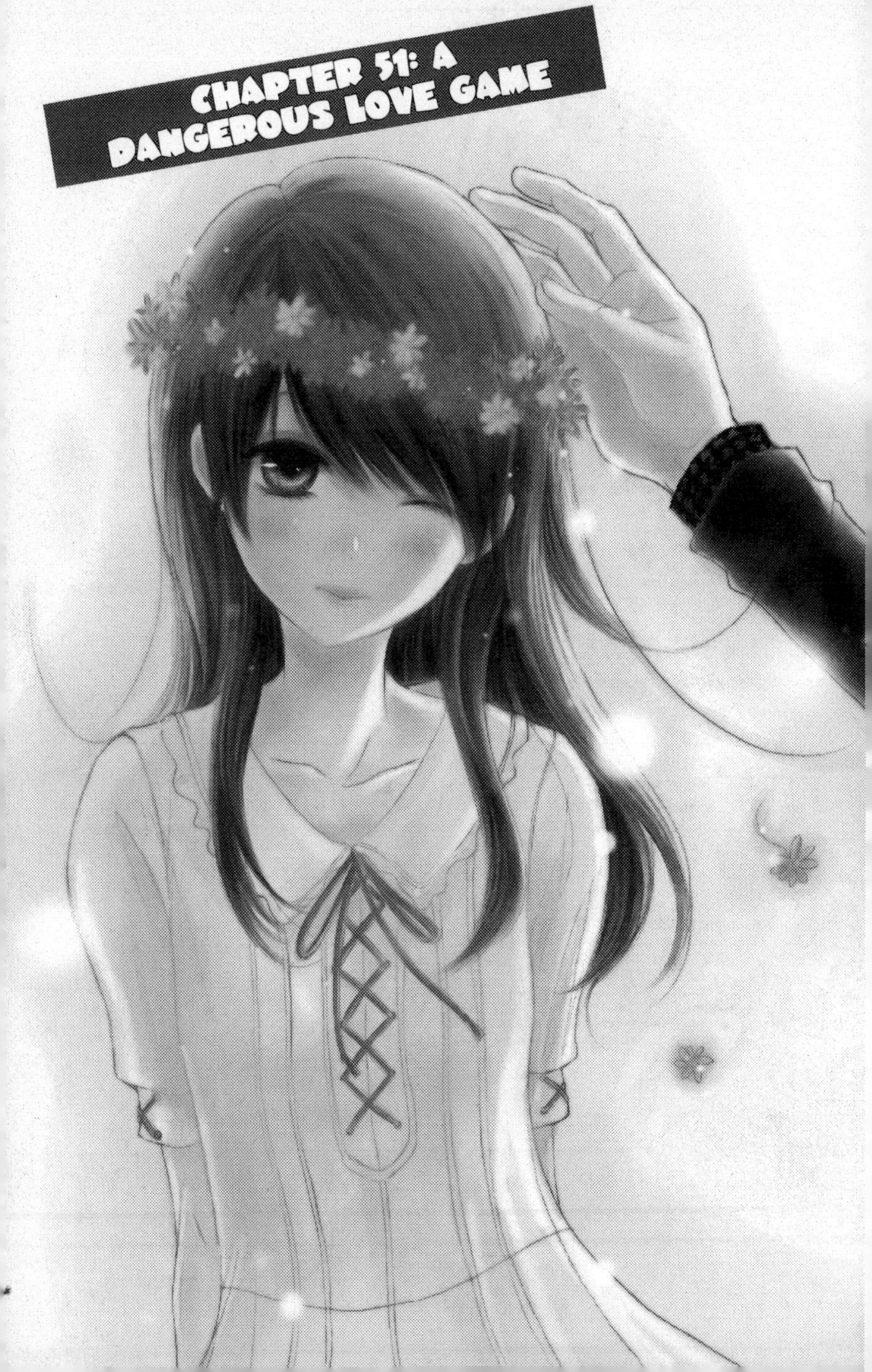
CHAPTER 51: A DANGEROUS LOVE GAME

DENGEKI DAISY QUESTION CORNER

RELOCATED

BALDLY ASK!!! ②

Q. WHEN YOU CARRY SOMEONE "PRINCESS-STYLE," I THOUGHT THE PERSON BEING CARRIED USUALLY DRAPES HER KNEES OVER THE ARMS OF THE PERSON CARRYING HER. BUT KUROSAKI IS TOUCHING TERU'S THIGHS. ISN'T IT DIFFICULT CARRYING SOMEONE THAT WAY? DID HE ENDURE IT SIMPLY BECAUSE HE WANTED TO TOUCH HER? KUROSAKI'S FINGERS ON HER THIGHS SEEMED A BIT LEWD, SO I HAD TO BALDLY ASK. (I'M TALKING ABOUT THE SCENE IN VOLUME 10, CHAPTER 49.)

(I.M., AICHI PREFECTURE)

A. THIS IS A GOOD QUESTION, VERY APPROPRIATE FOR THIS SECTION. THERE'S A REASON FOR THE PARTICULAR WAY IN WHICH HE CARRIED HER. HE'S DEFINITELY AT PAINS HOLDING HER IN THIS POSITION. I HAVE TO BE HONEST WITH YOU—THE AUTHOR MADE KUROSAKI CARRY TERU IN THIS AWKWARD MANNER TO PREVENT HER PANTIES FROM SHOWING. I DON'T HAVE ANYTHING AGAINST PANTIES. BUT I FELT THAT SHOWING UNDER-WEAR WOULD TAKE THE FOCUS AWAY FROM THE SERIOUSNESS OF THE SITUATION FOR BOTH THE READER AND KUROSAKI. SO WHILE KUROSAKI IS NOT TO BLAME HERE, IT'S NOT SURPRISING THAT EYEBROWS WERE RAISED CONSIDERING HOW HE USUALLY BEHAVES.

KEEP YOUR QUESTIONS COMING... DON'T HESITATE TO ASK.

Q. NATURALLY, KUROSAKI IS MORE SCIENCE-ORIENTED, BUT WHAT ABOUT TERU? IS SHE MORE INTO THE HUMANITIES OR SCIENCE?

(S.M., OKAYAMA PREFECTURE)

A.

TERU IS HUMANITIES-ORIENTED, AND SHE'S ESPECIALLY GOOD IN CLASSICAL LITERATURE AND LANGUAGES. SHE'S GOOD AT MATH, BUT NOT THE WAY KUROSAKI OR SOICHIRO ARE.

ON THE OTHER HAND, RATHER THAN BEING SCIENCE-ORIENTED, KUROSAKI PICKED UP ESSENTIAL KNOWLEDGE THROUGH SELF-STUDY. IN FACT, HIS CHARACTER IS SUPPOSED TO BE BAD AT READING AND WRITING KANJI CHARACTERS, BUT THAT DETAIL HASN'T MADE IT IN THE MANGA YET. THIS WEAKNESS HAS BOTHERED KUROSAKI, AND HE'S BEEN TRYING TO OVERCOME IT BY READING FAMOUS NOVELS. LIKE THE ***BROTHERS KARAMAZOV***.

D- Donragatana ...?
Donragatana? Oh, it's read "namakura-gatana," as in a dull sword.
HISTORICAL NOVEL

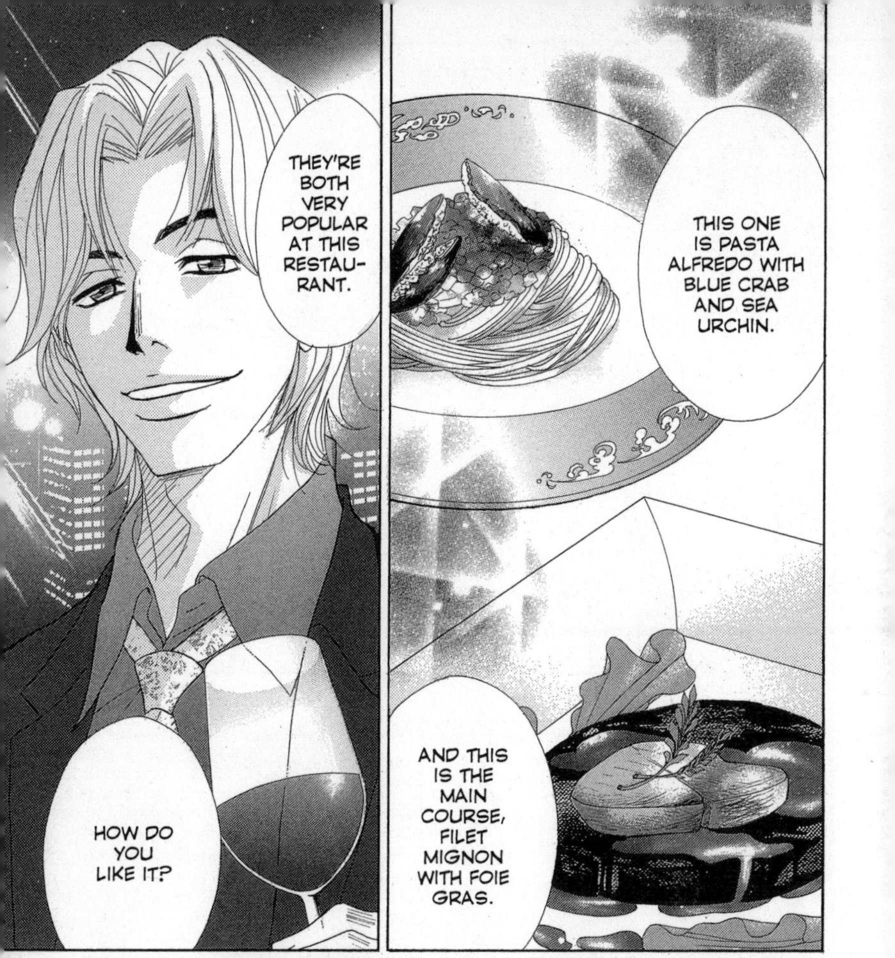

THIS ONE IS PASTA ALFREDO WITH BLUE CRAB AND SEA URCHIN.
AND THIS IS THE MAIN COURSE, FILET MIGNON WITH FOIE GRAS.
THEY'RE BOTH VERY POPULAR AT THIS RESTAURANT.
HOW DO YOU LIKE IT?

IN CHAPTER 50, KUROSAKI WEARS A TURTLENECK UNDER HIS WORK UNIFORM, BUT...IS THAT REALLY APPROPRIATE? (I MEAN FROM A MEN'S FASHION POINT OF VIEW.)
DUE TO THIS FAMOUS COMMERCIAL, TURTLENECKS EVOKE A REALLY STRONG IMAGE. I PERSONALLY THINK THAT GUYS WHO TEND TO BE ON THE FEMININE SIDE LOOK BETTER IN THEM... SO I WAS TORN ABOUT THIS. BUT, IT'S SIMPLY THE BEST THING TO WEAR WHEN IT'S COLD, SO I DECIDED TO PUT KUROSAKI IN A TURTLENECK. WHAT DO YOU ALL THINK?

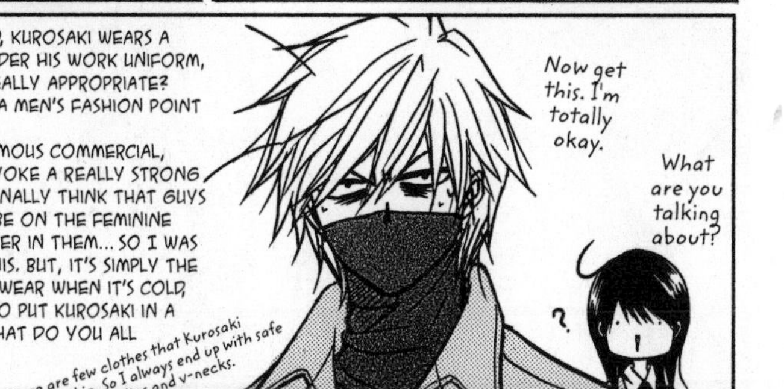

Now get this. I'm totally okay.
What are you talking about?
?
There are few clothes that Kurosaki looks good in. So I always end up with safe choices like hoodies and v-necks. Please tell me some new looks that would suit him.

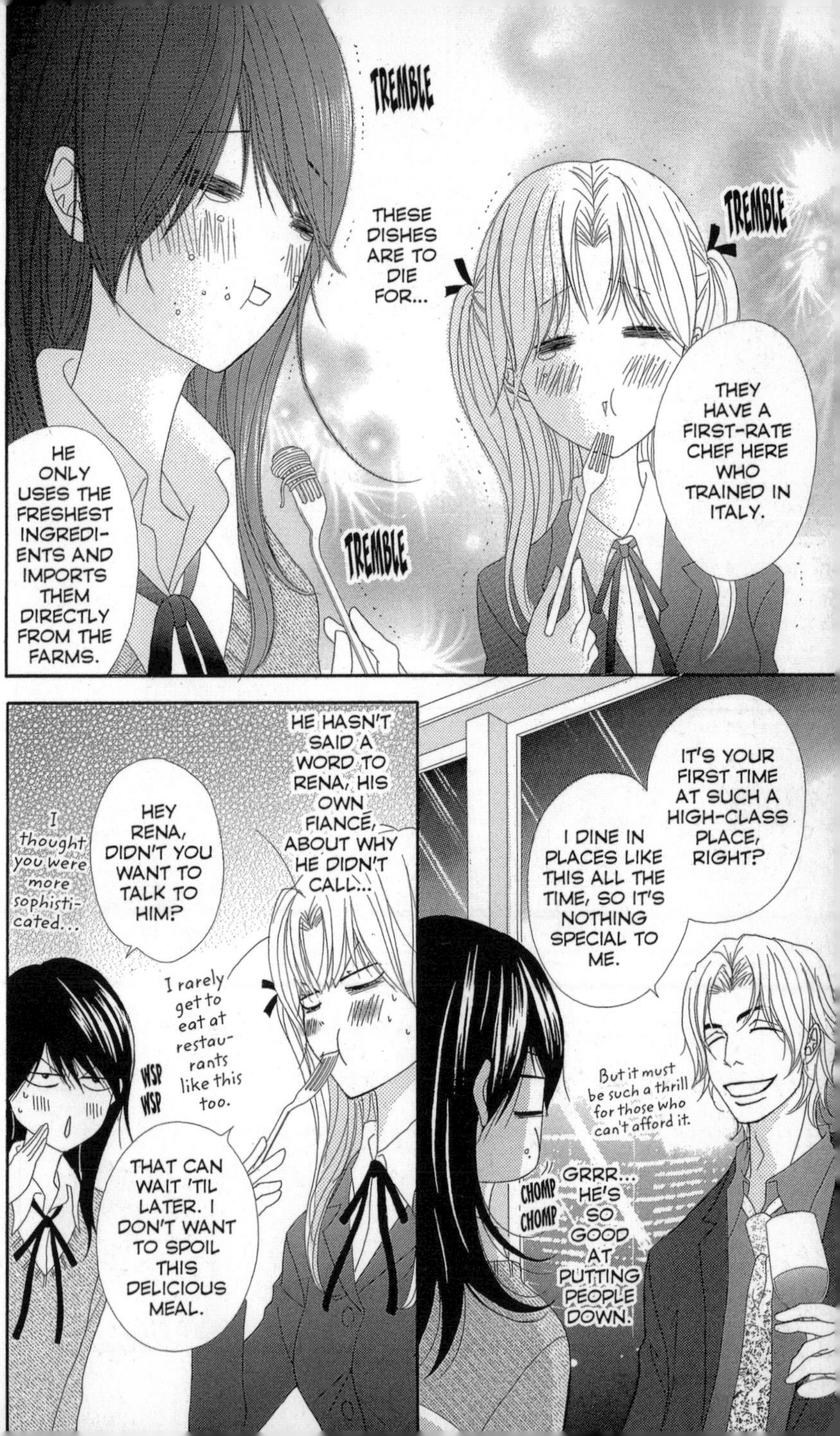
TREMBLE
THEY HAVE A FIRST-RATE CHEF HERE WHO TRAINED IN ITALY.
THESE DISHES ARE TO DIE FOR...
TREMBLE
HE ONLY USES THE FRESHEST INGREDI-ENTS AND IMPORTS THEM DIRECTLY FROM THE FARMS.
TREMBLE
IT'S YOUR FIRST TIME AT SUCH A HIGH-CLASS PLACE, RIGHT?
I DINE IN PLACES LIKE THIS ALL THE TIME, SO IT'S NOTHING SPECIAL TO ME.
But it must be such a thrill for those who can't afford it.
GRRR... HE'S SO GOOD AT PUTTING PEOPLE DOWN.
CHOMP CHOMP
HE HASN'T SAID A WORD TO RENA, HIS OWN FIANCÉ, ABOUT WHY HE DIDN'T CALL...
HEY RENA, DIDN'T YOU WANT TO TALK TO HIM?
I thought you were more sophisti-cated...
I rarely get to eat at restau-rants like this too.
WSP WSP
THAT CAN WAIT 'TIL LATER. I DON'T WANT TO SPOIL THIS DELICIOUS MEAL.

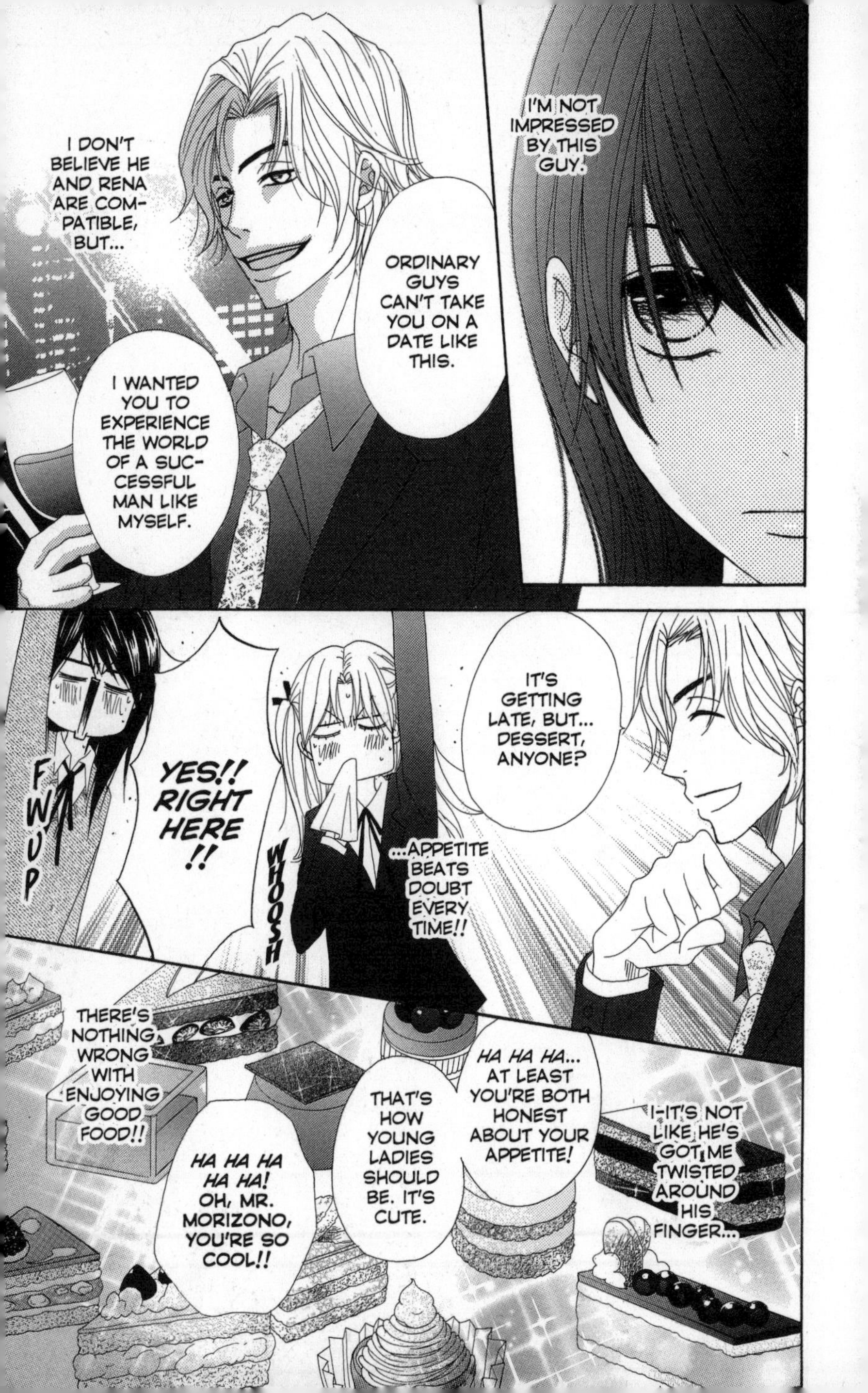
I'M NOT IMPRESSED BY THIS GUY.
ORDINARY GUYS CAN'T TAKE YOU ON A DATE LIKE THIS.
I WANTED YOU TO EXPERIENCE THE WORLD OF A SUC-CESSFUL MAN LIKE MYSELF.
I DON'T BELIEVE HE AND RENA ARE COM-PATIBLE, BUT...
IT'S GETTING LATE, BUT... DESSERT, ANYONE?
...APPETITE BEATS DOUBT EVERY TIME!!
WHOOSH
YES!! RIGHT HERE!!
FWUP
I-IT'S NOT LIKE HE'S GOT ME TWISTED AROUND HIS FINGER...
HA HA HA... AT LEAST YOU'RE BOTH HONEST ABOUT YOUR APPETITE!
THAT'S HOW YOUNG LADIES SHOULD BE. IT'S CUTE.
THERE'S NOTHING WRONG WITH ENJOYING GOOD FOOD!!
HA HA HA HA HA! OH, MR. MORIZONO, YOU'RE SO COOL!!

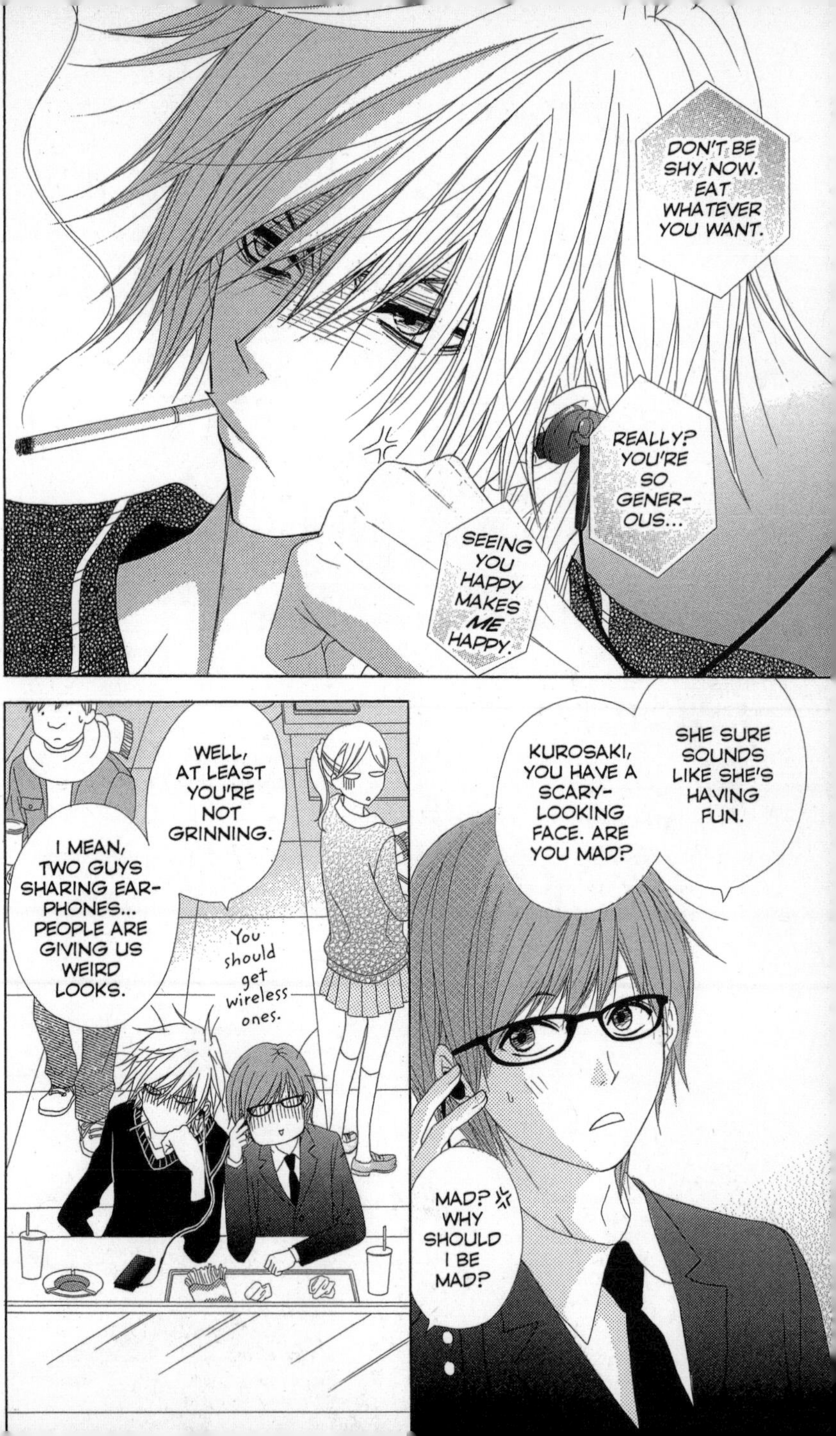
DON'T BE SHY NOW. EAT WHATEVER YOU WANT.
REALLY? YOU'RE SO GENER-OUS...
SEEING YOU HAPPY MAKES *ME* HAPPY.
SHE SURE SOUNDS LIKE SHE'S HAVING FUN.
KUROSAKI, YOU HAVE A SCARY-LOOKING FACE. ARE YOU MAD?
MAD? WHY SHOULD I BE MAD?
WELL, AT LEAST YOU'RE NOT GRINNING.
I MEAN, TWO GUYS SHARING EAR-PHONES... PEOPLE ARE GIVING US WEIRD LOOKS.
You should get wireless ones.

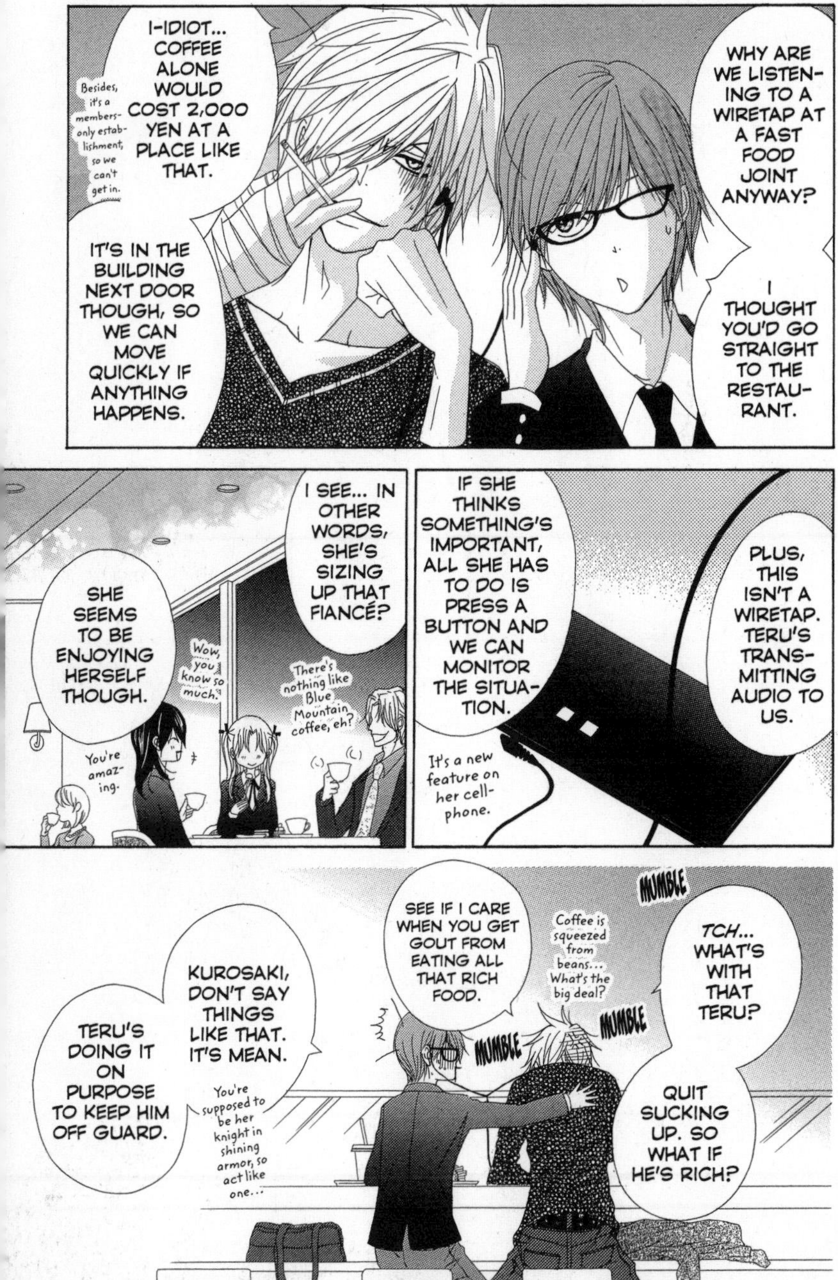
WHY ARE WE LISTENING TO A WIRETAP AT A FAST FOOD JOINT ANYWAY?
I THOUGHT YOU'D GO STRAIGHT TO THE RESTAURANT.
I-IDIOT... COFFEE ALONE WOULD COST 2,000 YEN AT A PLACE LIKE THAT.
Besides, it's a members-only establishment, so we can't get in.
IT'S IN THE BUILDING NEXT DOOR THOUGH, SO WE CAN MOVE QUICKLY IF ANYTHING HAPPENS.
PLUS, THIS ISN'T A WIRETAP. TERU'S TRANSMITTING AUDIO TO US.
IF SHE THINKS SOMETHING'S IMPORTANT, ALL SHE HAS TO DO IS PRESS A BUTTON AND WE CAN MONITOR THE SITUATION.
It's a new feature on her cellphone.
I SEE... IN OTHER WORDS, SHE'S SIZING UP THAT FIANCÉ?
There's nothing like Blue Mountain coffee, eh?
Wow, you know so much.
You're amazing.
SHE SEEMS TO BE ENJOYING HERSELF THOUGH.
MUMBLE
TCH... WHAT'S WITH THAT TERU?
Coffee is squeezed from beans... What's the big deal?
SEE IF I CARE WHEN YOU GET GOUT FROM EATING ALL THAT RICH FOOD.
MUMBLE
MUMBLE
QUIT SUCKING UP. SO WHAT IF HE'S RICH?
KUROSAKI, DON'T SAY THINGS LIKE THAT. IT'S MEAN.
TERU'S DOING IT ON PURPOSE TO KEEP HIM OFF GUARD.
You're supposed to be her knight in shining armor, so act like one...

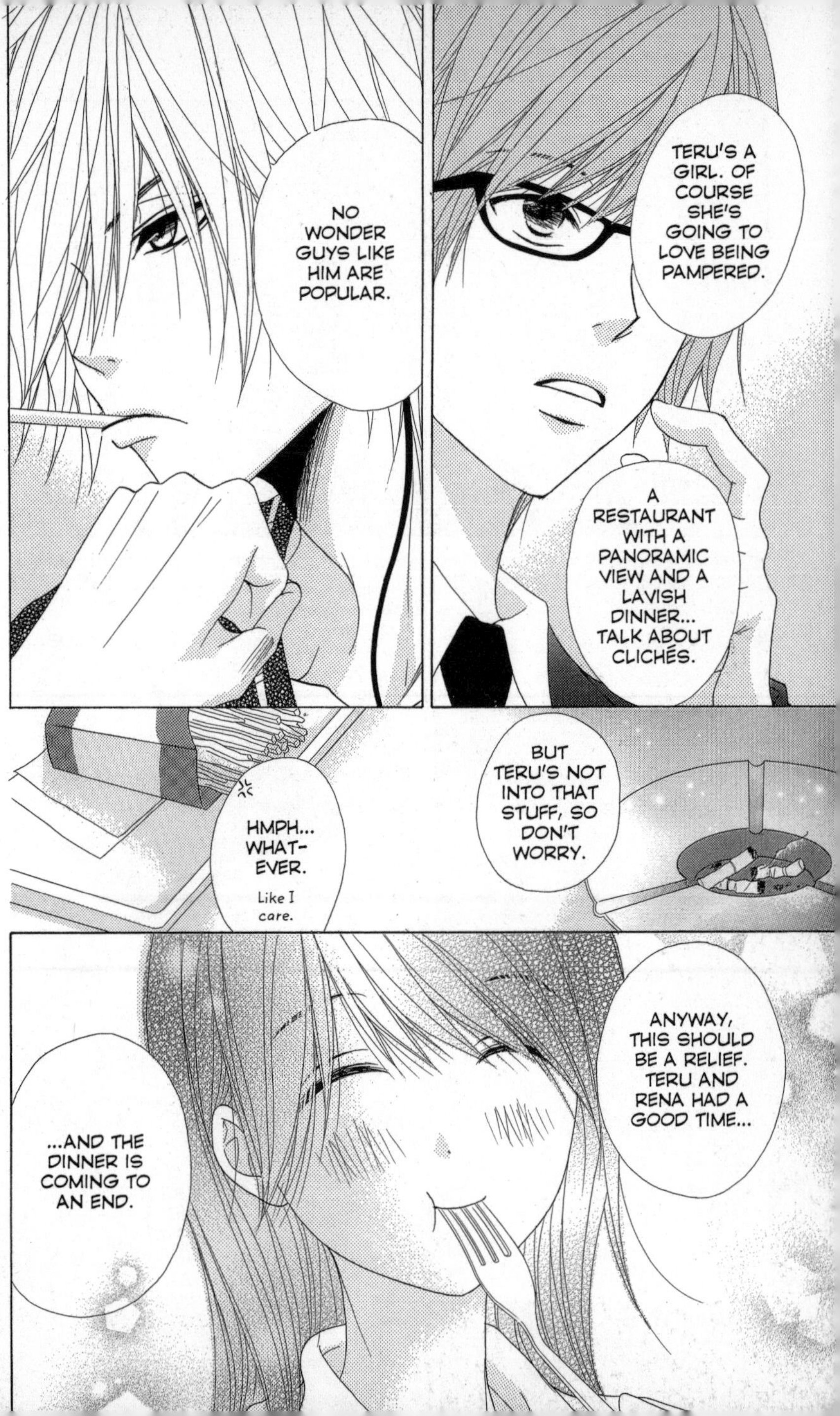
TERU'S A GIRL. OF COURSE SHE'S GOING TO LOVE BEING PAMPERED.
A RESTAURANT WITH A PANORAMIC VIEW AND A LAVISH DINNER... TALK ABOUT CLICHÉS.
NO WONDER GUYS LIKE HIM ARE POPULAR.
BUT TERU'S NOT INTO THAT STUFF, SO DON'T WORRY.
HMPH... WHAT-EVER.
Like I care.
ANYWAY, THIS SHOULD BE A RELIEF. TERU AND RENA HAD A GOOD TIME...
...AND THE DINNER IS COMING TO AN END.

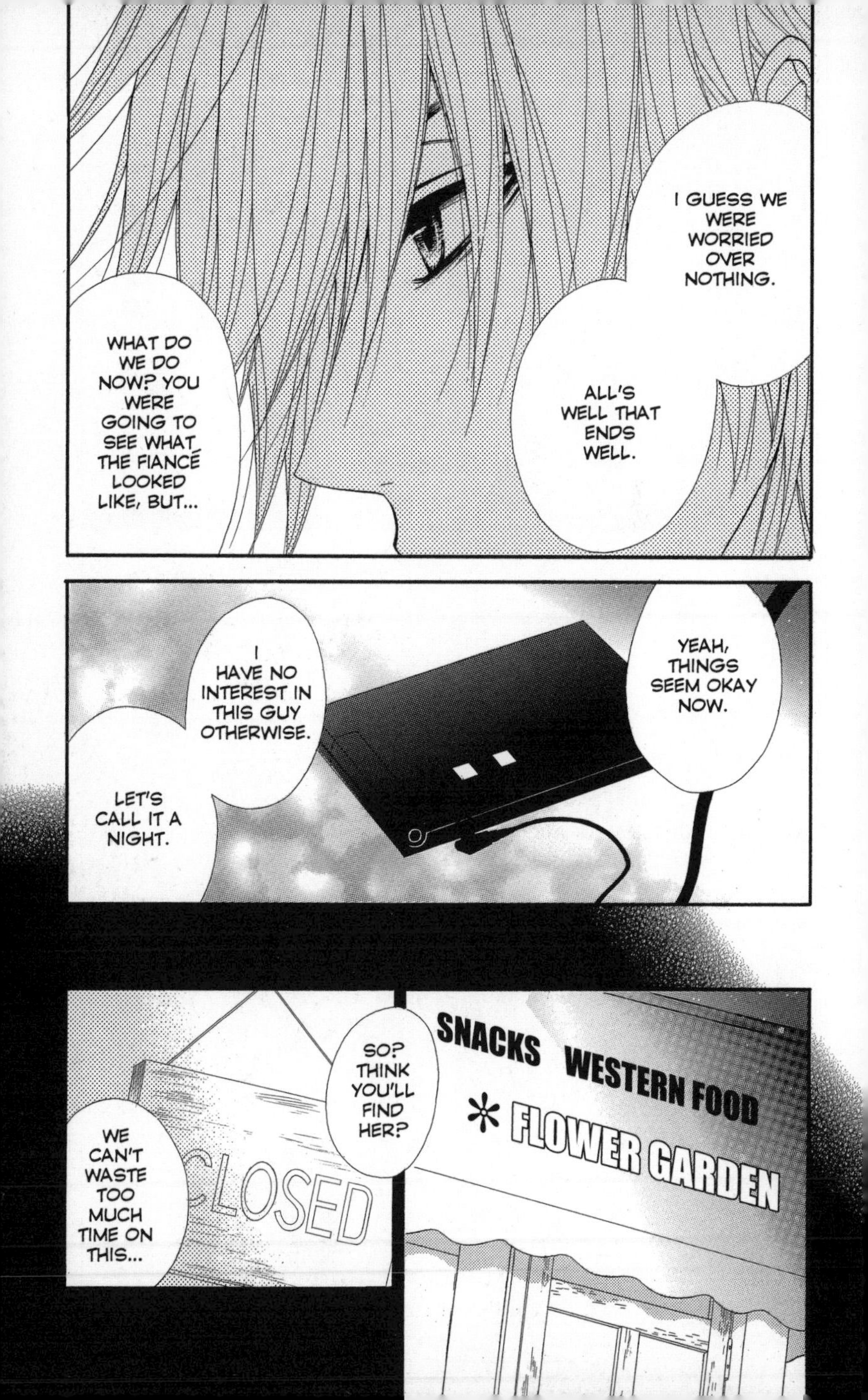
I GUESS WE WERE WORRIED OVER NOTHING.
ALL'S WELL THAT ENDS WELL.
WHAT DO WE DO NOW? YOU WERE GOING TO SEE WHAT THE FIANCÉ LOOKED LIKE, BUT...
YEAH, THINGS SEEM OKAY NOW.
I HAVE NO INTEREST IN THIS GUY OTHERWISE.
LET'S CALL IT A NIGHT.
SNACKS WESTERN FOOD
* FLOWER GARDEN
SO? THINK YOU'LL FIND HER?
CLOSED
WE CAN'T WASTE TOO MUCH TIME ON THIS...

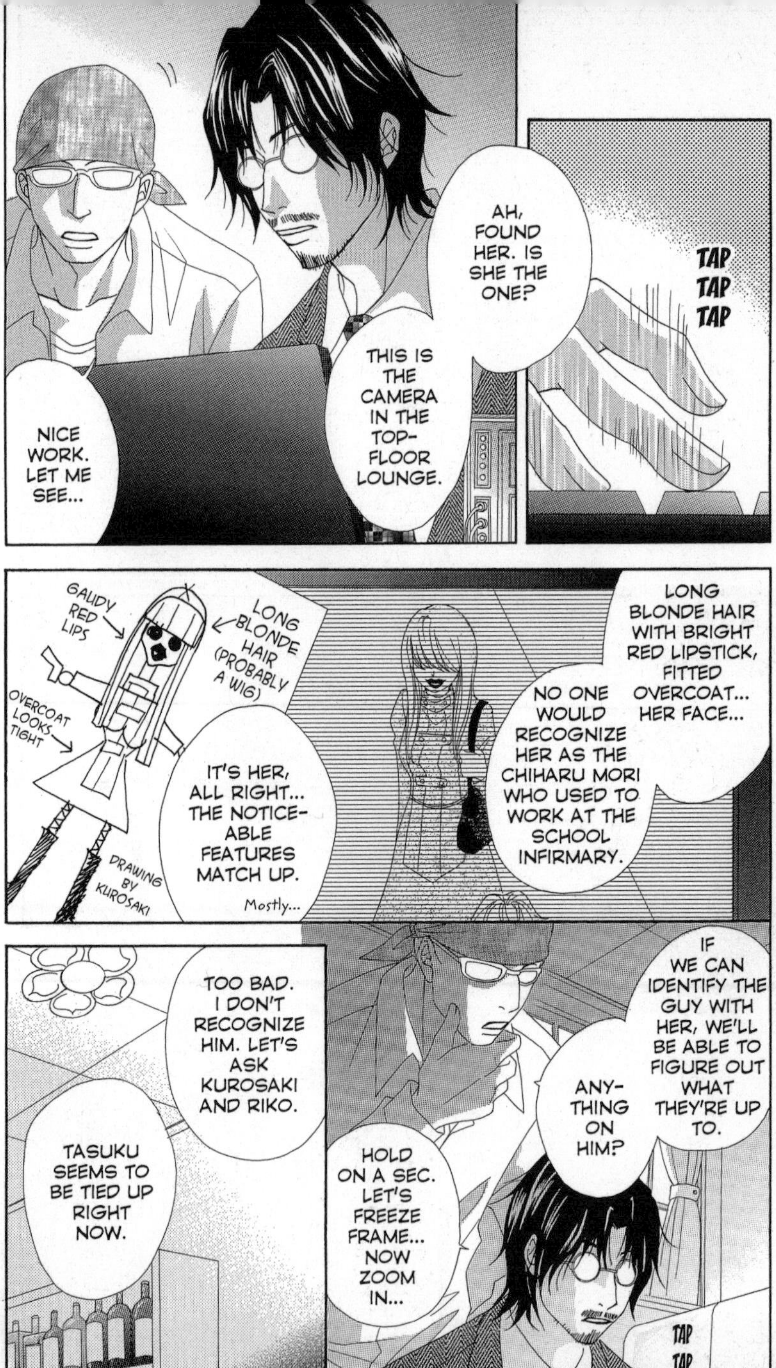
TAP TAP TAP
AH, FOUND HER. IS SHE THE ONE?
THIS IS THE CAMERA IN THE TOP-FLOOR LOUNGE.
NICE WORK. LET ME SEE...
LONG BLONDE HAIR WITH BRIGHT RED LIPSTICK, FITTED OVERCOAT... HER FACE...
NO ONE WOULD RECOGNIZE HER AS THE CHIHARU MORI WHO USED TO WORK AT THE SCHOOL INFIRMARY.
LONG BLONDE HAIR (PROBABLY A WIG)
GAUDY RED LIPS
OVERCOAT LOOKS TIGHT
IT'S HER, ALL RIGHT... THE NOTICE-ABLE FEATURES MATCH UP.
Mostly...
DRAWING BY KUROSAKI
IF WE CAN IDENTIFY THE GUY WITH HER, WE'LL BE ABLE TO FIGURE OUT WHAT THEY'RE UP TO.
ANY-THING ON HIM?
HOLD ON A SEC. LET'S FREEZE FRAME... NOW ZOOM IN...
TAP TAP
TOO BAD. I DON'T RECOGNIZE HIM. LET'S ASK KUROSAKI AND RIKO.
TASUKU SEEMS TO BE TIED UP RIGHT NOW.

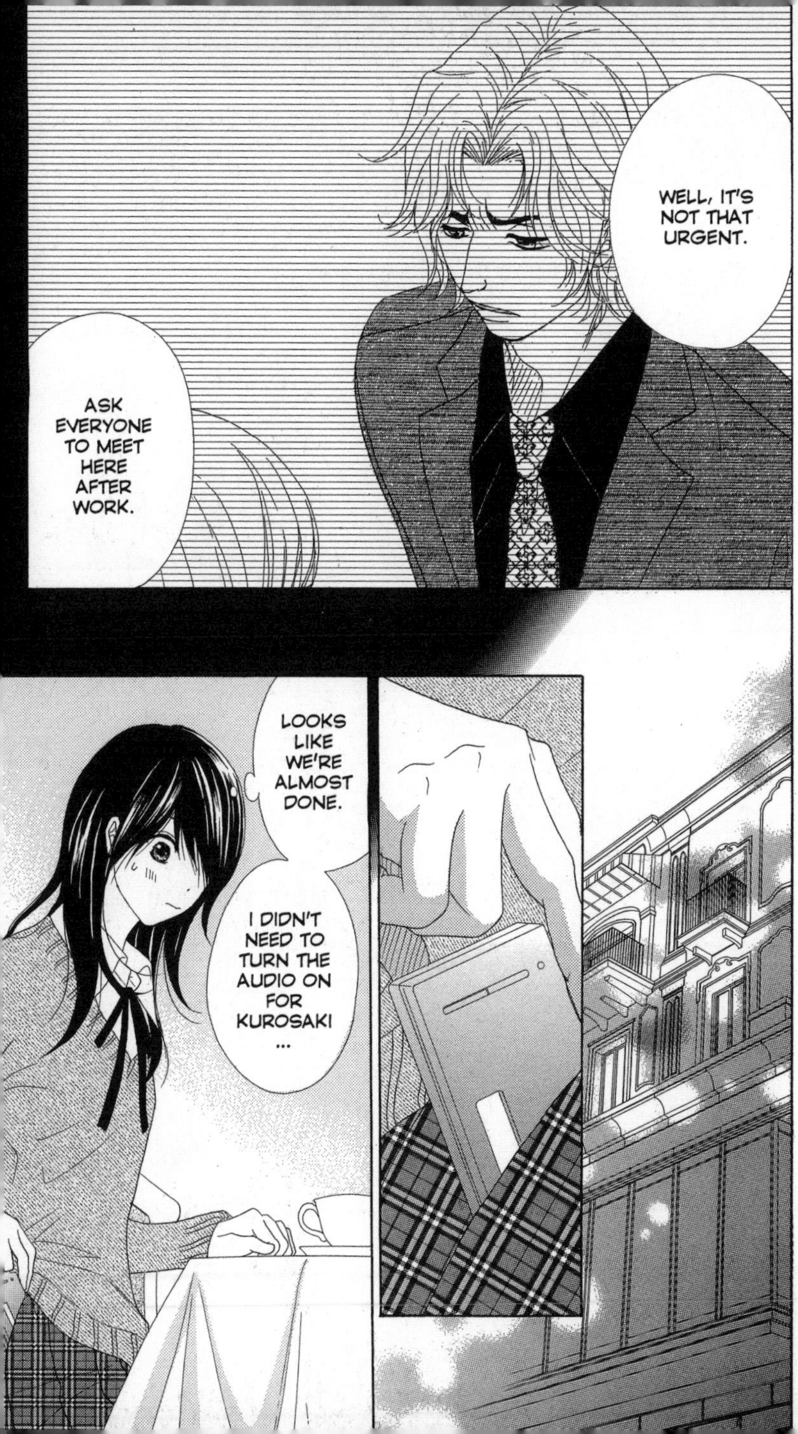
WELL, IT'S NOT THAT URGENT.
ASK EVERYONE TO MEET HERE AFTER WORK.
LOOKS LIKE WE'RE ALMOST DONE.
I DIDN'T NEED TO TURN THE AUDIO ON FOR KUROSAKI...

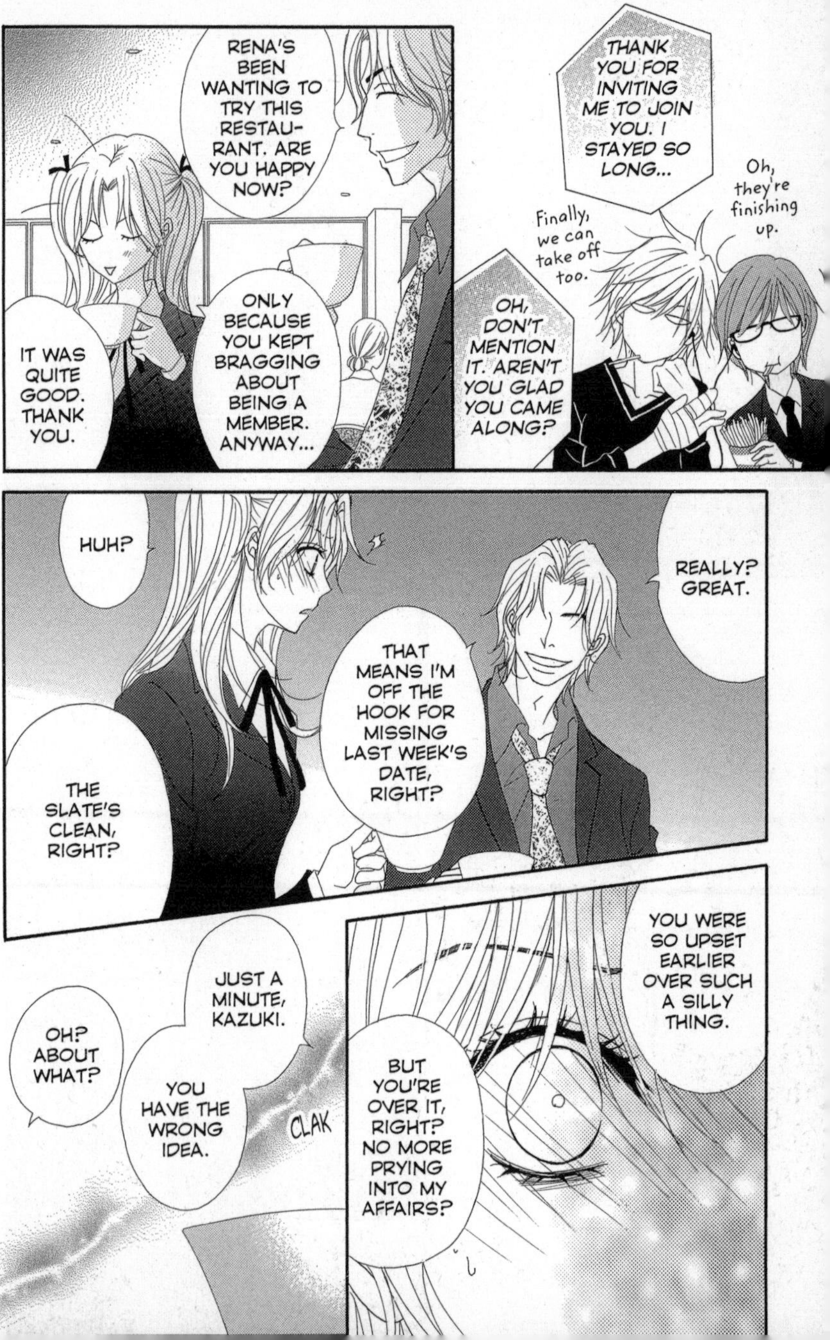
THANK YOU FOR INVITING ME TO JOIN YOU. I STAYED SO LONG...
Oh, they're finishing up.
Finally, we can take off too.
OH, DON'T MENTION IT. AREN'T YOU GLAD YOU CAME ALONG?
RENA'S BEEN WANTING TO TRY THIS RESTAU-RANT. ARE YOU HAPPY NOW?
ONLY BECAUSE YOU KEPT BRAGGING ABOUT BEING A MEMBER. ANYWAY...
IT WAS QUITE GOOD. THANK YOU.
REALLY? GREAT.
THAT MEANS I'M OFF THE HOOK FOR MISSING LAST WEEK'S DATE, RIGHT?
HUH?
THE SLATE'S CLEAN, RIGHT?
YOU WERE SO UPSET EARLIER OVER SUCH A SILLY THING.
BUT YOU'RE OVER IT, RIGHT? NO MORE PRYING INTO MY AFFAIRS?
CLAK
JUST A MINUTE, KAZUKI.
YOU HAVE THE WRONG IDEA.
OH? ABOUT WHAT?

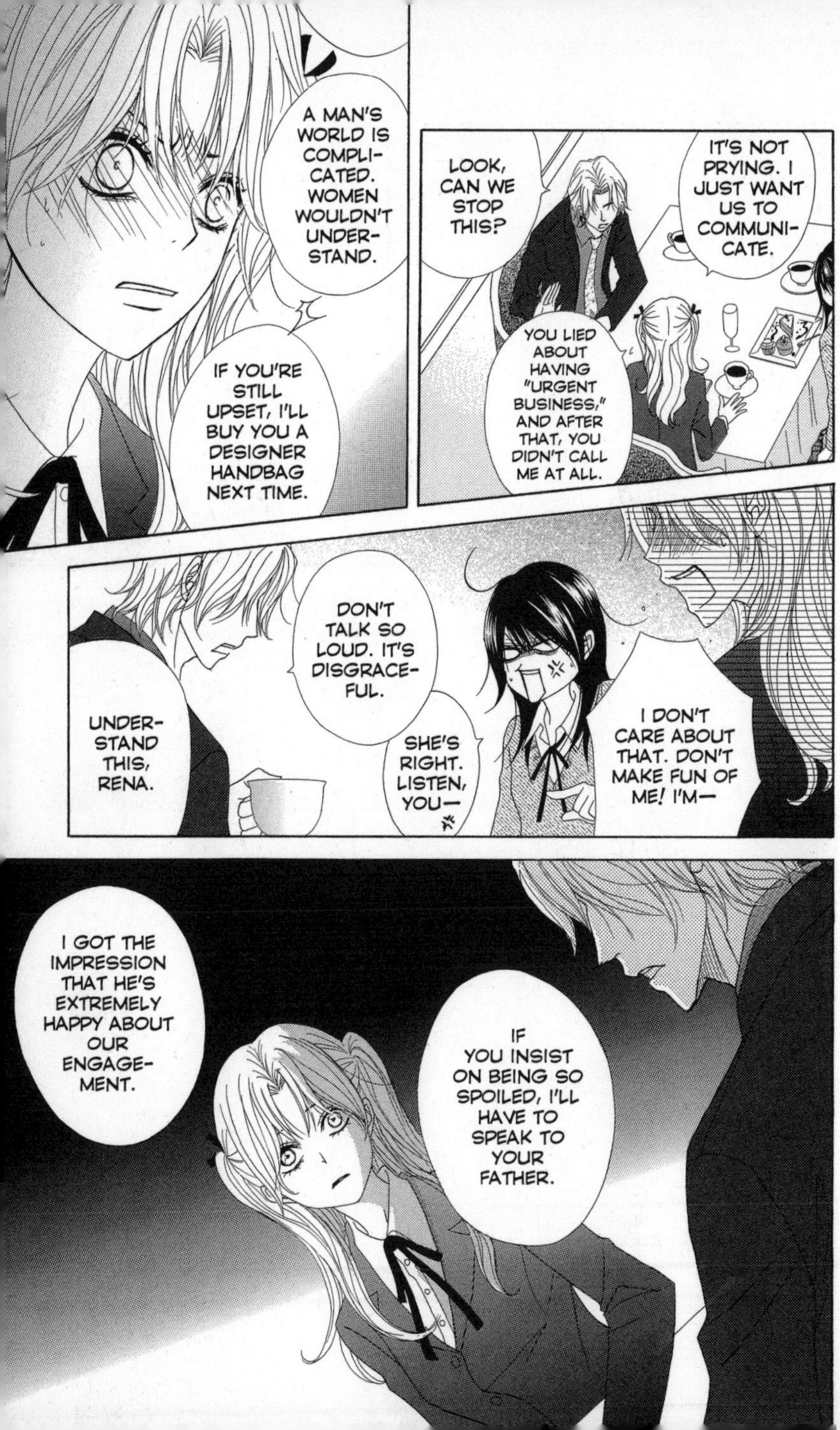
IT'S NOT PRYING. I JUST WANT US TO COMMUNICATE.
LOOK, CAN WE STOP THIS?
YOU LIED ABOUT HAVING "URGENT BUSINESS," AND AFTER THAT, YOU DIDN'T CALL ME AT ALL.
A MAN'S WORLD IS COMPLICATED. WOMEN WOULDN'T UNDERSTAND.
IF YOU'RE STILL UPSET, I'LL BUY YOU A DESIGNER HANDBAG NEXT TIME.
I DON'T CARE ABOUT THAT. DON'T MAKE FUN OF ME! I'M—
DON'T TALK SO LOUD. IT'S DISGRACEFUL.
SHE'S RIGHT. LISTEN, YOU—
UNDERSTAND THIS, RENA.
IF YOU INSIST ON BEING SO SPOILED, I'LL HAVE TO SPEAK TO YOUR FATHER.
I GOT THE IMPRESSION THAT HE'S EXTREMELY HAPPY ABOUT OUR ENGAGEMENT.

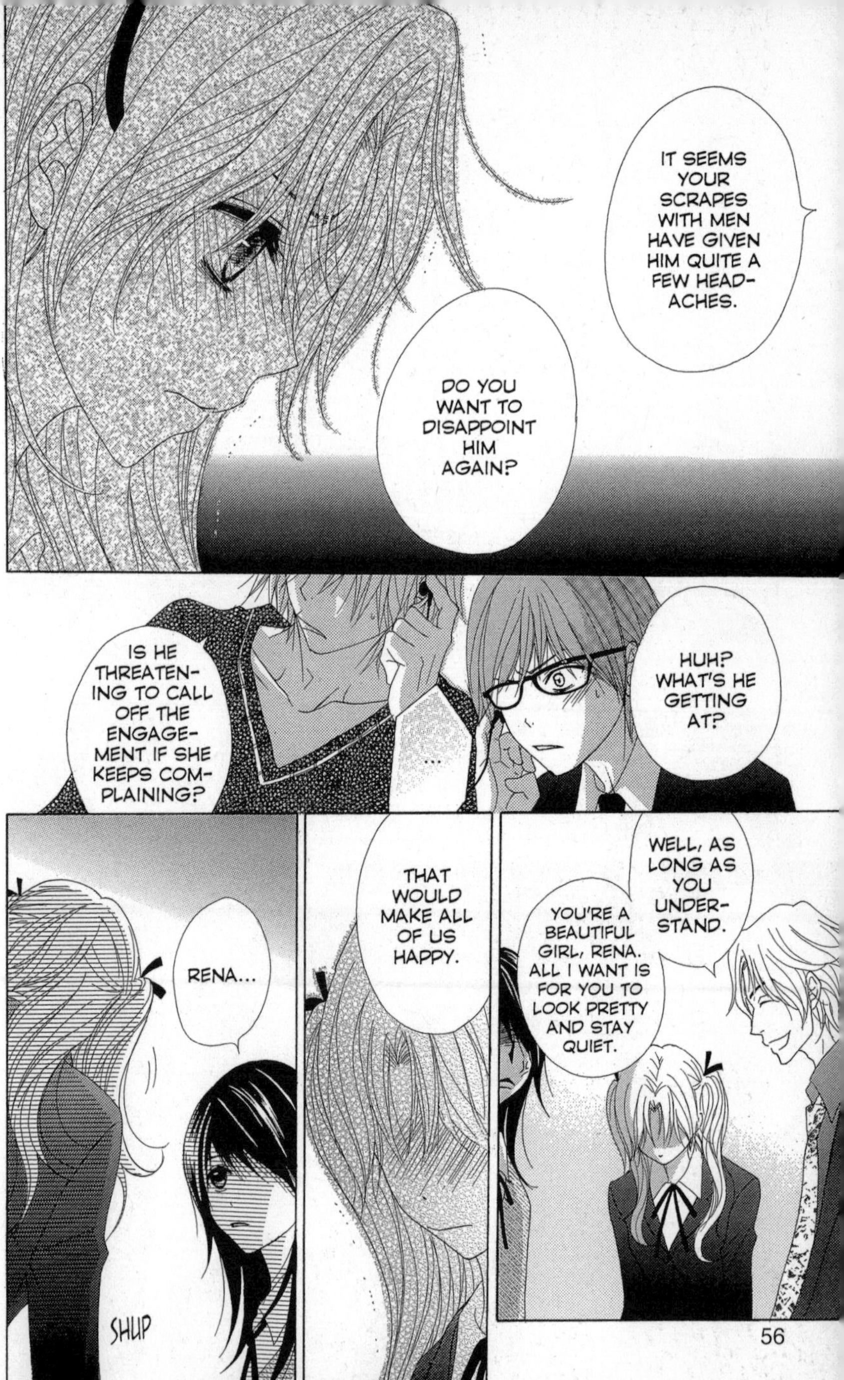
IT SEEMS YOUR SCRAPES WITH MEN HAVE GIVEN HIM QUITE A FEW HEAD-ACHES.
DO YOU WANT TO DISAPPOINT HIM AGAIN?
HUH? WHAT'S HE GETTING AT?
...
IS HE THREATEN-ING TO CALL OFF THE ENGAGE-MENT IF SHE KEEPS COM-PLAINING?
WELL, AS LONG AS YOU UNDER-STAND.
YOU'RE A BEAUTIFUL GIRL, RENA. ALL I WANT IS FOR YOU TO LOOK PRETTY AND STAY QUIET.
THAT WOULD MAKE ALL OF US HAPPY.
RENA...
SHUP

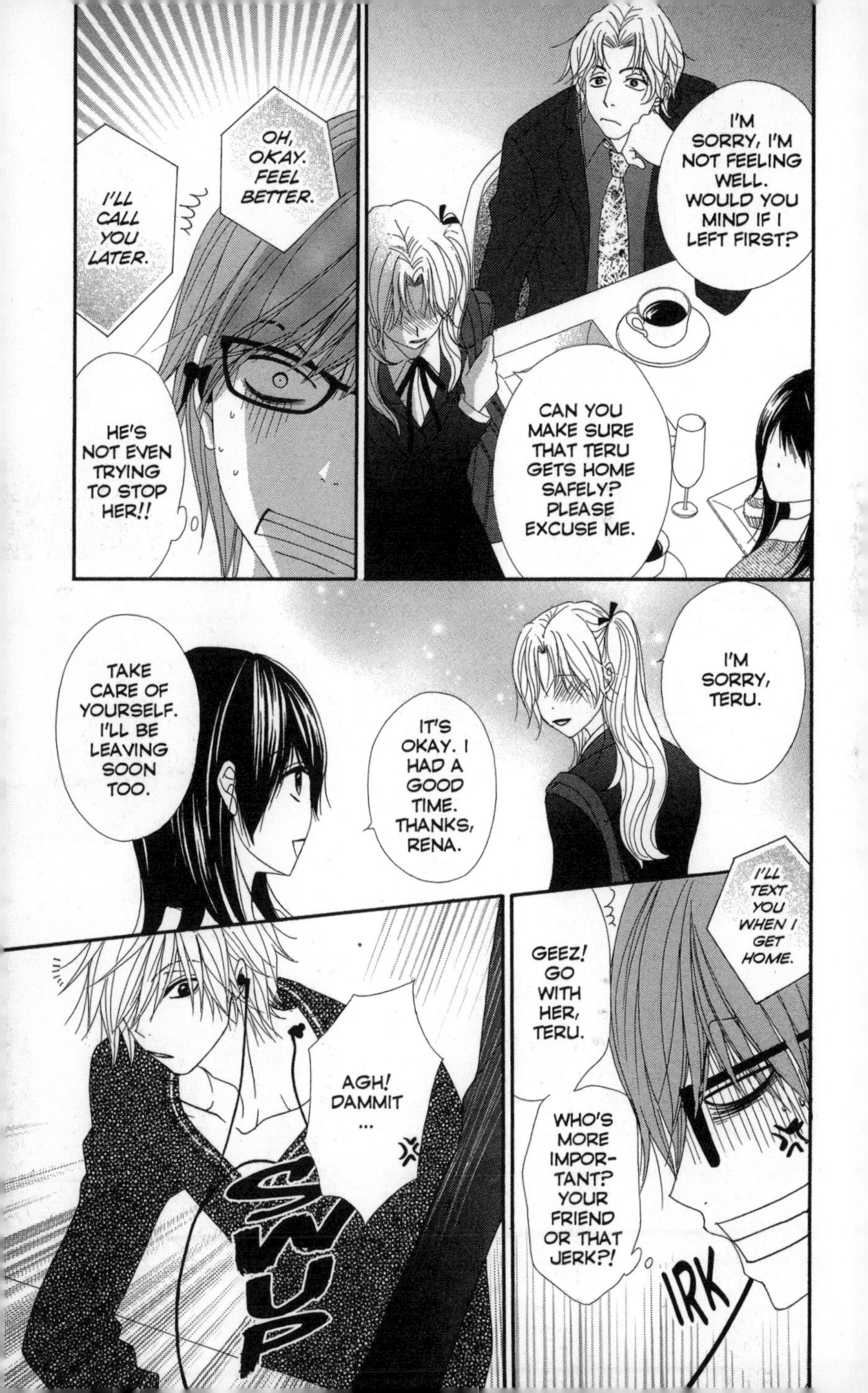
I'M SORRY, I'M NOT FEELING WELL. WOULD YOU MIND IF I LEFT FIRST?
CAN YOU MAKE SURE THAT TERU GETS HOME SAFELY? PLEASE EXCUSE ME.
OH, OKAY. FEEL BETTER.
I'LL CALL YOU LATER.
HE'S NOT EVEN TRYING TO STOP HER!!
I'M SORRY, TERU.
IT'S OKAY. I HAD A GOOD TIME. THANKS, RENA.
TAKE CARE OF YOURSELF. I'LL BE LEAVING SOON TOO.
I'LL TEXT YOU WHEN I GET HOME.
GEEZ! GO WITH HER, TERU.
WHO'S MORE IMPORTANT? YOUR FRIEND OR THAT JERK?!
IRK
AGH! DAMMIT ...
SWUP

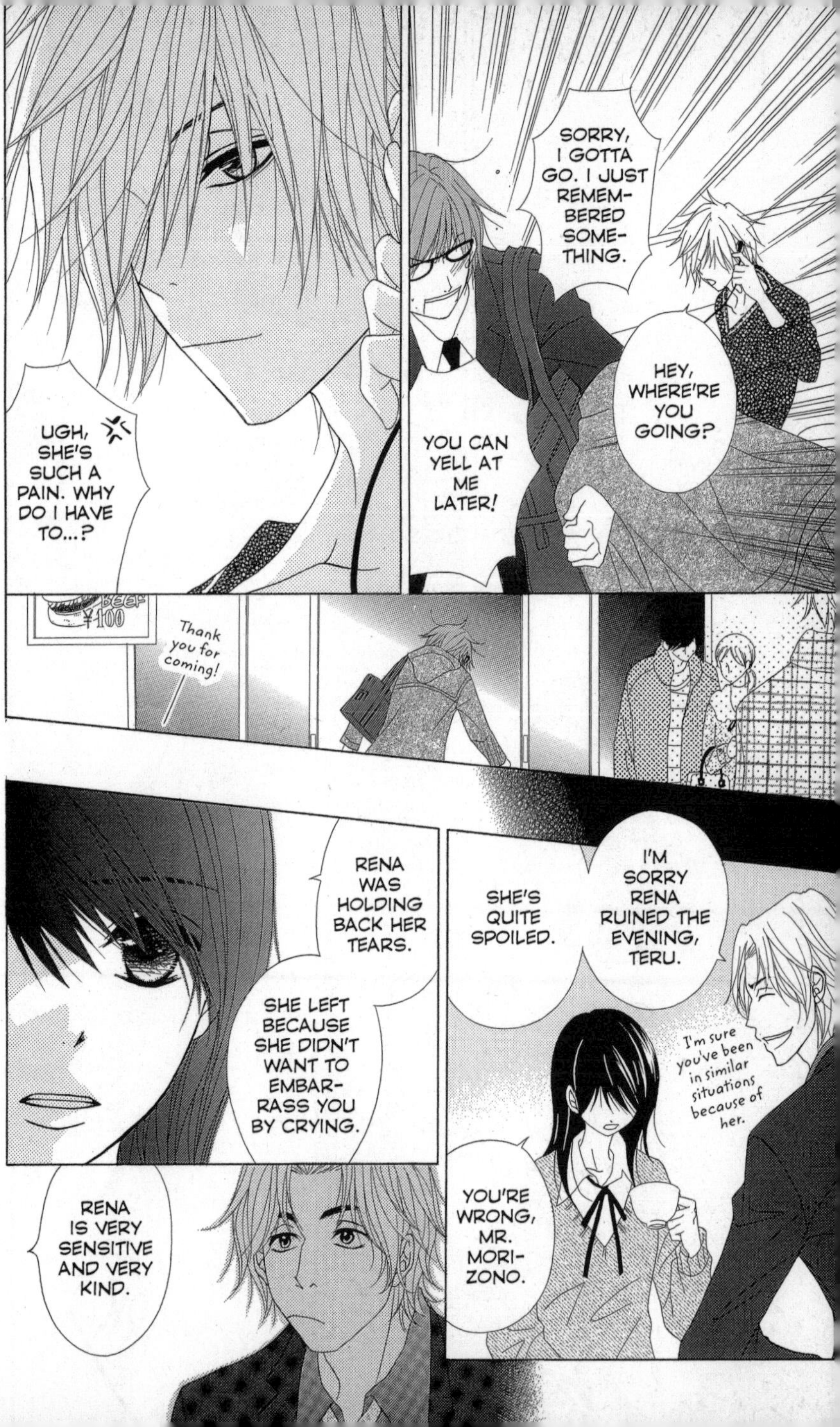
SORRY, I GOTTA GO. I JUST REMEMBERED SOMETHING.
HEY, WHERE'RE YOU GOING?
YOU CAN YELL AT ME LATER!
UGH, SHE'S SUCH A PAIN. WHY DO I HAVE TO...?
BEEF ¥100
Thank you for coming!
I'M SORRY RENA RUINED THE EVENING, TERU.
SHE'S QUITE SPOILED.
I'm sure you've been in similar situations because of her.
YOU'RE WRONG, MR. MORIZONO.
RENA WAS HOLDING BACK HER TEARS.
SHE LEFT BECAUSE SHE DIDN'T WANT TO EMBARRASS YOU BY CRYING.
RENA IS VERY SENSITIVE AND VERY KIND.

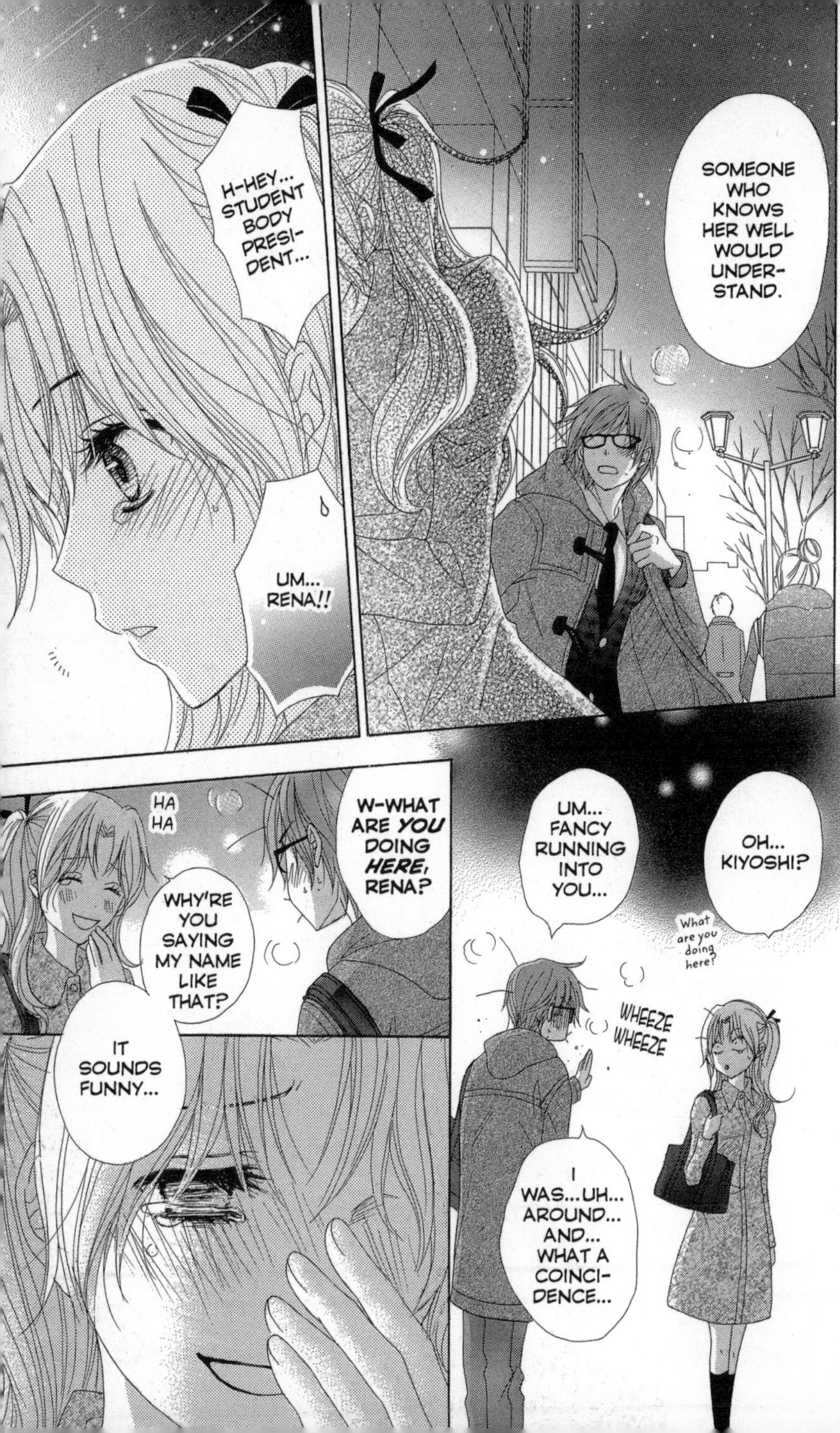
SOMEONE WHO KNOWS HER WELL WOULD UNDER-STAND.
H-HEY... STUDENT BODY PRESI-DENT...
UM... RENA!!
OH... KIYOSHI?
What are you doing here?
UM... FANCY RUNNING INTO YOU...
WHEEZE WHEEZE
I WAS...UH... AROUND... AND... WHAT A COINCI-DENCE...
W-WHAT ARE *YOU* DOING ***HERE***, RENA?
HA HA
WHY'RE YOU SAYING MY NAME LIKE THAT?
IT SOUNDS FUNNY...

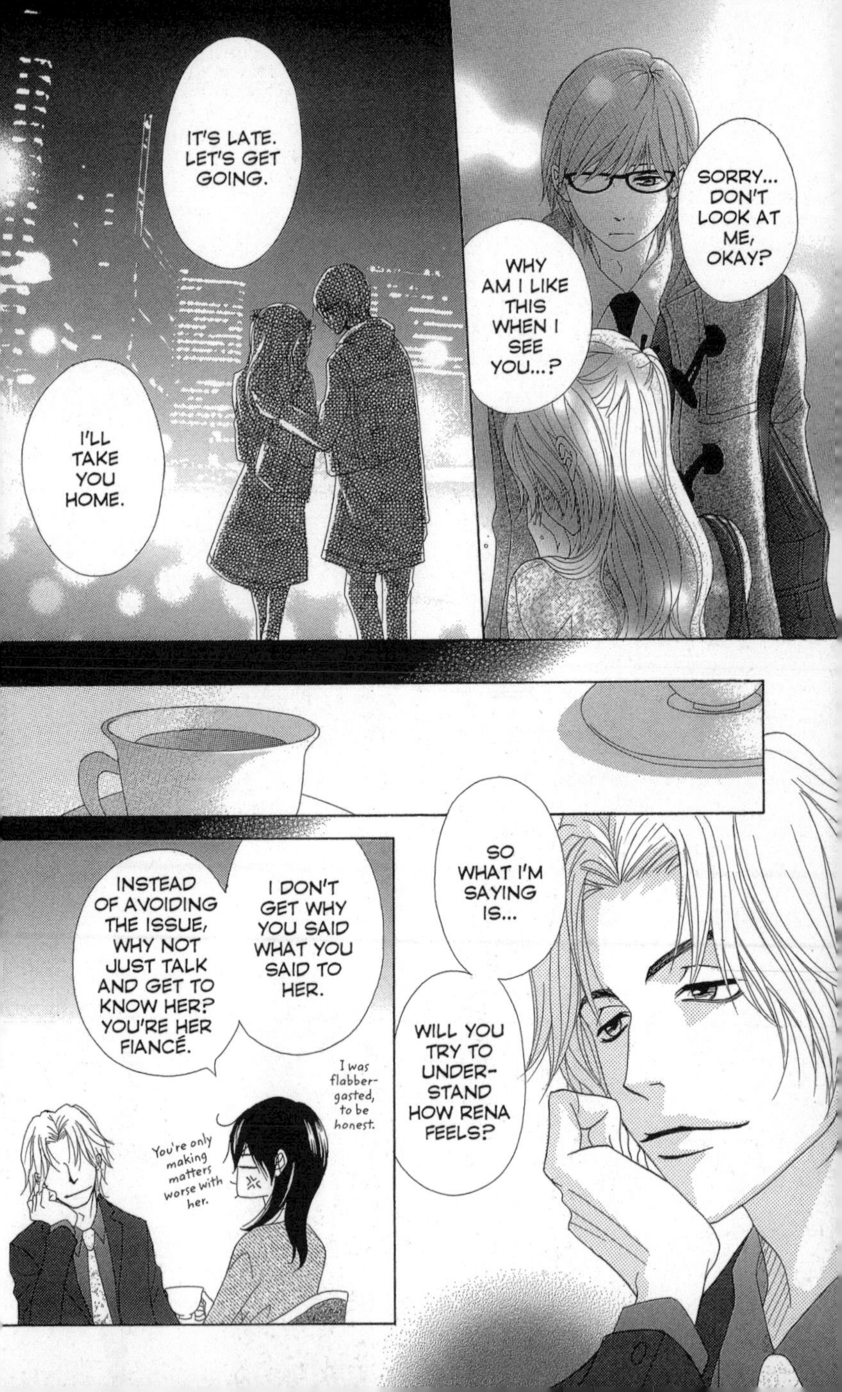
SORRY... DON'T LOOK AT ME, OKAY?
WHY AM I LIKE THIS WHEN I SEE YOU...?
IT'S LATE. LET'S GET GOING.
I'LL TAKE YOU HOME.
SO WHAT I'M SAYING IS...
WILL YOU TRY TO UNDER-STAND HOW RENA FEELS?
I DON'T GET WHY YOU SAID WHAT YOU SAID TO HER.
INSTEAD OF AVOIDING THE ISSUE, WHY NOT JUST TALK AND GET TO KNOW HER? YOU'RE HER FIANCÉ.
I was flabber-gasted, to be honest.
You're only making matters worse with her.

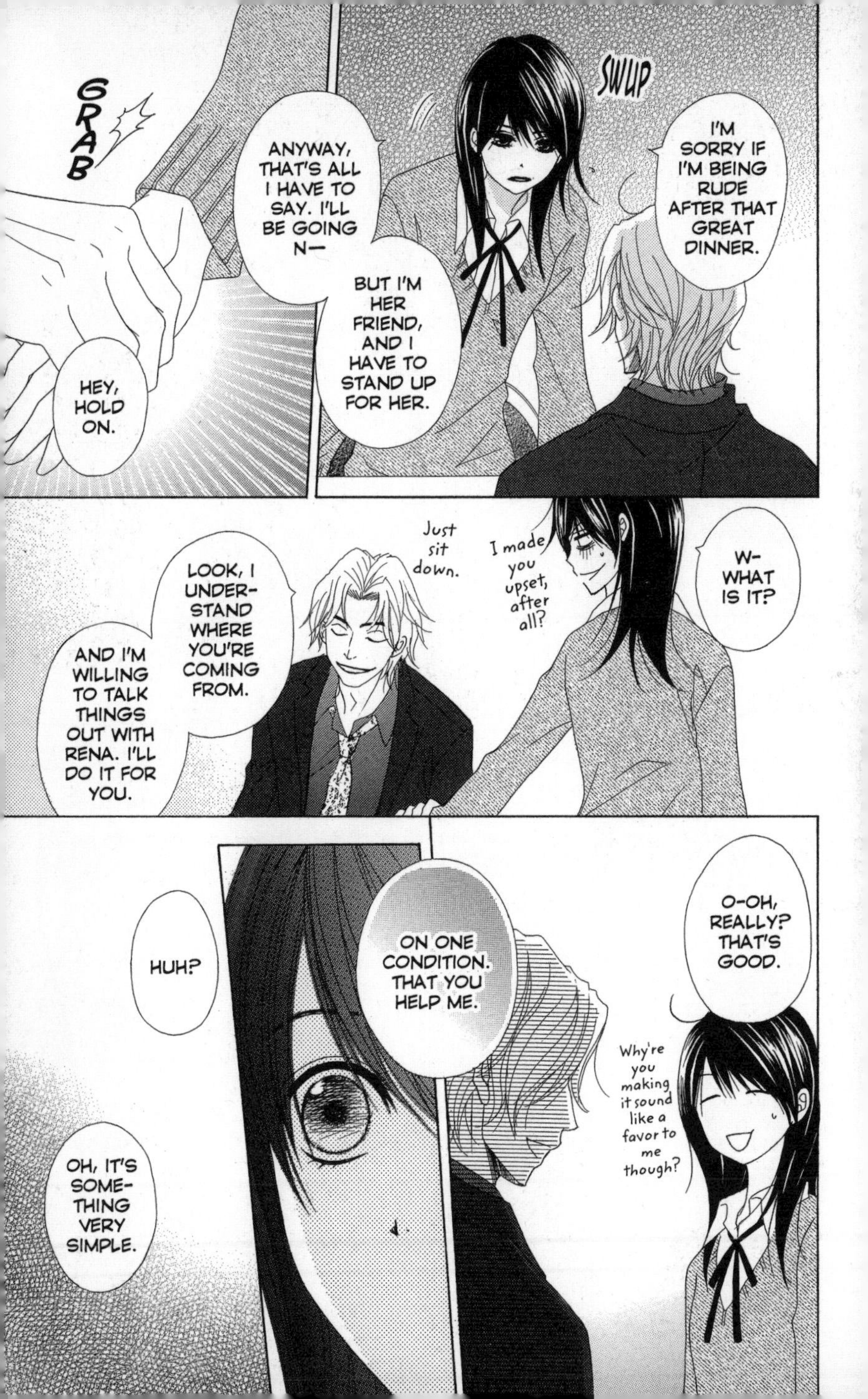
SWUP
I'M SORRY IF I'M BEING RUDE AFTER THAT GREAT DINNER.
BUT I'M HER FRIEND, AND I HAVE TO STAND UP FOR HER.
ANYWAY, THAT'S ALL I HAVE TO SAY. I'LL BE GOING N—
GRAB
HEY, HOLD ON.
W-WHAT IS IT?
I made you upset, after all?
Just sit down.
LOOK, I UNDER-STAND WHERE YOU'RE COMING FROM.
AND I'M WILLING TO TALK THINGS OUT WITH RENA. I'LL DO IT FOR YOU.
O-OH, REALLY? THAT'S GOOD.
Why're you making it sound like a favor to me though?
ON ONE CONDITION. THAT YOU HELP ME.
HUH?
OH, IT'S SOME-THING VERY SIMPLE.

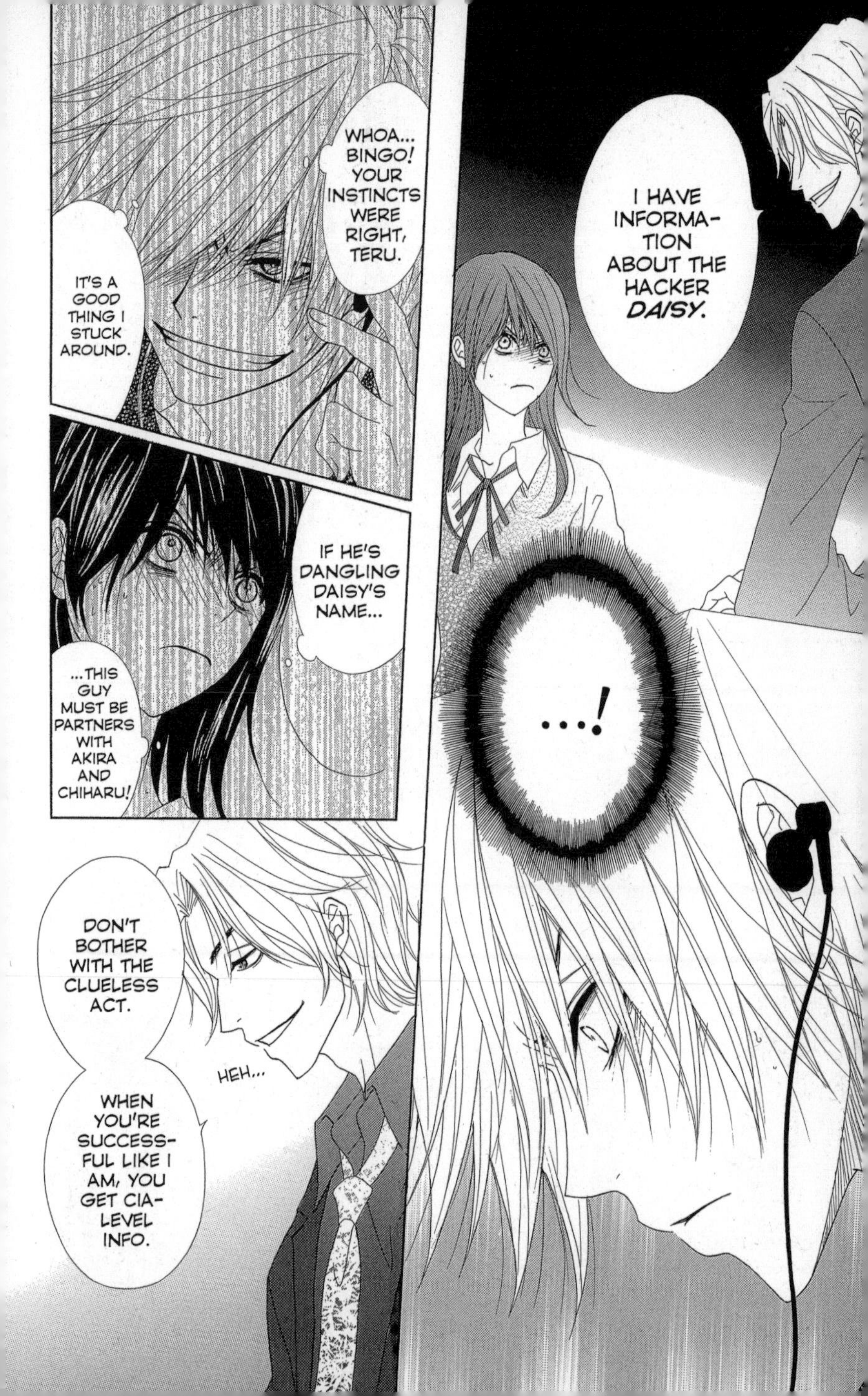
I HAVE INFORMATION ABOUT THE HACKER DAISY.
...!
WHOA... BINGO! YOUR INSTINCTS WERE RIGHT, TERU.
IT'S A GOOD THING I STUCK AROUND.
IF HE'S DANGLING DAISY'S NAME...
...THIS GUY MUST BE PARTNERS WITH AKIRA AND CHIHARU!
DON'T BOTHER WITH THE CLUELESS ACT.
HEH...
WHEN YOU'RE SUCCESSFUL LIKE I AM, YOU GET CIA-LEVEL INFO.

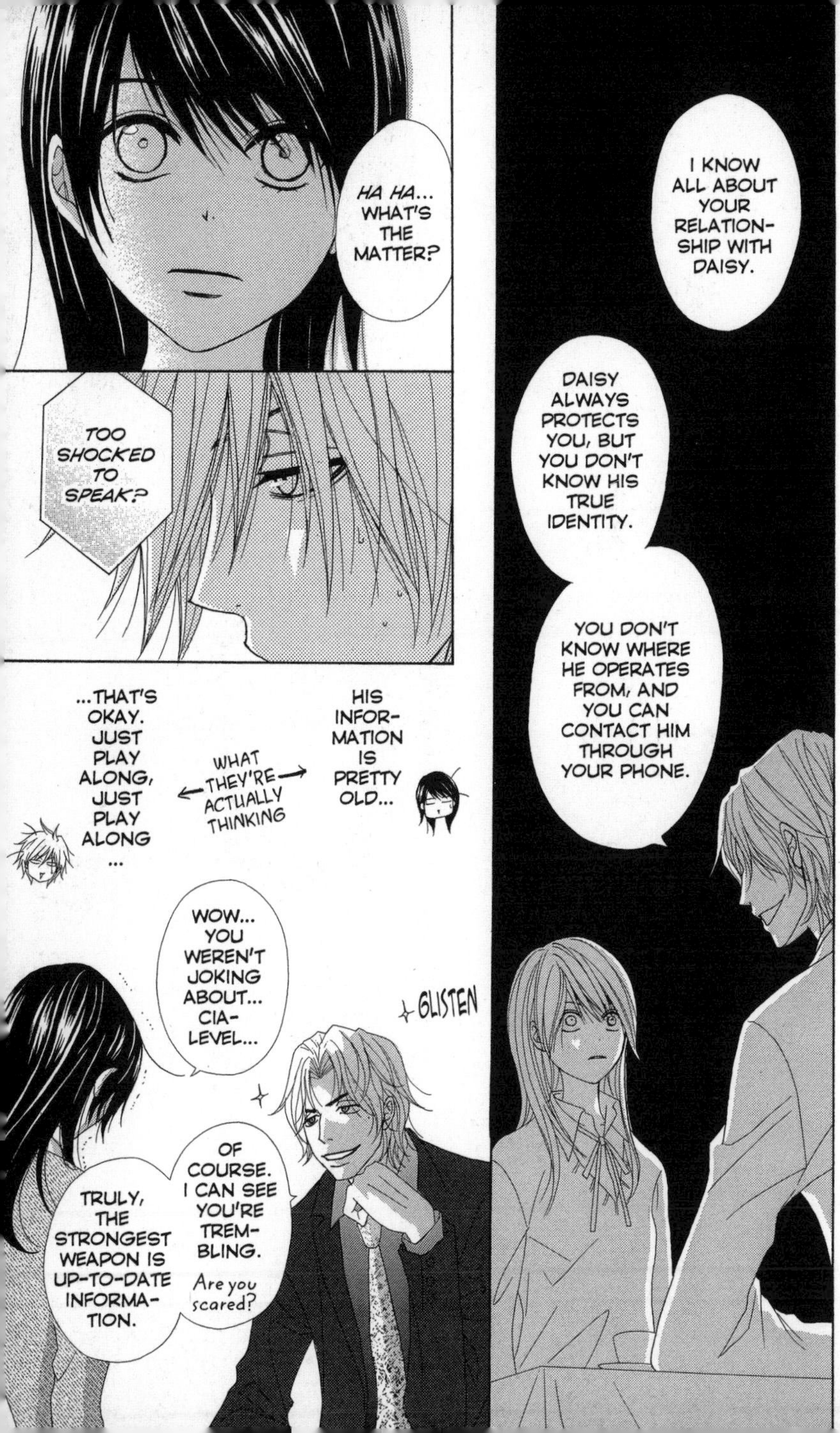
I KNOW ALL ABOUT YOUR RELATION-SHIP WITH DAISY.
DAISY ALWAYS PROTECTS YOU, BUT YOU DON'T KNOW HIS TRUE IDENTITY.
YOU DON'T KNOW WHERE HE OPERATES FROM, AND YOU CAN CONTACT HIM THROUGH YOUR PHONE.
HA HA... WHAT'S THE MATTER?
TOO SHOCKED TO SPEAK?
HIS INFOR-MATION IS PRETTY OLD...
WHAT THEY'RE ACTUALLY THINKING
...THAT'S OKAY. JUST PLAY ALONG, JUST PLAY ALONG ...
GLISTEN
WOW... YOU WEREN'T JOKING ABOUT... CIA-LEVEL...
OF COURSE. I CAN SEE YOU'RE TREM-BLING.
Are you scared?
TRULY, THE STRONGEST WEAPON IS UP-TO-DATE INFORMA-TION.

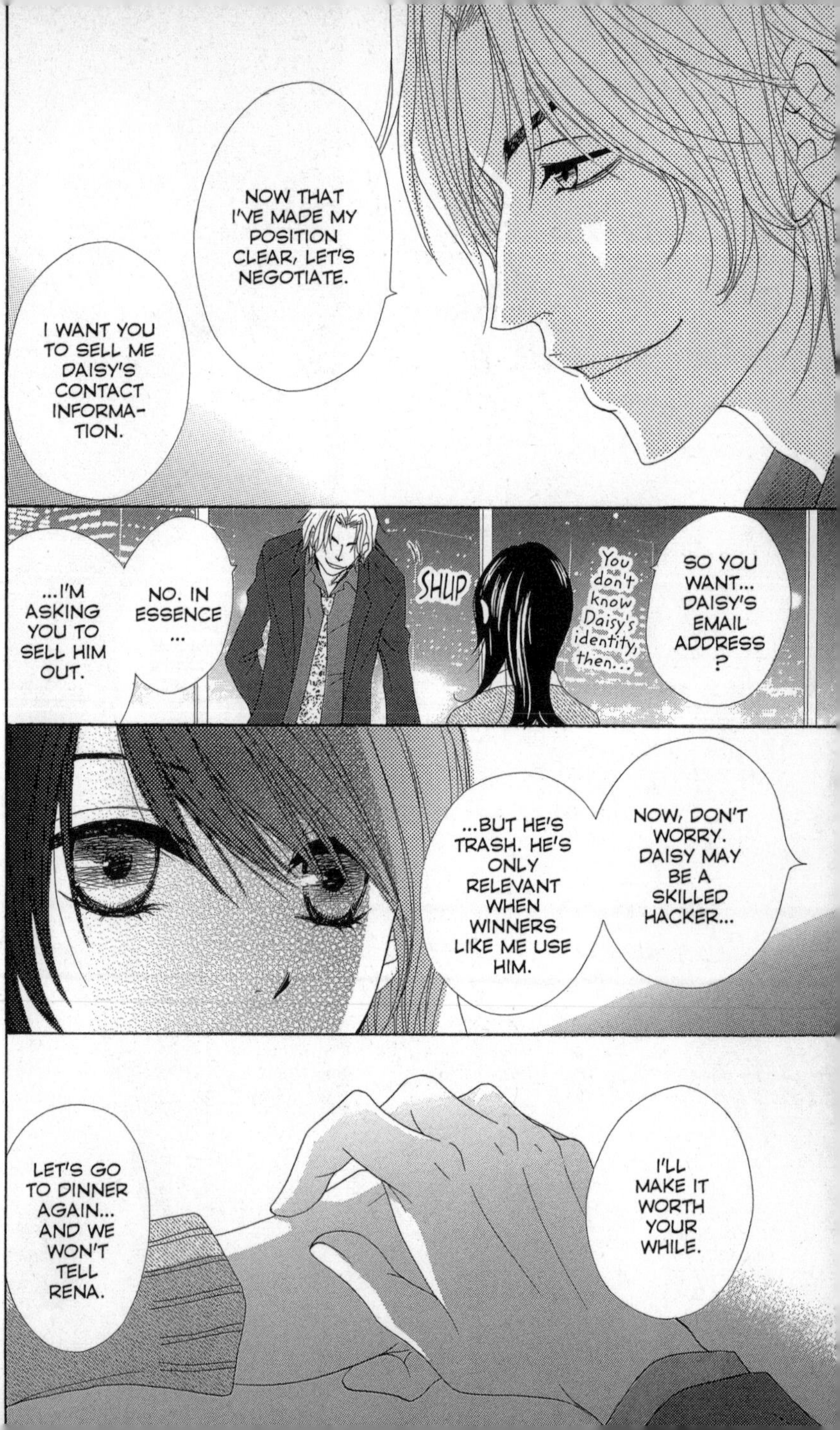
NOW THAT I'VE MADE MY POSITION CLEAR, LET'S NEGOTIATE.
I WANT YOU TO SELL ME DAISY'S CONTACT INFORMATION.
SO YOU WANT... DAISY'S EMAIL ADDRESS?
You don't know Daisy's identity, then...
SHUP
NO. IN ESSENCE...
...I'M ASKING YOU TO SELL HIM OUT.
NOW, DON'T WORRY. DAISY MAY BE A SKILLED HACKER...
...BUT HE'S TRASH. HE'S ONLY RELEVANT WHEN WINNERS LIKE ME USE HIM.
I'LL MAKE IT WORTH YOUR WHILE.
LET'S GO TO DINNER AGAIN... AND WE WON'T TELL RENA.

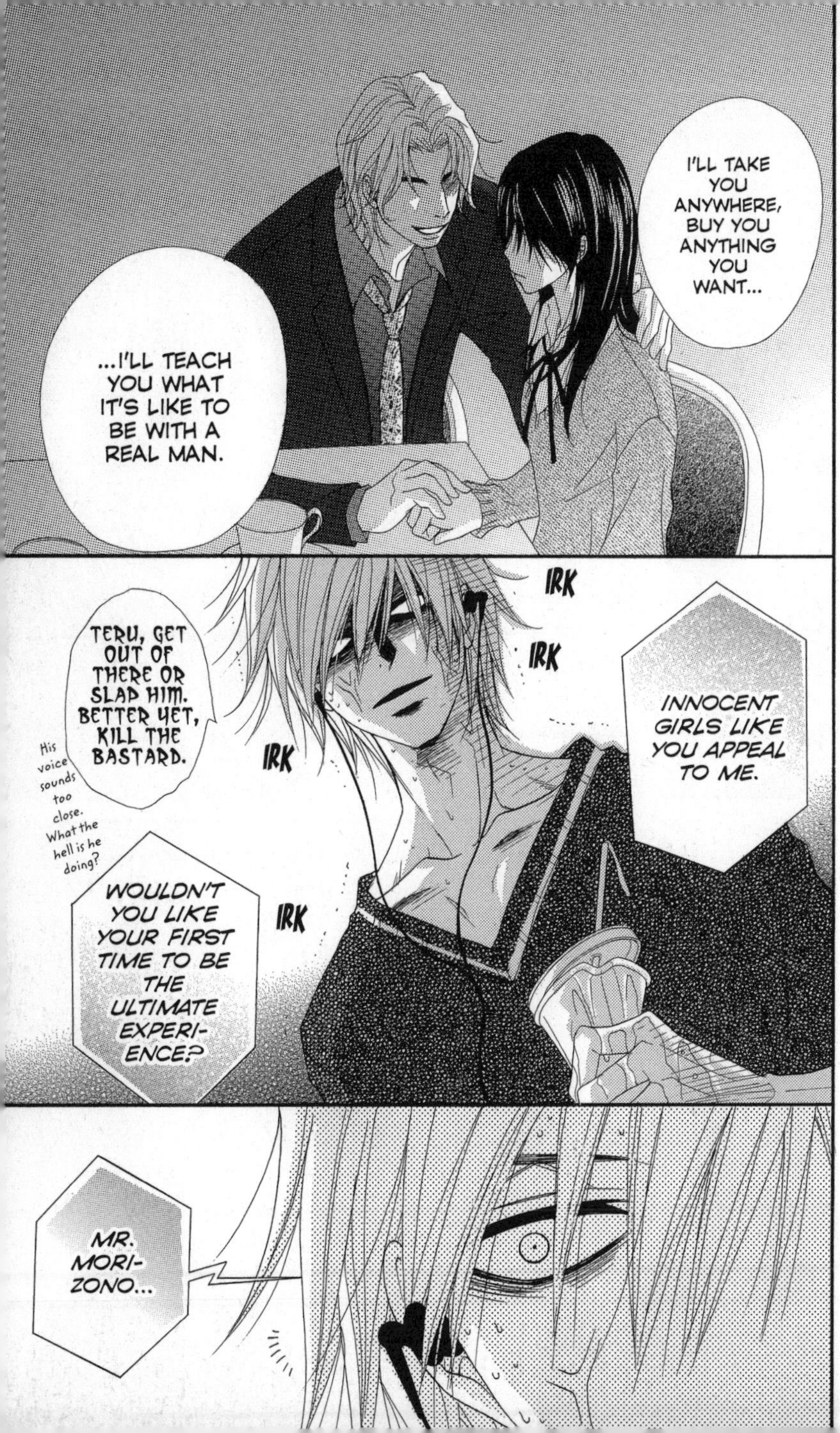
I'LL TAKE YOU ANYWHERE, BUY YOU ANYTHING YOU WANT...
...I'LL TEACH YOU WHAT IT'S LIKE TO BE WITH A REAL MAN.
IRK
INNOCENT GIRLS LIKE YOU APPEAL TO ME.
IRK
TERU, GET OUT OF THERE OR SLAP HIM. BETTER YET, KILL THE BASTARD.
His voice sounds too close. What the hell is he doing?
IRK
IRK
WOULDN'T YOU LIKE YOUR FIRST TIME TO BE THE ULTIMATE EXPERI-ENCE?
MR. MORI-ZONO...

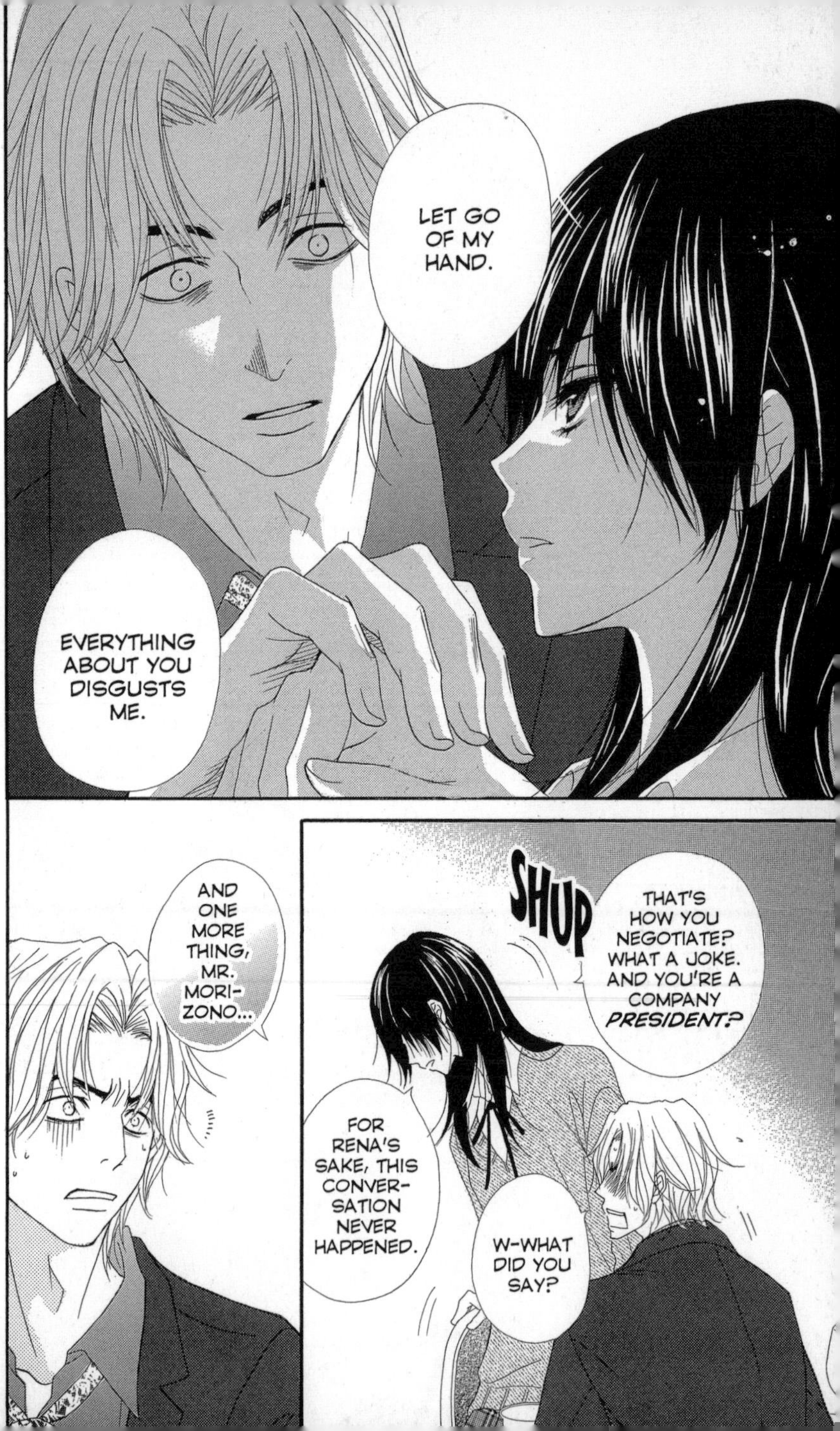
LET GO OF MY HAND.
EVERYTHING ABOUT YOU DISGUSTS ME.
SHUP
THAT'S HOW YOU NEGOTIATE? WHAT A JOKE. AND YOU'RE A COMPANY *PRESIDENT?*
FOR RENA'S SAKE, THIS CONVER-SATION NEVER HAPPENED.
W-WHAT DID YOU SAY?
AND ONE MORE THING, MR. MORI-ZONO...

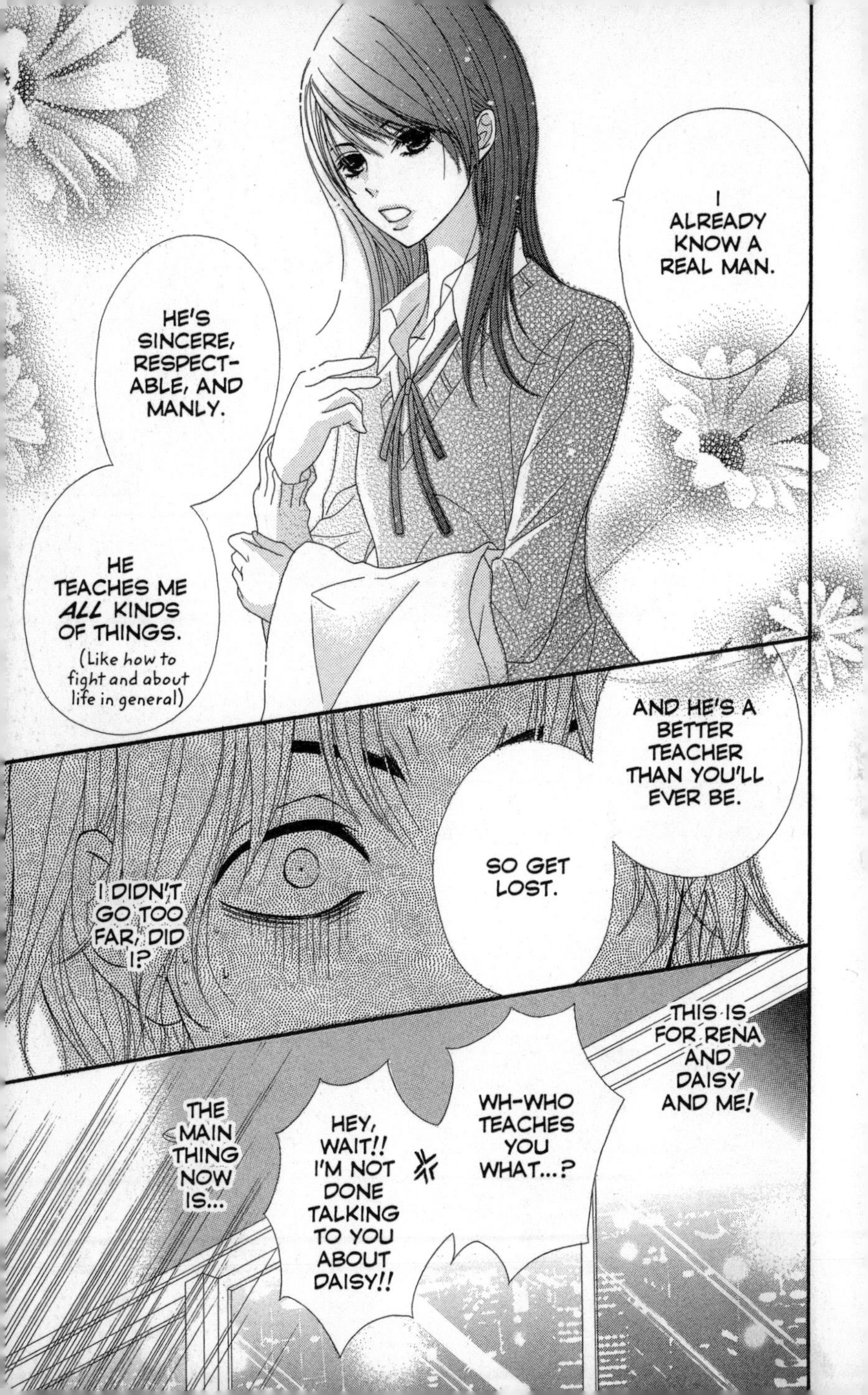
I ALREADY KNOW A REAL MAN.
HE'S SINCERE, RESPECT-ABLE, AND MANLY.
HE TEACHES ME *ALL* KINDS OF THINGS.
(Like how to fight and about life in general)
AND HE'S A BETTER TEACHER THAN YOU'LL EVER BE.
SO GET LOST.
I DIDN'T GO TOO FAR, DID I?
THIS IS FOR RENA AND DAISY AND ME!
WH-WHO TEACHES YOU WHAT...?
HEY, WAIT!! I'M NOT DONE TALKING TO YOU ABOUT DAISY!!
THE MAIN THING NOW IS...

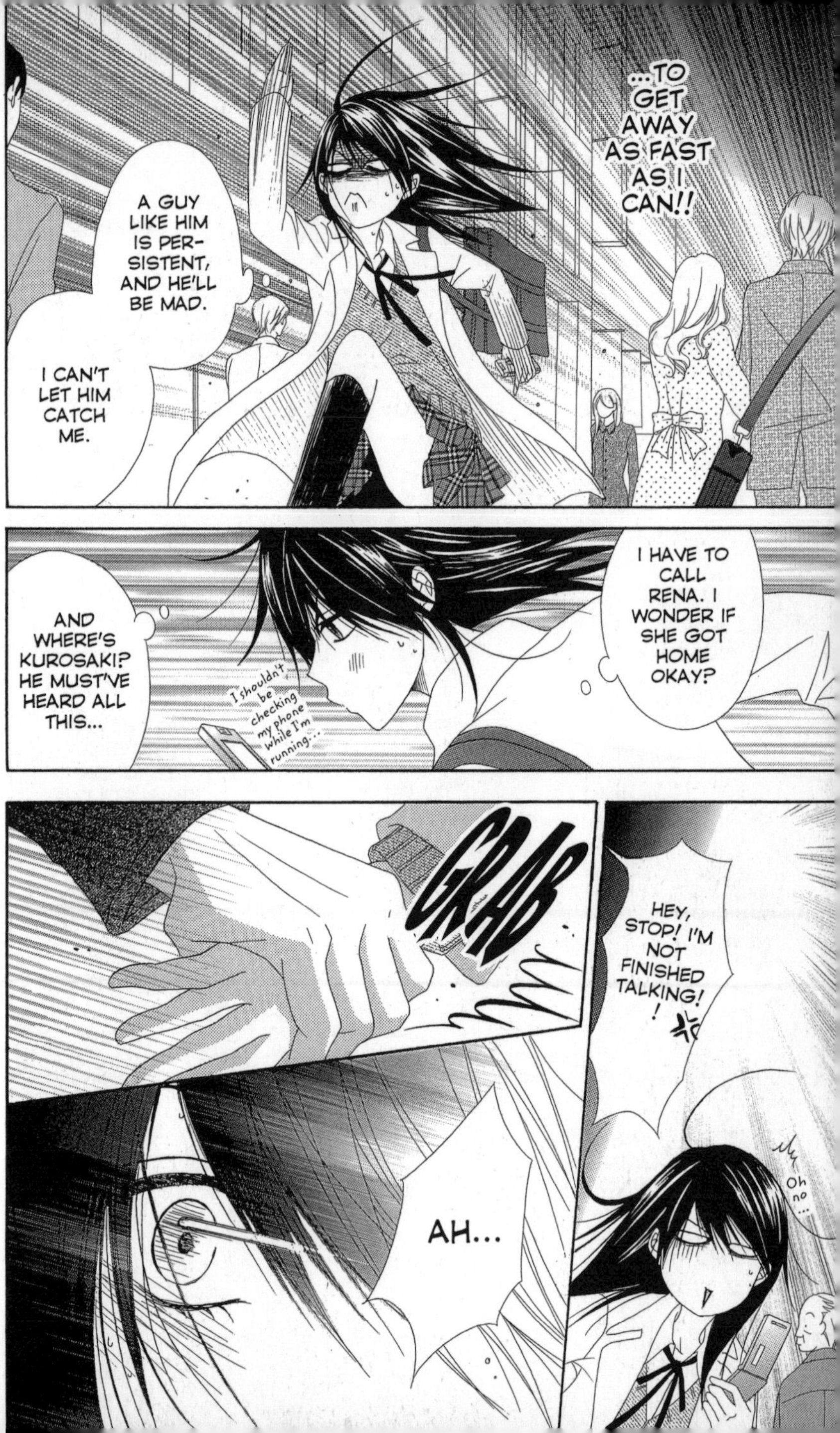
...TO GET AWAY AS FAST AS I CAN!!
A GUY LIKE HIM IS PER- SISTENT, AND HE'LL BE MAD.
I CAN'T LET HIM CATCH ME.
I HAVE TO CALL RENA. I WONDER IF SHE GOT HOME OKAY?
AND WHERE'S KUROSAKI? HE MUST'VE HEARD ALL THIS...
I shouldn't be checking my phone while I'm running...
HEY, STOP! I'M NOT FINISHED TALKING!!
GRAB
Oh no...
AH...

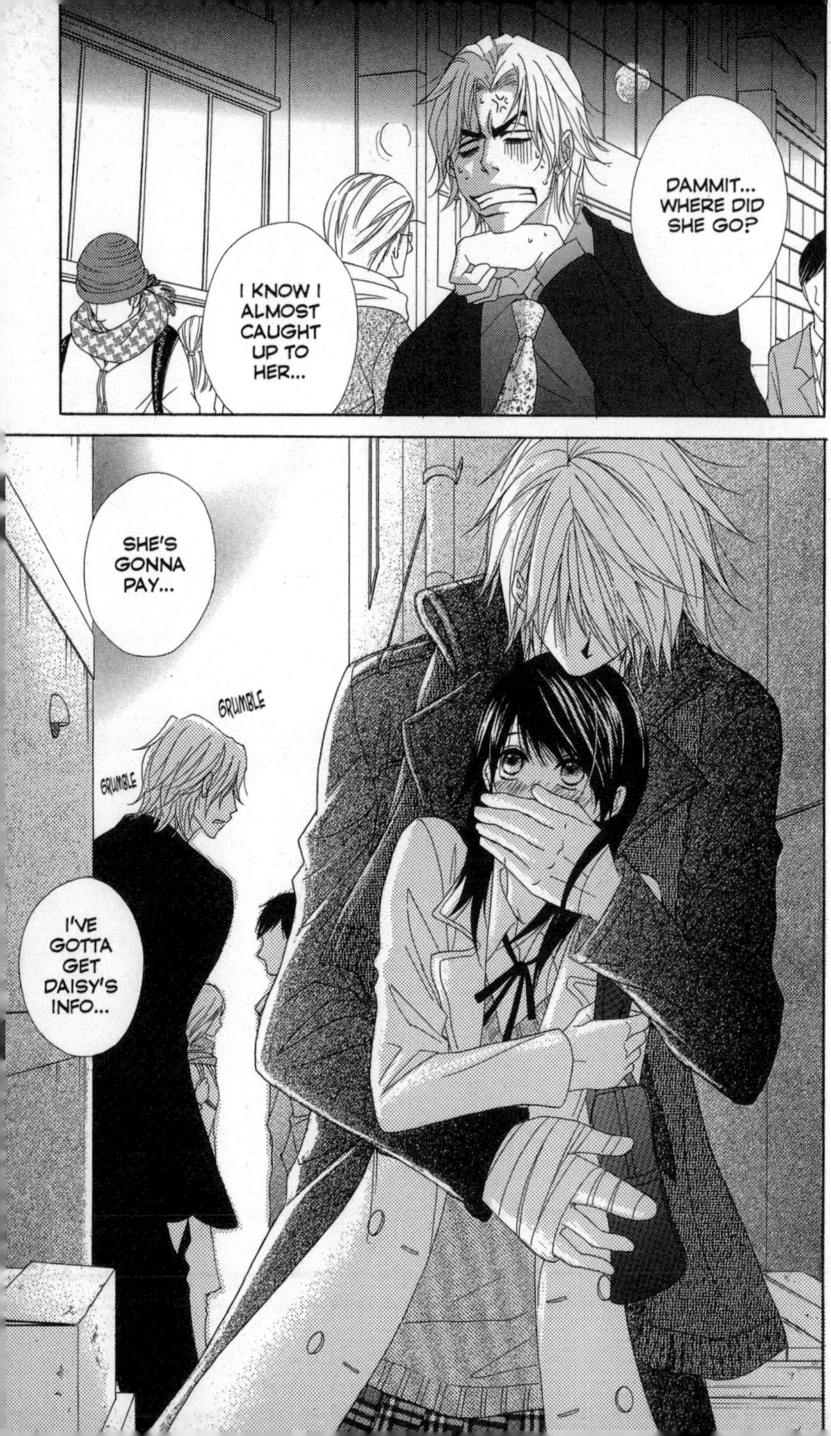
DAMMIT... WHERE DID SHE GO?
I KNOW I ALMOST CAUGHT UP TO HER...
SHE'S GONNA PAY...
GRUMBLE
GRUMBLE
I'VE GOTTA GET DAISY'S INFO...

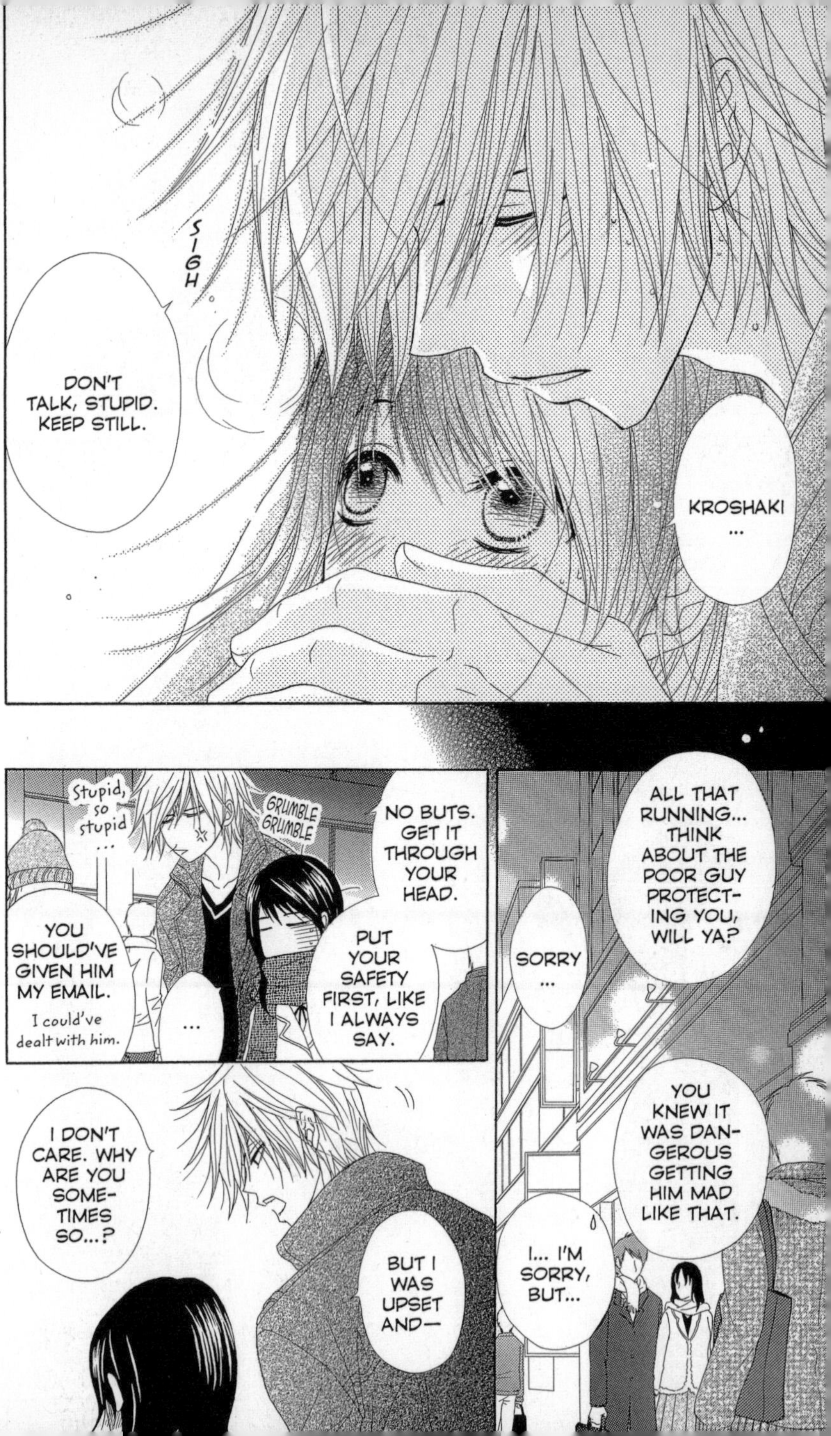
KROSHAKI ...
SIGH
DON'T TALK, STUPID. KEEP STILL.
ALL THAT RUNNING... THINK ABOUT THE POOR GUY PROTECT-ING YOU, WILL YA?
SORRY ...
YOU KNEW IT WAS DAN-GEROUS GETTING HIM MAD LIKE THAT.
I... I'M SORRY, BUT...
NO BUTS. GET IT THROUGH YOUR HEAD.
GRUMBLE GRUMBLE
Stupid, so stupid ...
PUT YOUR SAFETY FIRST, LIKE I ALWAYS SAY.
...
YOU SHOULD'VE GIVEN HIM MY EMAIL.
I could've dealt with him.
BUT I WAS UPSET AND—
I DON'T CARE. WHY ARE YOU SOME-TIMES SO...?

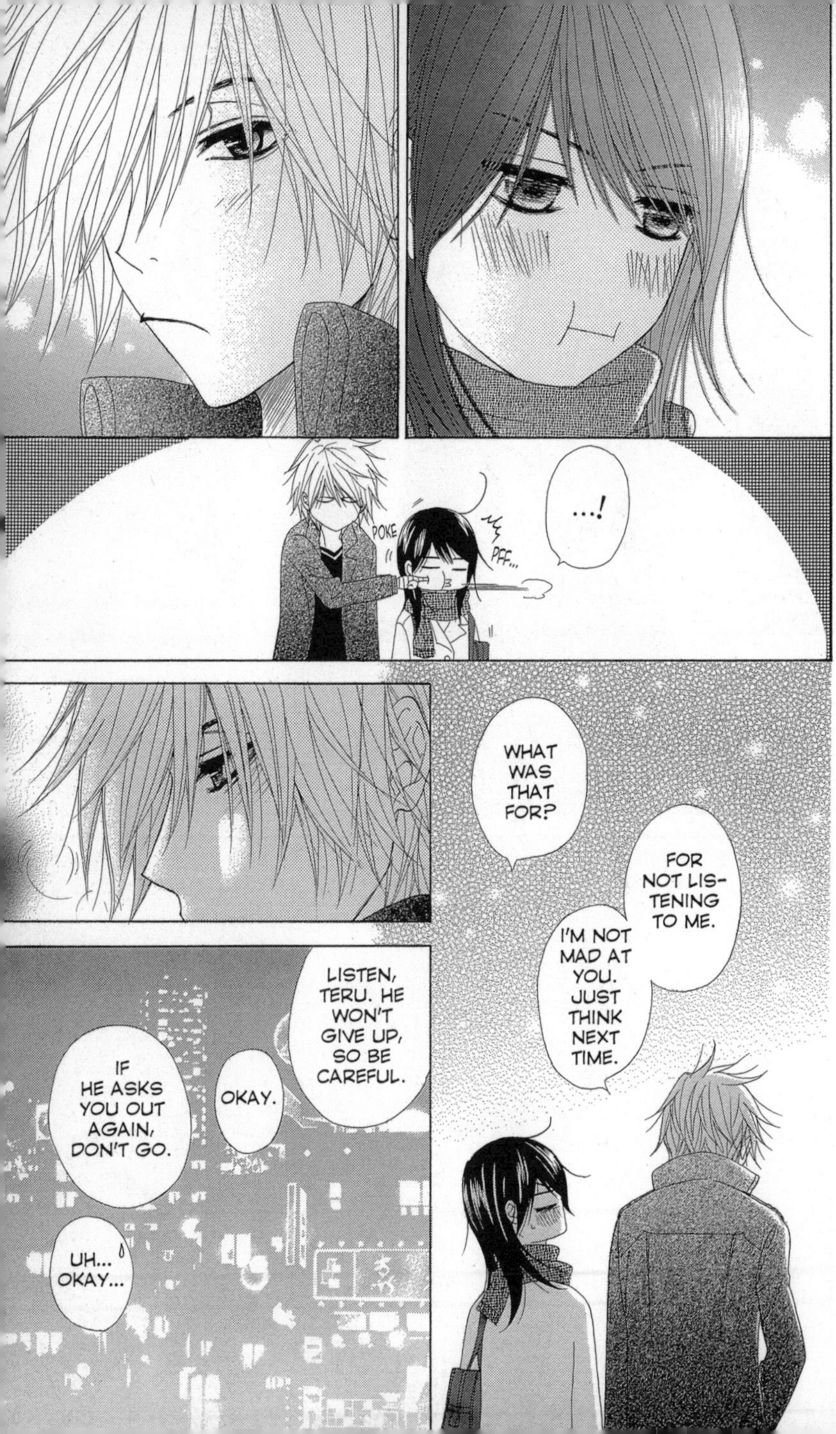
...!
PFF...
POKE
WHAT WAS THAT FOR?
FOR NOT LISTENING TO ME.
I'M NOT MAD AT YOU. JUST THINK NEXT TIME.
LISTEN, TERU. HE WON'T GIVE UP, SO BE CAREFUL.
OKAY.
IF HE ASKS YOU OUT AGAIN, DON'T GO.
UH... OKAY...

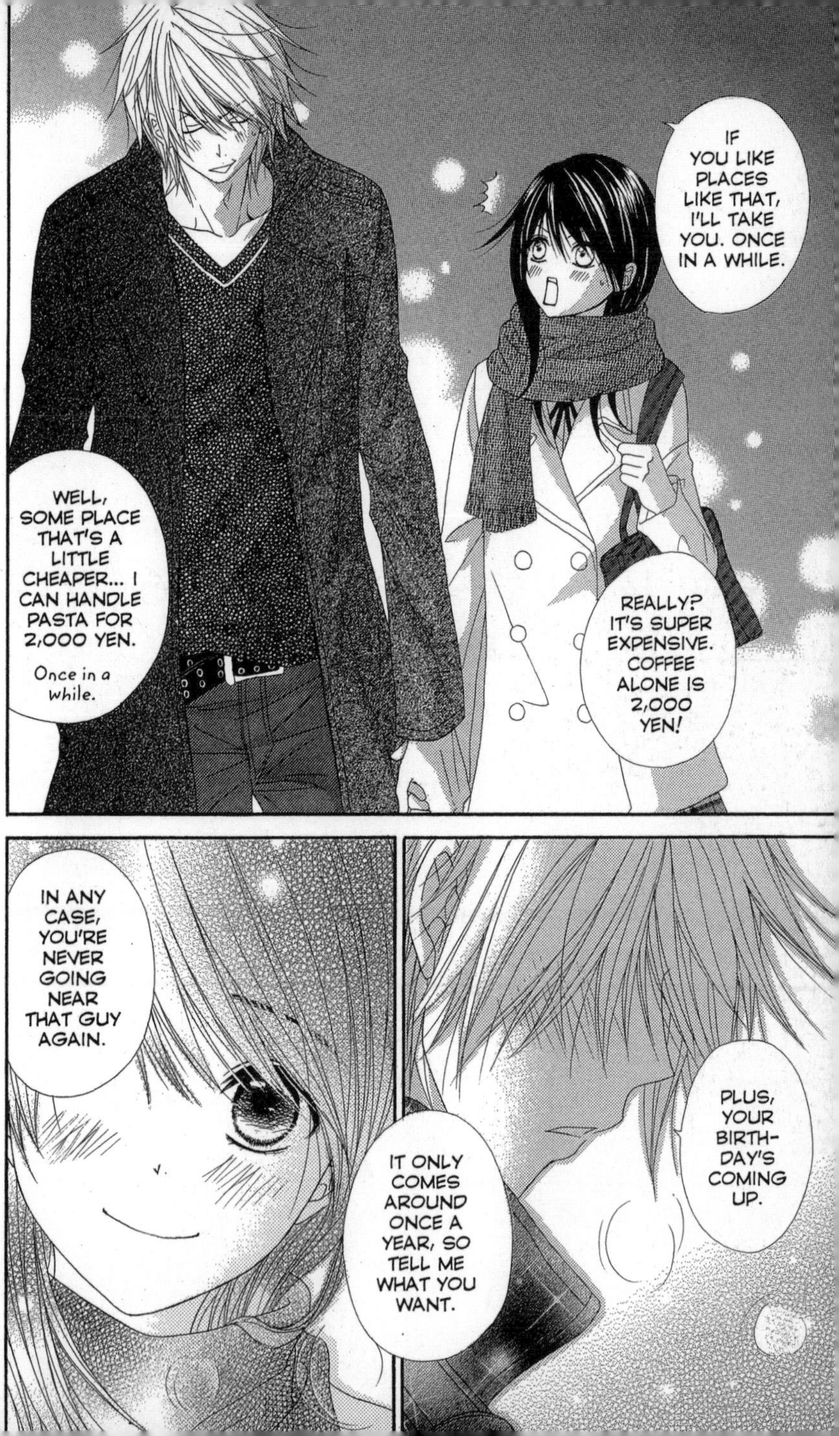
IF YOU LIKE PLACES LIKE THAT, I'LL TAKE YOU. ONCE IN A WHILE.
REALLY? IT'S SUPER EXPENSIVE. COFFEE ALONE IS 2,000 YEN!
WELL, SOME PLACE THAT'S A LITTLE CHEAPER... I CAN HANDLE PASTA FOR 2,000 YEN.
Once in a while.
PLUS, YOUR BIRTH-DAY'S COMING UP.
IT ONLY COMES AROUND ONCE A YEAR, SO TELL ME WHAT YOU WANT.
IN ANY CASE, YOU'RE NEVER GOING NEAR THAT GUY AGAIN.

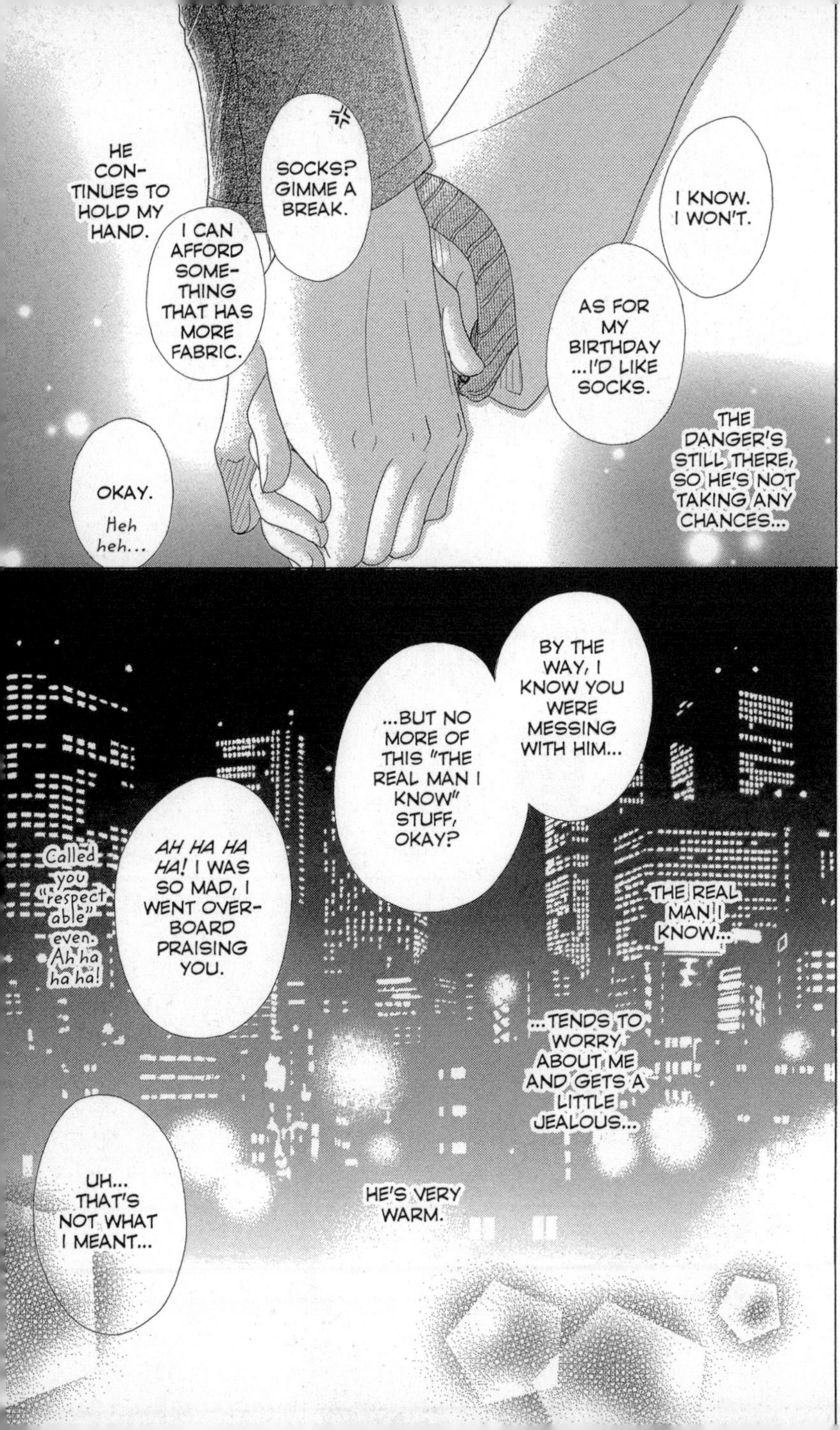
I KNOW. I WON'T.
HE CONTINUES TO HOLD MY HAND.
AS FOR MY BIRTHDAY ...I'D LIKE SOCKS.
SOCKS? GIMME A BREAK.
I CAN AFFORD SOMETHING THAT HAS MORE FABRIC.
THE DANGER'S STILL THERE, SO HE'S NOT TAKING ANY CHANCES...
OKAY.
Heh heh...
BY THE WAY, I KNOW YOU WERE MESSING WITH HIM...
...BUT NO MORE OF THIS "THE REAL MAN I KNOW" STUFF, OKAY?
THE REAL MAN I KNOW...
AH HA HA HA! I WAS SO MAD, I WENT OVERBOARD PRAISING YOU.
Called you "respectable" even. Ah ha ha ha!
...TENDS TO WORRY ABOUT ME AND GETS A LITTLE JEALOUS...
UH... THAT'S NOT WHAT I MEANT...
HE'S VERY WARM.

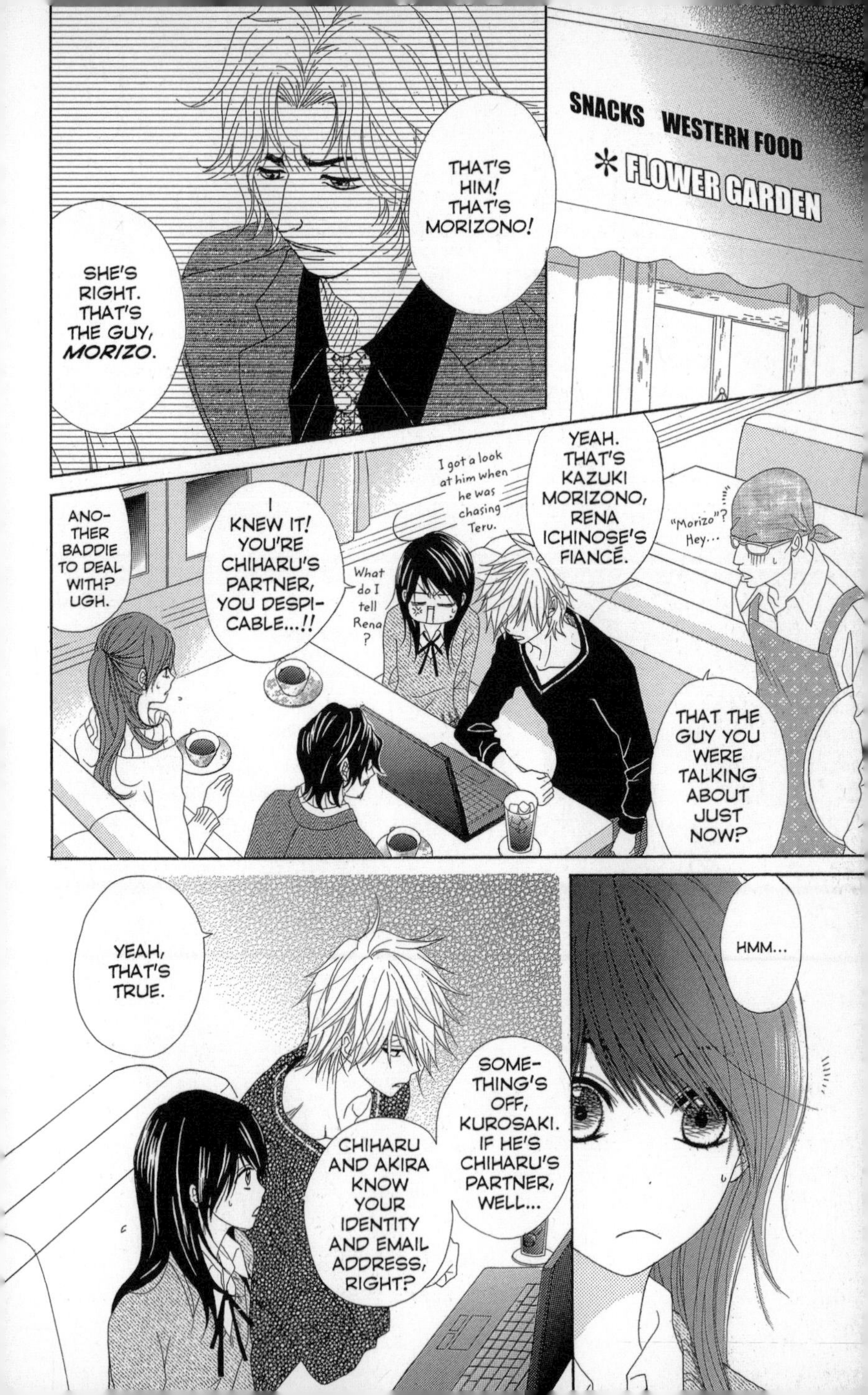
SNACKS WESTERN FOOD
* FLOWER GARDEN
THAT'S HIM! THAT'S MORIZONO!
SHE'S RIGHT. THAT'S THE GUY, *MORIZO*.
YEAH. THAT'S KAZUKI MORIZONO, RENA ICHINOSE'S FIANCÉ.
"Morizo"? Hey...
THAT THE GUY YOU WERE TALKING ABOUT JUST NOW?
I got a look at him when he was chasing Teru.
I KNEW IT! YOU'RE CHIHARU'S PARTNER, YOU DESPICABLE...!!
What do I tell Rena?
ANOTHER BADDIE TO DEAL WITH? UGH.
HMM...
SOMETHING'S OFF, KUROSAKI. IF HE'S CHIHARU'S PARTNER, WELL...
CHIHARU AND AKIRA KNOW YOUR IDENTITY AND EMAIL ADDRESS, RIGHT?
YEAH, THAT'S TRUE.

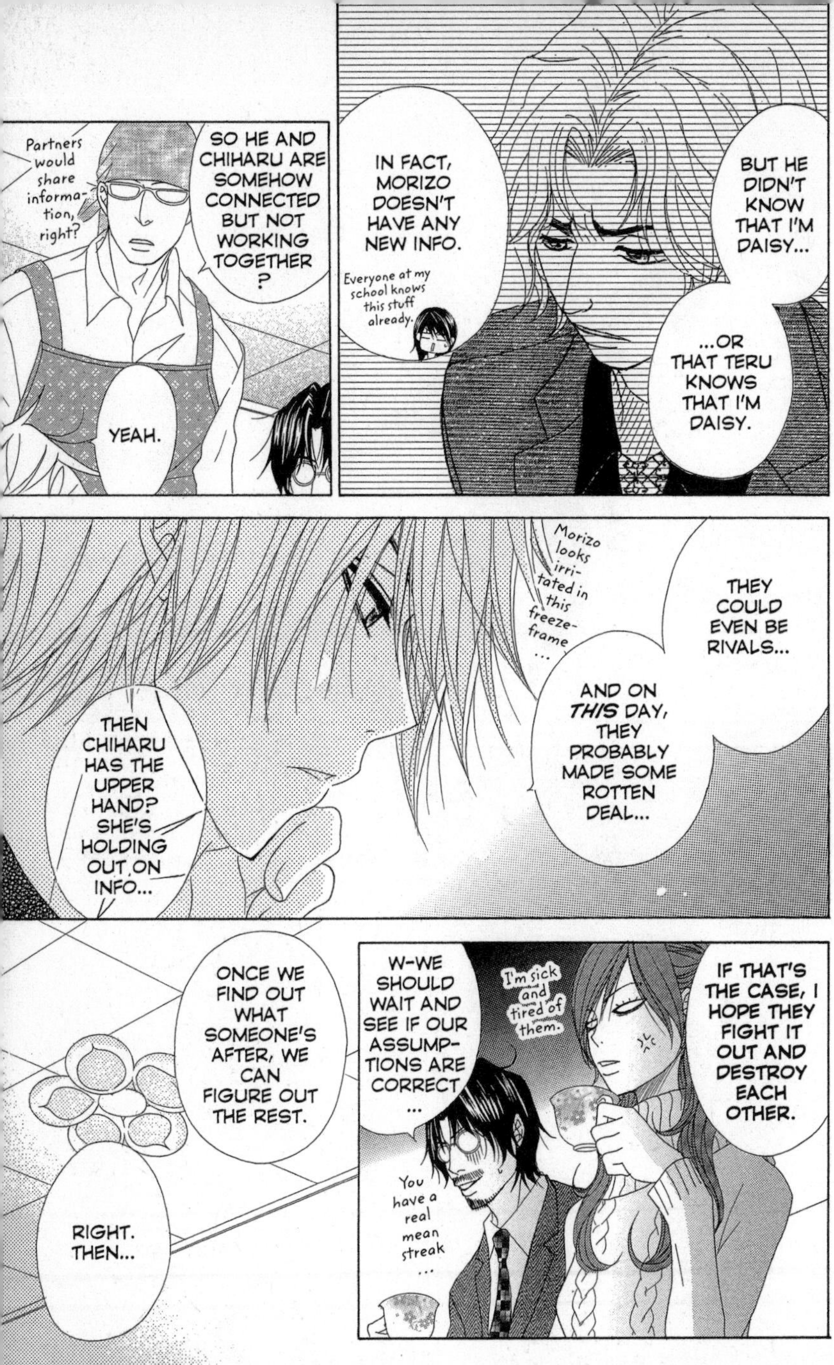
BUT HE DIDN'T KNOW THAT I'M DAISY...
...OR THAT TERU KNOWS THAT I'M DAISY.
IN FACT, MORIZO DOESN'T HAVE ANY NEW INFO.
Everyone at my school knows this stuff already.
SO HE AND CHIHARU ARE SOMEHOW CONNECTED BUT NOT WORKING TOGETHER?
Partners would share information, right?
YEAH.
THEY COULD EVEN BE RIVALS...
AND ON *THIS* DAY, THEY PROBABLY MADE SOME ROTTEN DEAL...
Morizo looks irritated in this freeze-frame...
THEN CHIHARU HAS THE UPPER HAND? SHE'S HOLDING OUT ON INFO...
IF THAT'S THE CASE, I HOPE THEY FIGHT IT OUT AND DESTROY EACH OTHER.
I'm sick and tired of them.
W-WE SHOULD WAIT AND SEE IF OUR ASSUMPTIONS ARE CORRECT...
You have a real mean streak...
ONCE WE FIND OUT WHAT SOMEONE'S AFTER, WE CAN FIGURE OUT THE REST.
RIGHT. THEN...

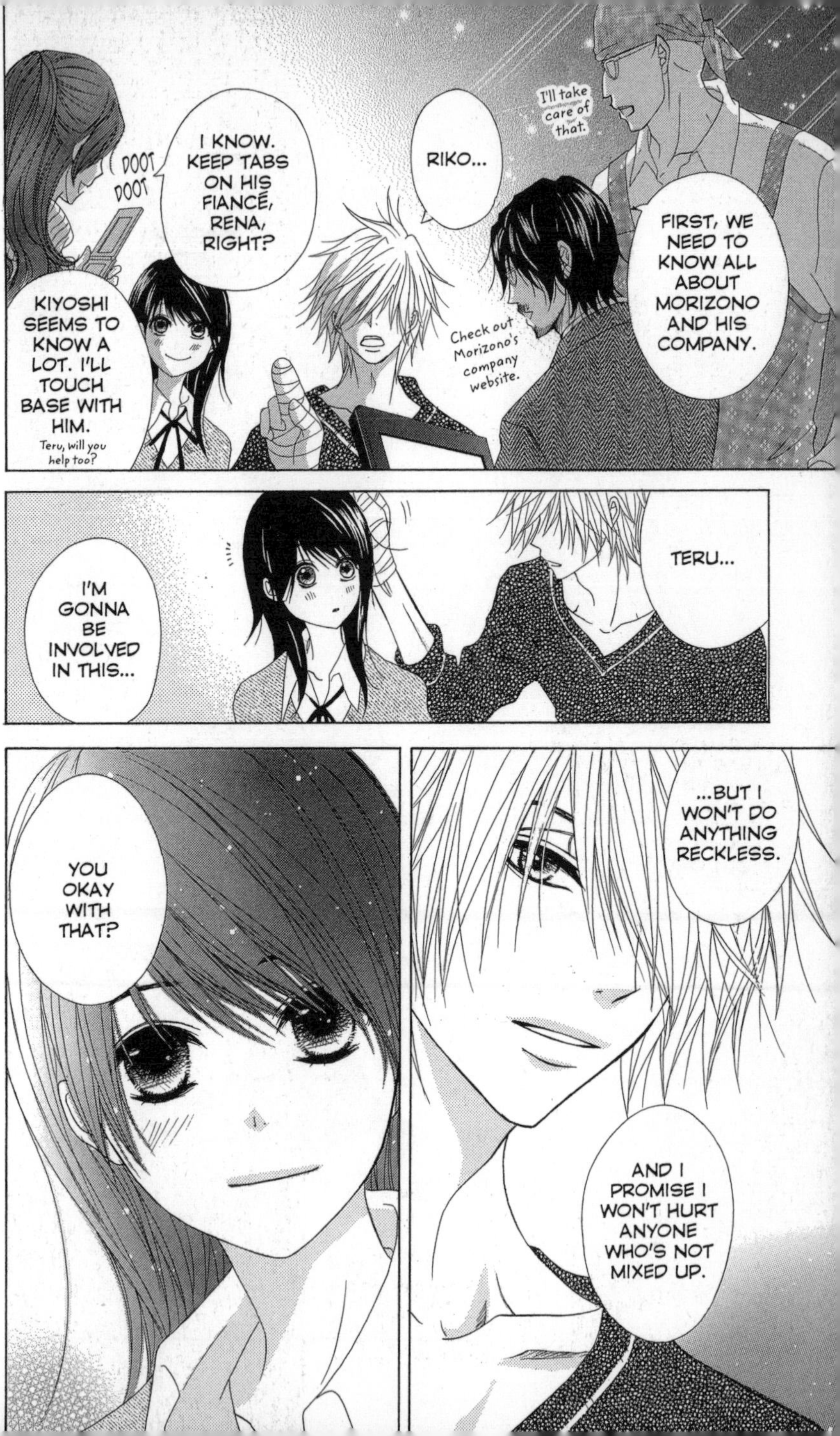
FIRST, WE NEED TO KNOW ALL ABOUT MORIZONO AND HIS COMPANY.
I'll take care of that.
Check out Morizono's company website.
RIKO...
I KNOW. KEEP TABS ON HIS FIANCÉ, RENA, RIGHT?
DOOT DOOT
KIYOSHI SEEMS TO KNOW A LOT. I'LL TOUCH BASE WITH HIM.
Teru, will you help too?
TERU...
I'M GONNA BE INVOLVED IN THIS...
...BUT I WON'T DO ANYTHING RECKLESS.
AND I PROMISE I WON'T HURT ANYONE WHO'S NOT MIXED UP.
YOU OKAY WITH THAT?

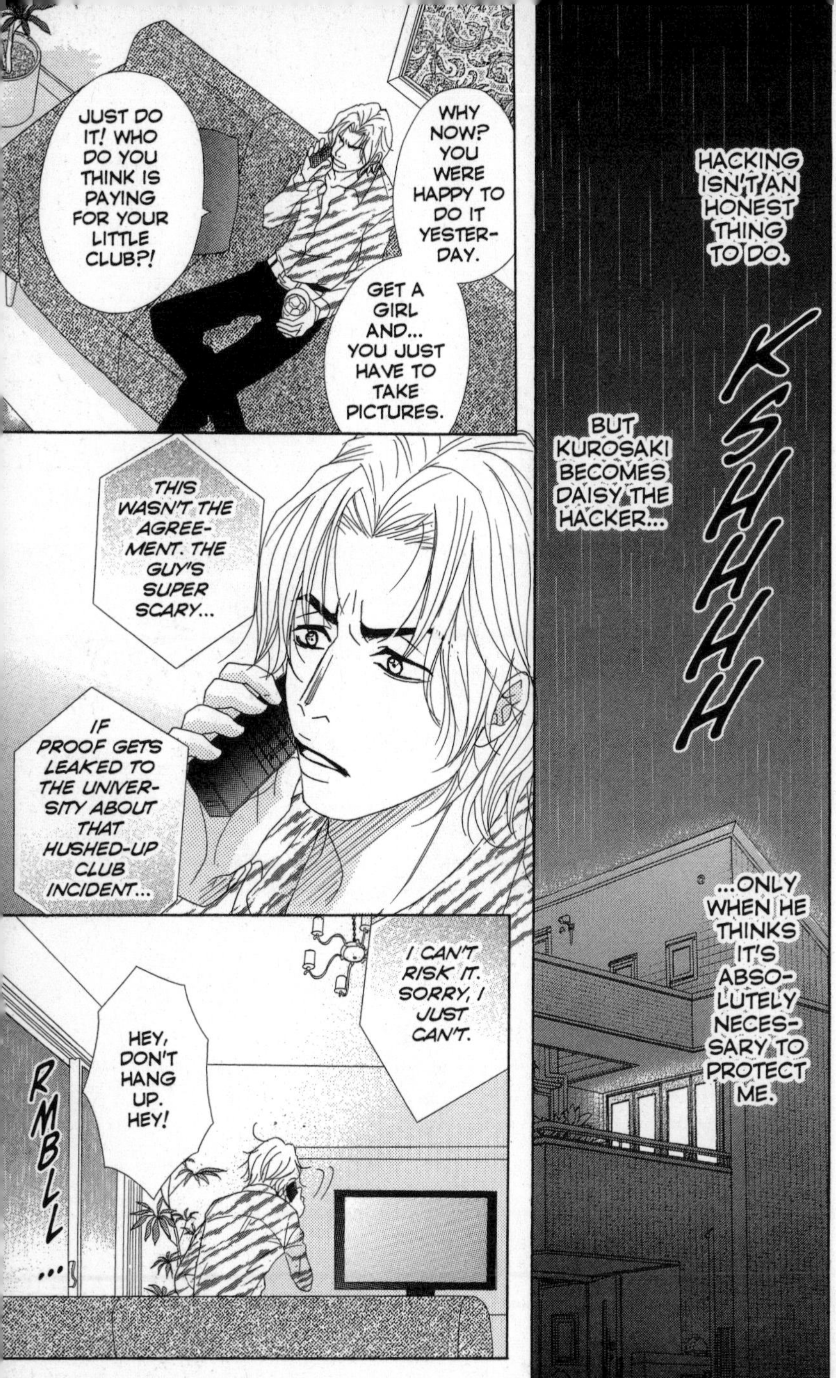
HACKING ISN'T AN HONEST THING TO DO.
KSHHHHH
BUT KUROSAKI BECOMES DAISY THE HACKER...
...ONLY WHEN HE THINKS IT'S ABSOLUTELY NECESSARY TO PROTECT ME.
WHY NOW? YOU WERE HAPPY TO DO IT YESTERDAY.
GET A GIRL AND... YOU JUST HAVE TO TAKE PICTURES.
JUST DO IT! WHO DO YOU THINK IS PAYING FOR YOUR LITTLE CLUB?!
THIS WASN'T THE AGREEMENT. THE GUY'S SUPER SCARY...
IF PROOF GETS LEAKED TO THE UNIVERSITY ABOUT THAT HUSHED-UP CLUB INCIDENT...
I CAN'T RISK IT. SORRY, I JUST CAN'T.
HEY, DON'T HANG UP. HEY!
RMBLL...

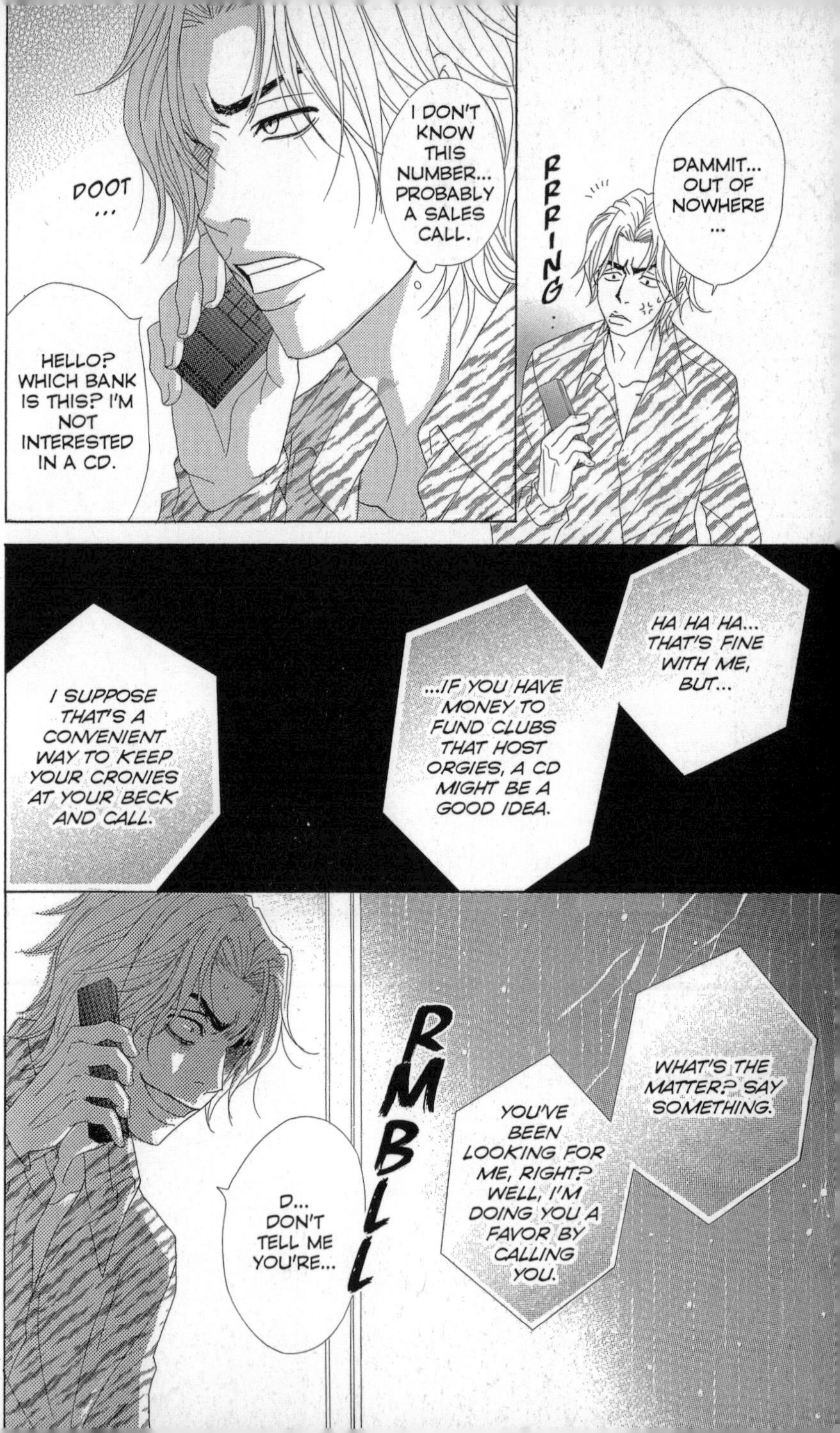
RRRING
DAMMIT... OUT OF NOWHERE ...
I DON'T KNOW THIS NUMBER... PROBABLY A SALES CALL.
DOOT ...
HELLO? WHICH BANK IS THIS? I'M NOT INTERESTED IN A CD.
HA HA HA... THAT'S FINE WITH ME, BUT...
...IF YOU HAVE MONEY TO FUND CLUBS THAT HOST ORGIES, A CD MIGHT BE A GOOD IDEA.
I SUPPOSE THAT'S A CONVENIENT WAY TO KEEP YOUR CRONIES AT YOUR BECK AND CALL.
WHAT'S THE MATTER? SAY SOMETHING.
YOU'VE BEEN LOOKING FOR ME, RIGHT? WELL, I'M DOING YOU A FAVOR BY CALLING YOU.
RMBLL
D... DON'T TELL ME YOU'RE...

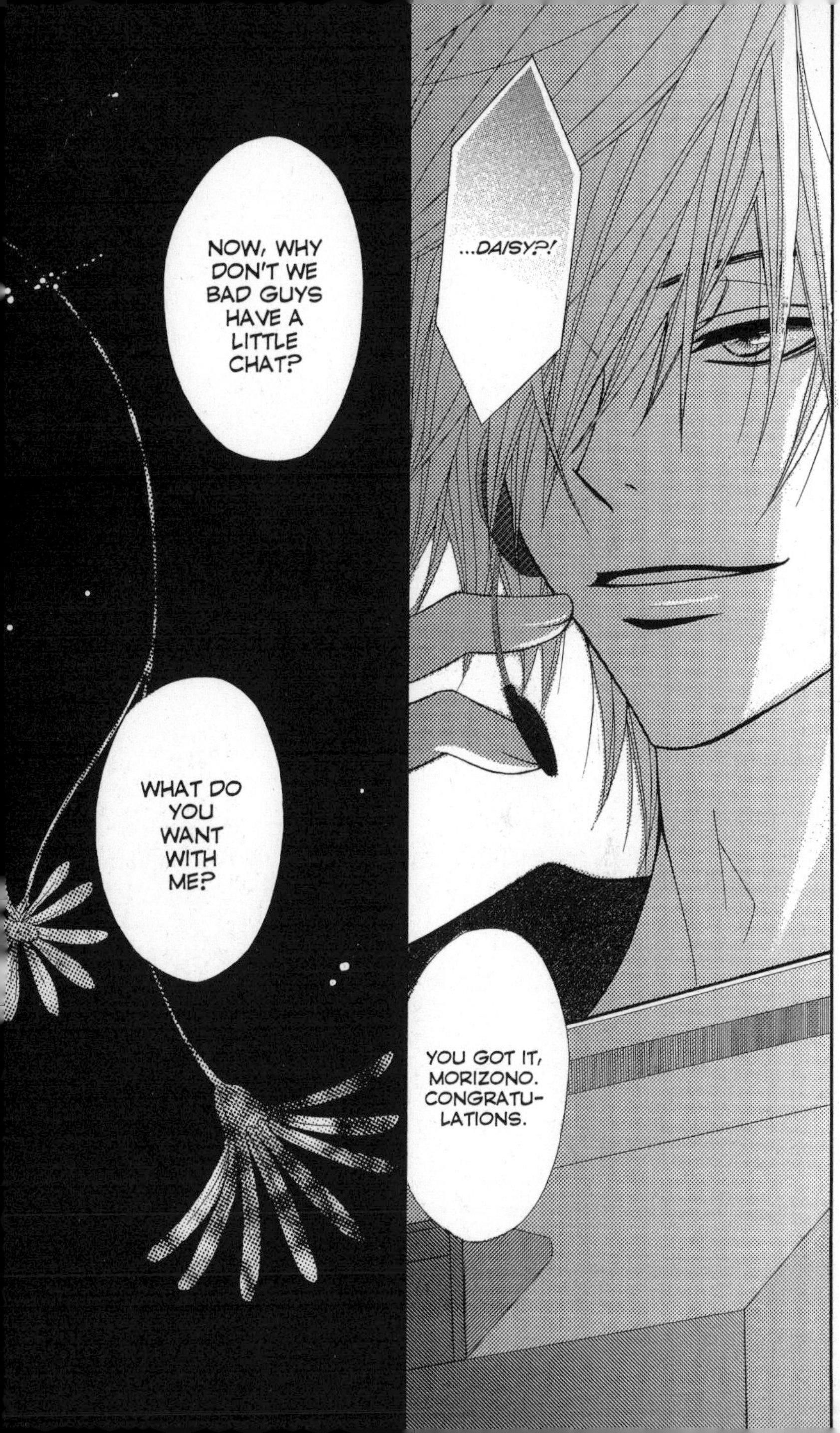
...DAISY?!
YOU GOT IT, MORIZONO. CONGRATU-LATIONS.
NOW, WHY DON'T WE BAD GUYS HAVE A LITTLE CHAT?
WHAT DO YOU WANT WITH ME?

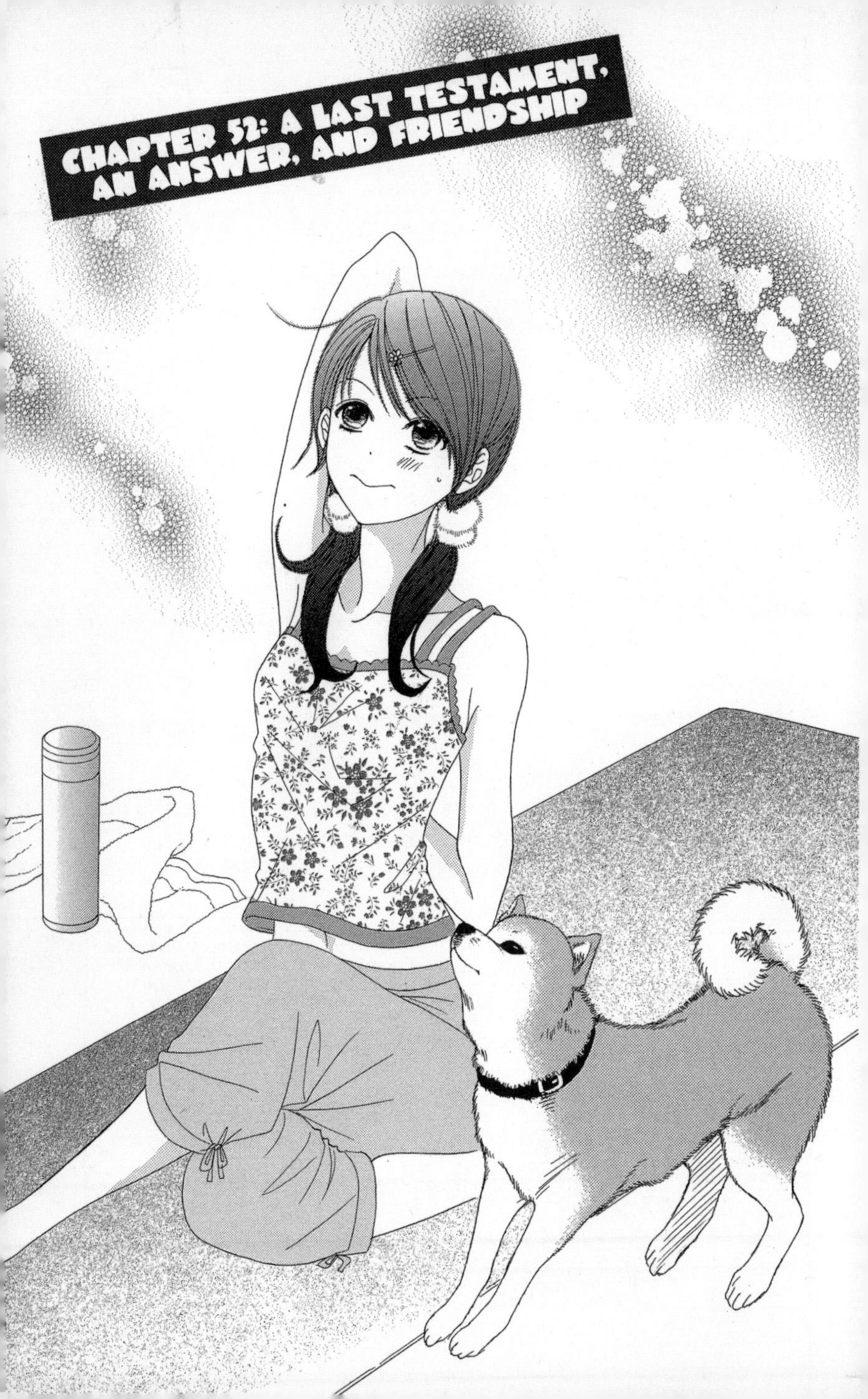
CHAPTER 52: A LAST TESTAMENT, AN ANSWER, AND FRIENDSHIP

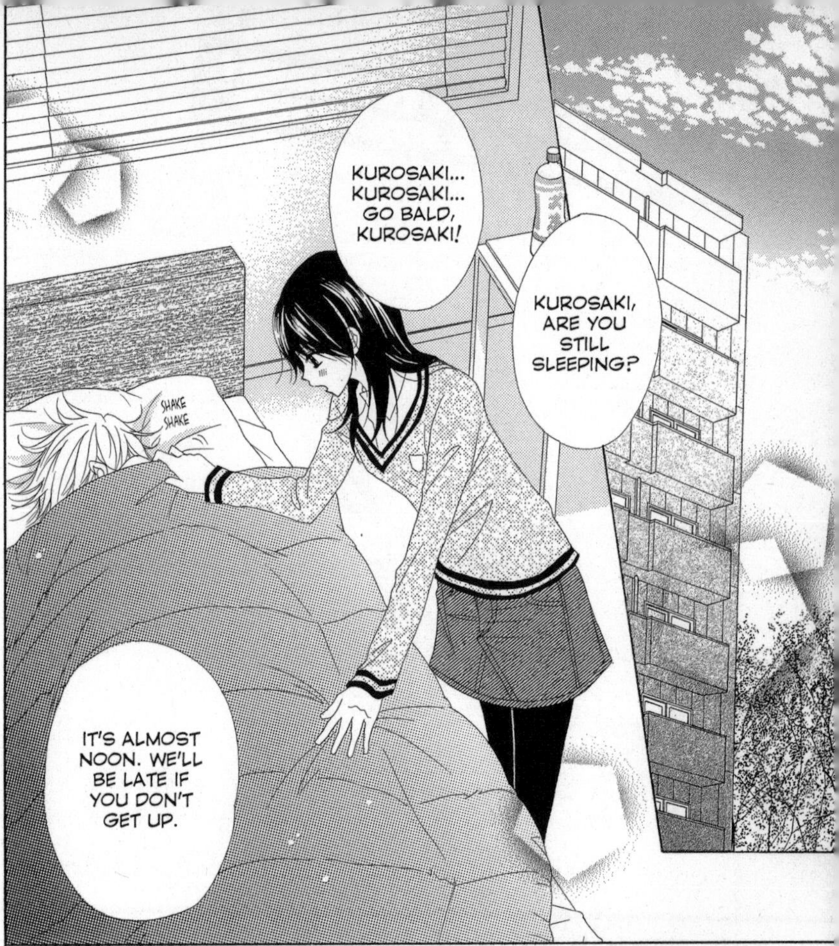
KUROSAKI, ARE YOU STILL SLEEPING?
KUROSAKI... KUROSAKI... GO BALD, KUROSAKI!
SHAKE SHAKE
IT'S ALMOST NOON. WE'LL BE LATE IF YOU DON'T GET UP.

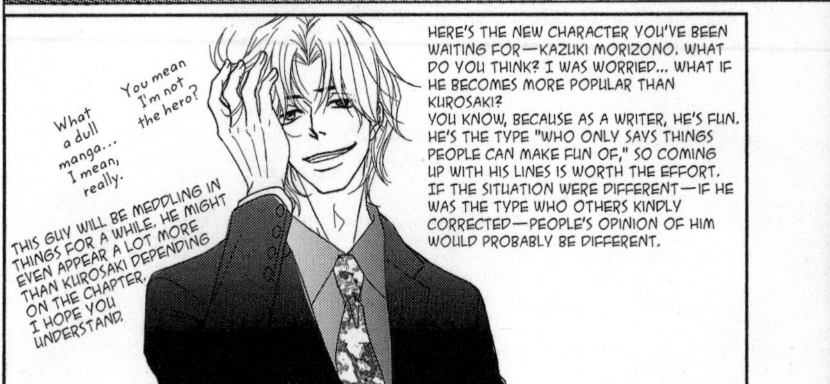
HERE'S THE NEW CHARACTER YOU'VE BEEN WAITING FOR—KAZUKI MORIZONO. WHAT DO YOU THINK? I WAS WORRIED... WHAT IF HE BECOMES MORE POPULAR THAN KUROSAKI?
YOU KNOW, BECAUSE AS A WRITER, HE'S FUN. HE'S THE TYPE "WHO ONLY SAYS THINGS PEOPLE CAN MAKE FUN OF," SO COMING UP WITH HIS LINES IS WORTH THE EFFORT. IF THE SITUATION WERE DIFFERENT—IF HE WAS THE TYPE WHO OTHERS KINDLY CORRECTED—PEOPLE'S OPINION OF HIM WOULD PROBABLY BE DIFFERENT.
You mean I'm not the hero?
What a dull manga... I mean, really.
THIS GUY WILL BE MEDDLING IN THINGS FOR A WHILE. HE MIGHT EVEN APPEAR A LOT MORE THAN KUROSAKI DEPENDING ON THE CHAPTER. I HOPE YOU UNDERSTAND.

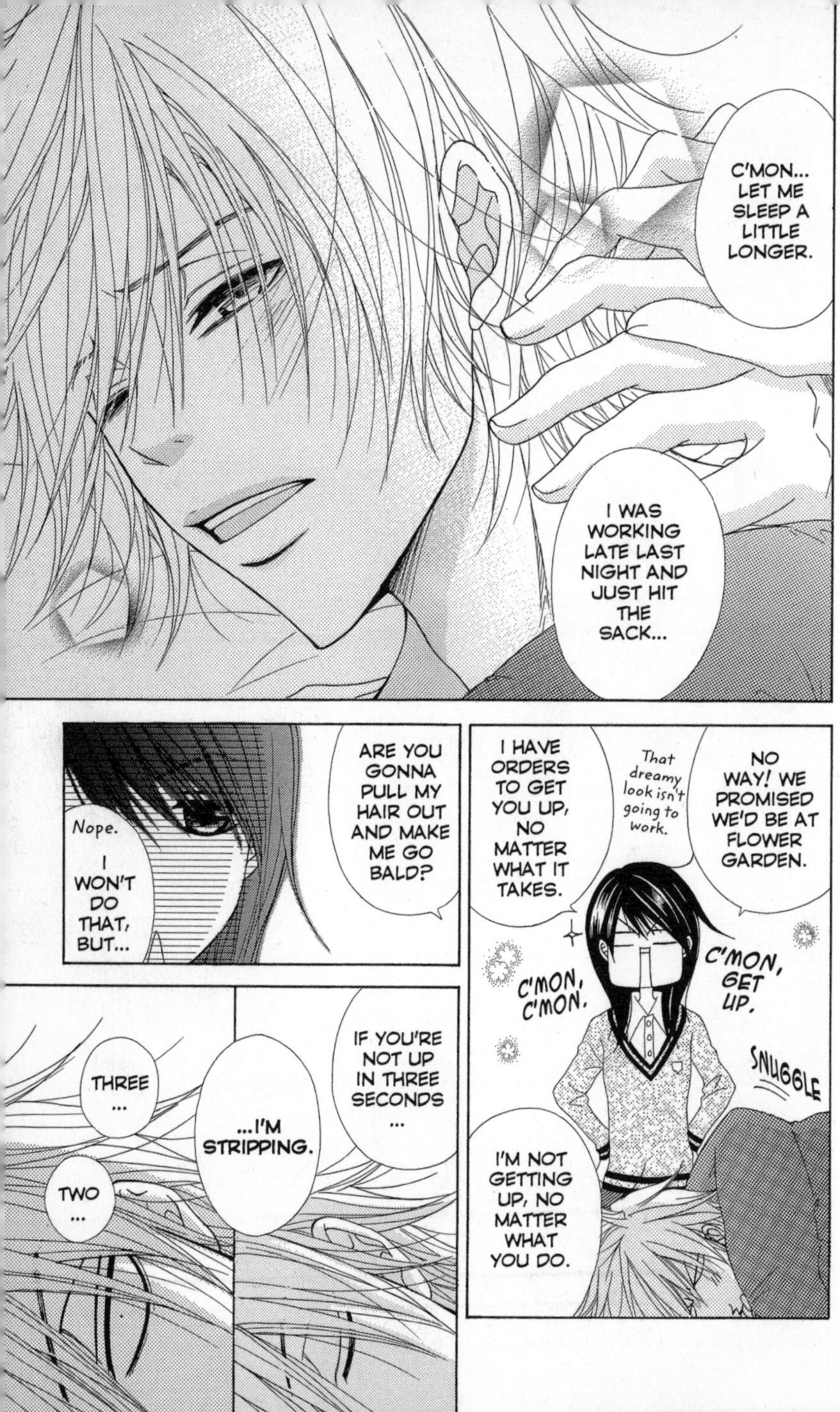
C'MON... LET ME SLEEP A LITTLE LONGER.
I WAS WORKING LATE LAST NIGHT AND JUST HIT THE SACK...
NO WAY! WE PROMISED WE'D BE AT FLOWER GARDEN.
That dreamy look isn't going to work.
I HAVE ORDERS TO GET YOU UP, NO MATTER WHAT IT TAKES.
C'MON, GET UP.
C'MON, C'MON.
SNUGGLE
I'M NOT GETTING UP, NO MATTER WHAT YOU DO.
ARE YOU GONNA PULL MY HAIR OUT AND MAKE ME GO BALD?
Nope.
I WON'T DO THAT, BUT...
IF YOU'RE NOT UP IN THREE SECONDS ...
...I'M STRIPPING.
THREE ...
TWO ...

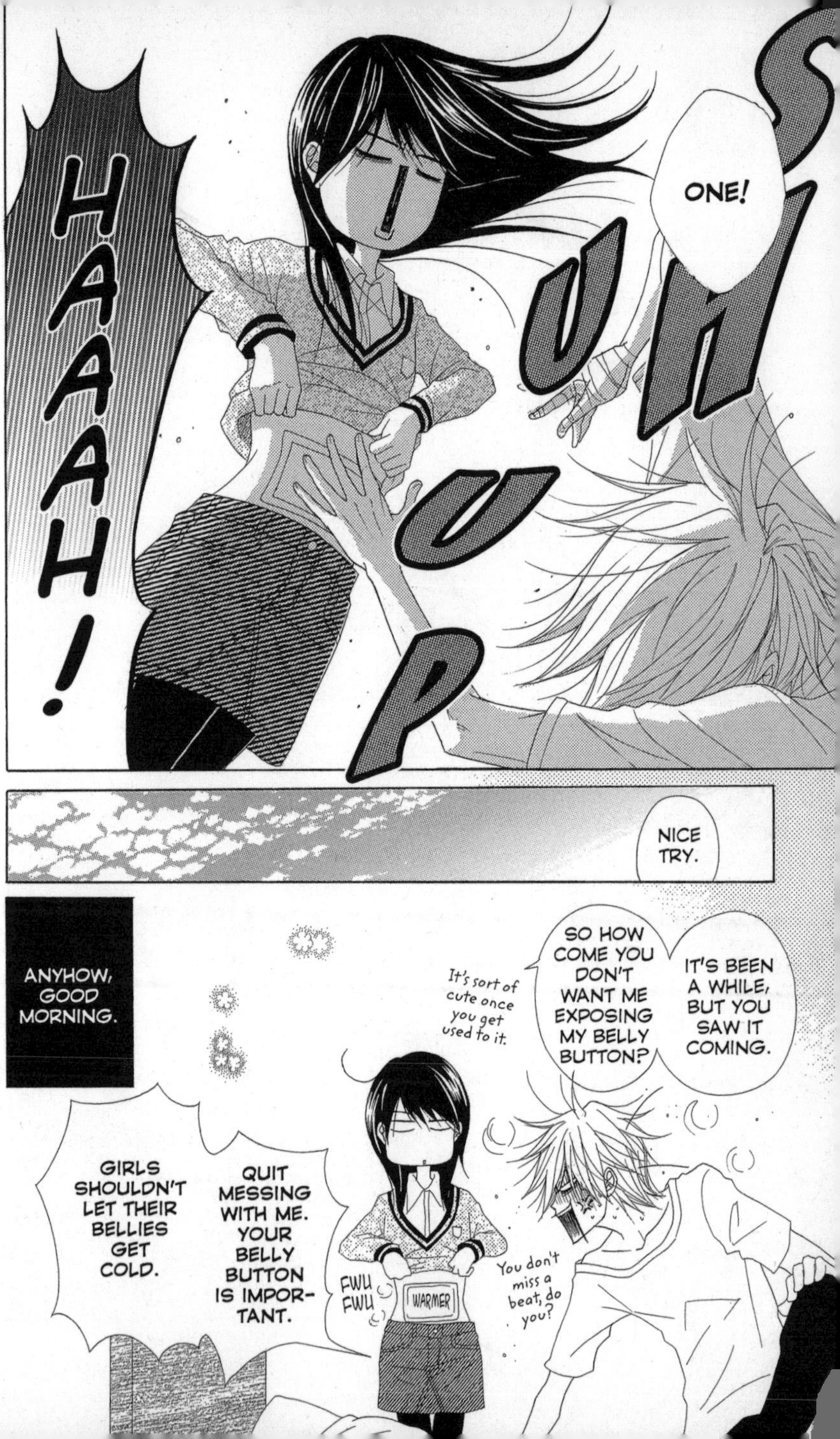
ONE!
SHUUP
HAAAH!
NICE TRY.
IT'S BEEN A WHILE, BUT YOU SAW IT COMING.
SO HOW COME YOU DON'T WANT ME EXPOSING MY BELLY BUTTON?
It's sort of cute once you get used to it.
ANYHOW, GOOD MORNING.
You don't miss a beat, do you?
FWU FWU
WARMER
QUIT MESSING WITH ME. YOUR BELLY BUTTON IS IMPOR-TANT.
GIRLS SHOULDN'T LET THEIR BELLIES GET COLD.

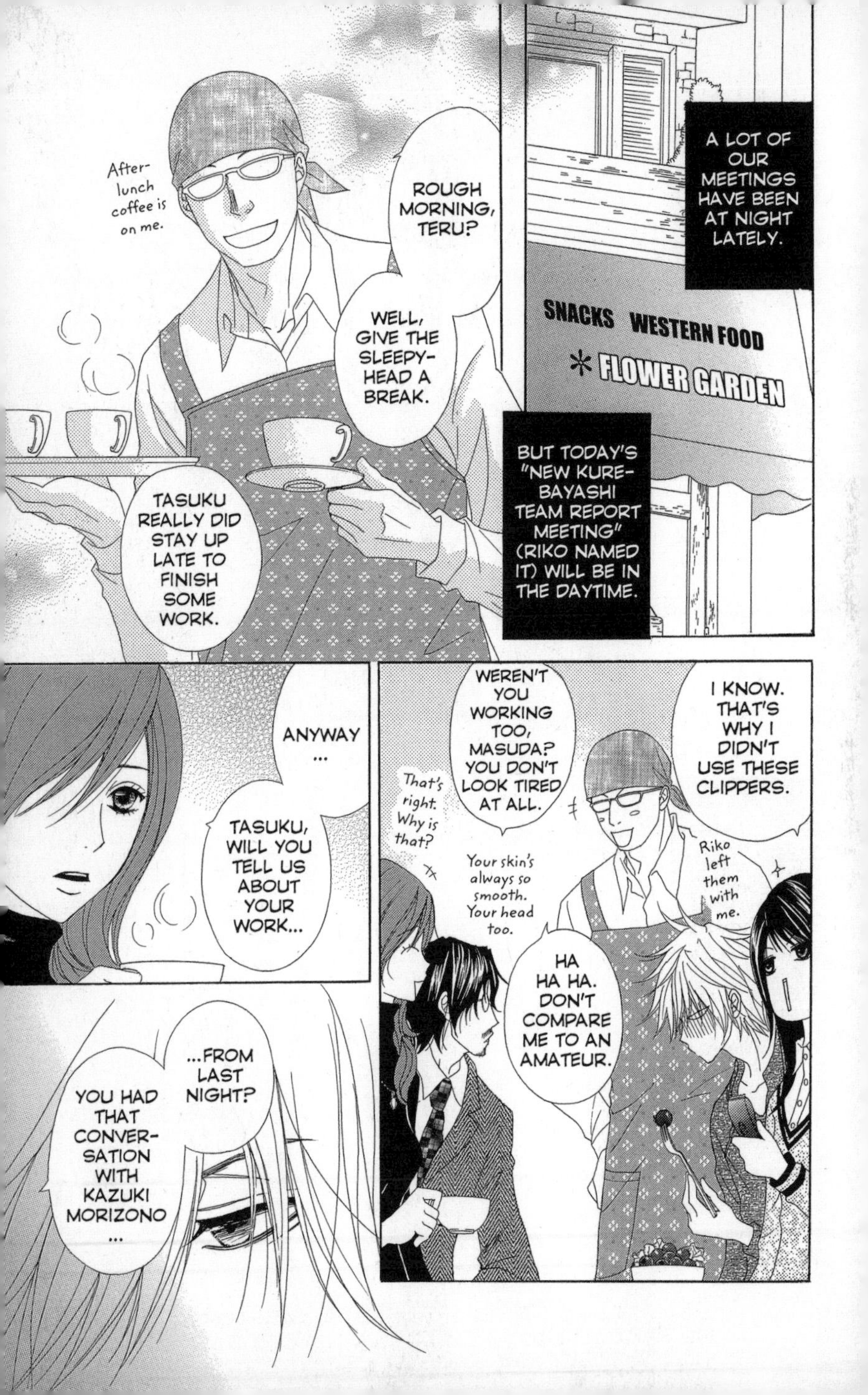
A LOT OF OUR MEETINGS HAVE BEEN AT NIGHT LATELY.
SNACKS WESTERN FOOD
FLOWER GARDEN
BUT TODAY'S "NEW KURE-BAYASHI TEAM REPORT MEETING" (RIKO NAMED IT) WILL BE IN THE DAYTIME.
ROUGH MORNING, TERU?
WELL, GIVE THE SLEEPY-HEAD A BREAK.
After-lunch coffee is on me.
TASUKU REALLY DID STAY UP LATE TO FINISH SOME WORK.
I KNOW. THAT'S WHY I DIDN'T USE THESE CLIPPERS.
WEREN'T YOU WORKING TOO, MASUDA? YOU DON'T LOOK TIRED AT ALL.
Riko left them with me.
That's right. Why is that?
Your skin's always so smooth. Your head too.
HA HA HA. DON'T COMPARE ME TO AN AMATEUR.
ANYWAY...
TASUKU, WILL YOU TELL US ABOUT YOUR WORK...
...FROM LAST NIGHT?
YOU HAD THAT CONVER-SATION WITH KAZUKI MORIZONO...

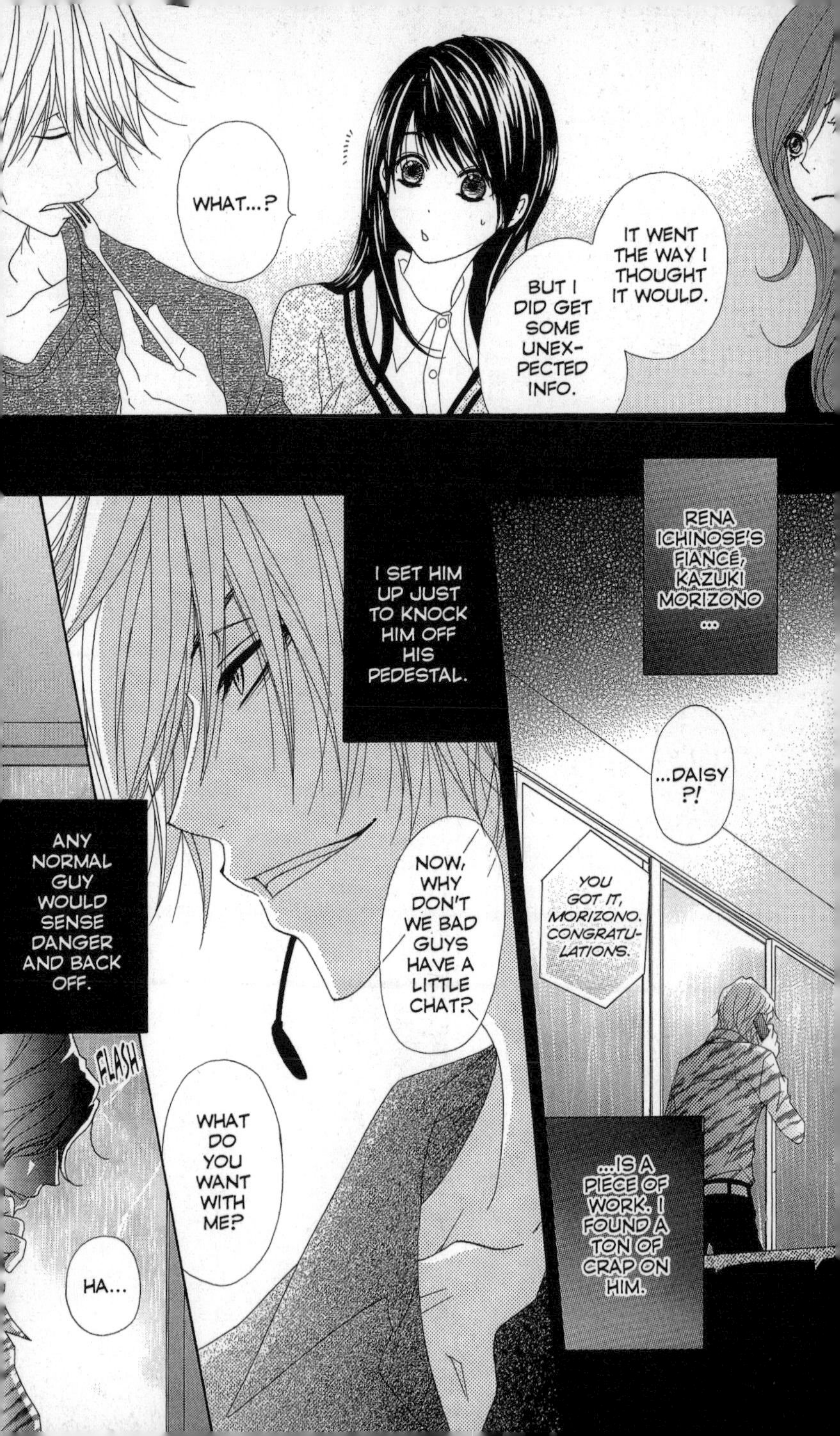
IT WENT THE WAY I THOUGHT IT WOULD.
BUT I DID GET SOME UNEX-PECTED INFO.
WHAT...?
RENA ICHINOSE'S FIANCÉ, KAZUKI MORIZONO ...
...DAISY ?!
YOU GOT IT, MORIZONO. CONGRATU-LATIONS.
...IS A PIECE OF WORK. I FOUND A TON OF CRAP ON HIM.
I SET HIM UP JUST TO KNOCK HIM OFF HIS PEDESTAL.
NOW, WHY DON'T WE BAD GUYS HAVE A LITTLE CHAT?
ANY NORMAL GUY WOULD SENSE DANGER AND BACK OFF.
FLASH
WHAT DO YOU WANT WITH ME?
HA...

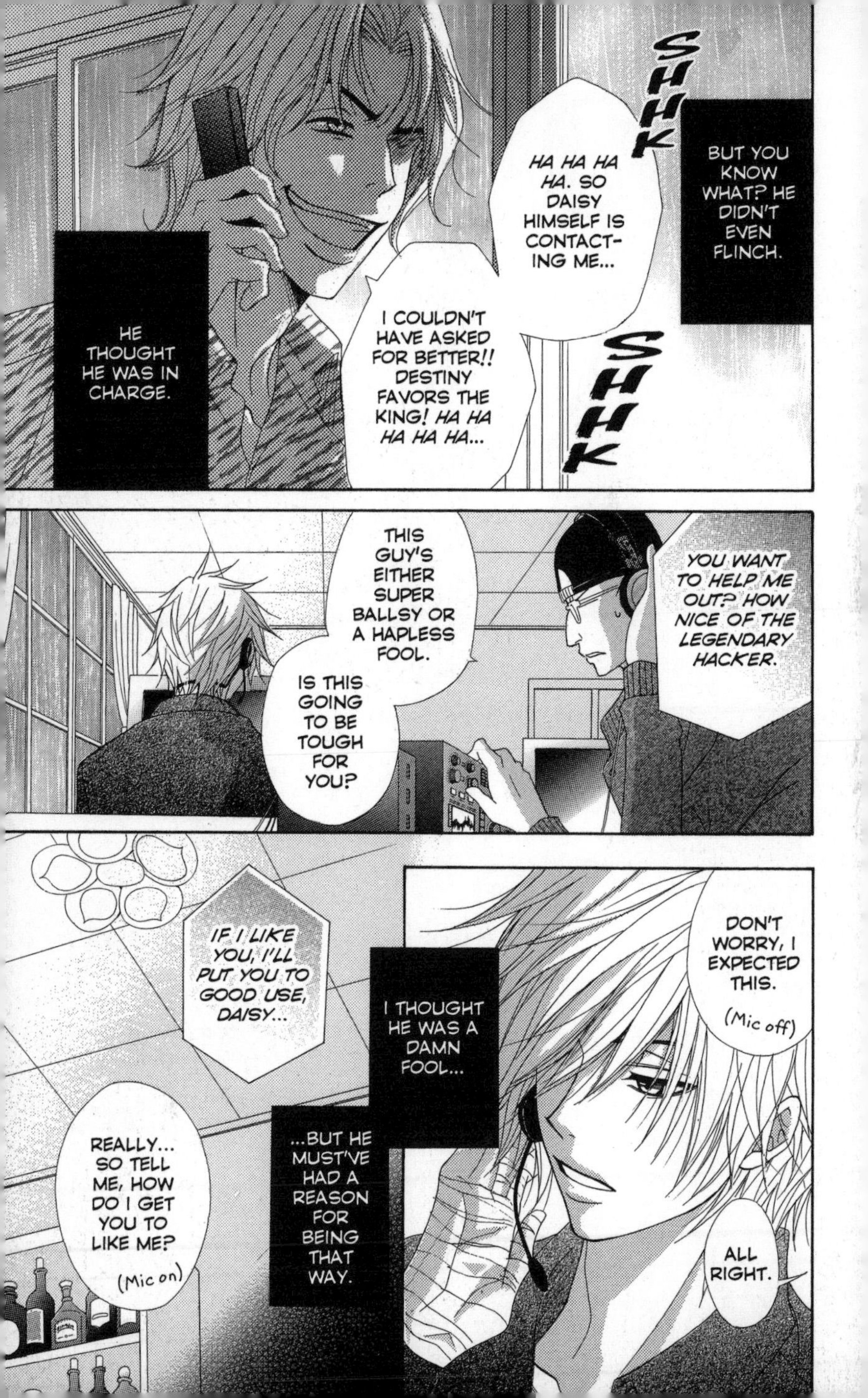
BUT YOU KNOW WHAT? HE DIDN'T EVEN FLINCH.
SHHK
HA HA HA HA. SO DAISY HIMSELF IS CONTACTING ME...
SHHK
I COULDN'T HAVE ASKED FOR BETTER!! DESTINY FAVORS THE KING! HA HA HA HA HA...
HE THOUGHT HE WAS IN CHARGE.
YOU WANT TO HELP ME OUT? HOW NICE OF THE LEGENDARY HACKER.
THIS GUY'S EITHER SUPER BALLSY OR A HAPLESS FOOL.
IS THIS GOING TO BE TOUGH FOR YOU?
DON'T WORRY, I EXPECTED THIS.
(Mic off)
IF I LIKE YOU, I'LL PUT YOU TO GOOD USE, DAISY...
I THOUGHT HE WAS A DAMN FOOL...
REALLY... SO TELL ME, HOW DO I GET YOU TO LIKE ME?
(Mic on)
...BUT HE MUST'VE HAD A REASON FOR BEING THAT WAY.
ALL RIGHT.

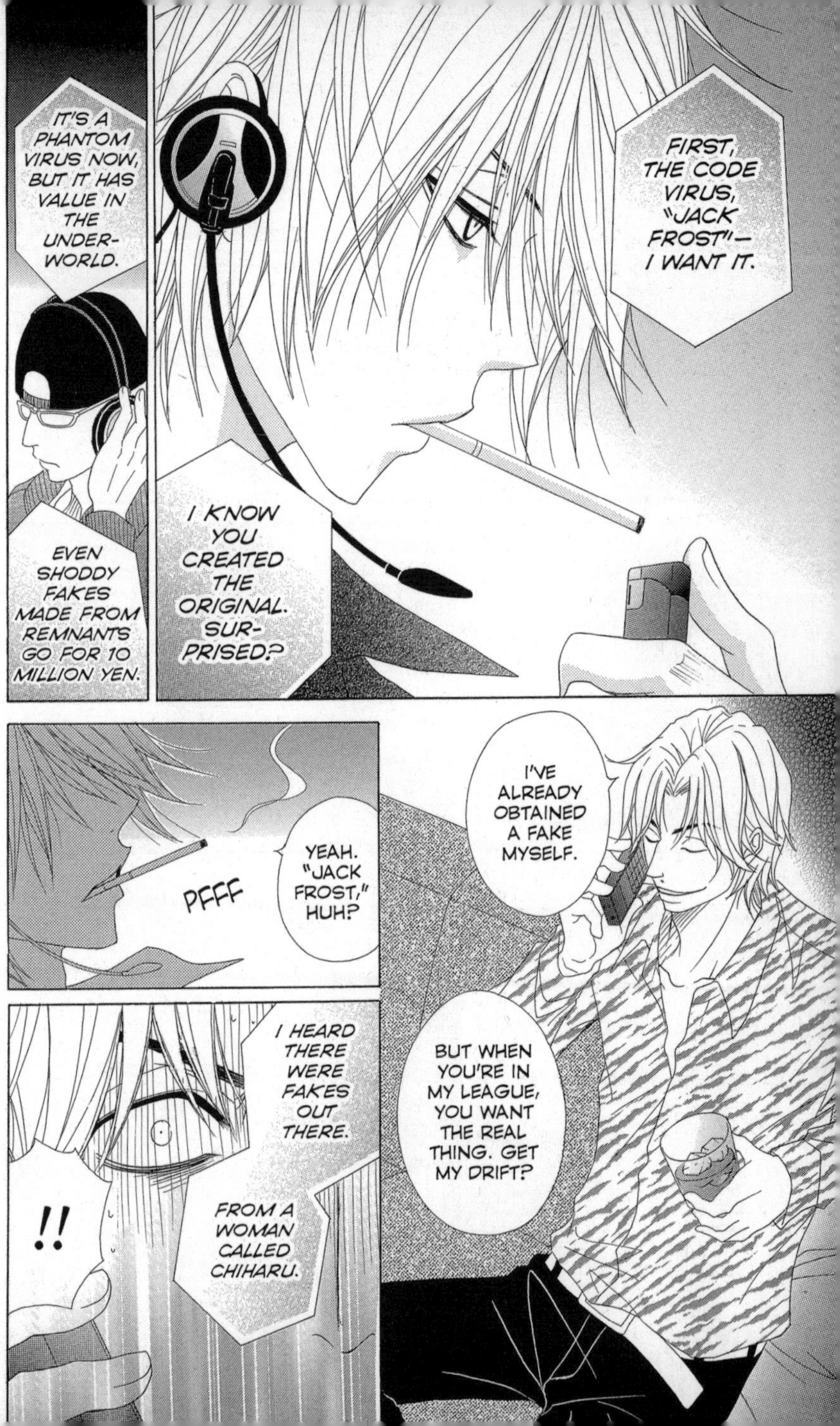
FIRST, THE CODE VIRUS, "JACK FROST"— I WANT IT.
I KNOW YOU CREATED THE ORIGINAL. SUR-PRISED?
IT'S A PHANTOM VIRUS NOW, BUT IT HAS VALUE IN THE UNDER-WORLD.
EVEN SHODDY FAKES MADE FROM REMNANTS GO FOR 10 MILLION YEN.
I'VE ALREADY OBTAINED A FAKE MYSELF.
BUT WHEN YOU'RE IN MY LEAGUE, YOU WANT THE REAL THING. GET MY DRIFT?
YEAH. "JACK FROST," HUH?
PFFF
I HEARD THERE WERE FAKES OUT THERE.
FROM A WOMAN CALLED CHIHARU.
!!

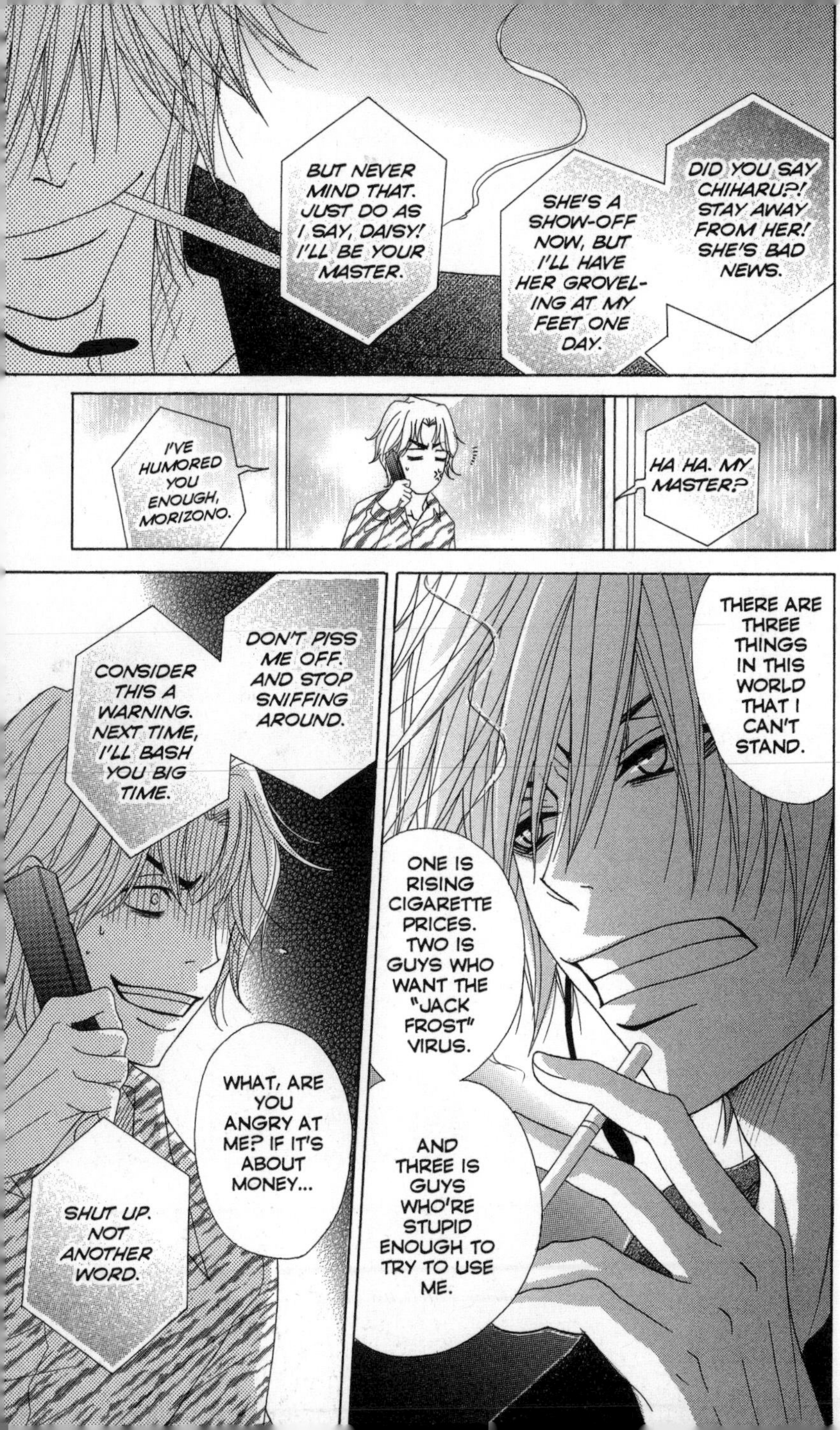
DID YOU SAY CHIHARU?! STAY AWAY FROM HER! SHE'S BAD NEWS.
SHE'S A SHOW-OFF NOW, BUT I'LL HAVE HER GROVELING AT MY FEET ONE DAY.
BUT NEVER MIND THAT. JUST DO AS I SAY, DAISY! I'LL BE YOUR MASTER.
HA HA. MY MASTER?
I'VE HUMORED YOU ENOUGH, MORIZONO.
THERE ARE THREE THINGS IN THIS WORLD THAT I CAN'T STAND.
ONE IS RISING CIGARETTE PRICES. TWO IS GUYS WHO WANT THE "JACK FROST" VIRUS.
AND THREE IS GUYS WHO'RE STUPID ENOUGH TO TRY TO USE ME.
DON'T PISS ME OFF. AND STOP SNIFFING AROUND.
CONSIDER THIS A WARNING. NEXT TIME, I'LL BASH YOU BIG TIME.
WHAT, ARE YOU ANGRY AT ME? IF IT'S ABOUT MONEY...
SHUT UP. NOT ANOTHER WORD.

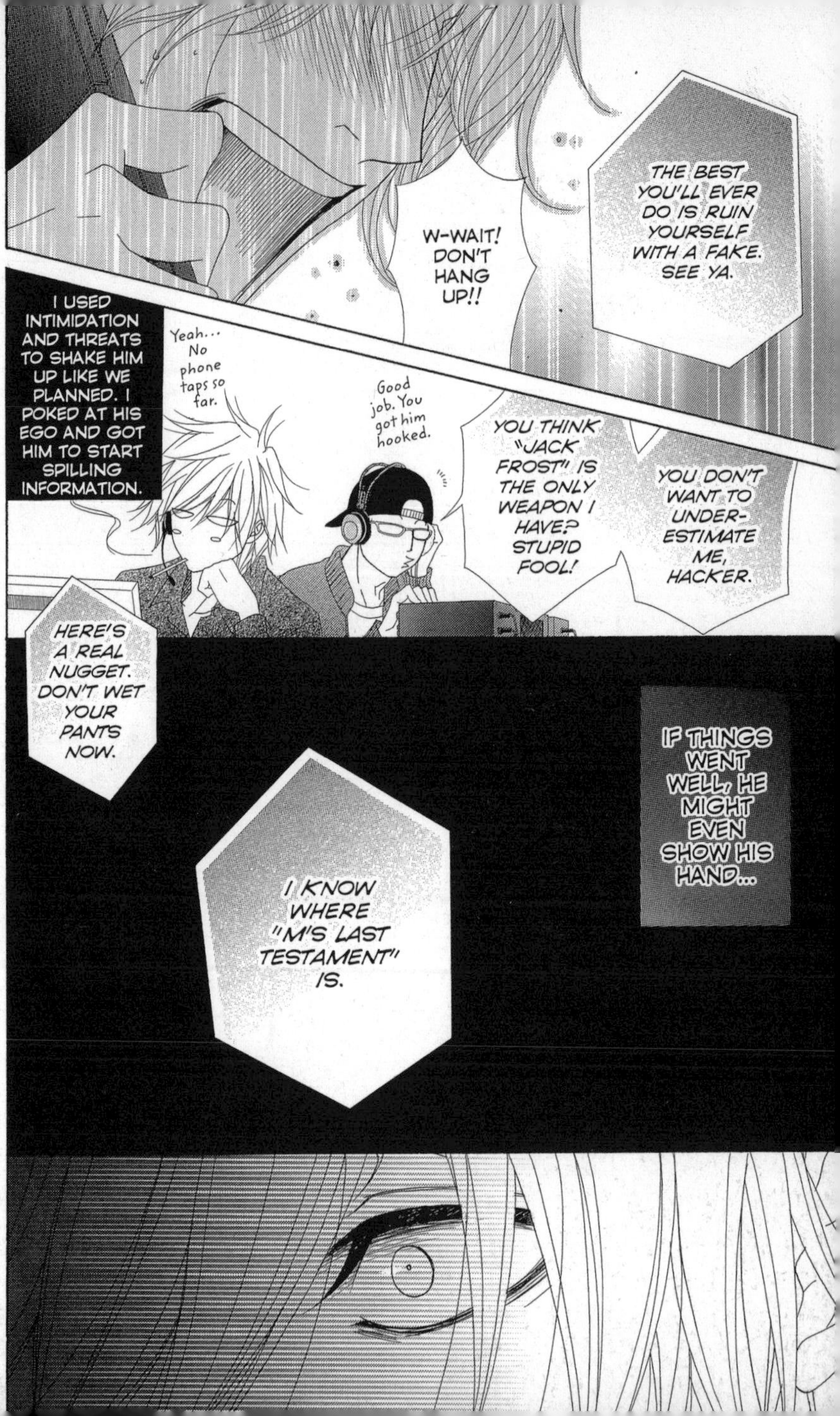
THE BEST YOU'LL EVER DO IS RUIN YOURSELF WITH A FAKE. SEE YA.
W-WAIT! DON'T HANG UP!!
YOU DON'T WANT TO UNDER-ESTIMATE ME, HACKER.
YOU THINK "JACK FROST" IS THE ONLY WEAPON I HAVE? STUPID FOOL!
Good job. You got him hooked.
Yeah... No phone taps so far.
I USED INTIMIDATION AND THREATS TO SHAKE HIM UP LIKE WE PLANNED. I POKED AT HIS EGO AND GOT HIM TO START SPILLING INFORMATION.
IF THINGS WENT WELL, HE MIGHT EVEN SHOW HIS HAND...
HERE'S A REAL NUGGET. DON'T WET YOUR PANTS NOW.
I KNOW WHERE "M'S LAST TESTAMENT" IS.

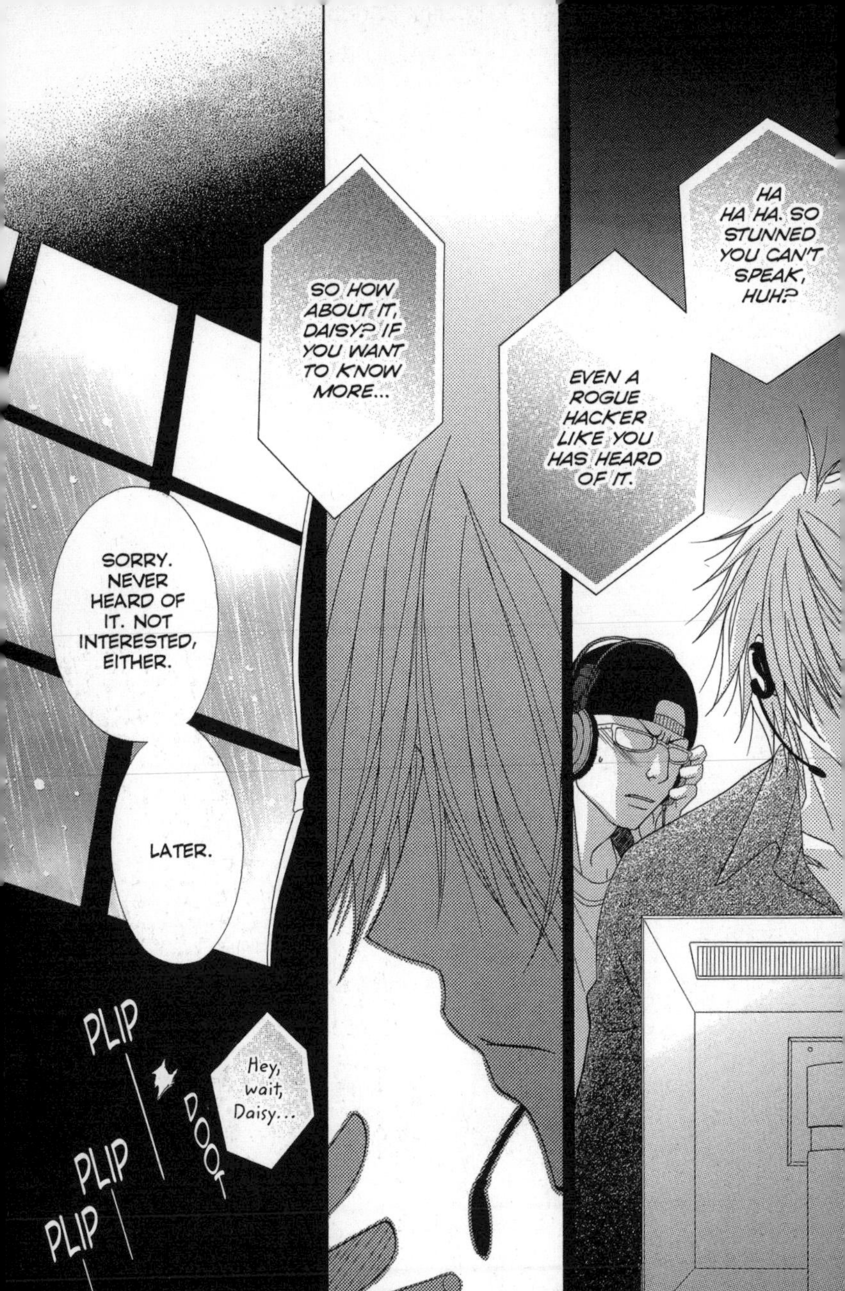
HA HA HA. SO STUNNED YOU CAN'T SPEAK, HUH?
EVEN A ROGUE HACKER LIKE YOU HAS HEARD OF IT.
SO HOW ABOUT IT, DAISY? IF YOU WANT TO KNOW MORE...
SORRY. NEVER HEARD OF IT. NOT INTERESTED, EITHER.
LATER.
Hey, wait, Daisy...
PLIP
DOOF
PLIP
PLIP

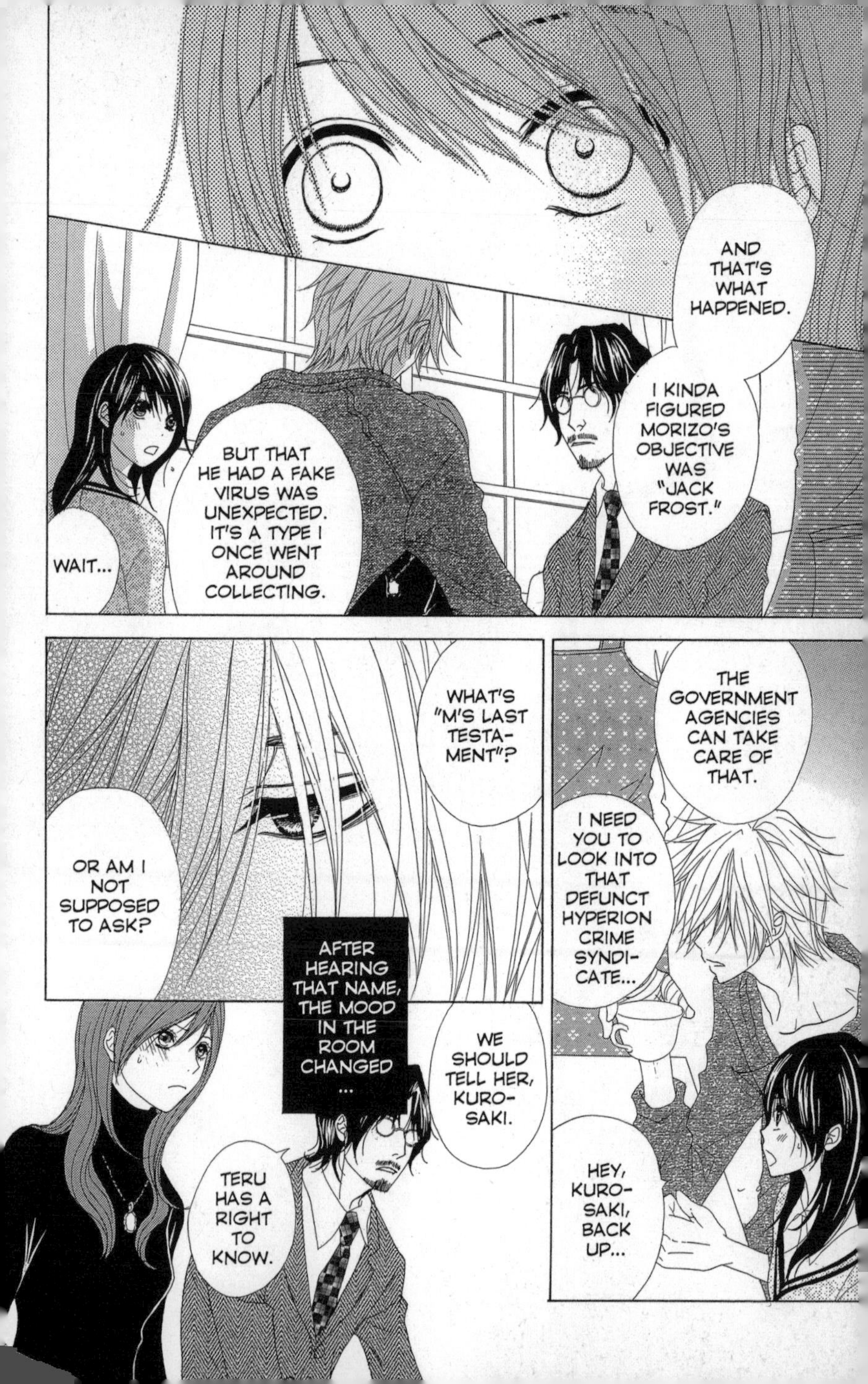
AND THAT'S WHAT HAPPENED.
I KINDA FIGURED MORIZO'S OBJECTIVE WAS "JACK FROST."
BUT THAT HE HAD A FAKE VIRUS WAS UNEXPECTED. IT'S A TYPE I ONCE WENT AROUND COLLECTING.
WAIT...
THE GOVERNMENT AGENCIES CAN TAKE CARE OF THAT.
I NEED YOU TO LOOK INTO THAT DEFUNCT HYPERION CRIME SYNDICATE...
HEY, KUROSAKI, BACK UP...
WHAT'S "M'S LAST TESTAMENT"?
OR AM I NOT SUPPOSED TO ASK?
AFTER HEARING THAT NAME, THE MOOD IN THE ROOM CHANGED...
WE SHOULD TELL HER, KUROSAKI.
TERU HAS A RIGHT TO KNOW.

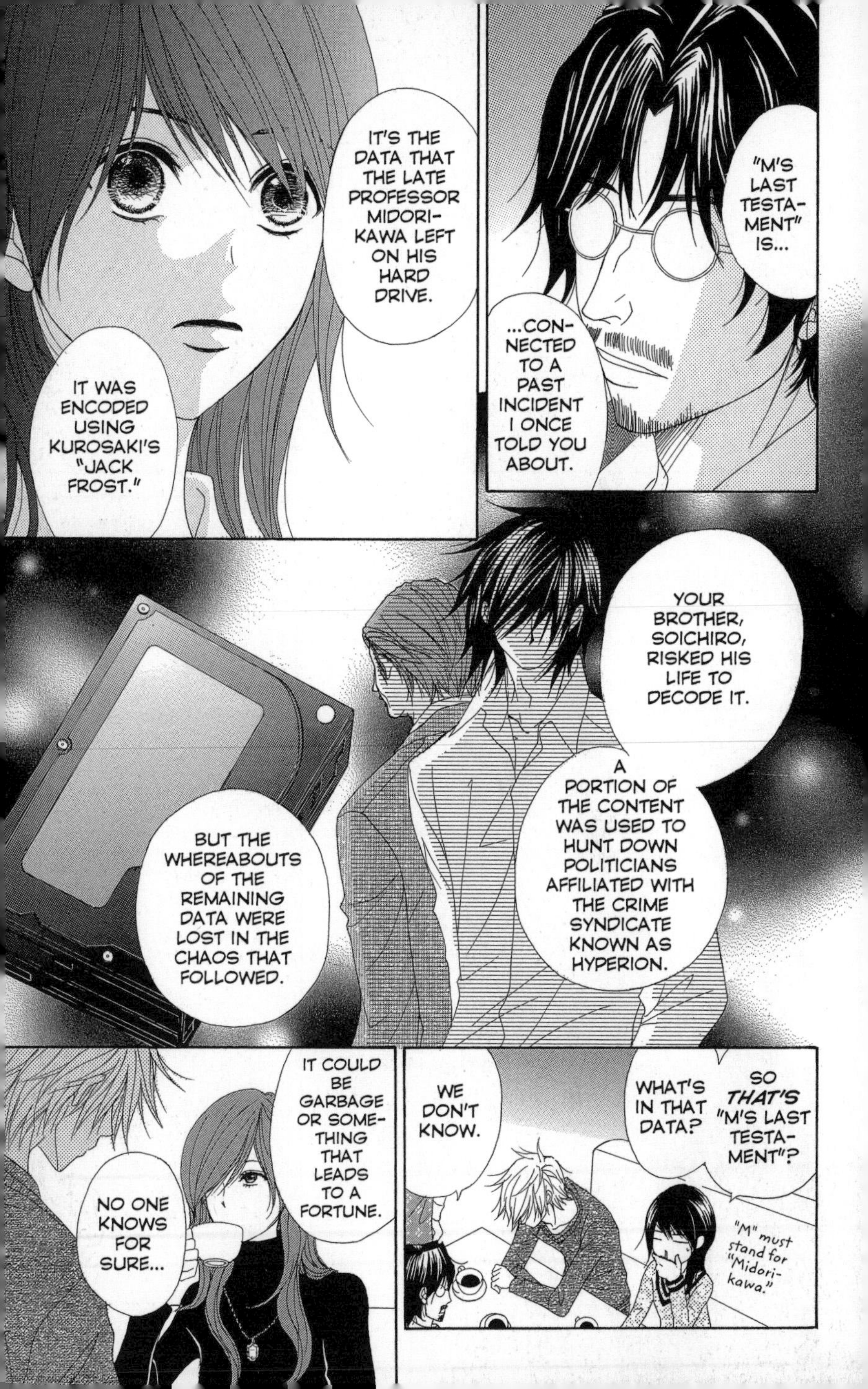
"M'S LAST TESTAMENT" IS...
...CONNECTED TO A PAST INCIDENT I ONCE TOLD YOU ABOUT.
IT'S THE DATA THAT THE LATE PROFESSOR MIDORIKAWA LEFT ON HIS HARD DRIVE.
IT WAS ENCODED USING KUROSAKI'S "JACK FROST."
YOUR BROTHER, SOICHIRO, RISKED HIS LIFE TO DECODE IT.
A PORTION OF THE CONTENT WAS USED TO HUNT DOWN POLITICIANS AFFILIATED WITH THE CRIME SYNDICATE KNOWN AS HYPERION.
BUT THE WHEREABOUTS OF THE REMAINING DATA WERE LOST IN THE CHAOS THAT FOLLOWED.
SO *THAT'S* "M'S LAST TESTAMENT"?
WHAT'S IN THAT DATA?
WE DON'T KNOW.
"M" must stand for "Midorikawa."
IT COULD BE GARBAGE OR SOMETHING THAT LEADS TO A FORTUNE.
NO ONE KNOWS FOR SURE...

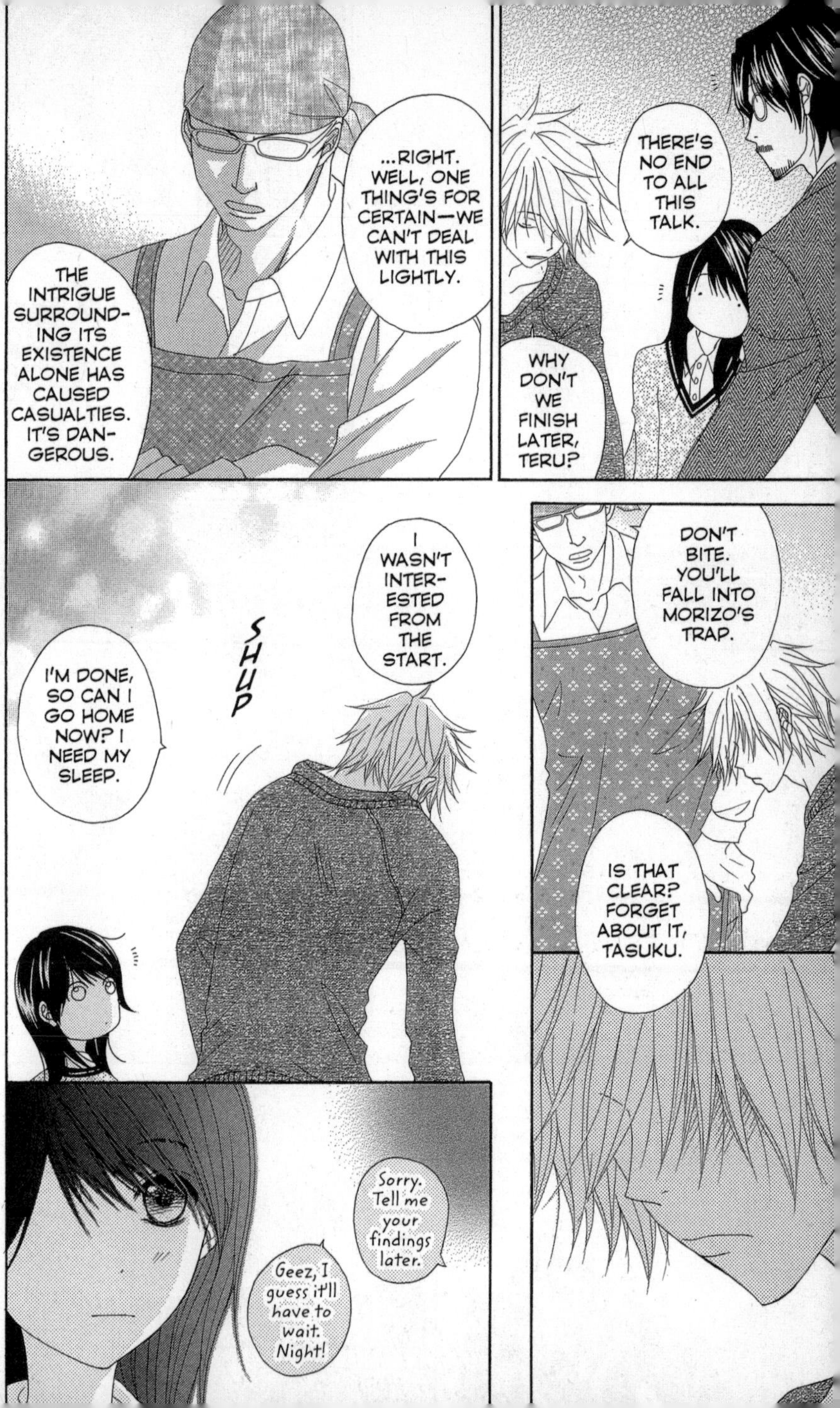
THERE'S NO END TO ALL THIS TALK.
WHY DON'T WE FINISH LATER, TERU?
...RIGHT. WELL, ONE THING'S FOR CERTAIN—WE CAN'T DEAL WITH THIS LIGHTLY.
THE INTRIGUE SURROUND-ING ITS EXISTENCE ALONE HAS CAUSED CASUALTIES. IT'S DAN-GEROUS.
DON'T BITE. YOU'LL FALL INTO MORIZO'S TRAP.
IS THAT CLEAR? FORGET ABOUT IT, TASUKU.
I WASN'T INTER-ESTED FROM THE START.
SHUP
I'M DONE, SO CAN I GO HOME NOW? I NEED MY SLEEP.
Sorry. Tell me your findings later.
Geez, I guess it'll have to wait. Night!

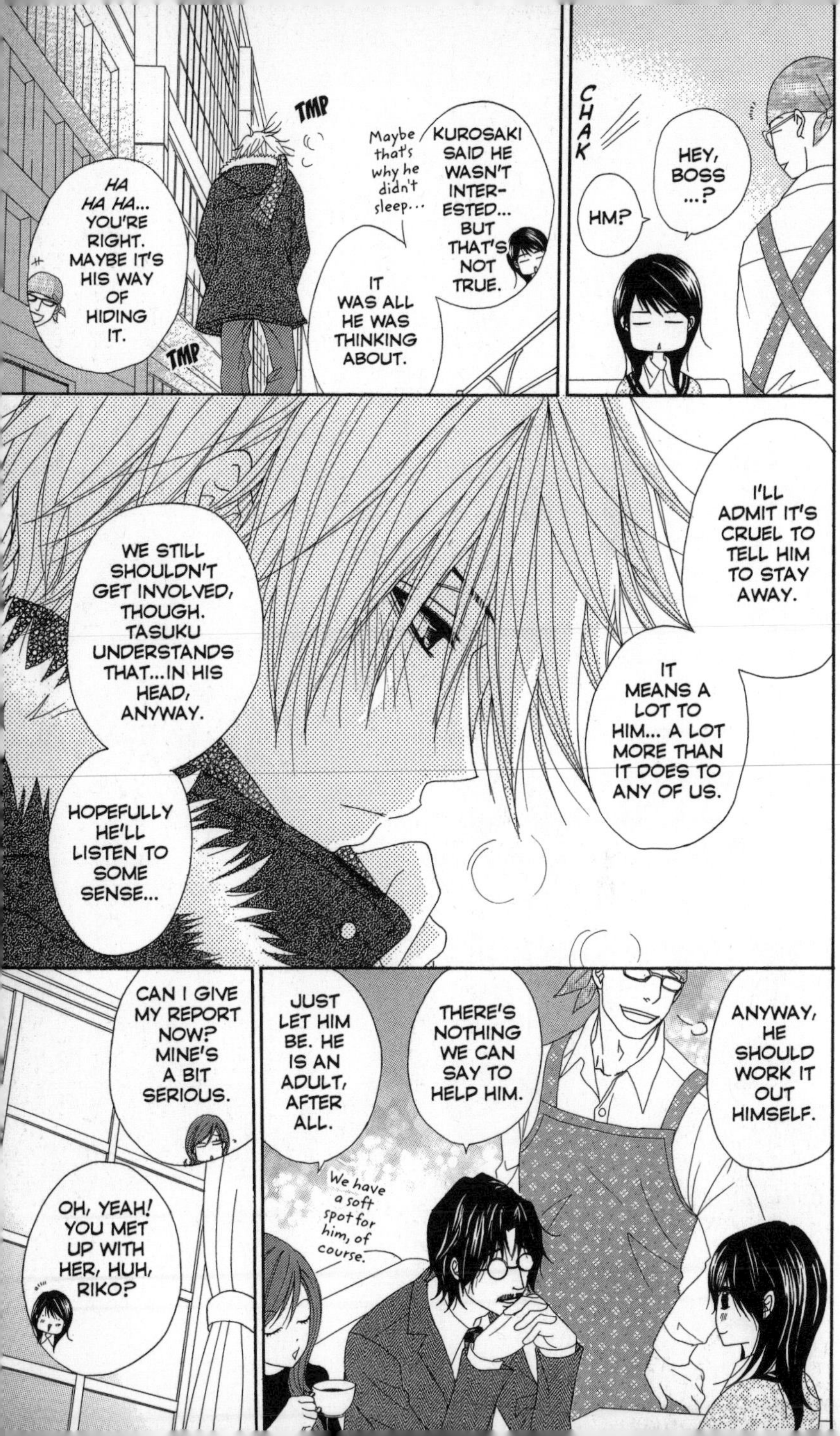
CHAK
HEY, BOSS ...?
HM?
TMP
KUROSAKI SAID HE WASN'T INTERESTED... BUT THAT'S NOT TRUE.
Maybe that's why he didn't sleep...
IT WAS ALL HE WAS THINKING ABOUT.
HA HA HA... YOU'RE RIGHT. MAYBE IT'S HIS WAY OF HIDING IT.
TMP
I'LL ADMIT IT'S CRUEL TO TELL HIM TO STAY AWAY.
IT MEANS A LOT TO HIM... A LOT MORE THAN IT DOES TO ANY OF US.
WE STILL SHOULDN'T GET INVOLVED, THOUGH. TASUKU UNDERSTANDS THAT...IN HIS HEAD, ANYWAY.
HOPEFULLY HE'LL LISTEN TO SOME SENSE...
ANYWAY, HE SHOULD WORK IT OUT HIMSELF.
THERE'S NOTHING WE CAN SAY TO HELP HIM.
JUST LET HIM BE. HE IS AN ADULT, AFTER ALL.
We have a soft spot for him, of course.
CAN I GIVE MY REPORT NOW? MINE'S A BIT SERIOUS.
OH, YEAH! YOU MET UP WITH HER, HUH, RIKO?

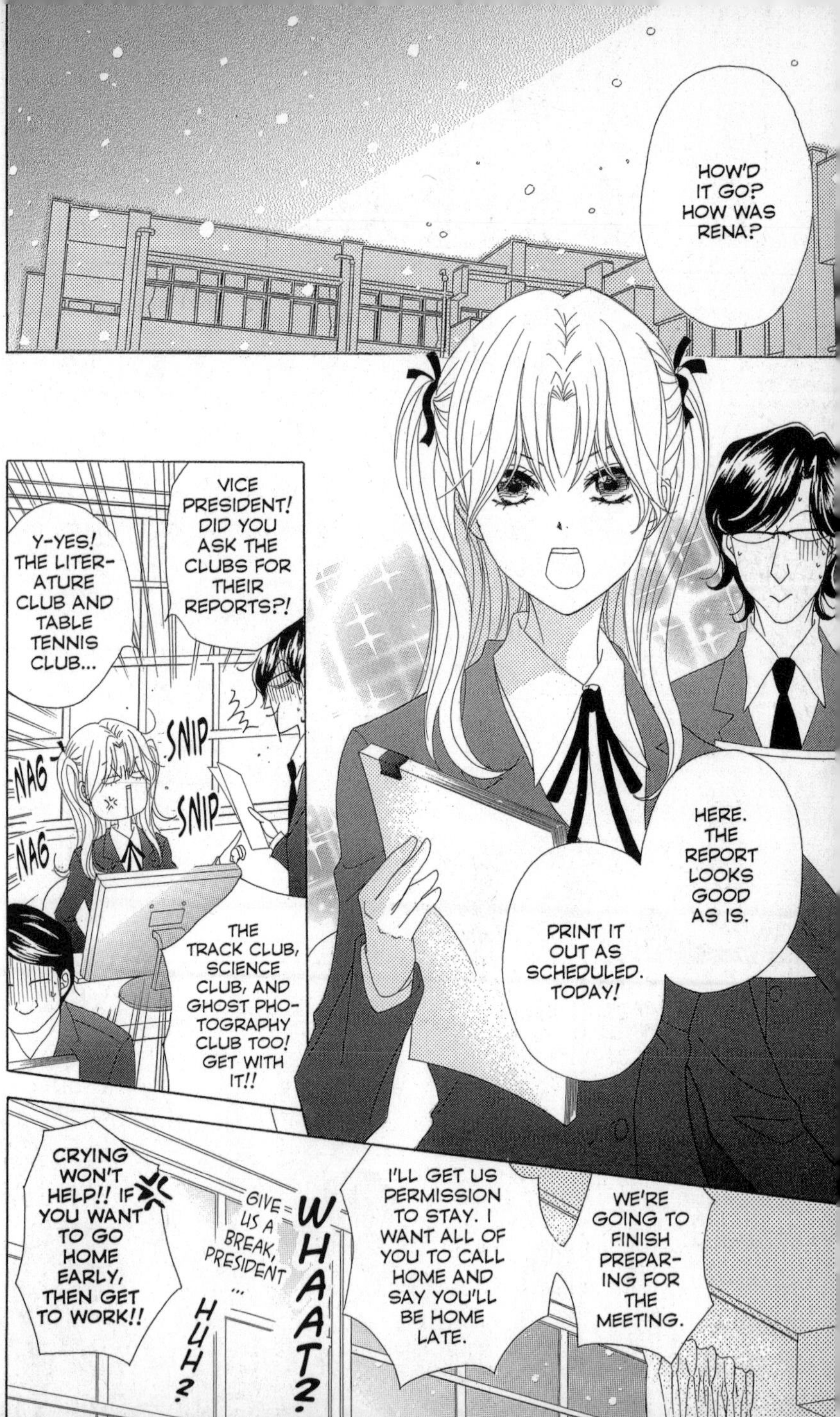
HOW'D IT GO? HOW WAS RENA?
HERE. THE REPORT LOOKS GOOD AS IS.
PRINT IT OUT AS SCHEDULED. TODAY!
VICE PRESIDENT! DID YOU ASK THE CLUBS FOR THEIR REPORTS?!
Y-YES! THE LITERATURE CLUB AND TABLE TENNIS CLUB...
SNIP
SNIP
NAG
NAG
THE TRACK CLUB, SCIENCE CLUB, AND GHOST PHOTOGRAPHY CLUB TOO! GET WITH IT!!
WE'RE GOING TO FINISH PREPARING FOR THE MEETING.
I'LL GET US PERMISSION TO STAY. I WANT ALL OF YOU TO CALL HOME AND SAY YOU'LL BE HOME LATE.
WHAAT?
HUH?
GIVE US A BREAK, PRESIDENT...
CRYING WON'T HELP!! IF YOU WANT TO GO HOME EARLY, THEN GET TO WORK!!

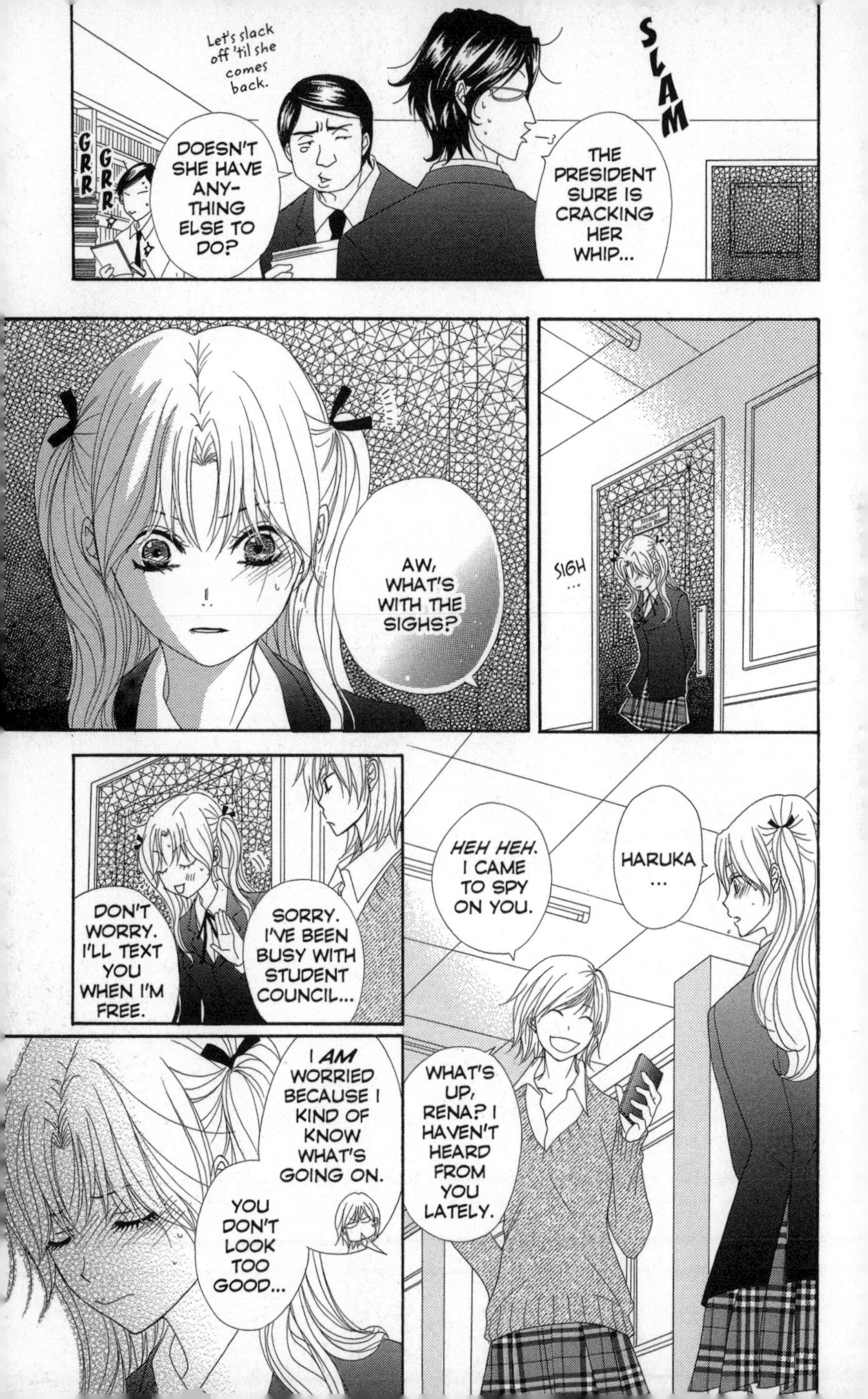
SLAM
THE PRESIDENT SURE IS CRACKING HER WHIP...
Let's slack off 'til she comes back.
DOESN'T SHE HAVE ANY-THING ELSE TO DO?
GRR GRR
SIGH...
AW, WHAT'S WITH THE SIGHS?
HARUKA...
HEH HEH. I CAME TO SPY ON YOU.
WHAT'S UP, RENA? I HAVEN'T HEARD FROM YOU LATELY.
SORRY. I'VE BEEN BUSY WITH STUDENT COUNCIL...
DON'T WORRY. I'LL TEXT YOU WHEN I'M FREE.
I ***AM*** WORRIED BECAUSE I KIND OF KNOW WHAT'S GOING ON.
YOU DON'T LOOK TOO GOOD...

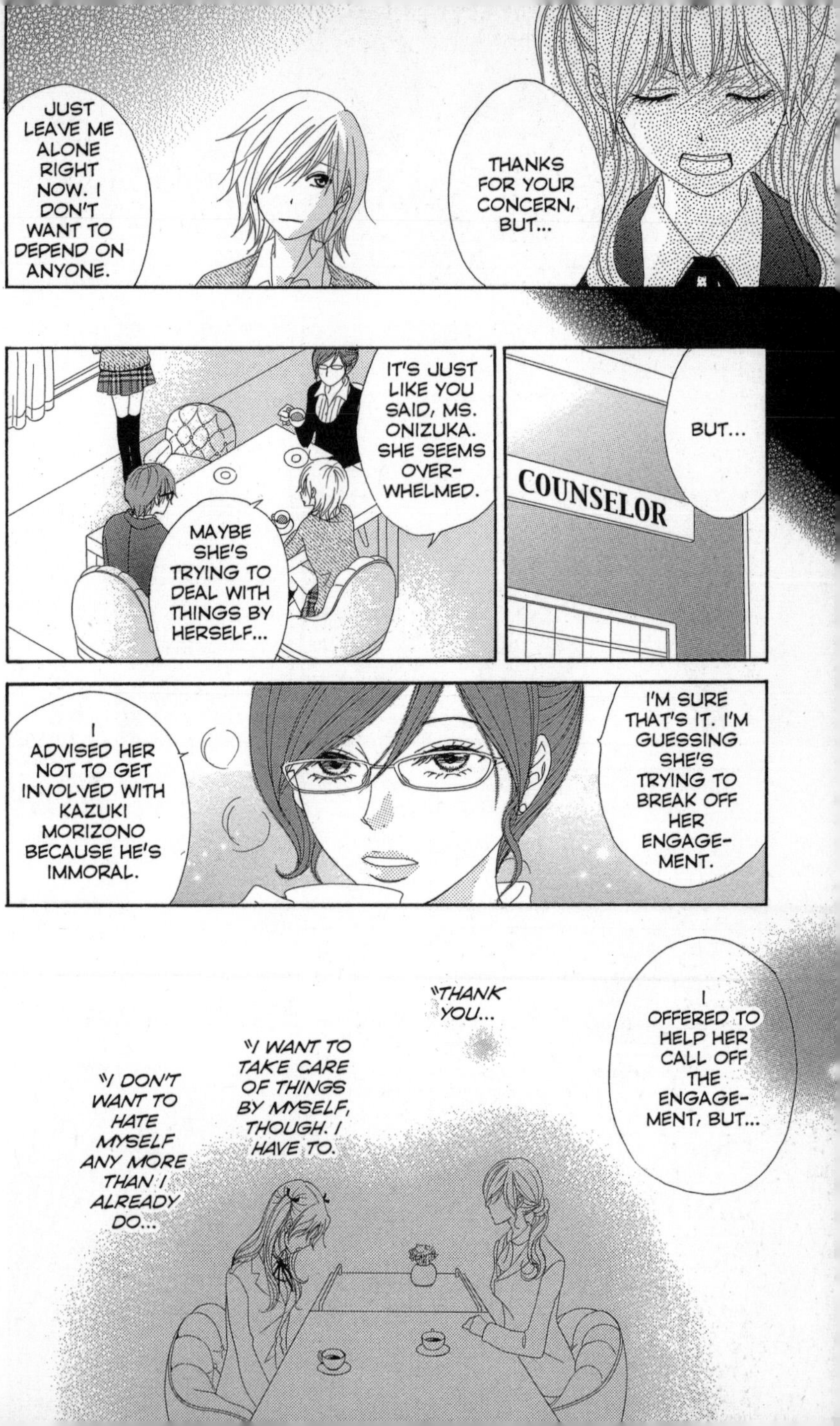
THANKS FOR YOUR CONCERN, BUT...
JUST LEAVE ME ALONE RIGHT NOW. I DON'T WANT TO DEPEND ON ANYONE.
BUT...
COUNSELOR
IT'S JUST LIKE YOU SAID, MS. ONIZUKA. SHE SEEMS OVER-WHELMED.
MAYBE SHE'S TRYING TO DEAL WITH THINGS BY HERSELF...
I'M SURE THAT'S IT. I'M GUESSING SHE'S TRYING TO BREAK OFF HER ENGAGE-MENT.
I ADVISED HER NOT TO GET INVOLVED WITH KAZUKI MORIZONO BECAUSE HE'S IMMORAL.
I OFFERED TO HELP HER CALL OFF THE ENGAGE-MENT, BUT...
"THANK YOU...
"I WANT TO TAKE CARE OF THINGS BY MYSELF, THOUGH. I HAVE TO.
"I DON'T WANT TO HATE MYSELF ANY MORE THAN I ALREADY DO...

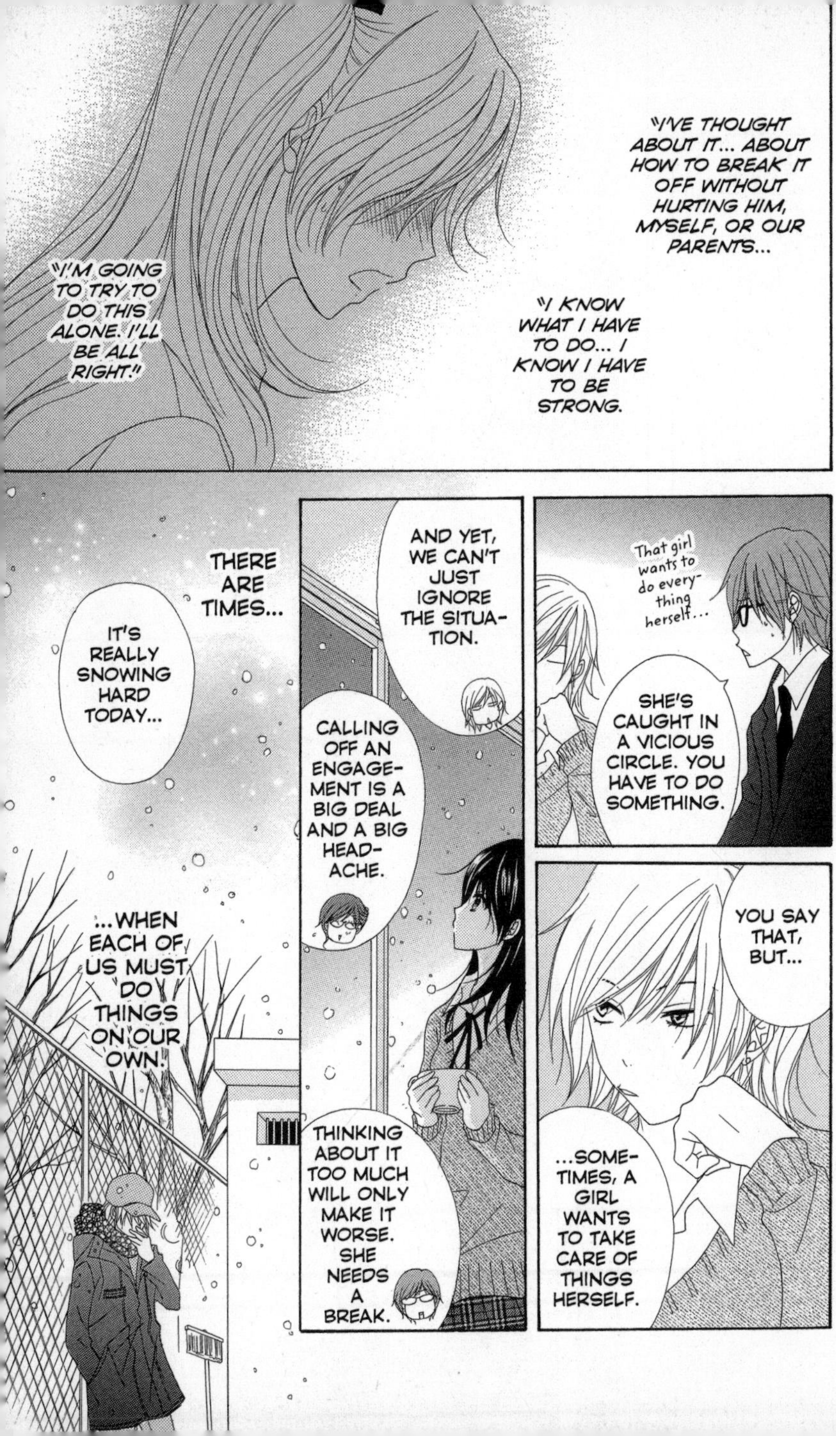
"I'VE THOUGHT ABOUT IT... ABOUT HOW TO BREAK IT OFF WITHOUT HURTING HIM, MYSELF, OR OUR PARENTS...
"I KNOW WHAT I HAVE TO DO... I KNOW I HAVE TO BE STRONG.
"I'M GOING TO TRY TO DO THIS ALONE. I'LL BE ALL RIGHT."
That girl wants to do everything herself...
SHE'S CAUGHT IN A VICIOUS CIRCLE. YOU HAVE TO DO SOMETHING.
YOU SAY THAT, BUT...
...SOMETIMES, A GIRL WANTS TO TAKE CARE OF THINGS HERSELF.
AND YET, WE CAN'T JUST IGNORE THE SITUATION.
CALLING OFF AN ENGAGEMENT IS A BIG DEAL AND A BIG HEADACHE.
THINKING ABOUT IT TOO MUCH WILL ONLY MAKE IT WORSE. SHE NEEDS A BREAK.
THERE ARE TIMES...
IT'S REALLY SNOWING HARD TODAY...
...WHEN EACH OF US MUST "DO THINGS ON OUR OWN."

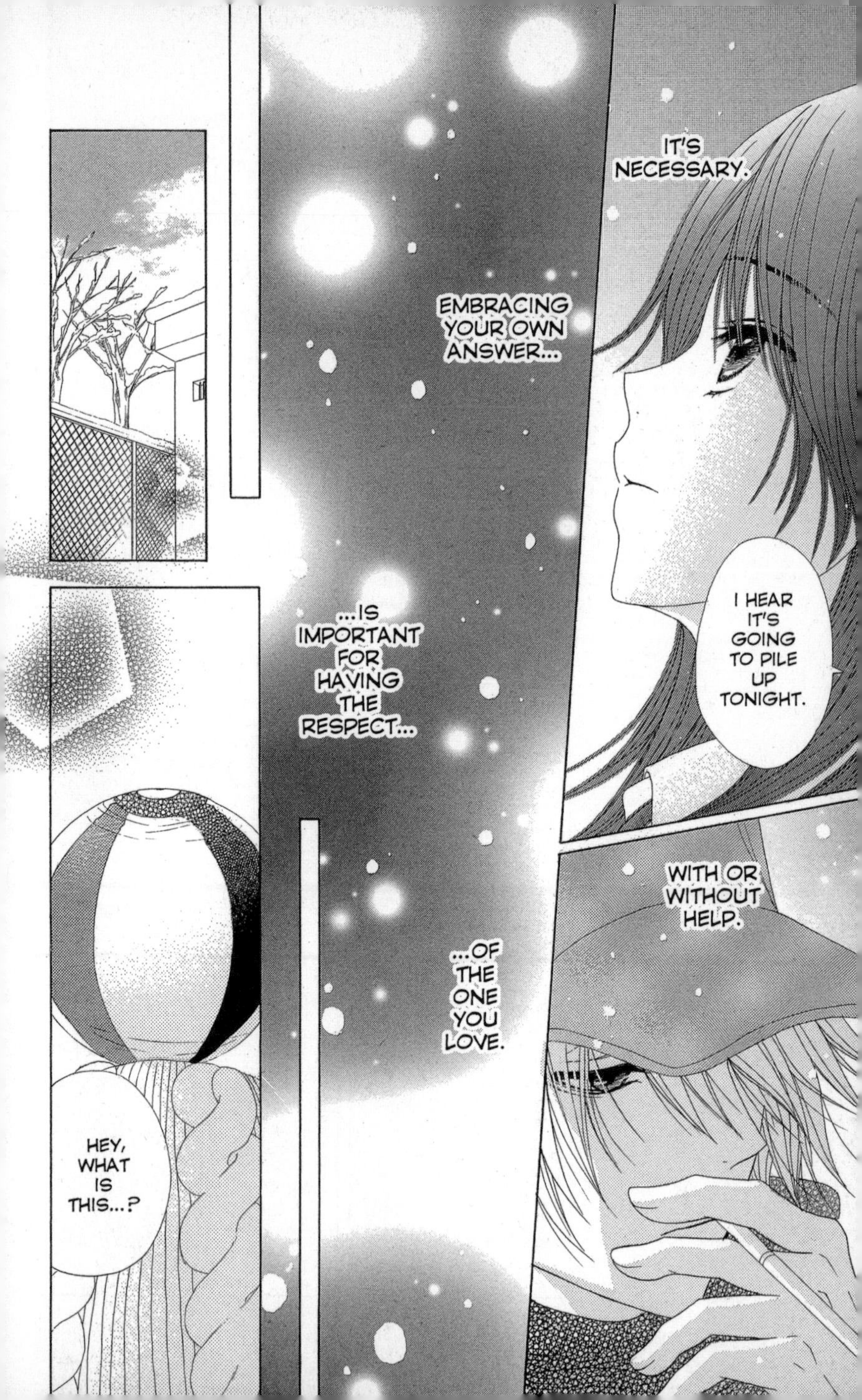
IT'S NECESSARY.
I HEAR IT'S GOING TO PILE UP TONIGHT.
EMBRACING YOUR OWN ANSWER...
...IS IMPORTANT FOR HAVING THE RESPECT...
WITH OR WITHOUT HELP.
...OF THE ONE YOU LOVE.
HEY, WHAT IS THIS...?

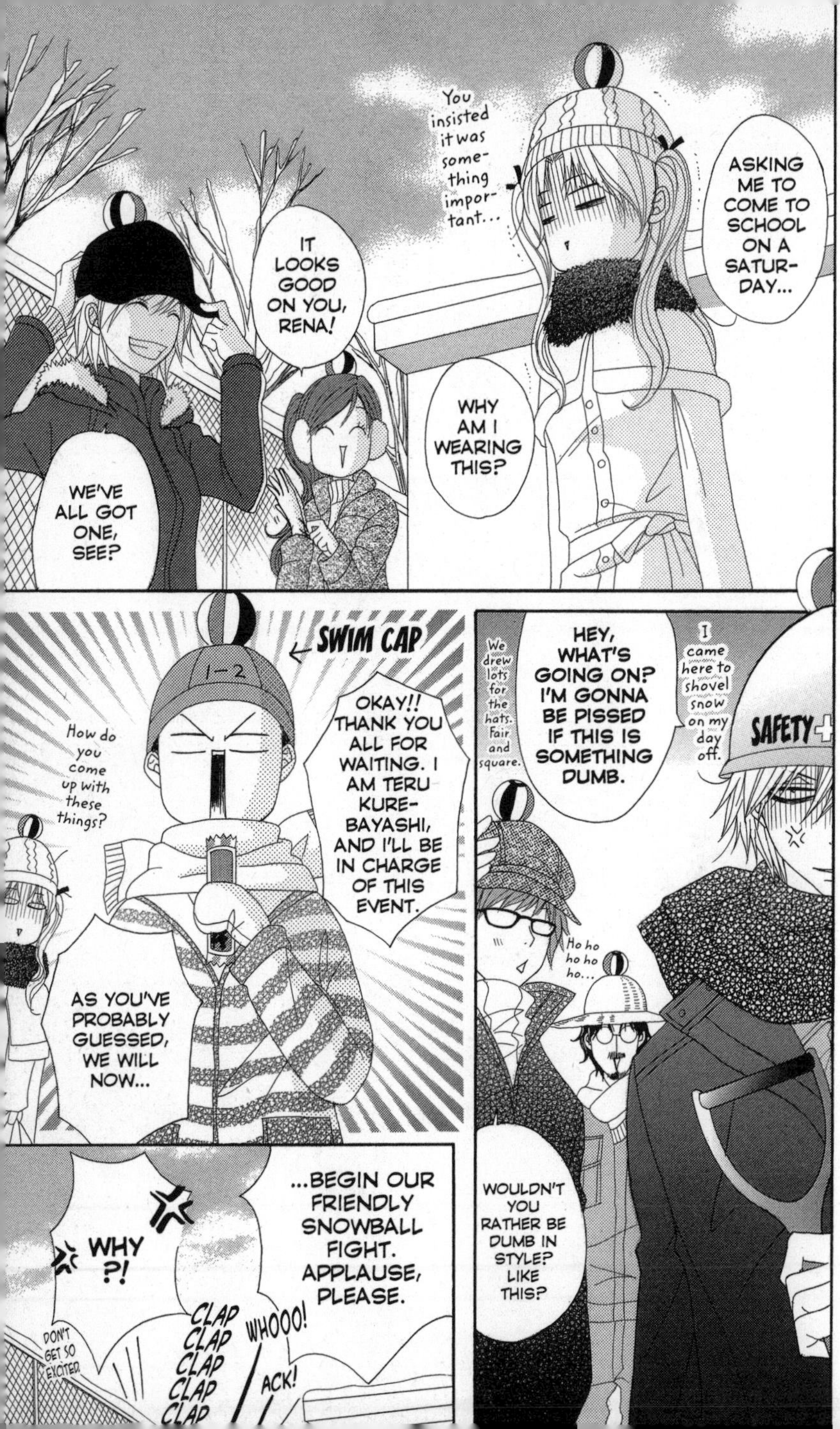
ASKING ME TO COME TO SCHOOL ON A SATURDAY...
You insisted it was something important...
WHY AM I WEARING THIS?
IT LOOKS GOOD ON YOU, RENA!
WE'VE ALL GOT ONE, SEE?
I came here to shovel snow on my day off.
SAFETY
HEY, WHAT'S GOING ON? I'M GONNA BE PISSED IF THIS IS SOMETHING DUMB.
We drew lots for the hats. Fair and square.
Ho ho ho ho ho...
WOULDN'T YOU RATHER BE DUMB IN STYLE? LIKE THIS?
SWIM CAP
1-2
OKAY!! THANK YOU ALL FOR WAITING. I AM TERU KUREBAYASHI, AND I'LL BE IN CHARGE OF THIS EVENT.
How do you come up with these things?
AS YOU'VE PROBABLY GUESSED, WE WILL NOW...
...BEGIN OUR FRIENDLY SNOWBALL FIGHT. APPLAUSE, PLEASE.
WHY?!
WHOOO!
CLAP CLAP CLAP CLAP CLAP
ACK!
DON'T GET SO EXCITED.

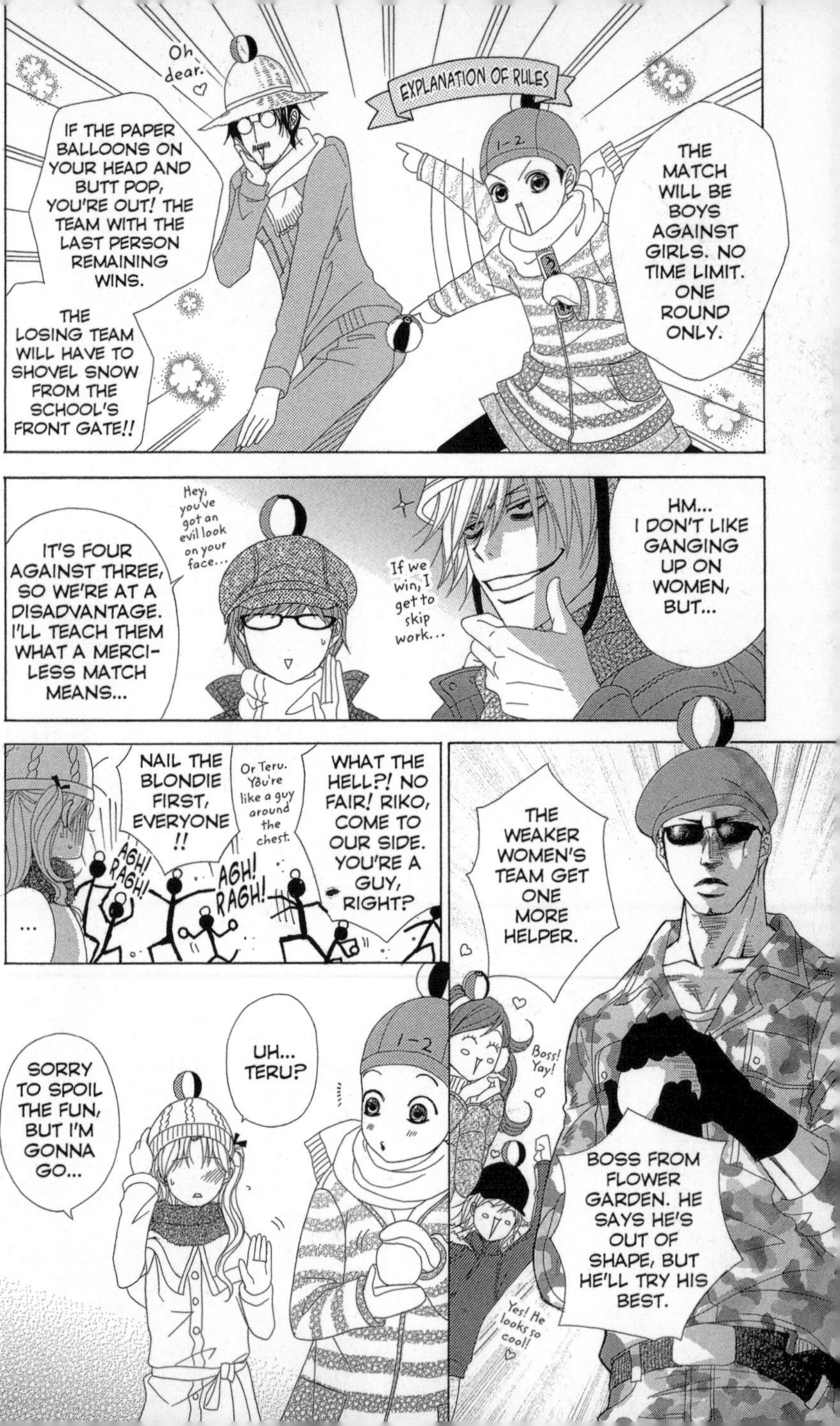
EXPLANATION OF RULES
THE MATCH WILL BE BOYS AGAINST GIRLS. NO TIME LIMIT. ONE ROUND ONLY.
Oh dear. ♡
IF THE PAPER BALLOONS ON YOUR HEAD AND BUTT POP, YOU'RE OUT! THE TEAM WITH THE LAST PERSON REMAINING WINS.
THE LOSING TEAM WILL HAVE TO SHOVEL SNOW FROM THE SCHOOL'S FRONT GATE!!
HM... I DON'T LIKE GANGING UP ON WOMEN, BUT...
If we win, I get to skip work...
Hey, you've got an evil look on your face...
IT'S FOUR AGAINST THREE, SO WE'RE AT A DISADVANTAGE. I'LL TEACH THEM WHAT A MERCILESS MATCH MEANS...
THE WEAKER WOMEN'S TEAM GET ONE MORE HELPER.
Boss! Yay!
BOSS FROM FLOWER GARDEN. HE SAYS HE'S OUT OF SHAPE, BUT HE'LL TRY HIS BEST.
Yes! He looks so cool! ♡
WHAT THE HELL?! NO FAIR! RIKO, COME TO OUR SIDE. YOU'RE A GUY, RIGHT?
Or Teru. You're like a guy around the chest.
NAIL THE BLONDIE FIRST, EVERYONE!!
AGH! RAGH!
AGH! RAGH!
...
UH... TERU?
SORRY TO SPOIL THE FUN, BUT I'M GONNA GO...

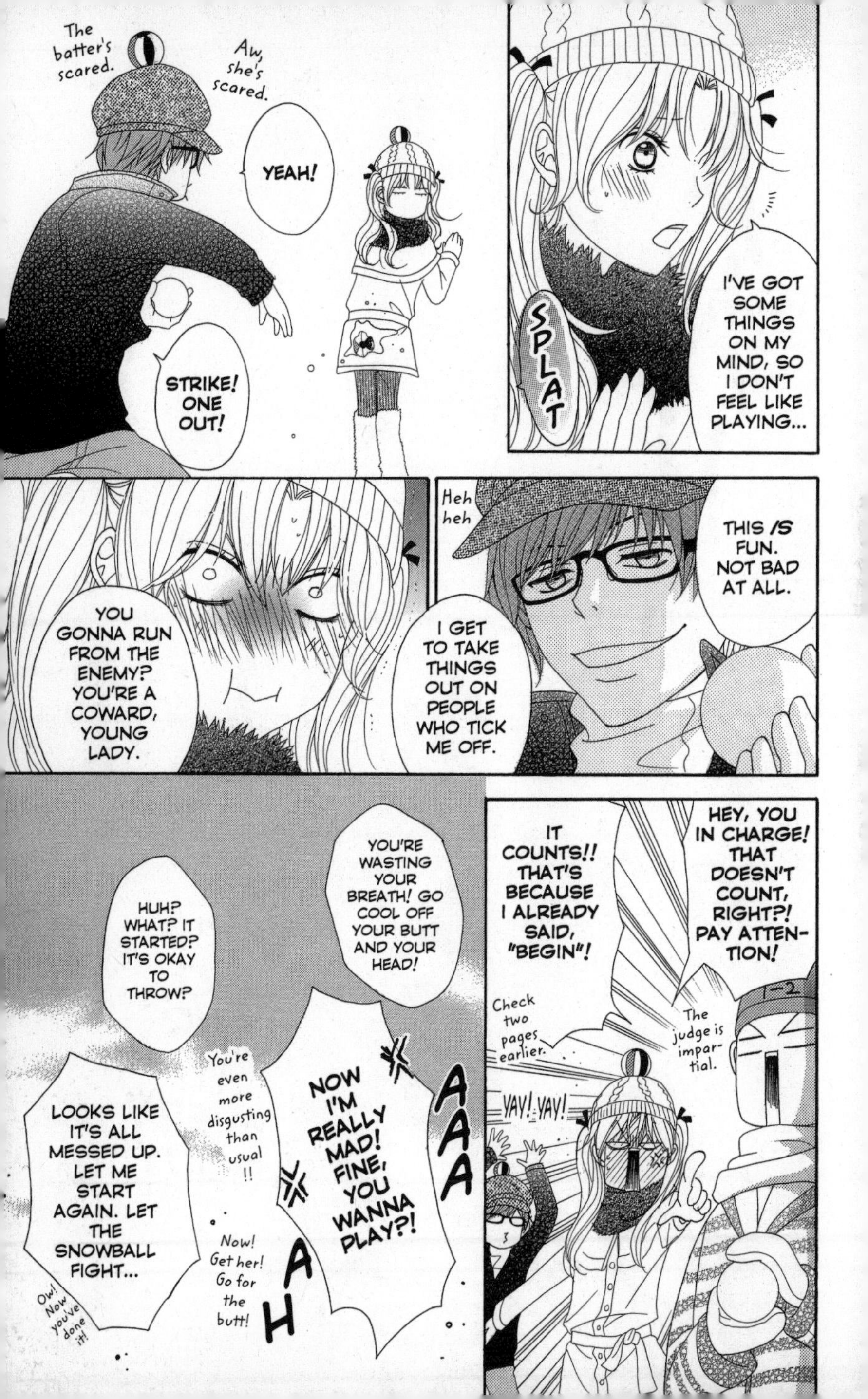
I'VE GOT SOME THINGS ON MY MIND, SO I DON'T FEEL LIKE PLAYING...
SPLAT
Aw, she's scared.
The batter's scared.
YEAH!
STRIKE! ONE OUT!
Heh heh
THIS IS FUN. NOT BAD AT ALL.
I GET TO TAKE THINGS OUT ON PEOPLE WHO TICK ME OFF.
YOU GONNA RUN FROM THE ENEMY? YOU'RE A COWARD, YOUNG LADY.
HEY, YOU IN CHARGE! THAT DOESN'T COUNT, RIGHT?! PAY ATTEN-TION!
IT COUNTS!! THAT'S BECAUSE I ALREADY SAID, "BEGIN"!
The judge is impar-tial.
Check two pages earlier.
YAY! YAY!
YOU'RE WASTING YOUR BREATH! GO COOL OFF YOUR BUTT AND YOUR HEAD!
HUH? WHAT? IT STARTED? IT'S OKAY TO THROW?
NOW I'M REALLY MAD! FINE, YOU WANNA PLAY?!
AAAAH
You're even more disgusting than usual!!
LOOKS LIKE IT'S ALL MESSED UP. LET ME START AGAIN. LET THE SNOWBALL FIGHT...
Now! Get her! Go for the butt!
Ow! Now you've done it!

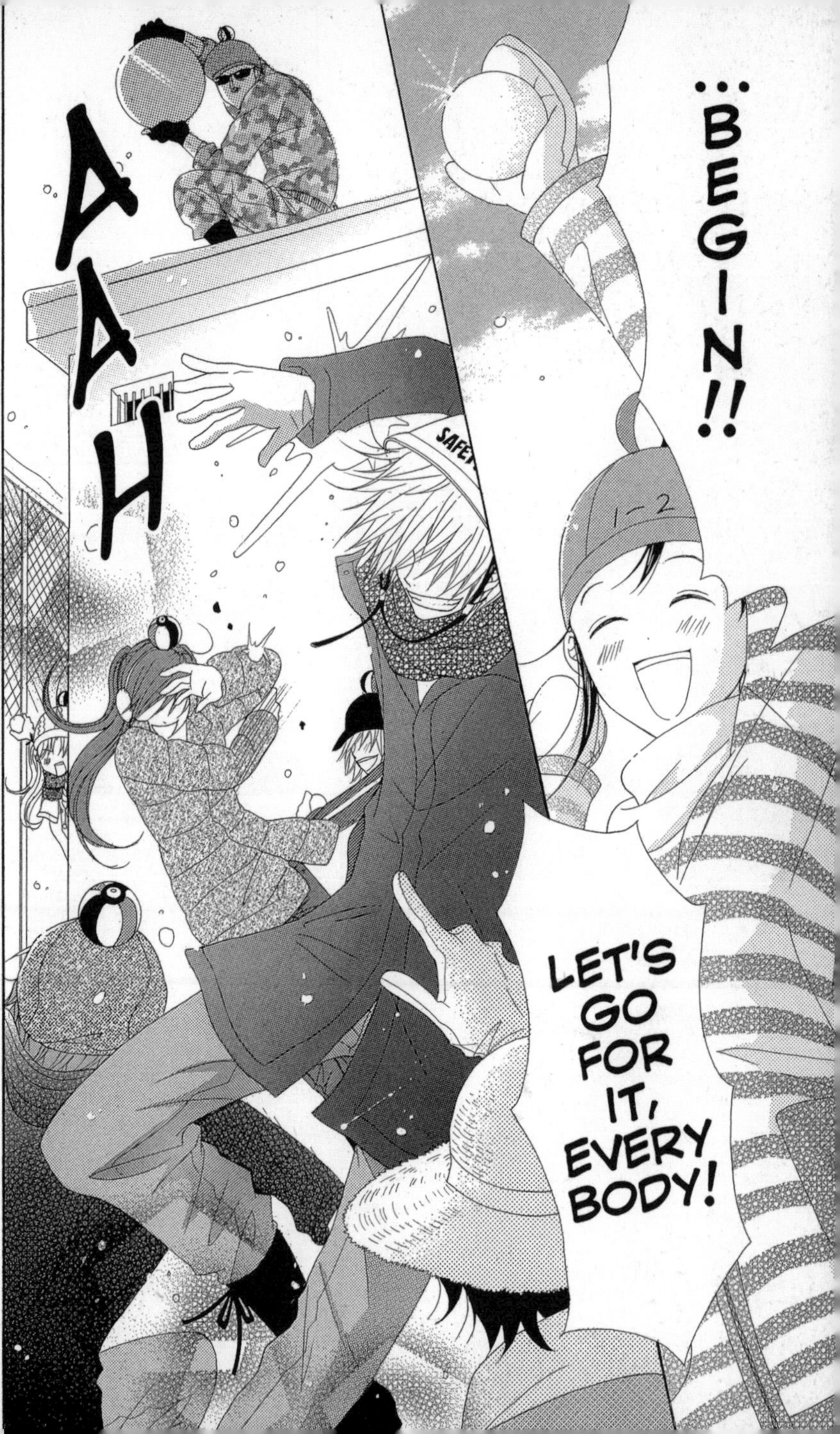
...BEGIN!!
LET'S GO FOR IT, EVERY BODY!
AAH

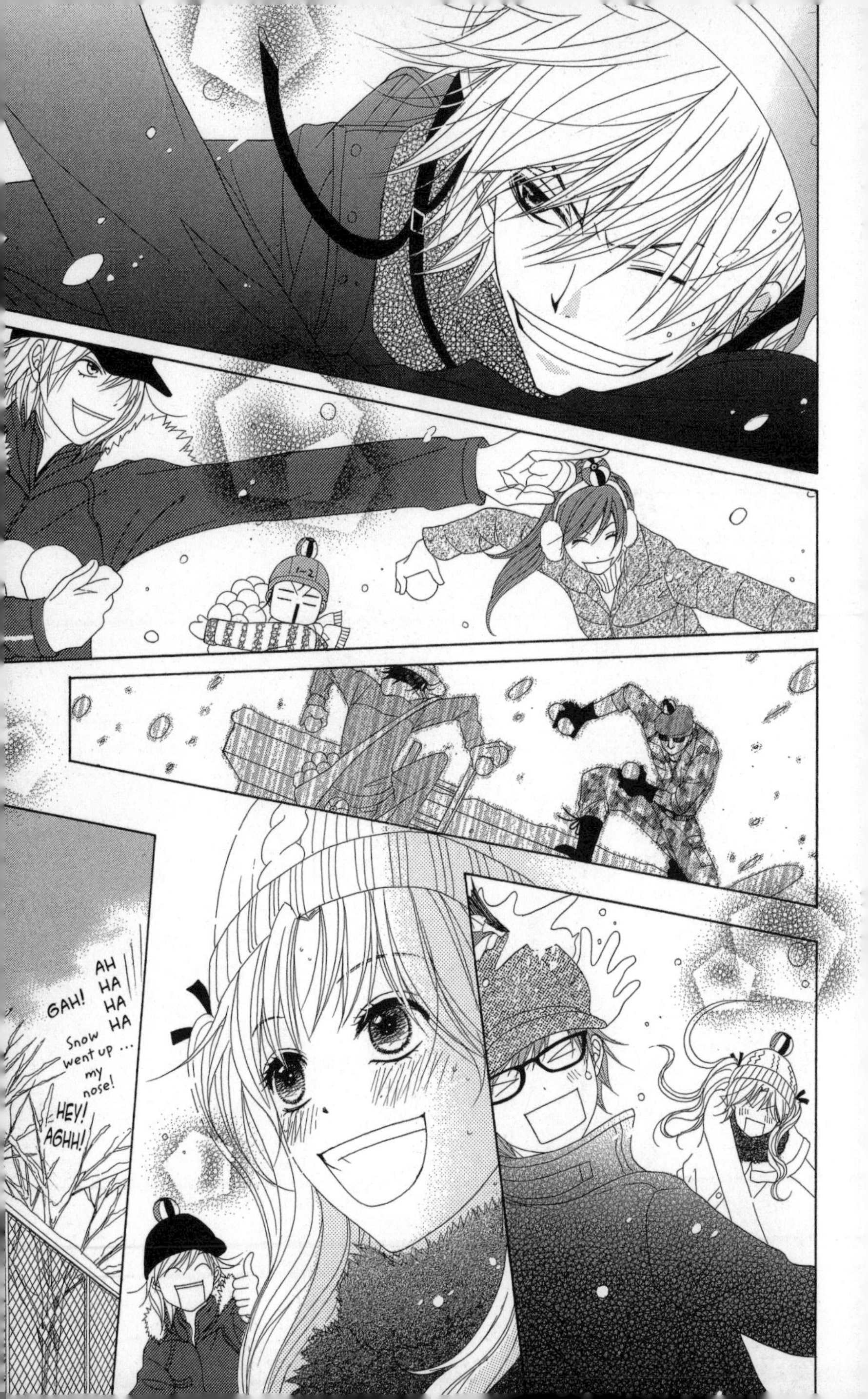
AH HA HA HA
GAH!
Snow went up ... my nose!
HEY! AGHH!

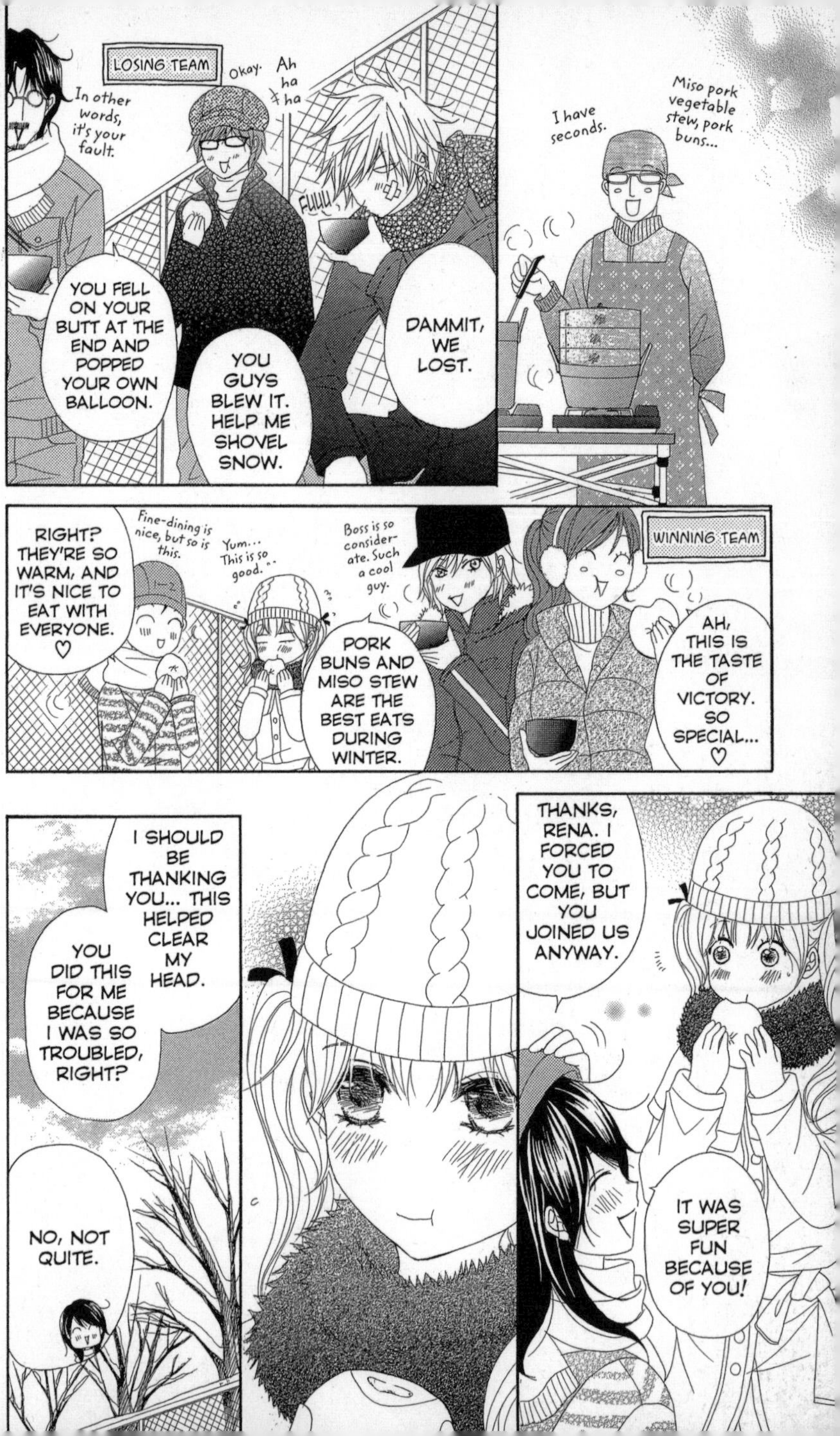
Miso pork vegetable stew, pork buns...
I have seconds.
LOSING TEAM
Ah ha ha
Okay.
In other words, it's your fault.
FUUU
DAMMIT, WE LOST.
YOU GUYS BLEW IT. HELP ME SHOVEL SNOW.
YOU FELL ON YOUR BUTT AT THE END AND POPPED YOUR OWN BALLOON.
WINNING TEAM
AH, THIS IS THE TASTE OF VICTORY. SO SPECIAL... ♡
Boss is so considerate. Such a cool guy.
PORK BUNS AND MISO STEW ARE THE BEST EATS DURING WINTER.
Yum... This is so good. ^^
Fine-dining is nice, but so is this.
RIGHT? THEY'RE SO WARM, AND IT'S NICE TO EAT WITH EVERYONE. ♡
THANKS, RENA. I FORCED YOU TO COME, BUT YOU JOINED US ANYWAY.
IT WAS SUPER FUN BECAUSE OF YOU!
I SHOULD BE THANKING YOU... THIS HELPED CLEAR MY HEAD.
YOU DID THIS FOR ME BECAUSE I WAS SO TROUBLED, RIGHT?
NO, NOT QUITE.

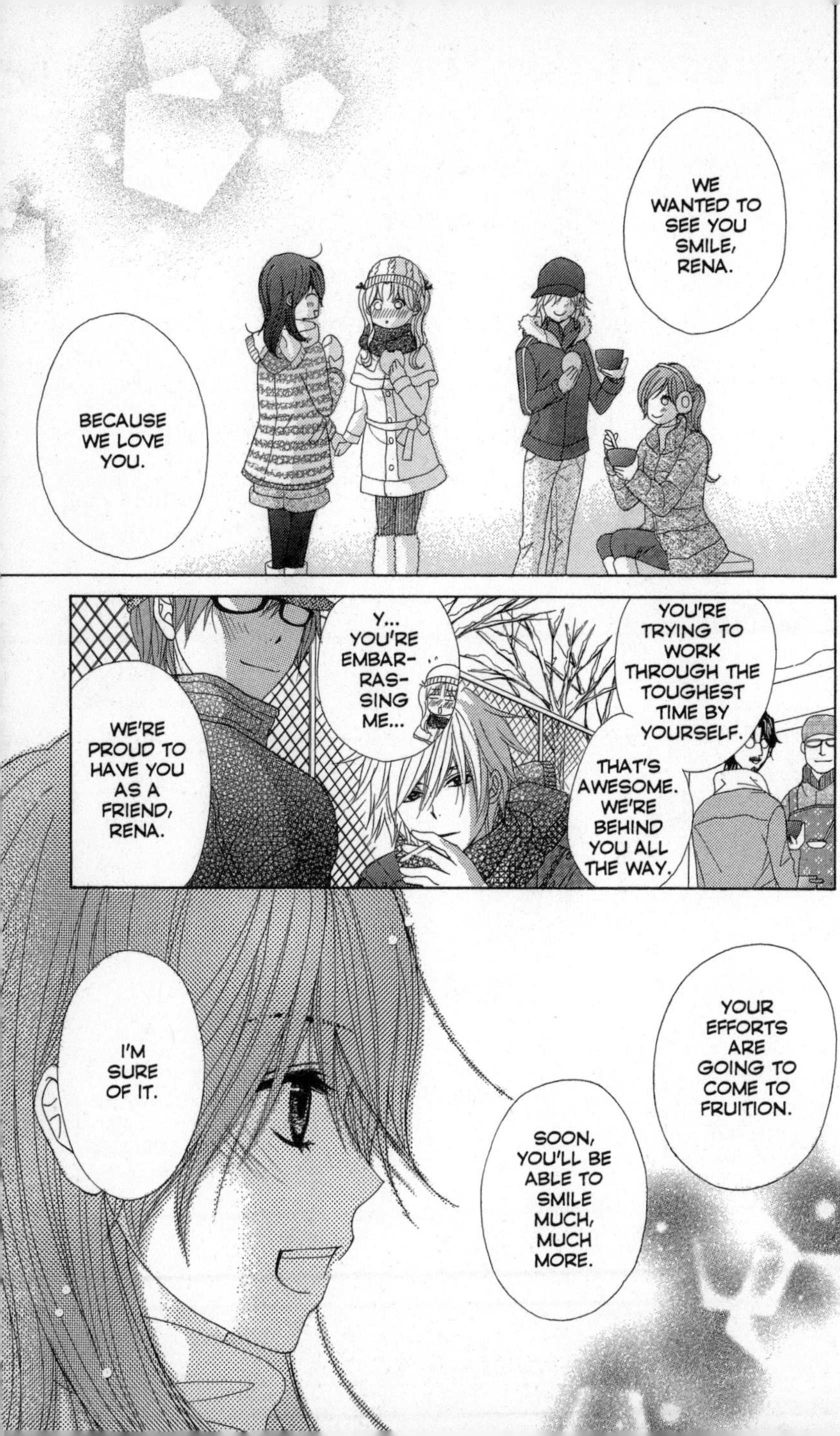
WE WANTED TO SEE YOU SMILE, RENA.
BECAUSE WE LOVE YOU.
YOU'RE TRYING TO WORK THROUGH THE TOUGHEST TIME BY YOURSELF.
THAT'S AWESOME. WE'RE BEHIND YOU ALL THE WAY.
Y... YOU'RE EMBARRASSING ME...
WE'RE PROUD TO HAVE YOU AS A FRIEND, RENA.
YOUR EFFORTS ARE GOING TO COME TO FRUITION.
SOON, YOU'LL BE ABLE TO SMILE MUCH, MUCH MORE.
I'M SURE OF IT.

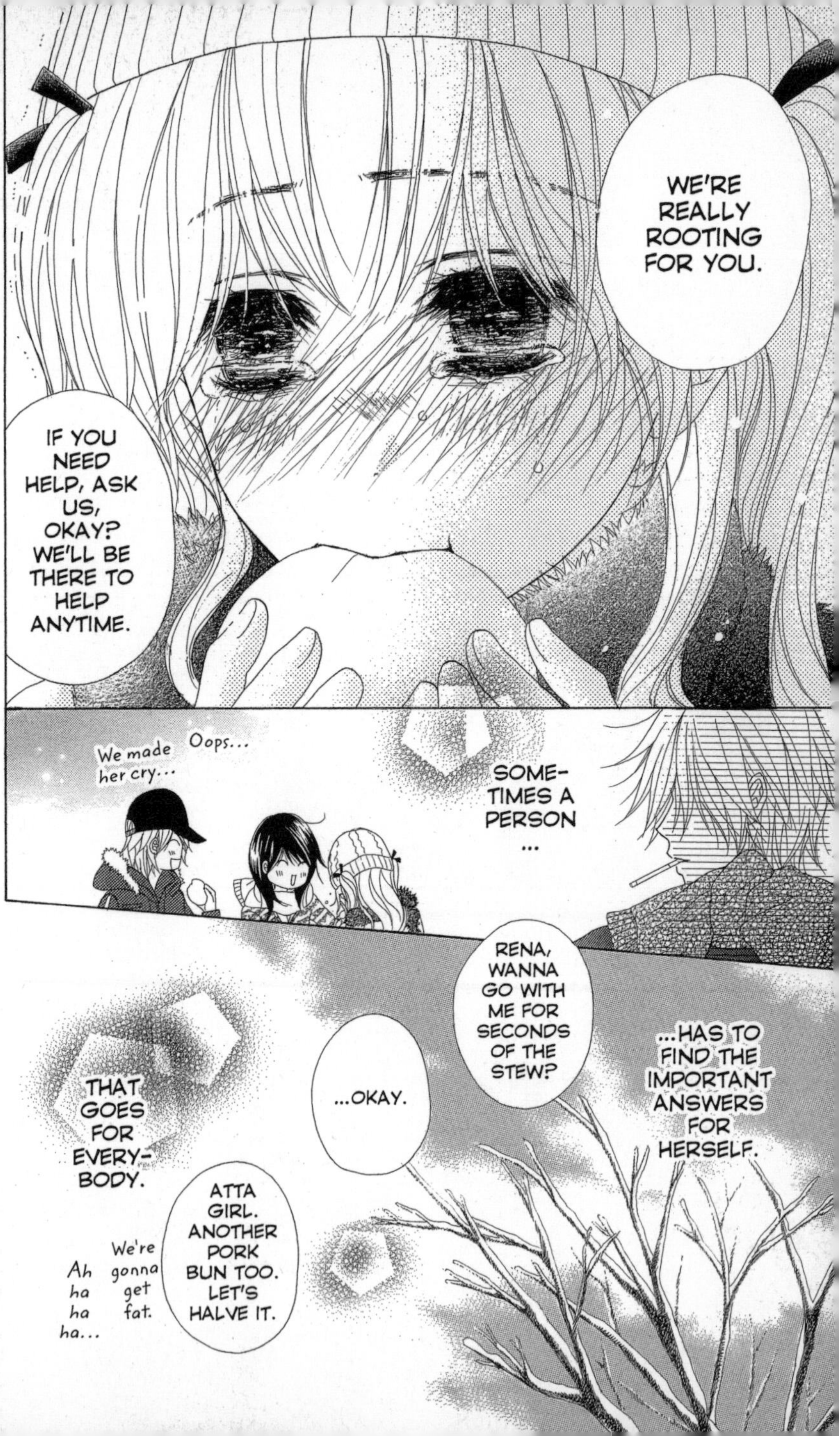
WE'RE REALLY ROOTING FOR YOU.
IF YOU NEED HELP, ASK US, OKAY? WE'LL BE THERE TO HELP ANYTIME.
SOME-TIMES A PERSON...
Oops...
We made her cry...
...HAS TO FIND THE IMPORTANT ANSWERS FOR HERSELF.
RENA, WANNA GO WITH ME FOR SECONDS OF THE STEW?
...OKAY.
THAT GOES FOR EVERY-BODY.
ATTA GIRL. ANOTHER PORK BUN TOO. LET'S HALVE IT.
We're gonna get fat.
Ah ha ha ha...

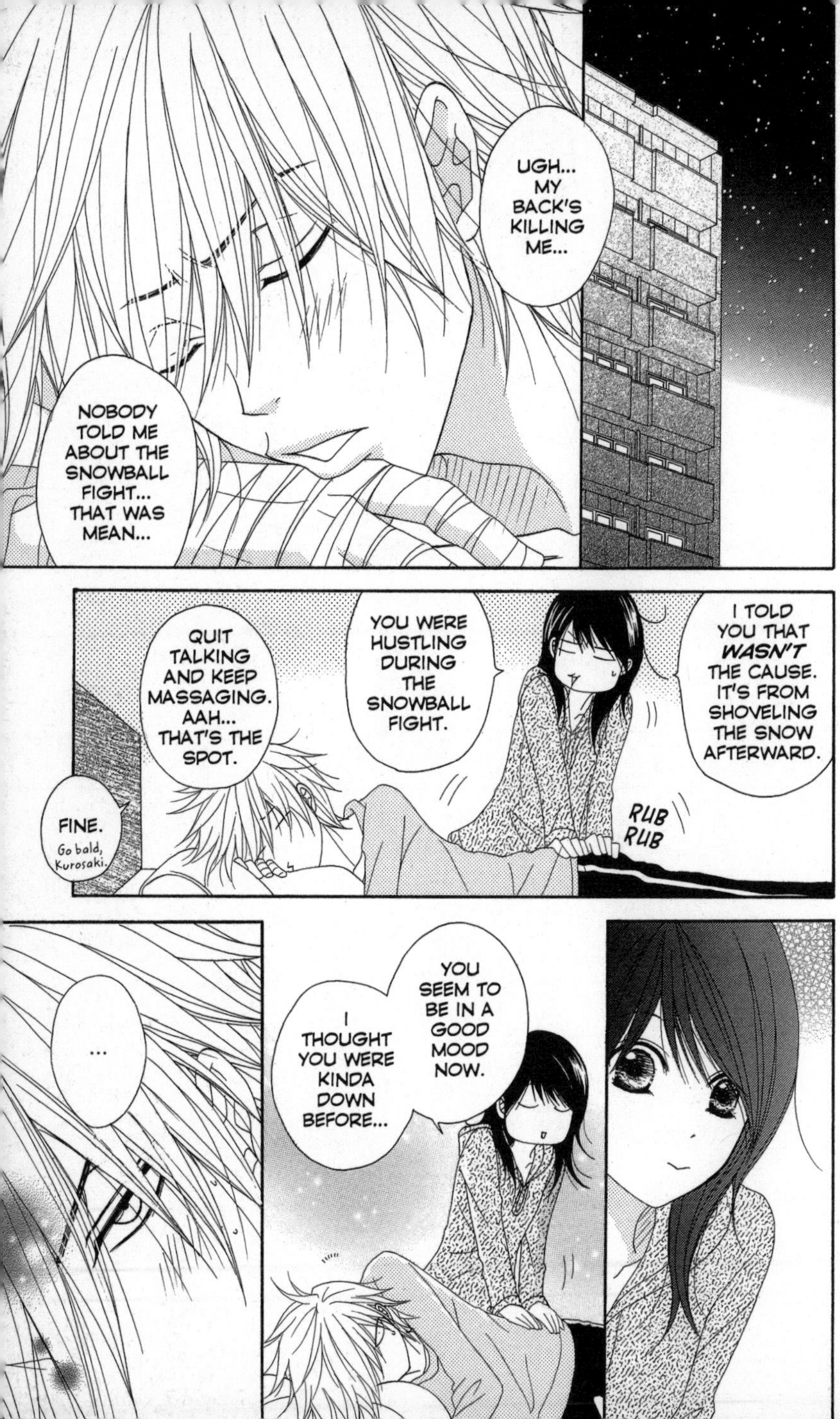
UGH... MY BACK'S KILLING ME...
NOBODY TOLD ME ABOUT THE SNOWBALL FIGHT... THAT WAS MEAN...
YOU WERE HUSTLING DURING THE SNOWBALL FIGHT.
I TOLD YOU THAT ***WASN'T*** THE CAUSE. IT'S FROM SHOVELING THE SNOW AFTERWARD.
RUB RUB
QUIT TALKING AND KEEP MASSAGING. AAH... THAT'S THE SPOT.
FINE.
Go bald, Kurosaki.
YOU SEEM TO BE IN A GOOD MOOD NOW.
I THOUGHT YOU WERE KINDA DOWN BEFORE...
...

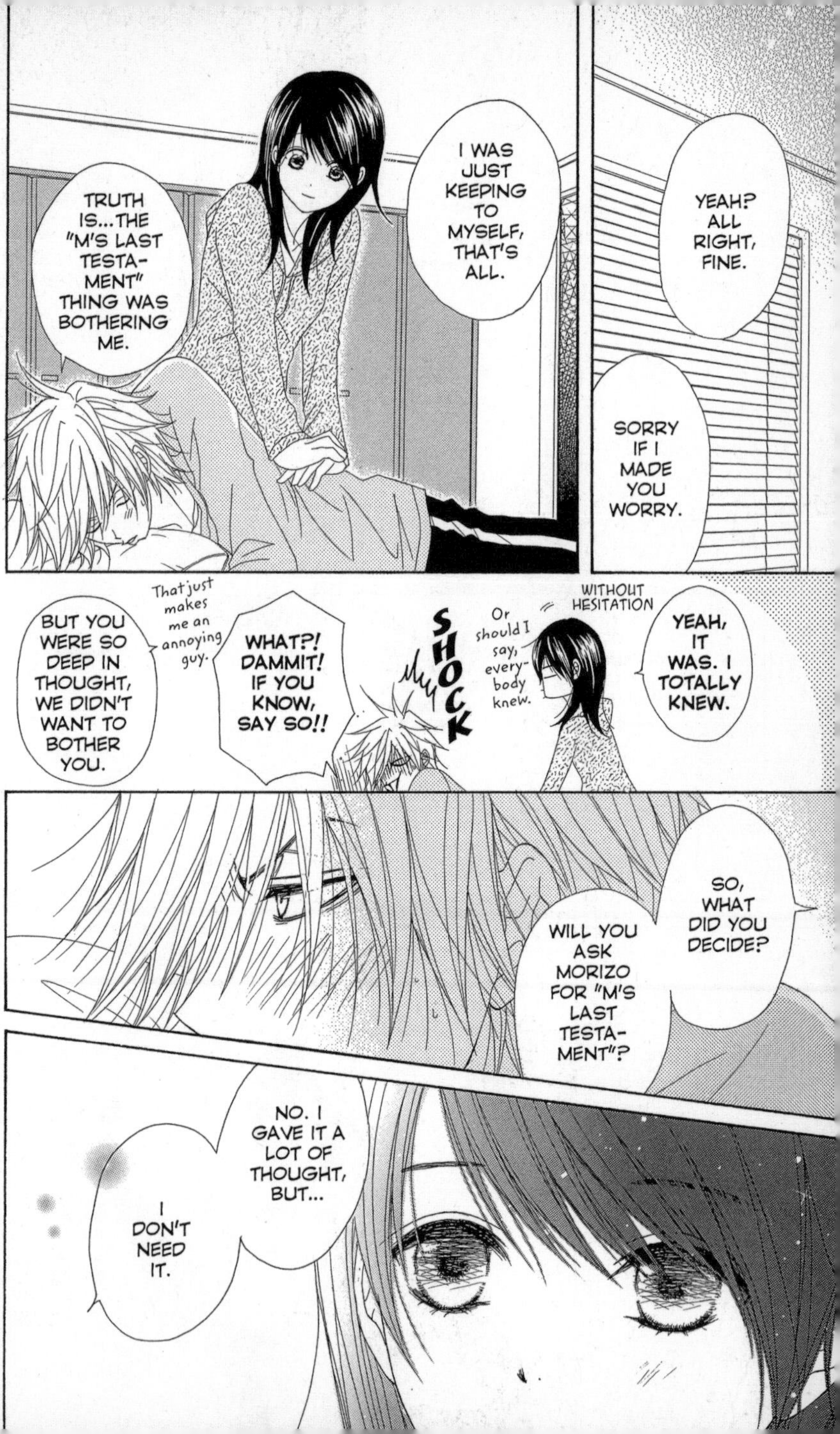
YEAH? ALL RIGHT, FINE.
SORRY IF I MADE YOU WORRY.
I WAS JUST KEEPING TO MYSELF, THAT'S ALL.
TRUTH IS...THE "M'S LAST TESTAMENT" THING WAS BOTHERING ME.
YEAH, IT WAS. I TOTALLY KNEW.
WITHOUT HESITATION
Or should I say, everybody knew.
SHOCK
WHAT?! DAMMIT! IF YOU KNOW, SAY SO!!
That just makes me an annoying guy.
BUT YOU WERE SO DEEP IN THOUGHT, WE DIDN'T WANT TO BOTHER YOU.
SO, WHAT DID YOU DECIDE?
WILL YOU ASK MORIZO FOR "M'S LAST TESTAMENT"?
NO. I GAVE IT A LOT OF THOUGHT, BUT...
I DON'T NEED IT.

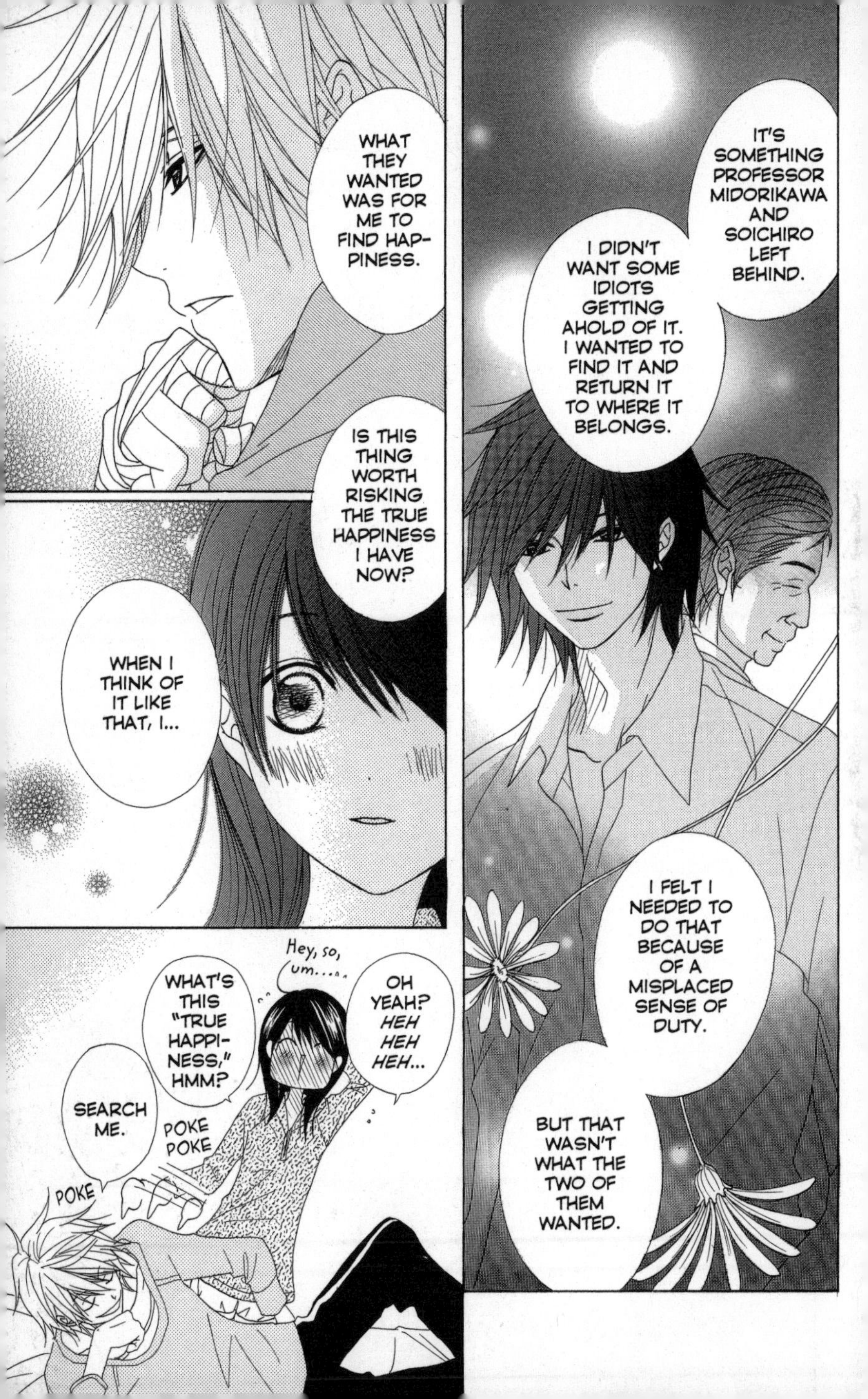
IT'S SOMETHING PROFESSOR MIDORIKAWA AND SOICHIRO LEFT BEHIND.
I DIDN'T WANT SOME IDIOTS GETTING AHOLD OF IT. I WANTED TO FIND IT AND RETURN IT TO WHERE IT BELONGS.
I FELT I NEEDED TO DO THAT BECAUSE OF A MISPLACED SENSE OF DUTY.
BUT THAT WASN'T WHAT THE TWO OF THEM WANTED.
WHAT THEY WANTED WAS FOR ME TO FIND HAP-PINESS.
IS THIS THING WORTH RISKING THE TRUE HAPPINESS I HAVE NOW?
WHEN I THINK OF IT LIKE THAT, I...
Hey, so, um...
OH YEAH? *HEH HEH HEH...*
WHAT'S THIS "TRUE HAPPI-NESS," HMM?
POKE POKE
SEARCH ME.
POKE

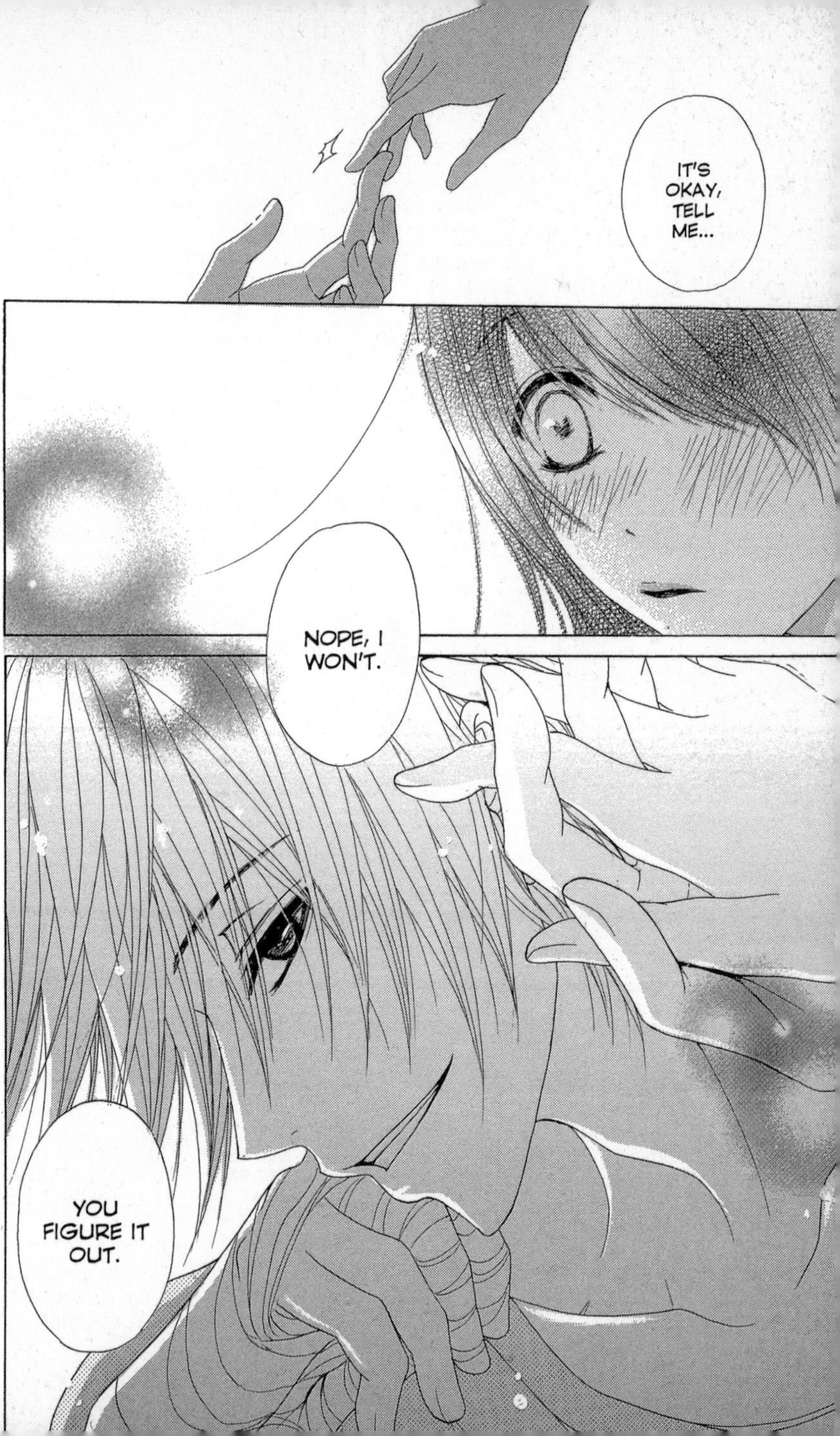
IT'S OKAY, TELL ME...
NOPE, I WON'T.
YOU FIGURE IT OUT.

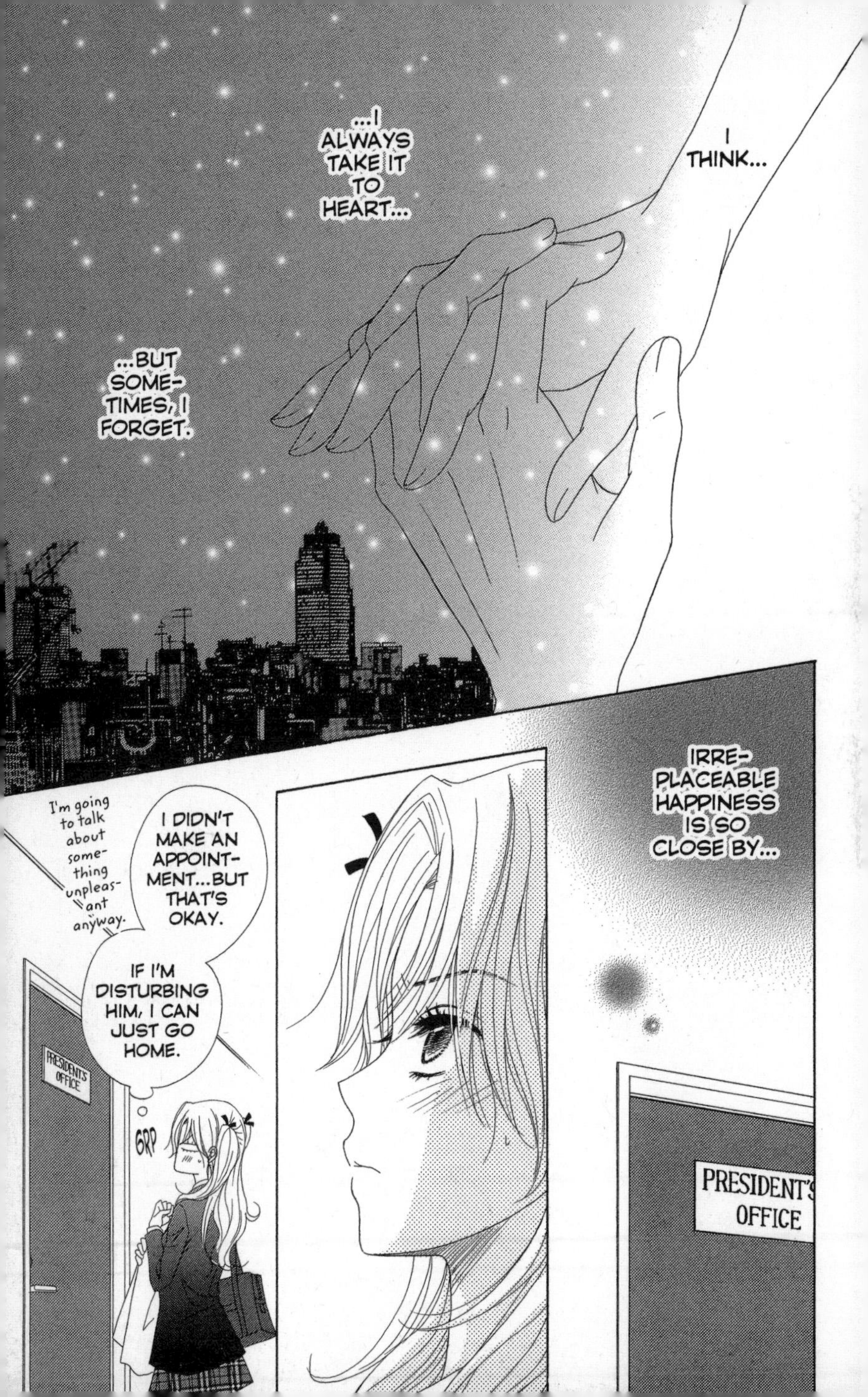
I THINK...
...I ALWAYS TAKE IT TO HEART...
...BUT SOME-TIMES, I FORGET.
IRRE-PLACEABLE HAPPINESS IS SO CLOSE BY...
PRESIDENT'S OFFICE
I DIDN'T MAKE AN APPOINT-MENT...BUT THAT'S OKAY.
I'm going to talk about some-thing unpleas-ant anyway.
IF I'M DISTURBING HIM, I CAN JUST GO HOME.
PRESIDENT'S OFFICE
GRP

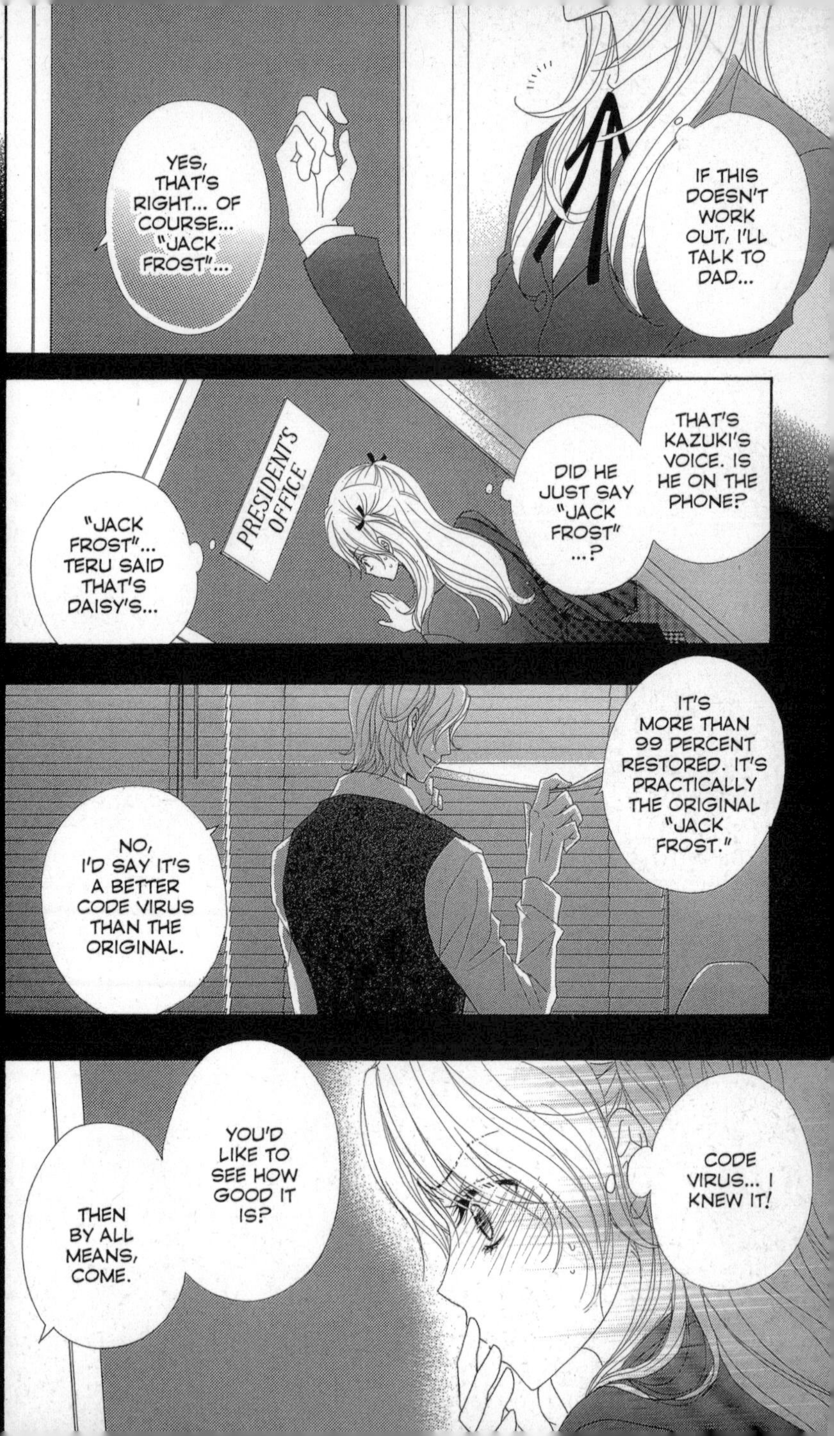
IF THIS DOESN'T WORK OUT, I'LL TALK TO DAD...
YES, THAT'S RIGHT... OF COURSE... "JACK FROST"...
THAT'S KAZUKI'S VOICE. IS HE ON THE PHONE?
DID HE JUST SAY "JACK FROST" ...?
PRESIDENT'S OFFICE
"JACK FROST"... TERU SAID THAT'S DAISY'S...
IT'S MORE THAN 99 PERCENT RESTORED. IT'S PRACTICALLY THE ORIGINAL "JACK FROST."
NO, I'D SAY IT'S A BETTER CODE VIRUS THAN THE ORIGINAL.
CODE VIRUS... I KNEW IT!
YOU'D LIKE TO SEE HOW GOOD IT IS?
THEN BY ALL MEANS, COME.

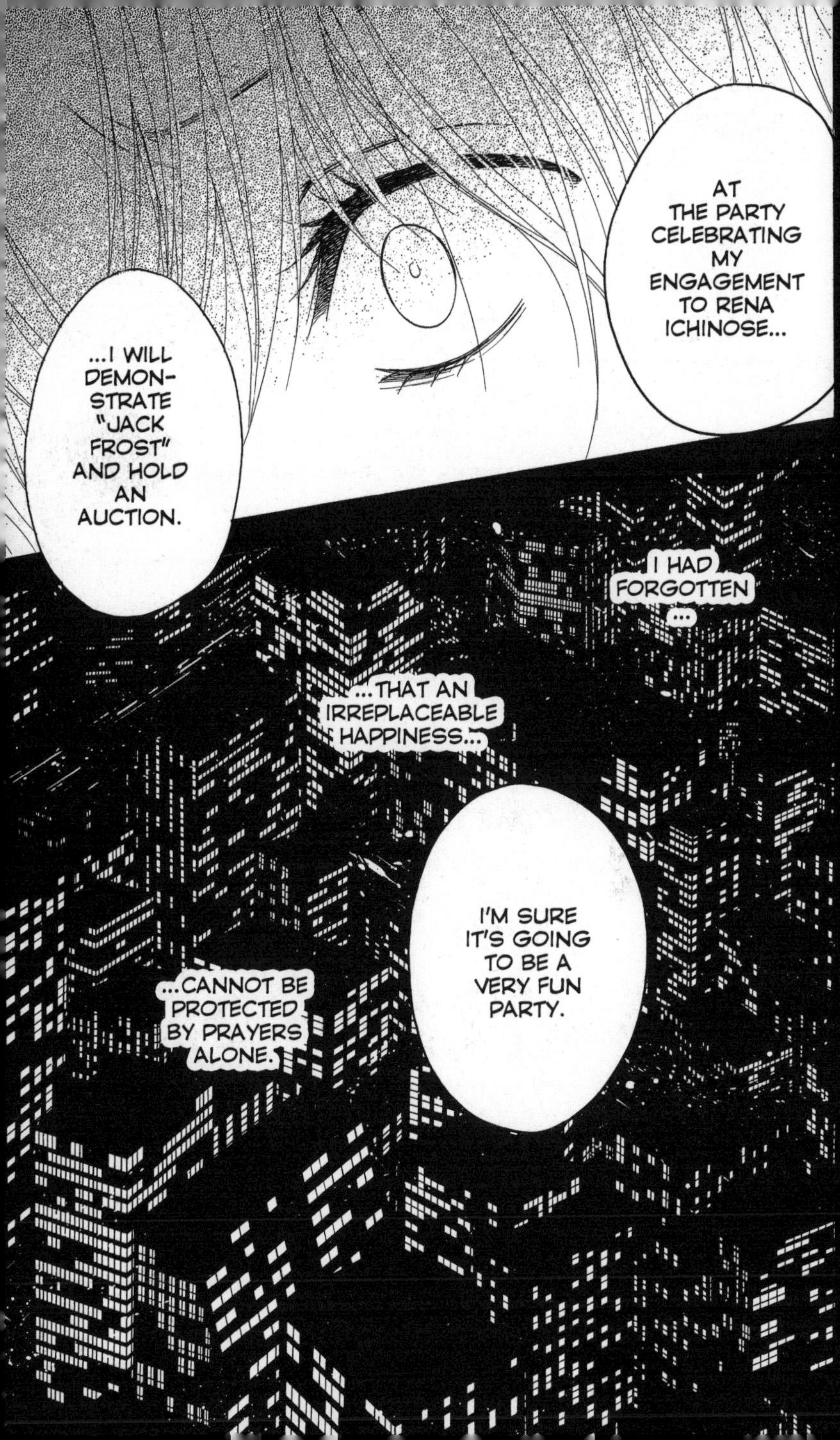
AT THE PARTY CELEBRATING MY ENGAGEMENT TO RENA ICHINOSE...
...I WILL DEMON-STRATE "JACK FROST" AND HOLD AN AUCTION.
I HAD FORGOTTEN...
...THAT AN IRREPLACEABLE HAPPINESS...
I'M SURE IT'S GOING TO BE A VERY FUN PARTY.
...CANNOT BE PROTECTED BY PRAYERS ALONE.

DENGEKI DAISY
QUESTION CORNER

RELOCATED

BALDLY ASK!!! ③

Q. I HAVE A LOT OF FREE TIME DURING THIS CLASS, SO I WANT TO DRAW KUROSAKI IN THE CORNER OF MY NOTEBOOK, BUT I'M FINDING IT VERY DIFFICULT. WHAT DO I NEED TO DO TO DRAW HIM EASILY? IF THERE IS ONE, PLEASE TEACH ME A DRAWING SONG TO GO WITH IT!!

(AN 8TH-GRADE GIRL THEY CALL "BALDY," TOKYO)

A. THAT'S QUITE A DIFFICULT QUESTION... I KNOW WHAT YOU MEAN ABOUT KUROSAKI BEING DIFFICULT TO DRAW. I HAVE TROUBLE DRAWING HIM TOO. A DRAWING SONG, EH? HAD TO THINK ABOUT THAT ONE...

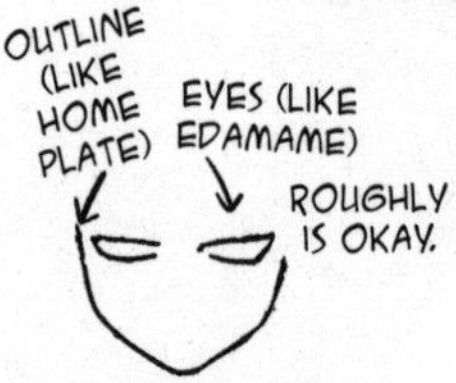
OUTLINE (LIKE HOME PLATE)
EYES (LIKE EDAMAME)
ROUGHLY IS OKAY.
① (TO THE TUNE OF "UMI") ON TOP OF HOME PLATE... PLACE EDAMAME...

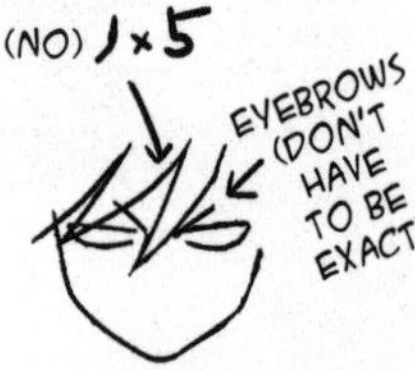
(NO) ノ×5
EYEBROWS (DON'T HAVE TO BE EXACT)
② EYEBROWS LIKE WOODEN CHOPSTICKS NO NO NO—NO—NO—

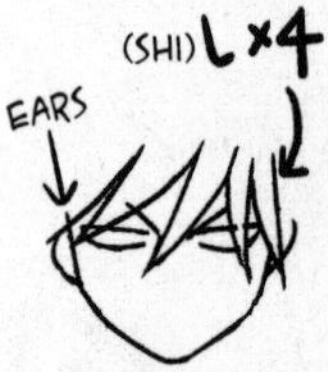
(SHI) し×4
EARS
③ (SECOND VERSE) DRAW IN THE EARS SHI SHI SHI—SHI—

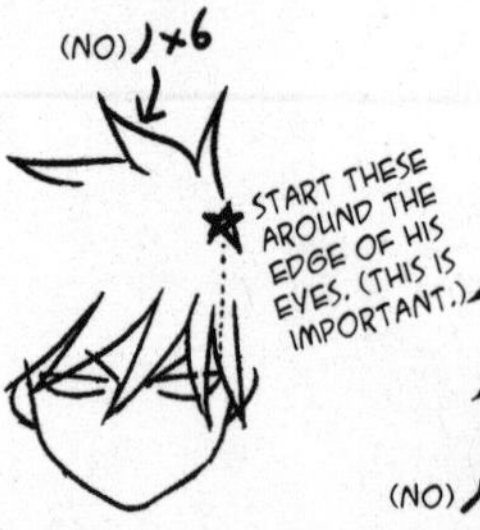
(NO) ノ×6
START THESE AROUND THE EDGE OF HIS EYES. (THIS IS IMPORTANT.)
④ NO NO NO NO NO—NO—

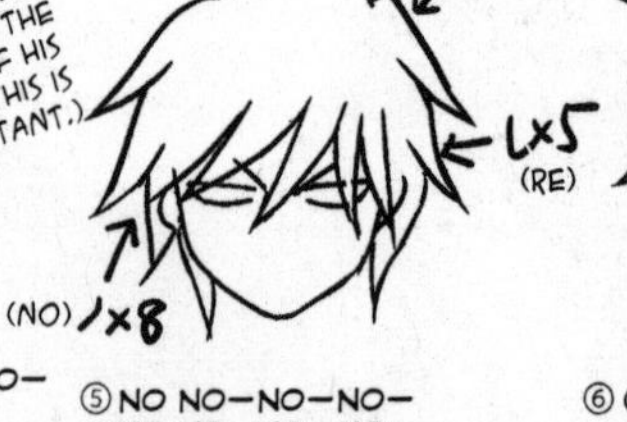
ヘ (HE)
レ×5 (RE)
(NO) ノ×8
⑤ NO NO—NO—NO— NO NO—NO—NO— HE SHI SHI SHI SHI—SHI—

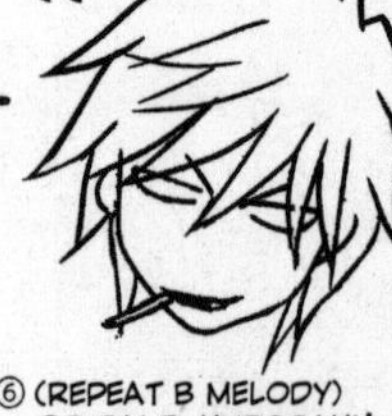
HMPH. IDIOT.
⑥ (REPEAT B MELODY) GO BALD, KUROSAKI! AND WE'RE DONE~~ (THE END)

I HAVEN'T BEEN SLEEPING LATELY. FORGIVE ME!!!!!

THAT'S THE END OF THIS INSTALLMENT!!!

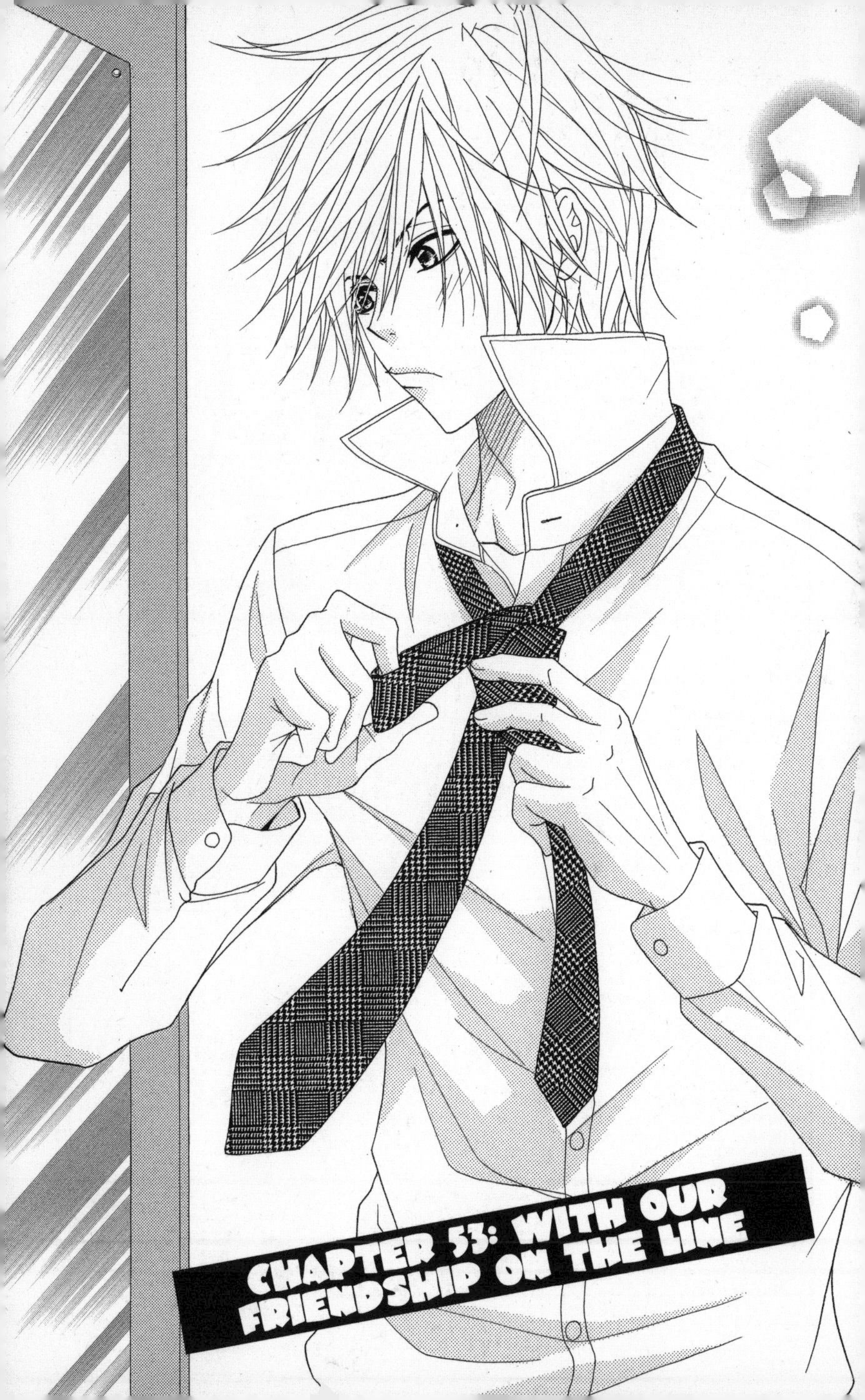
CHAPTER 53: WITH OUR FRIENDSHIP ON THE LINE

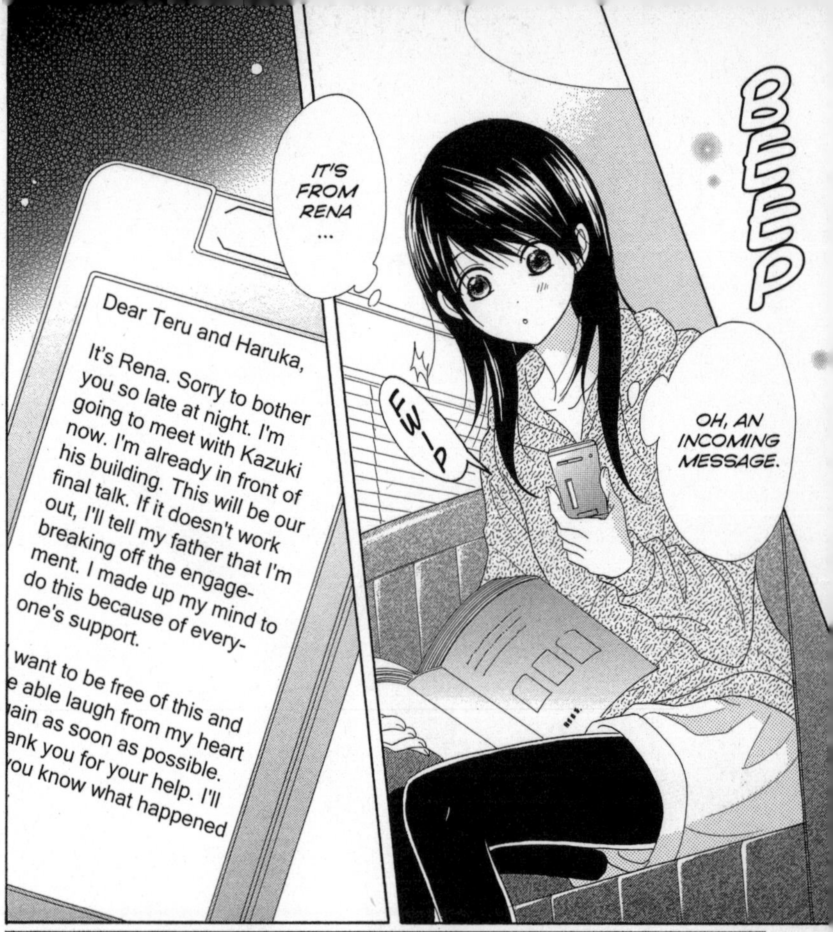
BEEP
OH, AN INCOMING MESSAGE.
FWIP
IT'S FROM RENA ...
Dear Teru and Haruka,
It's Rena. Sorry to bother you so late at night. I'm going to meet with Kazuki now. I'm already in front of his building. This will be our final talk. If it doesn't work out, I'll tell my father that I'm breaking off the engagement. I made up my mind to do this because of everyone's support.
want to be free of this and
e able laugh from my heart
ain as soon as possible.
ank you for your help. I'll
ou know what happened

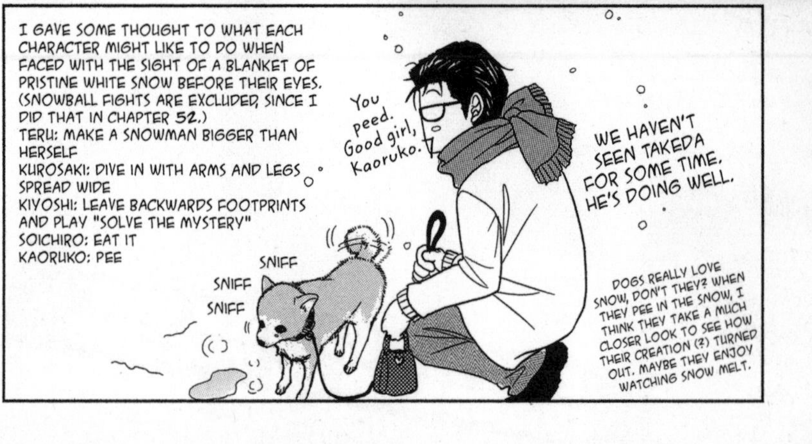
WE HAVEN'T SEEN TAKEDA FOR SOME TIME. HE'S DOING WELL.
You peed. Good girl, Kaoruko.
I GAVE SOME THOUGHT TO WHAT EACH CHARACTER MIGHT LIKE TO DO WHEN FACED WITH THE SIGHT OF A BLANKET OF PRISTINE WHITE SNOW BEFORE THEIR EYES. (SNOWBALL FIGHTS ARE EXCLUDED, SINCE I DID THAT IN CHAPTER 52.)
TERU: MAKE A SNOWMAN BIGGER THAN HERSELF
KUROSAKI: DIVE IN WITH ARMS AND LEGS SPREAD WIDE
KIYOSHI: LEAVE BACKWARDS FOOTPRINTS AND PLAY "SOLVE THE MYSTERY"
SOICHIRO: EAT IT
KAORUKO: PEE
DOGS REALLY LOVE SNOW, DON'T THEY? WHEN THEY PEE IN THE SNOW, I THINK THEY TAKE A MUCH CLOSER LOOK TO SEE HOW THEIR CREATION (?) TURNED OUT. MAYBE THEY ENJOY WATCHING SNOW MELT.
SNIFF
SNIFF
SNIFF

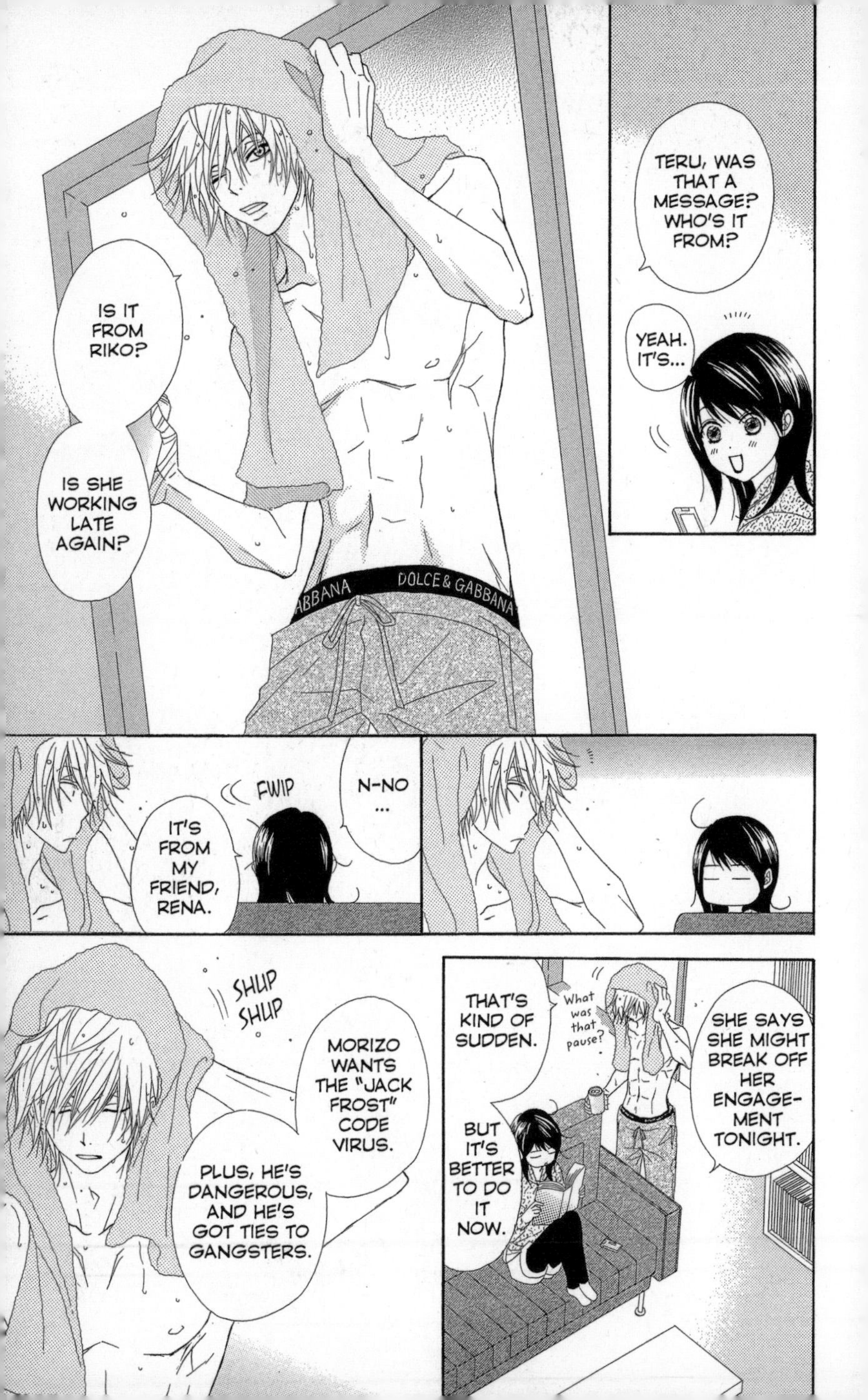
TERU, WAS THAT A MESSAGE? WHO'S IT FROM?
YEAH. IT'S...
IS IT FROM RIKO?
IS SHE WORKING LATE AGAIN?
DOLCE&GABBANA
N-NO...
FWIP
IT'S FROM MY FRIEND, RENA.
SHE SAYS SHE MIGHT BREAK OFF HER ENGAGE-MENT TONIGHT.
What was that pause?
THAT'S KIND OF SUDDEN.
BUT IT'S BETTER TO DO IT NOW.
SHUP SHUP
MORIZO WANTS THE "JACK FROST" CODE VIRUS.
PLUS, HE'S DANGEROUS, AND HE'S GOT TIES TO GANGSTERS.

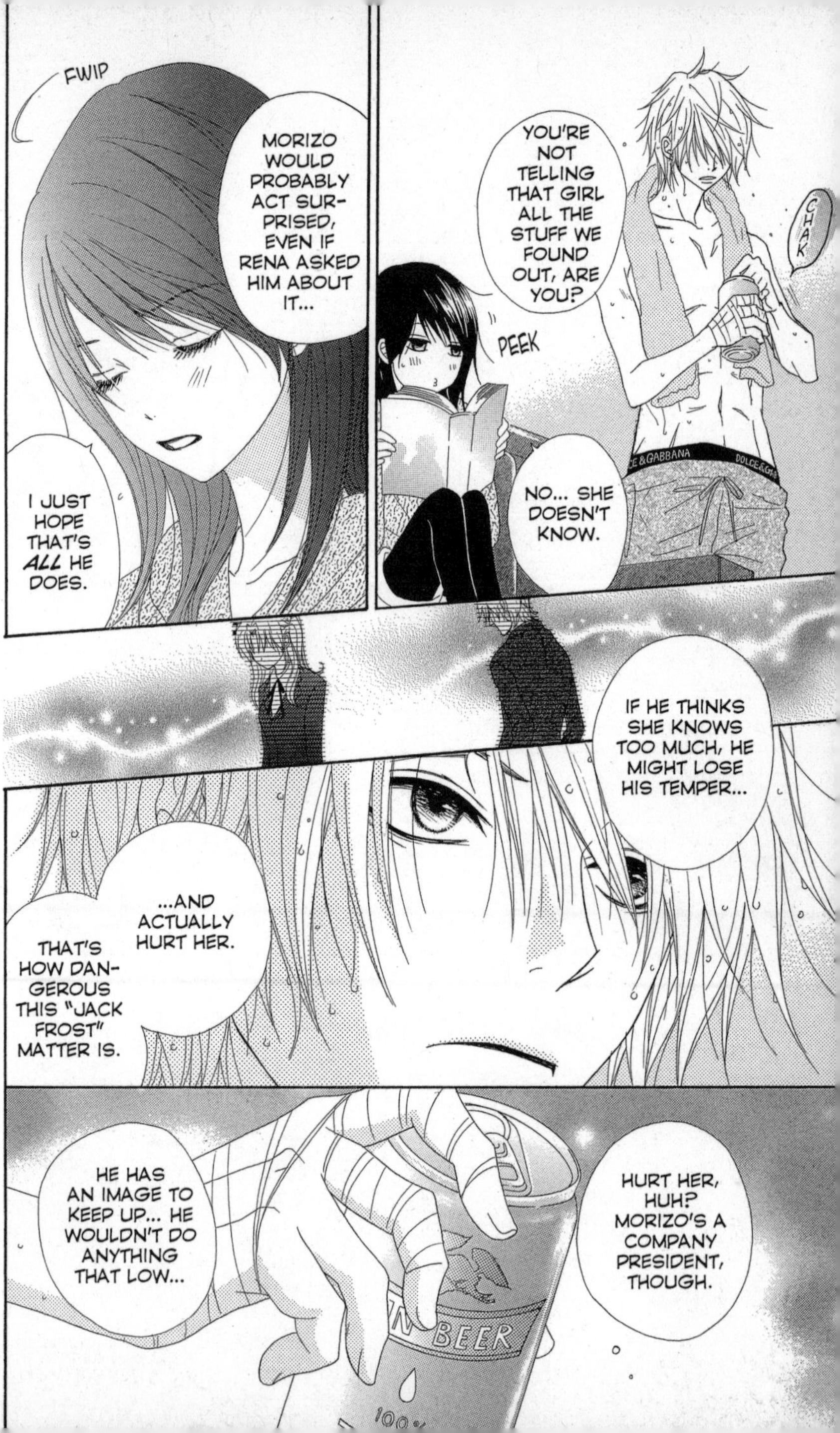
CHAK
YOU'RE NOT TELLING THAT GIRL ALL THE STUFF WE FOUND OUT, ARE YOU?
PEEK
NO... SHE DOESN'T KNOW.
FWIP
MORIZO WOULD PROBABLY ACT SUR-PRISED, EVEN IF RENA ASKED HIM ABOUT IT...
I JUST HOPE THAT'S ALL HE DOES.
IF HE THINKS SHE KNOWS TOO MUCH, HE MIGHT LOSE HIS TEMPER...
...AND ACTUALLY HURT HER.
THAT'S HOW DAN-GEROUS THIS "JACK FROST" MATTER IS.
HURT HER, HUH? MORIZO'S A COMPANY PRESIDENT, THOUGH.
HE HAS AN IMAGE TO KEEP UP... HE WOULDN'T DO ANYTHING THAT LOW...
BEER

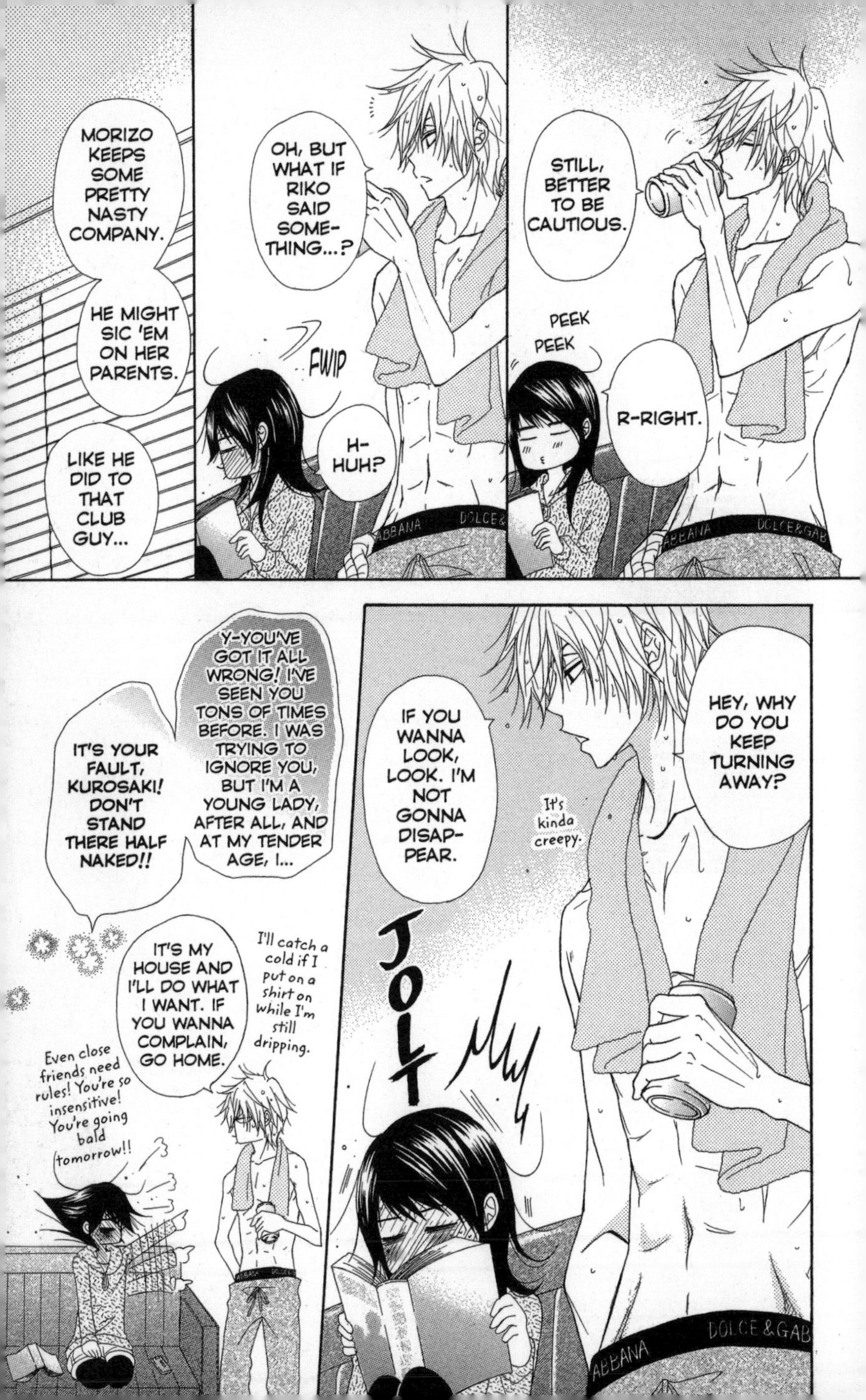
STILL, BETTER TO BE CAUTIOUS.
PEEK PEEK
R-RIGHT.
OH, BUT WHAT IF RIKO SAID SOME-THING...?
FWIP
H-HUH?
MORIZO KEEPS SOME PRETTY NASTY COMPANY.
HE MIGHT SIC 'EM ON HER PARENTS.
LIKE HE DID TO THAT CLUB GUY...
DOLCE&GABBANA
HEY, WHY DO YOU KEEP TURNING AWAY?
It's kinda creepy.
IF YOU WANNA LOOK, LOOK. I'M NOT GONNA DISAP-PEAR.
JOLT
DOLCE&GABBANA
Y-YOU'VE GOT IT ALL WRONG! I'VE SEEN YOU TONS OF TIMES BEFORE. I WAS TRYING TO IGNORE YOU, BUT I'M A YOUNG LADY, AFTER ALL, AND AT MY TENDER AGE, I...
IT'S YOUR FAULT, KUROSAKI! DON'T STAND THERE HALF NAKED!!
I'll catch a cold if I put on a shirt on while I'm still dripping.
IT'S MY HOUSE AND I'LL DO WHAT I WANT. IF YOU WANNA COMPLAIN, GO HOME.
Even close friends need rules! You're so insensitive! You're going bald tomorrow!!

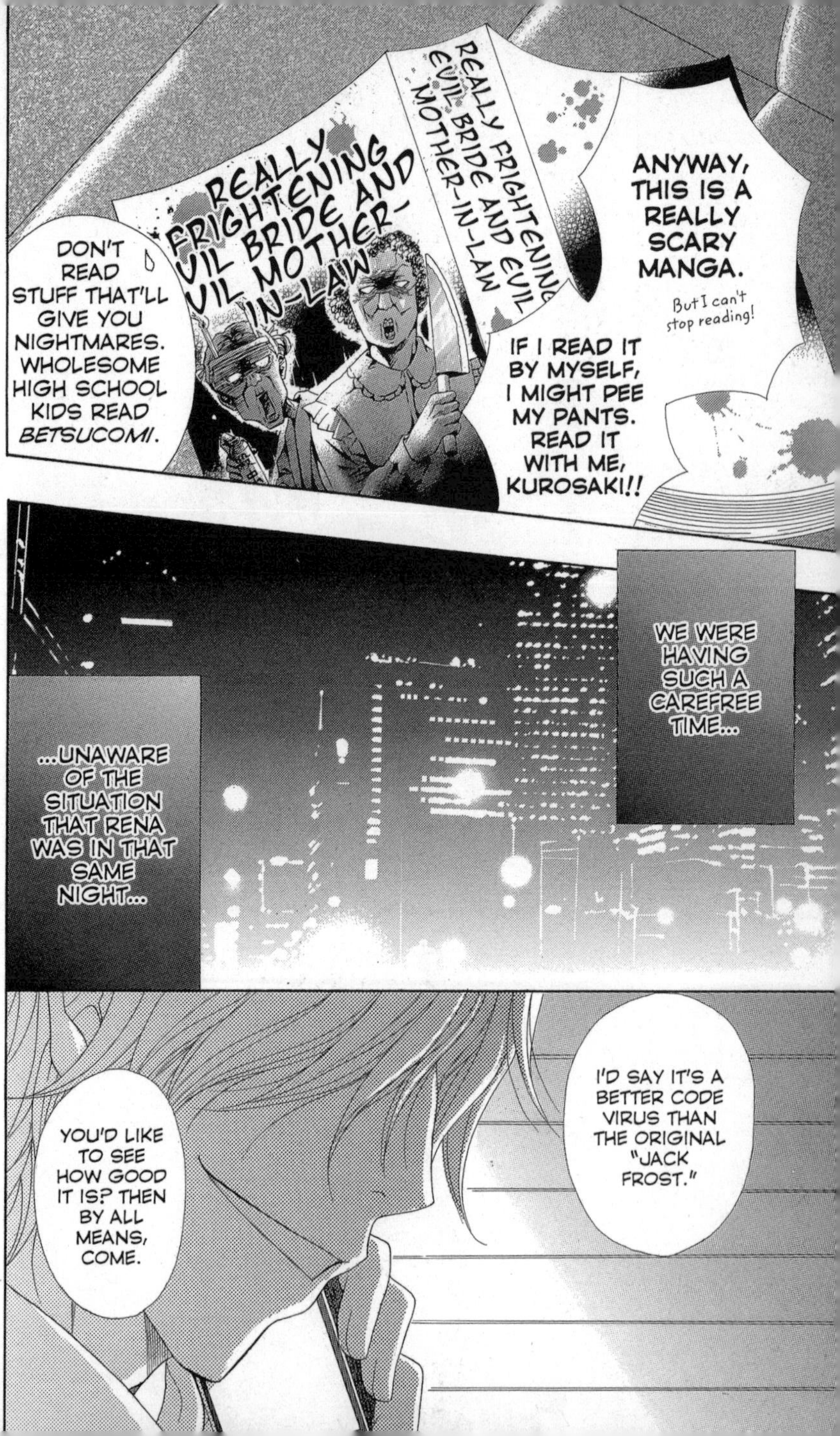
ANYWAY, THIS IS A REALLY SCARY MANGA.
But I can't stop reading!
REALLY FRIGHTENING EVIL BRIDE AND EVIL MOTHER-IN-LAW
REALLY FRIGHTENING VIL BRIDE AND VIL MOTHER-IN-LAW
IF I READ IT BY MYSELF, I MIGHT PEE MY PANTS. READ IT WITH ME, KUROSAKI!!
DON'T READ STUFF THAT'LL GIVE YOU NIGHTMARES. WHOLESOME HIGH SCHOOL KIDS READ *BETSUCOMI*.
WE WERE HAVING SUCH A CAREFREE TIME...
...UNAWARE OF THE SITUATION THAT RENA WAS IN THAT SAME NIGHT...
I'D SAY IT'S A BETTER CODE VIRUS THAN THE ORIGINAL "JACK FROST."
YOU'D LIKE TO SEE HOW GOOD IT IS? THEN BY ALL MEANS, COME.

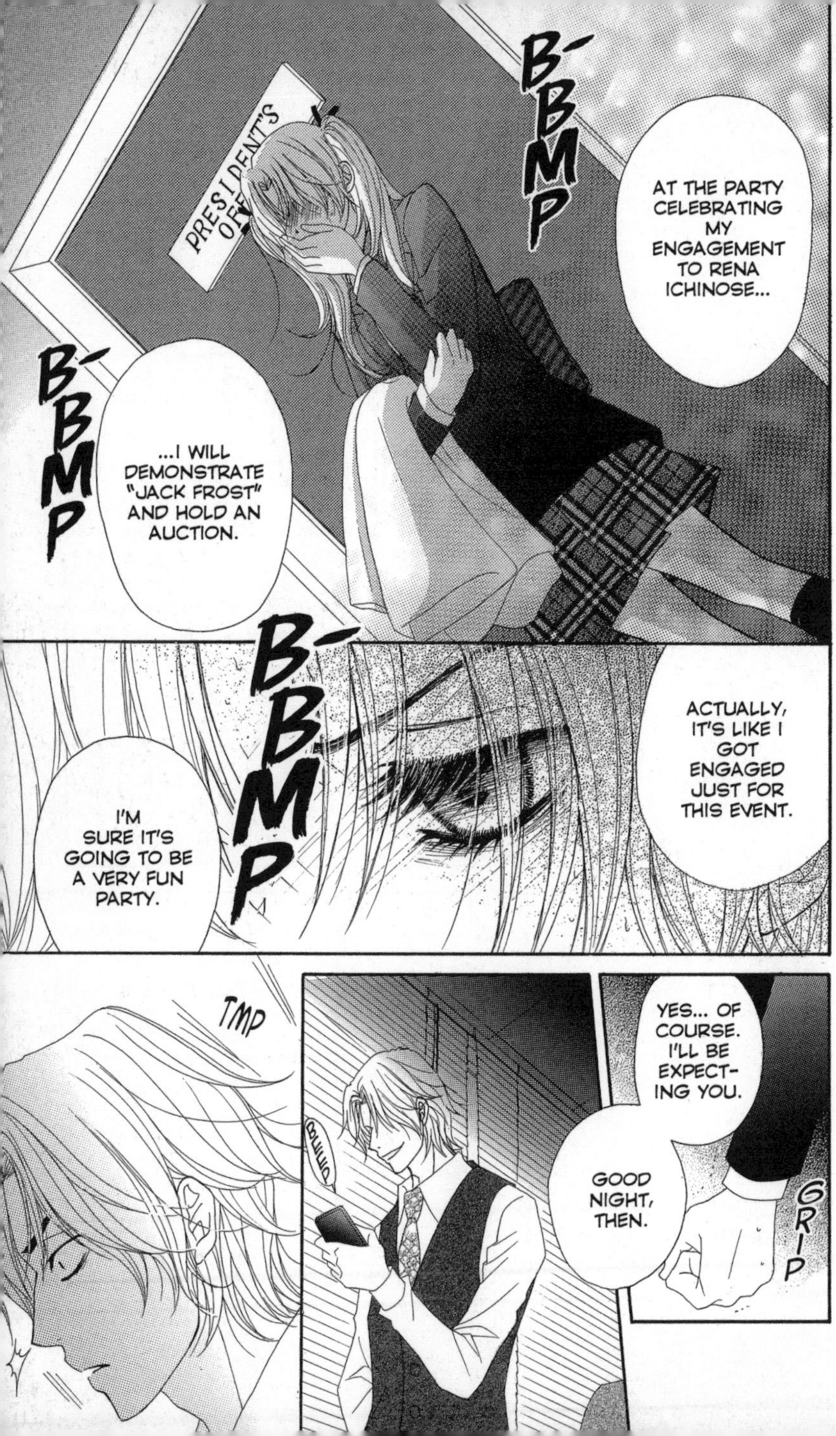
B-BBMP
AT THE PARTY CELEBRATING MY ENGAGEMENT TO RENA ICHINOSE...
PRESIDENT'S
...I WILL DEMONSTRATE "JACK FROST" AND HOLD AN AUCTION.
B-BBMP
ACTUALLY, IT'S LIKE I GOT ENGAGED JUST FOR THIS EVENT.
B-BBMP
I'M SURE IT'S GOING TO BE A VERY FUN PARTY.
YES... OF COURSE. I'LL BE EXPECTING YOU.
GOOD NIGHT, THEN.
GRIP
TMP

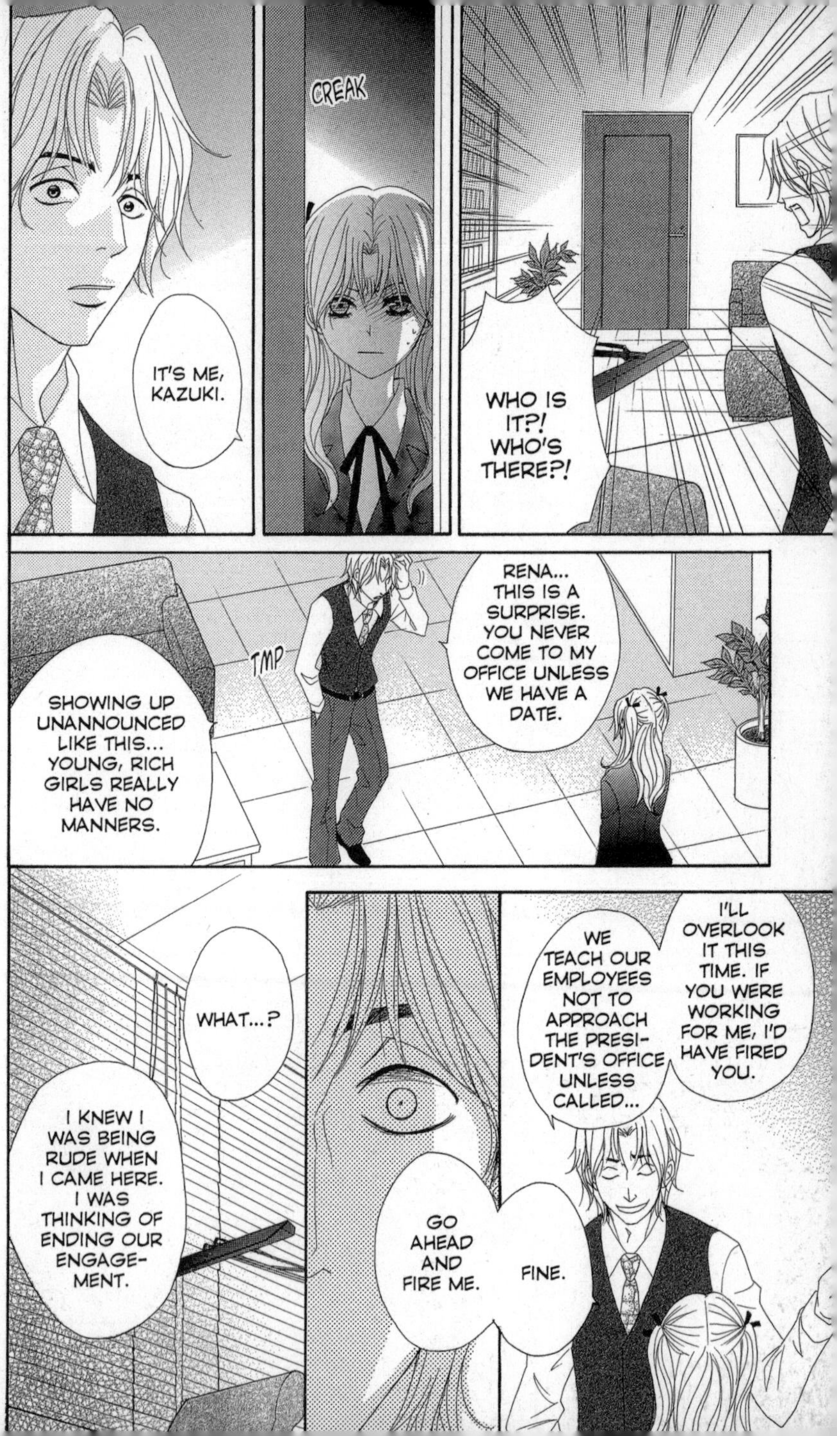
WHO IS IT?! WHO'S THERE?!
CREAK
IT'S ME, KAZUKI.
RENA... THIS IS A SURPRISE. YOU NEVER COME TO MY OFFICE UNLESS WE HAVE A DATE.
TMP
SHOWING UP UNANNOUNCED LIKE THIS... YOUNG, RICH GIRLS REALLY HAVE NO MANNERS.
I'LL OVERLOOK IT THIS TIME. IF YOU WERE WORKING FOR ME, I'D HAVE FIRED YOU.
WE TEACH OUR EMPLOYEES NOT TO APPROACH THE PRESI-DENT'S OFFICE UNLESS CALLED...
FINE.
GO AHEAD AND FIRE ME.
WHAT...?
I KNEW I WAS BEING RUDE WHEN I CAME HERE. I WAS THINKING OF ENDING OUR ENGAGE-MENT.

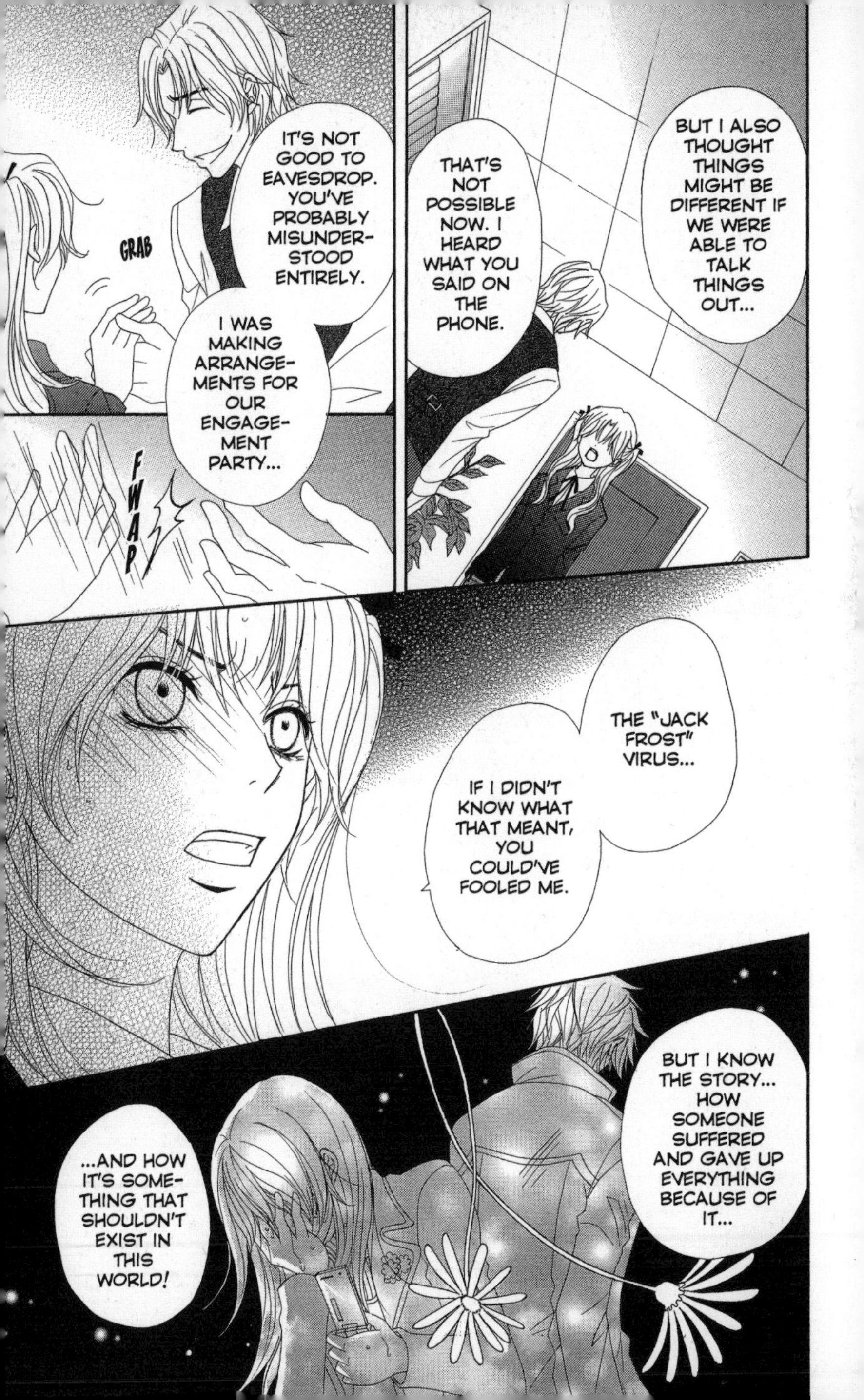
BUT I ALSO THOUGHT THINGS MIGHT BE DIFFERENT IF WE WERE ABLE TO TALK THINGS OUT...
THAT'S NOT POSSIBLE NOW. I HEARD WHAT YOU SAID ON THE PHONE.
IT'S NOT GOOD TO EAVESDROP. YOU'VE PROBABLY MISUNDER-STOOD ENTIRELY.
GRAB
I WAS MAKING ARRANGE-MENTS FOR OUR ENGAGE-MENT PARTY...
FWAP
THE "JACK FROST" VIRUS...
IF I DIDN'T KNOW WHAT THAT MEANT, YOU COULD'VE FOOLED ME.
BUT I KNOW THE STORY... HOW SOMEONE SUFFERED AND GAVE UP EVERYTHING BECAUSE OF IT...
...AND HOW IT'S SOME-THING THAT SHOULDN'T EXIST IN THIS WORLD!

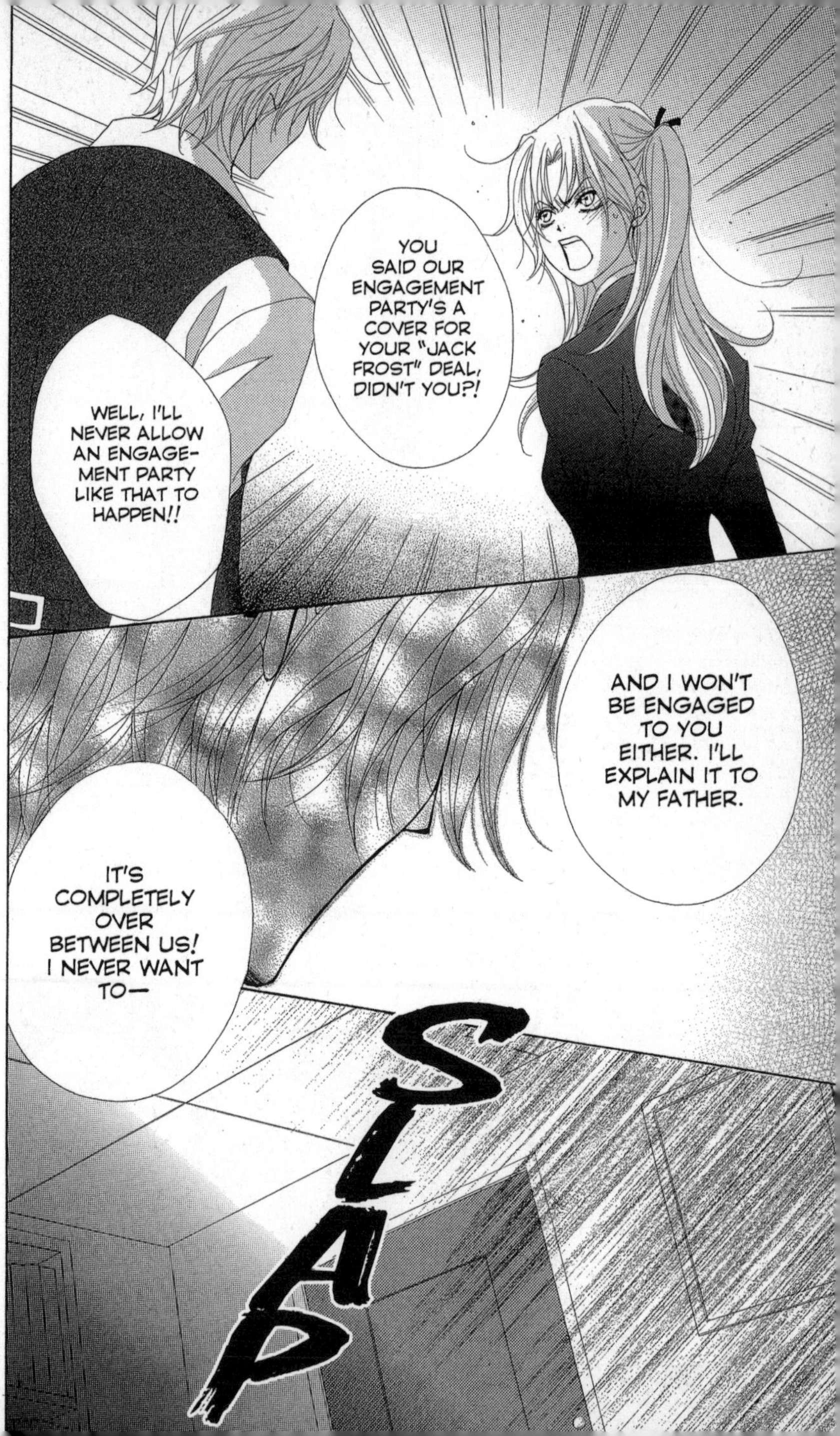
YOU SAID OUR ENGAGEMENT PARTY'S A COVER FOR YOUR "JACK FROST" DEAL, DIDN'T YOU?!
WELL, I'LL NEVER ALLOW AN ENGAGE-MENT PARTY LIKE THAT TO HAPPEN!!
AND I WON'T BE ENGAGED TO YOU EITHER. I'LL EXPLAIN IT TO MY FATHER.
IT'S COMPLETELY OVER BETWEEN US! I NEVER WANT TO—
SLAP

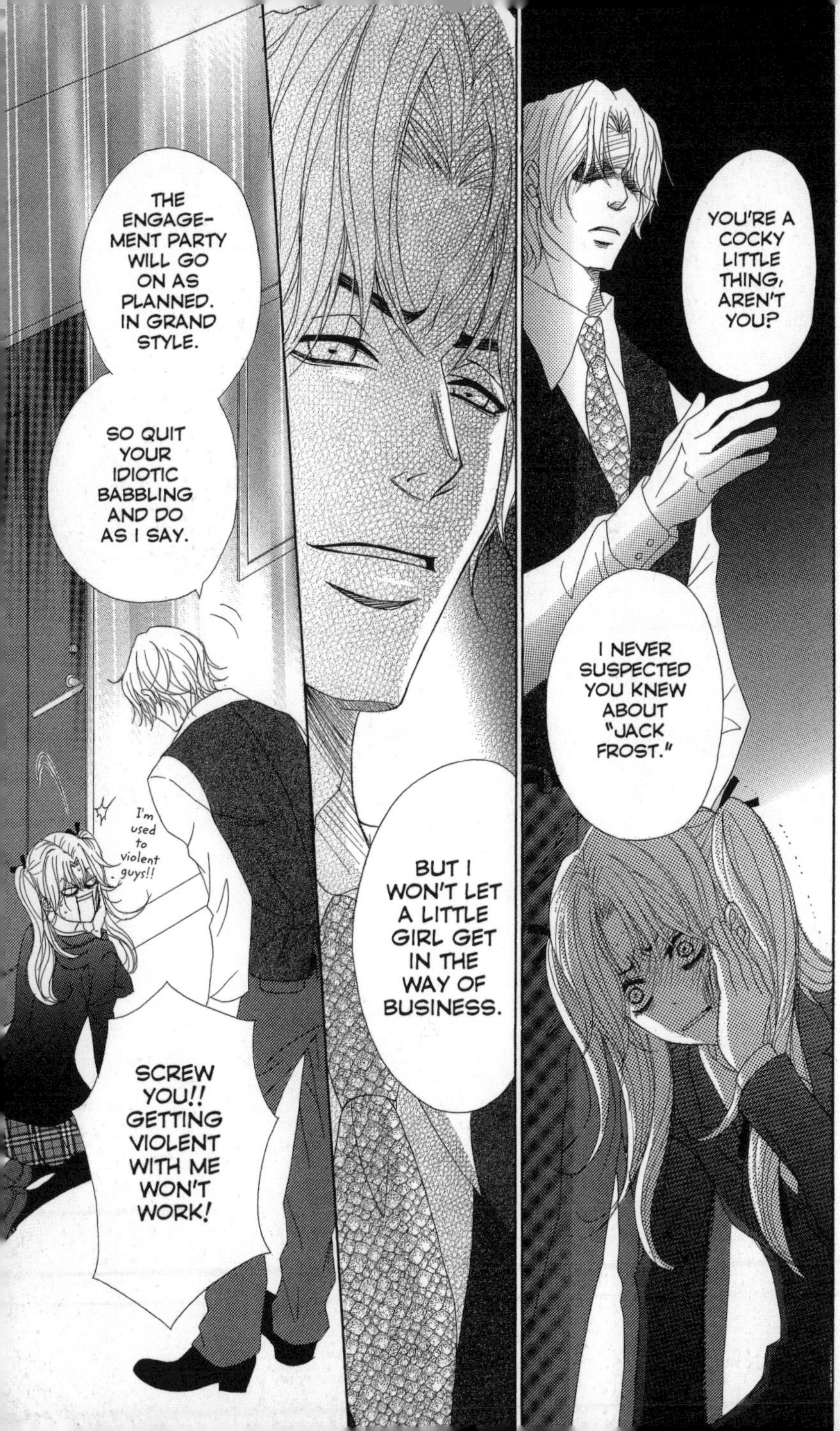
YOU'RE A COCKY LITTLE THING, AREN'T YOU?
I NEVER SUSPECTED YOU KNEW ABOUT "JACK FROST."
BUT I WON'T LET A LITTLE GIRL GET IN THE WAY OF BUSINESS.
THE ENGAGEMENT PARTY WILL GO ON AS PLANNED. IN GRAND STYLE.
SO QUIT YOUR IDIOTIC BABBLING AND DO AS I SAY.
I'm used to violent guys!!
SCREW YOU!! GETTING VIOLENT WITH ME WON'T WORK!

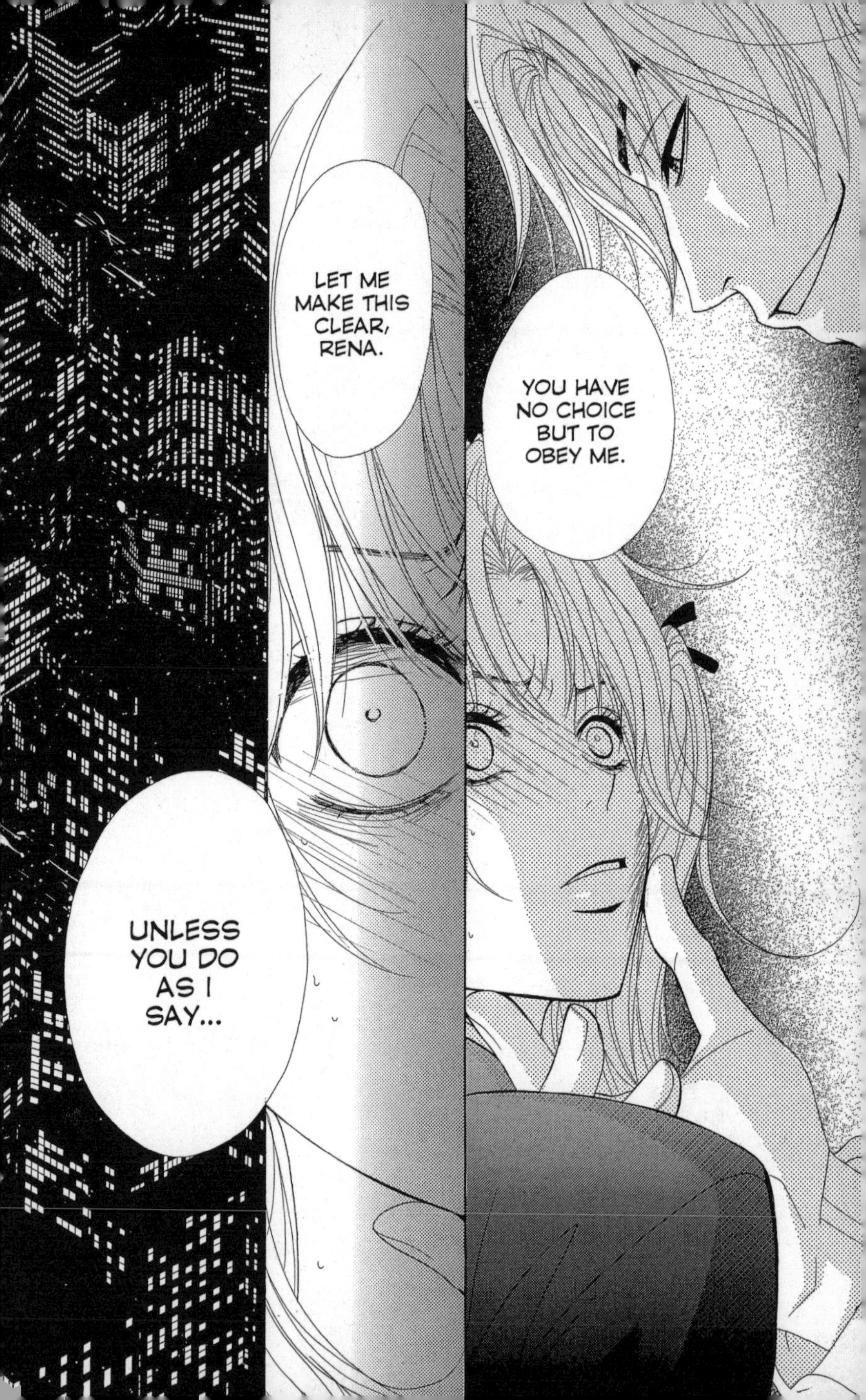
YOU HAVE NO CHOICE BUT TO OBEY ME.
LET ME MAKE THIS CLEAR, RENA.
UNLESS YOU DO AS I SAY...

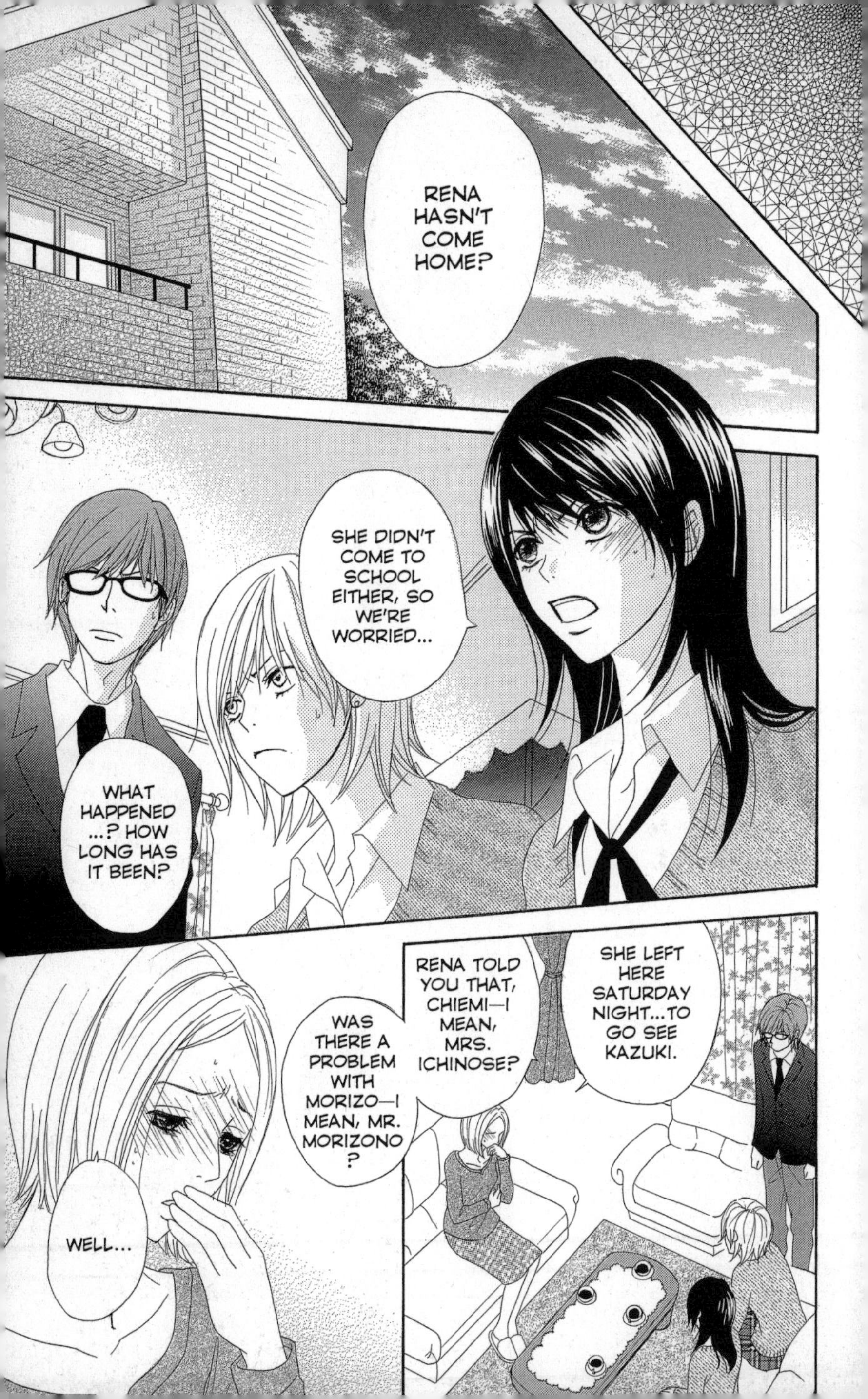
RENA HASN'T COME HOME?
SHE DIDN'T COME TO SCHOOL EITHER, SO WE'RE WORRIED...
WHAT HAPPENED ...? HOW LONG HAS IT BEEN?
SHE LEFT HERE SATURDAY NIGHT...TO GO SEE KAZUKI.
RENA TOLD YOU THAT, CHIEMI—I MEAN, MRS. ICHINOSE?
WAS THERE A PROBLEM WITH MORIZO—I MEAN, MR. MORIZONO ?
WELL...

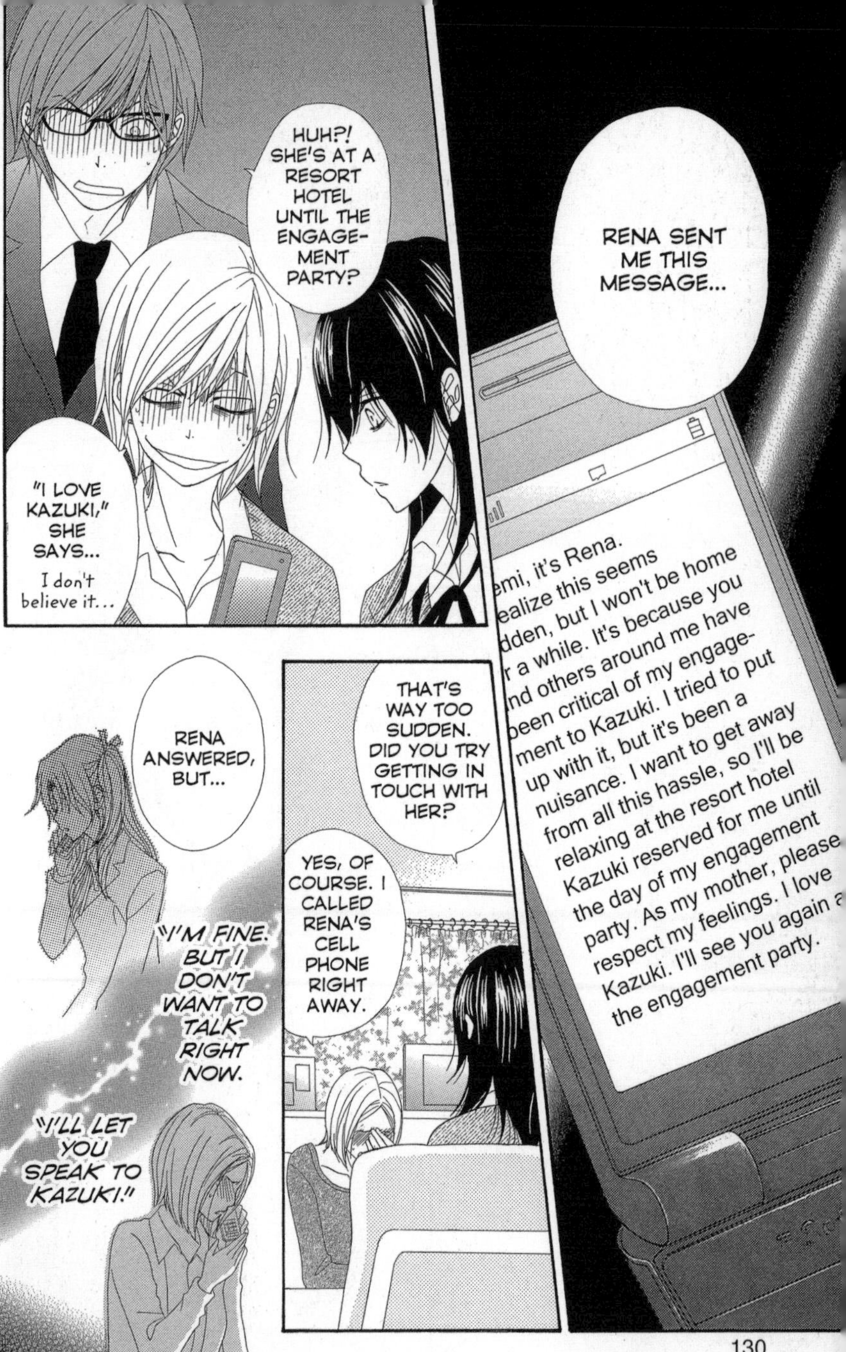
RENA SENT ME THIS MESSAGE...
emi, it's Rena.
ealize this seems
dden, but I won't be home
r a while. It's because you
nd others around me have
been critical of my engage-
ment to Kazuki. I tried to put
up with it, but it's been a
nuisance. I want to get away
from all this hassle, so I'll be
relaxing at the resort hotel
Kazuki reserved for me until
the day of my engagement
party. As my mother, please
respect my feelings. I love
Kazuki. I'll see you again a
the engagement party.
HUH?! SHE'S AT A RESORT HOTEL UNTIL THE ENGAGE-MENT PARTY?
"I LOVE KAZUKI," SHE SAYS...
I don't believe it...
THAT'S WAY TOO SUDDEN. DID YOU TRY GETTING IN TOUCH WITH HER?
YES, OF COURSE. I CALLED RENA'S CELL PHONE RIGHT AWAY.
RENA ANSWERED, BUT...
"I'M FINE. BUT I DON'T WANT TO TALK RIGHT NOW.
"I'LL LET YOU SPEAK TO KAZUKI."

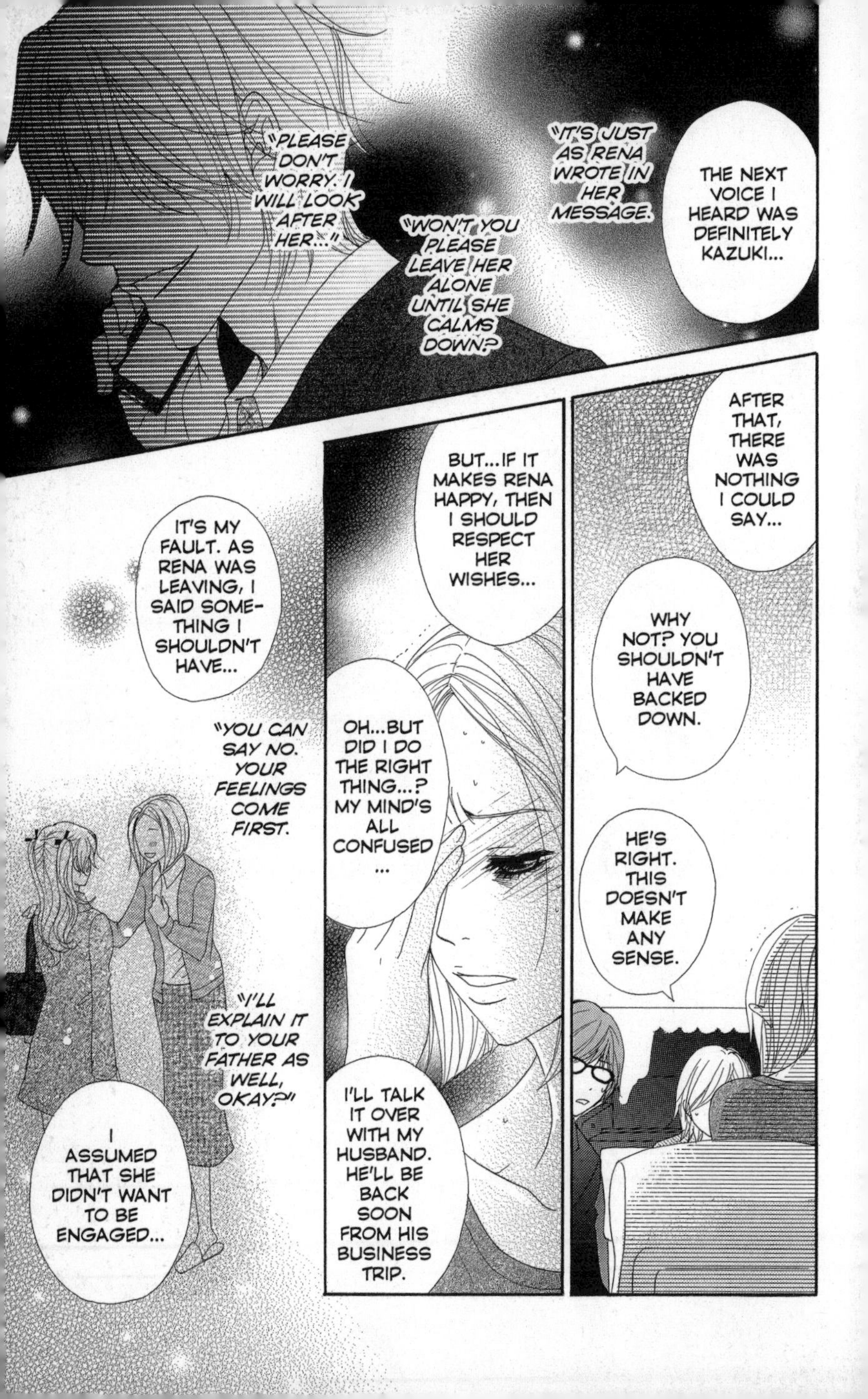
THE NEXT VOICE I HEARD WAS DEFINITELY KAZUKI...
"IT'S JUST AS RENA WROTE IN HER MESSAGE.
"WON'T YOU PLEASE LEAVE HER ALONE UNTIL SHE CALMS DOWN?
"PLEASE DON'T WORRY. I WILL LOOK AFTER HER..."
AFTER THAT, THERE WAS NOTHING I COULD SAY...
WHY NOT? YOU SHOULDN'T HAVE BACKED DOWN.
HE'S RIGHT. THIS DOESN'T MAKE ANY SENSE.
BUT...IF IT MAKES RENA HAPPY, THEN I SHOULD RESPECT HER WISHES...
OH...BUT DID I DO THE RIGHT THING...? MY MIND'S ALL CONFUSED...
I'LL TALK IT OVER WITH MY HUSBAND. HE'LL BE BACK SOON FROM HIS BUSINESS TRIP.
IT'S MY FAULT. AS RENA WAS LEAVING, I SAID SOME-THING I SHOULDN'T HAVE...
"YOU CAN SAY NO. YOUR FEELINGS COME FIRST.
"I'LL EXPLAIN IT TO YOUR FATHER AS WELL, OKAY?"
I ASSUMED THAT SHE DIDN'T WANT TO BE ENGAGED...

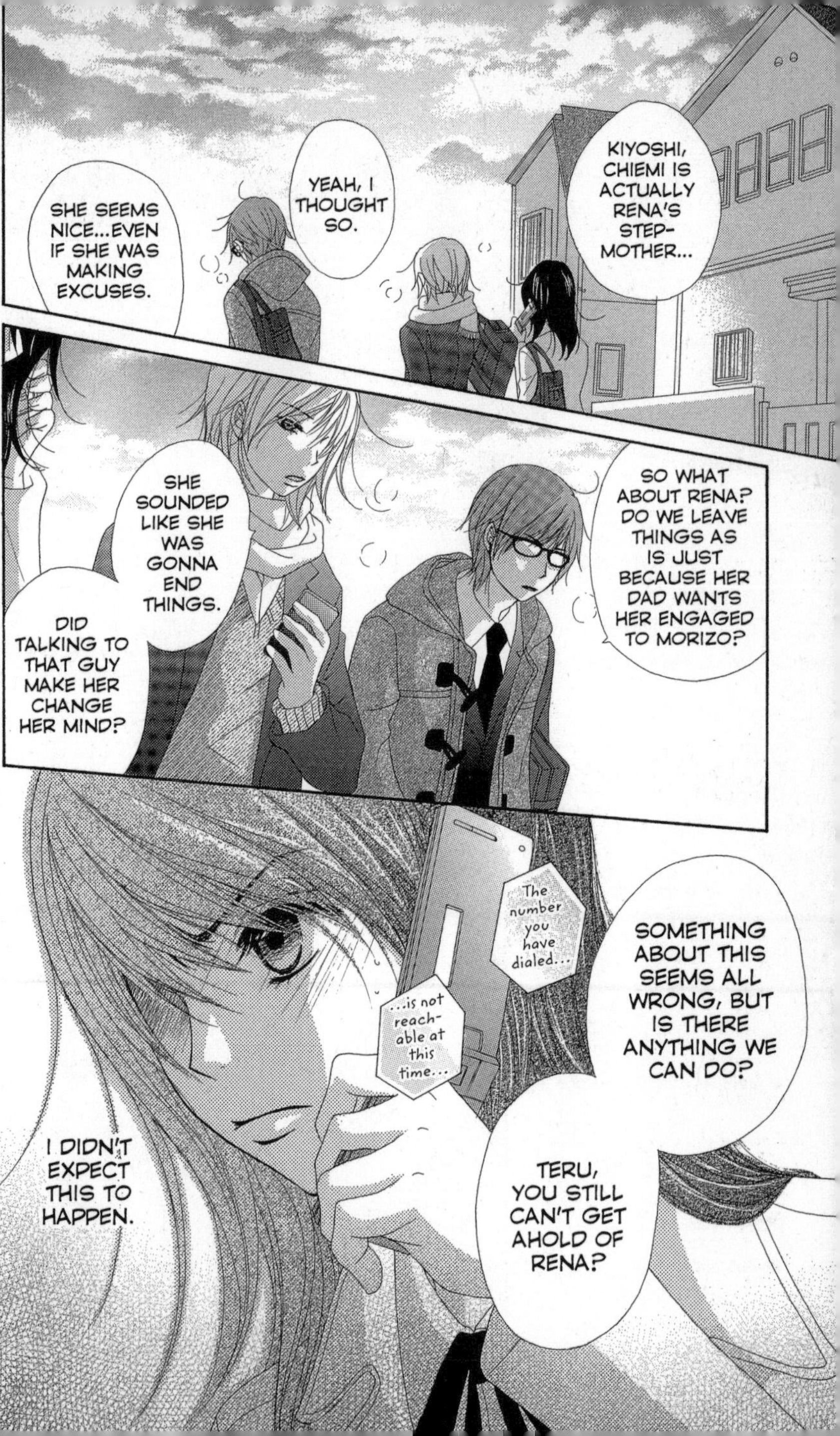
KIYOSHI, CHIEMI IS ACTUALLY RENA'S STEP-MOTHER...
YEAH, I THOUGHT SO.
SHE SEEMS NICE...EVEN IF SHE WAS MAKING EXCUSES.
SO WHAT ABOUT RENA? DO WE LEAVE THINGS AS IS JUST BECAUSE HER DAD WANTS HER ENGAGED TO MORIZO?
SHE SOUNDED LIKE SHE WAS GONNA END THINGS.
DID TALKING TO THAT GUY MAKE HER CHANGE HER MIND?
SOMETHING ABOUT THIS SEEMS ALL WRONG, BUT IS THERE ANYTHING WE CAN DO?
The number you have dialed...
...is not reachable at this time...
TERU, YOU STILL CAN'T GET AHOLD OF RENA?
I DIDN'T EXPECT THIS TO HAPPEN.

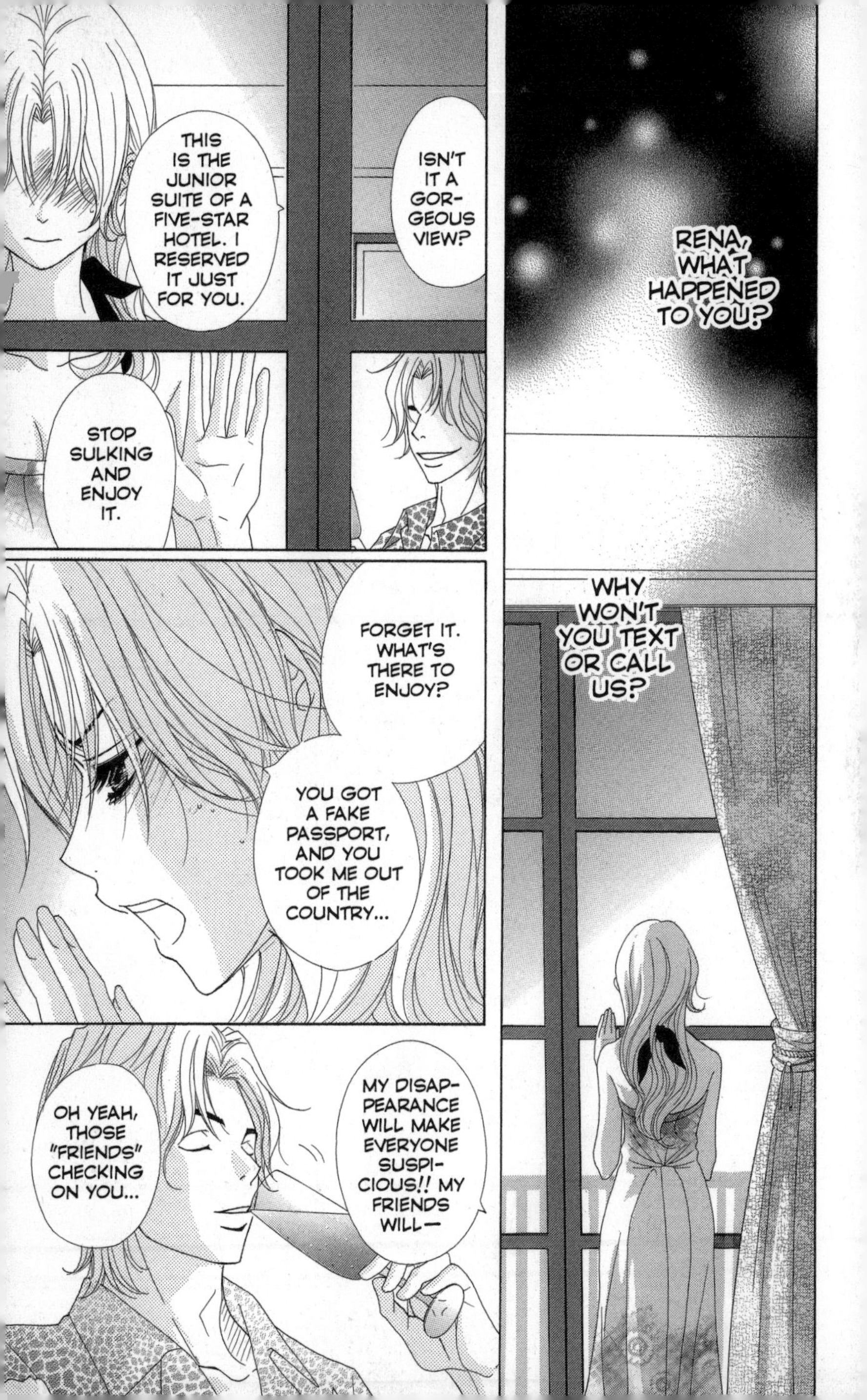
RENA, WHAT HAPPENED TO YOU?
WHY WON'T YOU TEXT OR CALL US?
ISN'T IT A GORGEOUS VIEW?
THIS IS THE JUNIOR SUITE OF A FIVE-STAR HOTEL. I RESERVED IT JUST FOR YOU.
STOP SULKING AND ENJOY IT.
FORGET IT. WHAT'S THERE TO ENJOY?
YOU GOT A FAKE PASSPORT, AND YOU TOOK ME OUT OF THE COUNTRY...
MY DISAPPEARANCE WILL MAKE EVERYONE SUSPICIOUS!! MY FRIENDS WILL—
OH YEAH, THOSE "FRIENDS" CHECKING ON YOU...

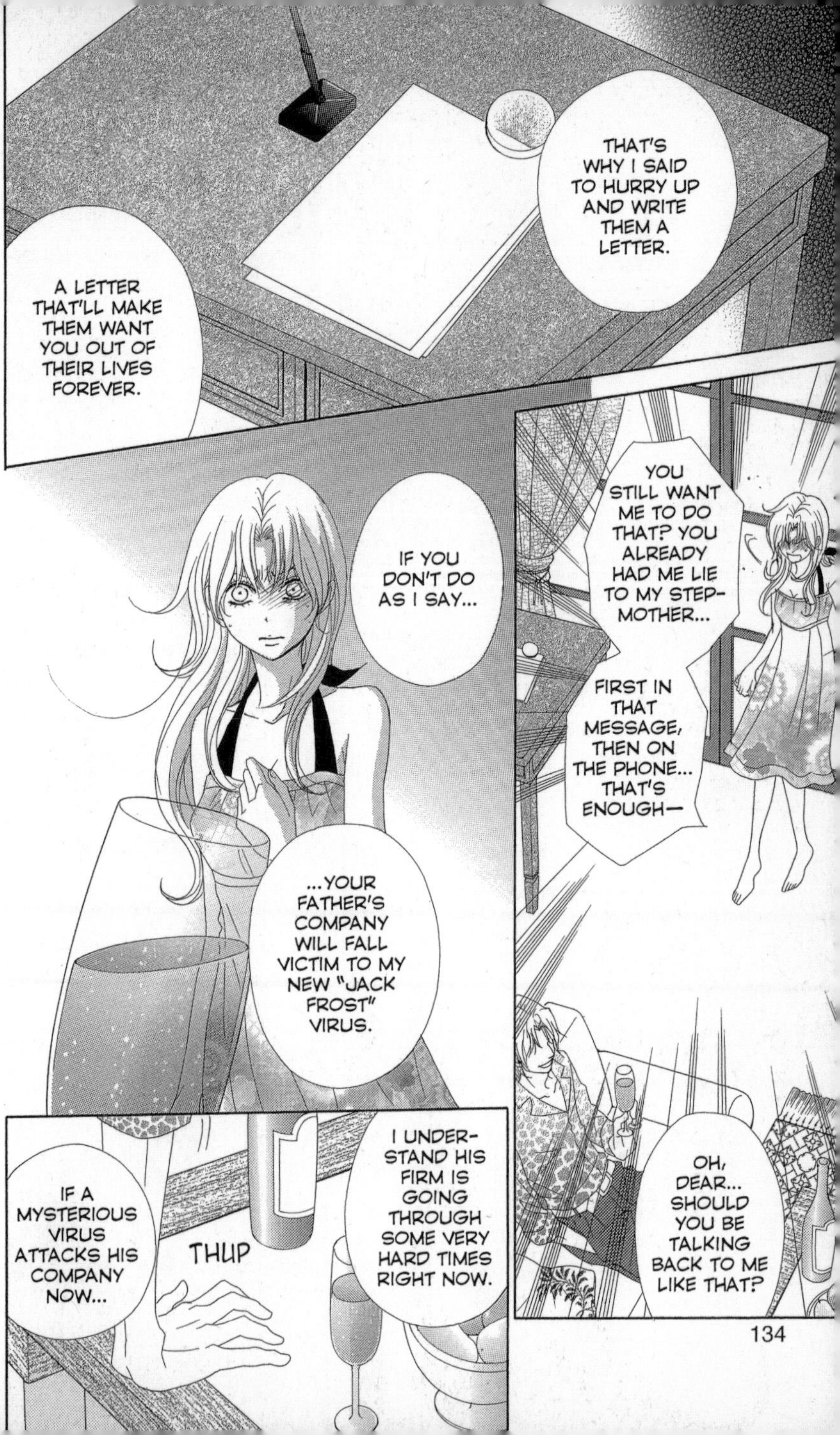
THAT'S WHY I SAID TO HURRY UP AND WRITE THEM A LETTER.
A LETTER THAT'LL MAKE THEM WANT YOU OUT OF THEIR LIVES FOREVER.
YOU STILL WANT ME TO DO THAT? YOU ALREADY HAD ME LIE TO MY STEP-MOTHER...
FIRST IN THAT MESSAGE, THEN ON THE PHONE... THAT'S ENOUGH—
OH, DEAR... SHOULD YOU BE TALKING BACK TO ME LIKE THAT?
IF YOU DON'T DO AS I SAY...
...YOUR FATHER'S COMPANY WILL FALL VICTIM TO MY NEW "JACK FROST" VIRUS.
I UNDER-STAND HIS FIRM IS GOING THROUGH SOME VERY HARD TIMES RIGHT NOW.
THUP
IF A MYSTERIOUS VIRUS ATTACKS HIS COMPANY NOW...

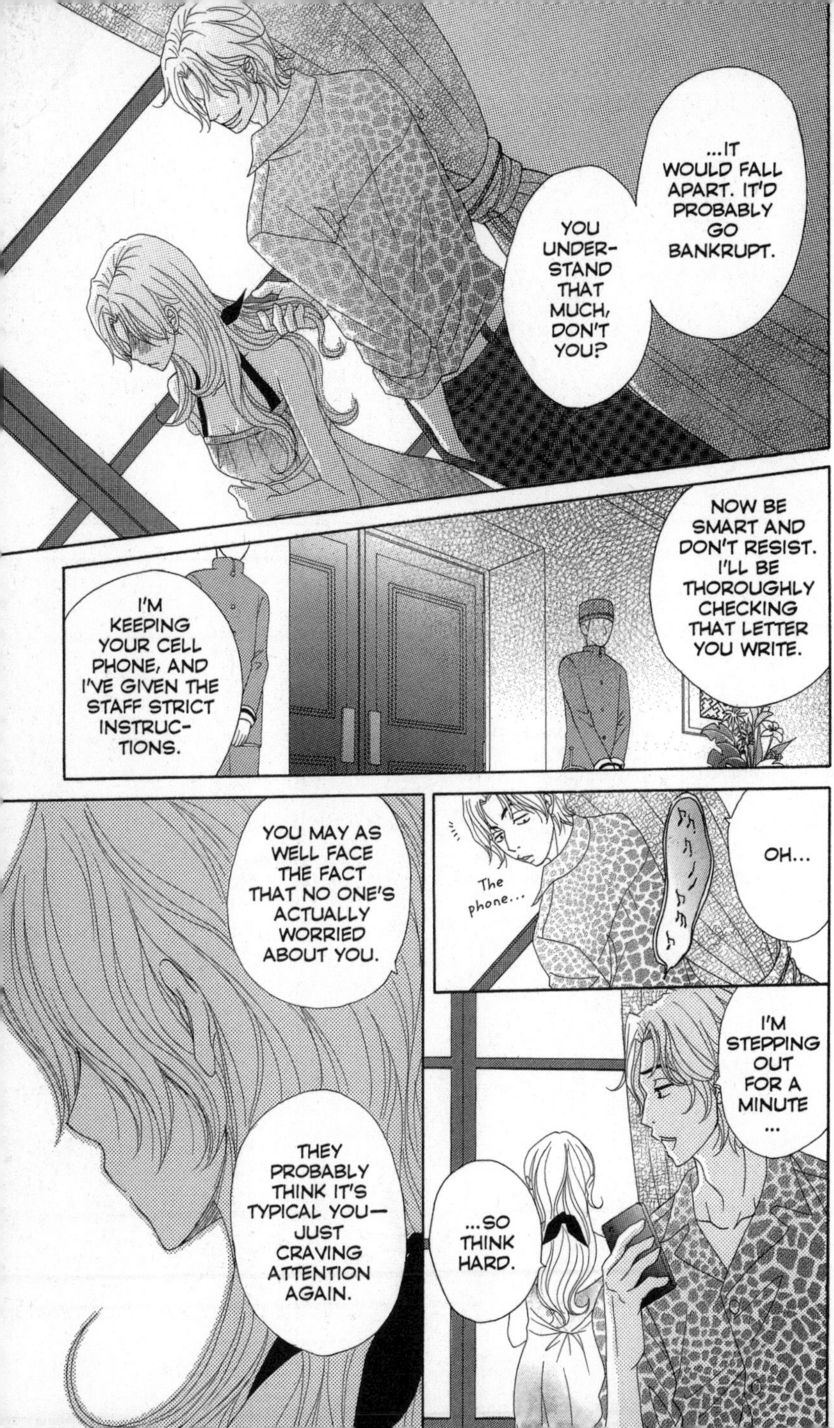
...IT WOULD FALL APART. IT'D PROBABLY GO BANKRUPT.
YOU UNDER-STAND THAT MUCH, DON'T YOU?
NOW BE SMART AND DON'T RESIST. I'LL BE THOROUGHLY CHECKING THAT LETTER YOU WRITE.
I'M KEEPING YOUR CELL PHONE, AND I'VE GIVEN THE STAFF STRICT INSTRUC-TIONS.
OH...
The phone...
I'M STEPPING OUT FOR A MINUTE...
...SO THINK HARD.
YOU MAY AS WELL FACE THE FACT THAT NO ONE'S ACTUALLY WORRIED ABOUT YOU.
THEY PROBABLY THINK IT'S TYPICAL YOU—JUST CRAVING ATTENTION AGAIN.

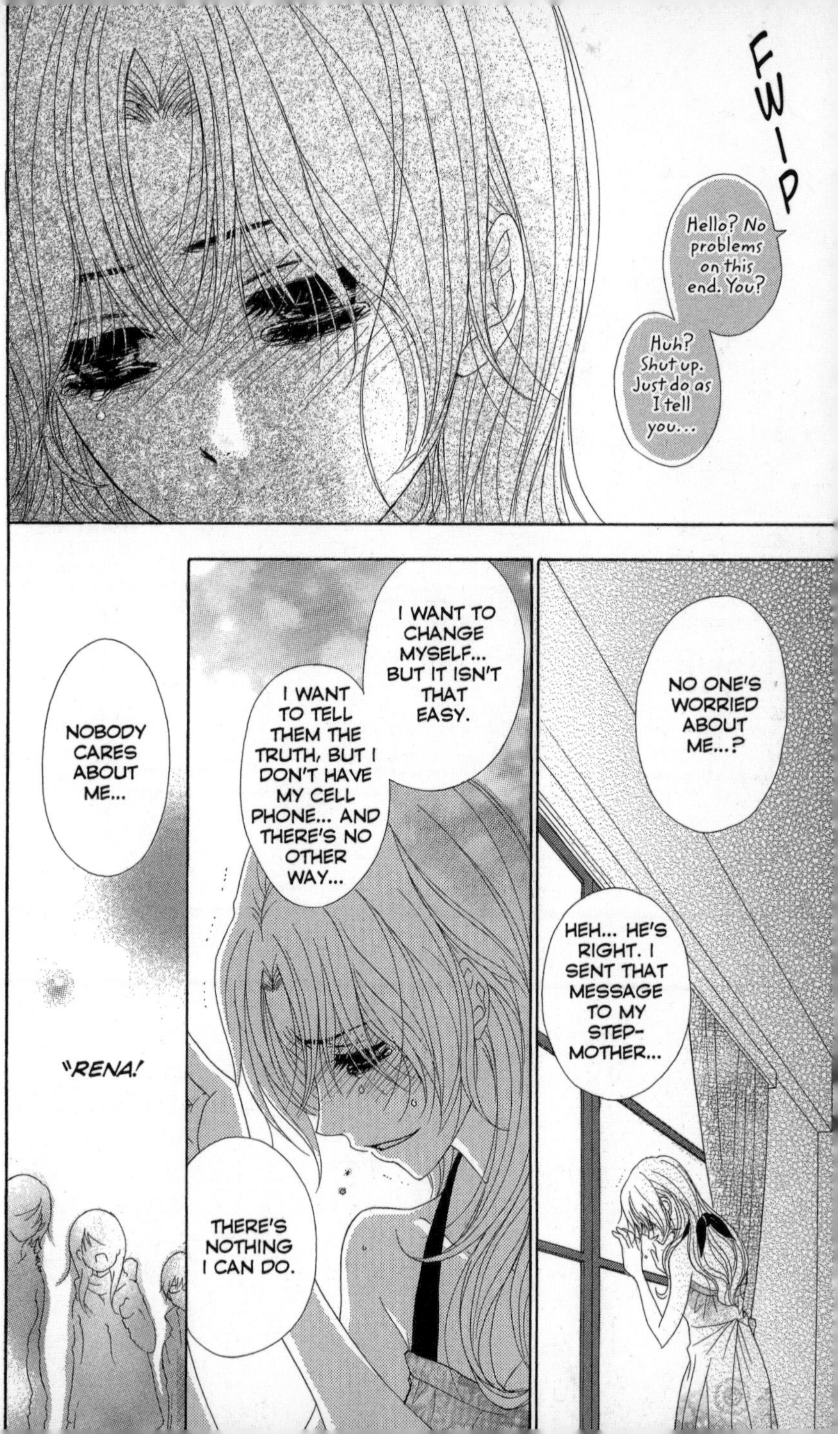
FWIP
Hello? No problems on this end. You?
Huh? Shut up. Just do as I tell you...
NO ONE'S WORRIED ABOUT ME...?
HEH... HE'S RIGHT. I SENT THAT MESSAGE TO MY STEP-MOTHER...
I WANT TO CHANGE MYSELF... BUT IT ISN'T THAT EASY.
I WANT TO TELL THEM THE TRUTH, BUT I DON'T HAVE MY CELL PHONE... AND THERE'S NO OTHER WAY...
THERE'S NOTHING I CAN DO.
NOBODY CARES ABOUT ME...
"RENA!

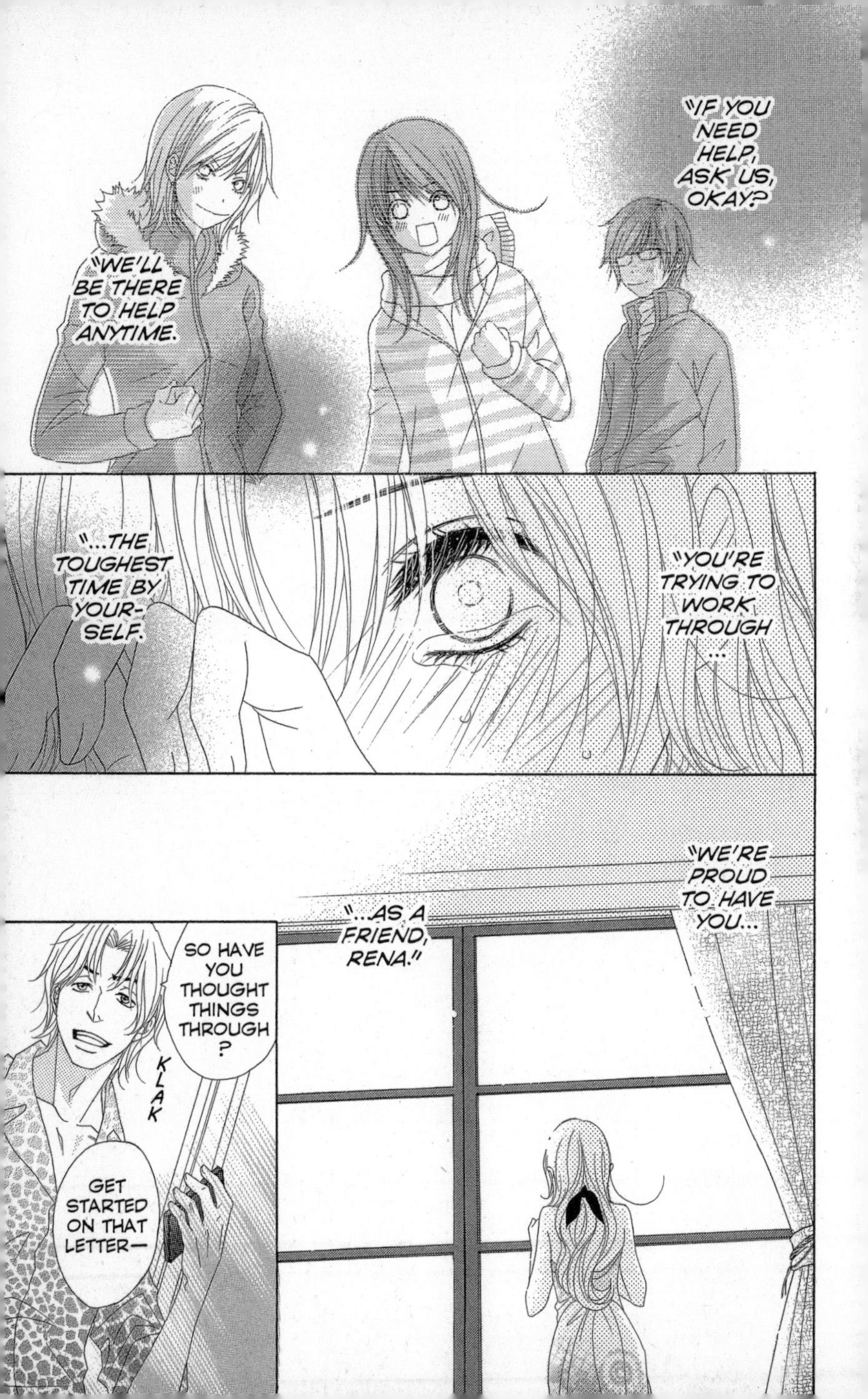
"IF YOU NEED HELP, ASK US, OKAY?
"WE'LL BE THERE TO HELP ANYTIME.
"YOU'RE TRYING TO WORK THROUGH ...
"...THE TOUGHEST TIME BY YOUR-SELF.
"WE'RE PROUD TO HAVE YOU...
"...AS A FRIEND, RENA."
SO HAVE YOU THOUGHT THINGS THROUGH ?
KLAK
GET STARTED ON THAT LETTER—

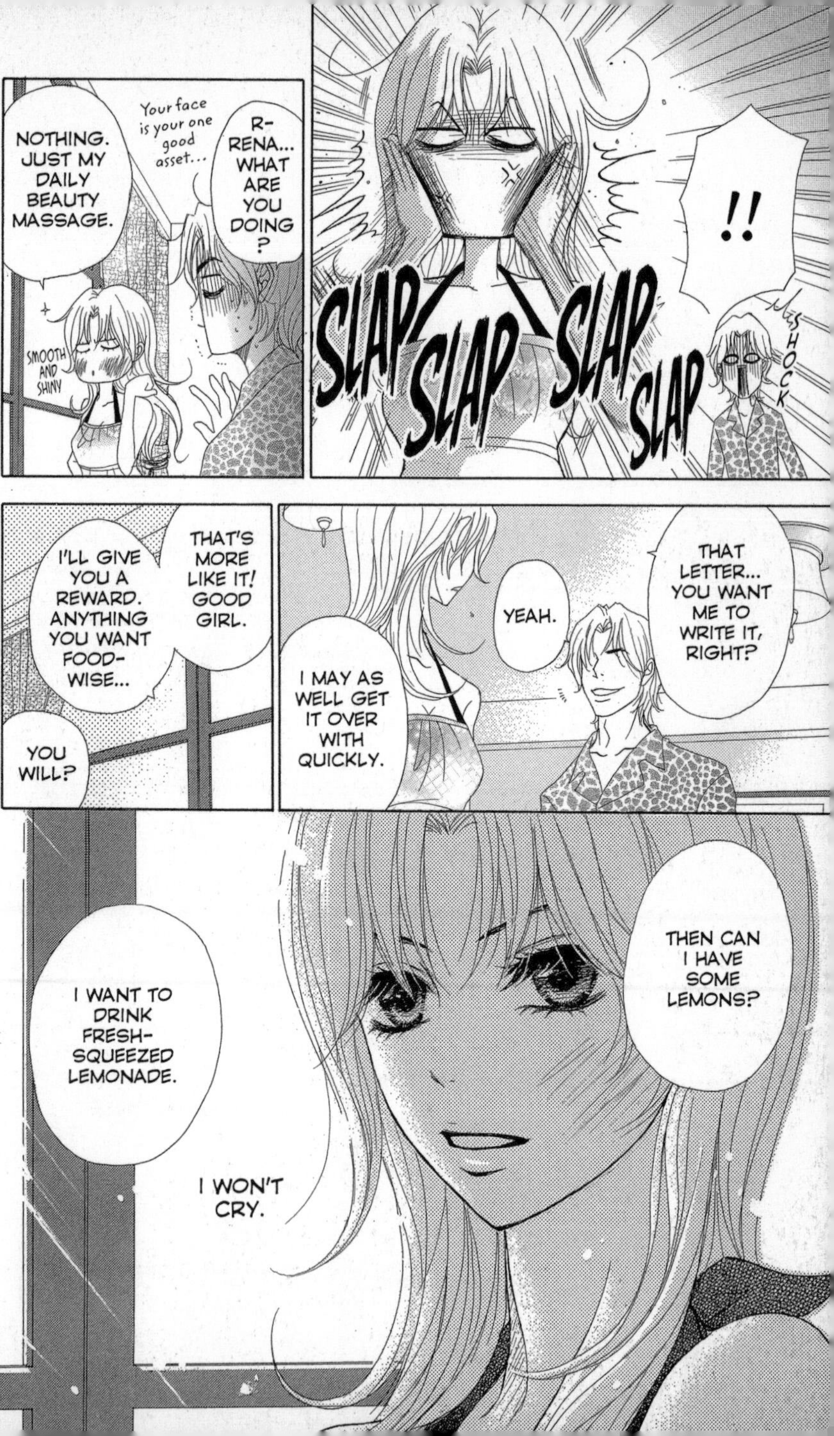
!!
SLAP SLAP SLAP SLAP
SHOCK
R-RENA... WHAT ARE YOU DOING?
Your face is your one good asset...
NOTHING. JUST MY DAILY BEAUTY MASSAGE.
SMOOTH AND SHINY
THAT LETTER... YOU WANT ME TO WRITE IT, RIGHT?
YEAH.
I MAY AS WELL GET IT OVER WITH QUICKLY.
THAT'S MORE LIKE IT! GOOD GIRL.
I'LL GIVE YOU A REWARD. ANYTHING YOU WANT FOOD-WISE...
YOU WILL?
THEN CAN I HAVE SOME LEMONS?
I WANT TO DRINK FRESH-SQUEEZED LEMONADE.
I WON'T CRY.

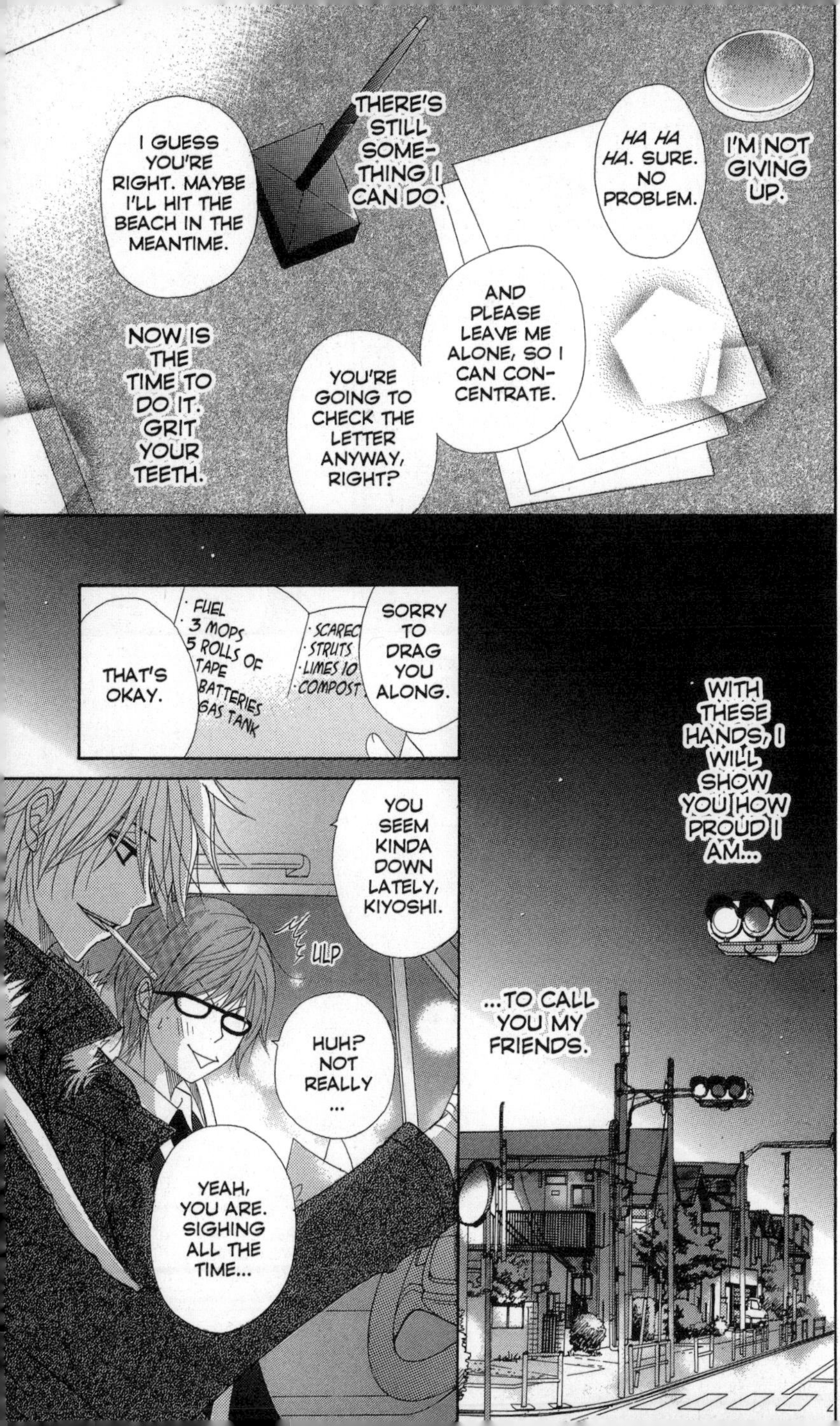
I'M NOT GIVING UP.
HA HA HA. SURE. NO PROBLEM.
THERE'S STILL SOMETHING I CAN DO.
I GUESS YOU'RE RIGHT. MAYBE I'LL HIT THE BEACH IN THE MEANTIME.
AND PLEASE LEAVE ME ALONE, SO I CAN CONCENTRATE.
YOU'RE GOING TO CHECK THE LETTER ANYWAY, RIGHT?
NOW IS THE TIME TO DO IT. GRIT YOUR TEETH.
WITH THESE HANDS, I WILL SHOW YOU HOW PROUD I AM...
...TO CALL YOU MY FRIENDS.
SORRY TO DRAG YOU ALONG.
· SCAREC · STRUTS · LIMES 10 · COMPOST
· FUEL · 3 MOPS · 5 ROLLS OF TAPE · BATTERIES · GAS TANK
THAT'S OKAY.
YOU SEEM KINDA DOWN LATELY, KIYOSHI.
ULP
HUH? NOT REALLY ...
YEAH, YOU ARE. SIGHING ALL THE TIME...

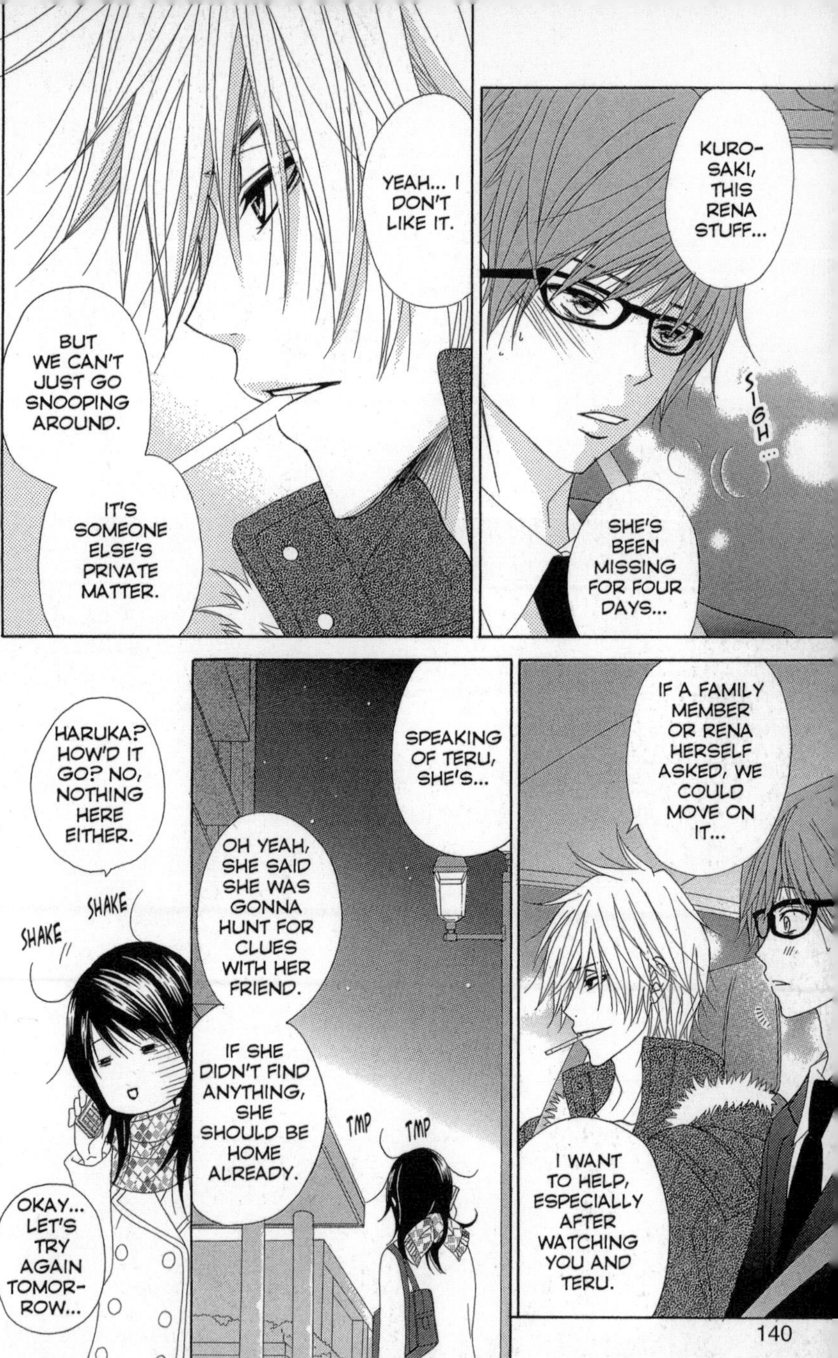
KURO-SAKI, THIS RENA STUFF...
SIGH...
SHE'S BEEN MISSING FOR FOUR DAYS...
YEAH... I DON'T LIKE IT.
BUT WE CAN'T JUST GO SNOOPING AROUND.
IT'S SOMEONE ELSE'S PRIVATE MATTER.
IF A FAMILY MEMBER OR RENA HERSELF ASKED, WE COULD MOVE ON IT...
I WANT TO HELP, ESPECIALLY AFTER WATCHING YOU AND TERU.
SPEAKING OF TERU, SHE'S...
OH YEAH, SHE SAID SHE WAS GONNA HUNT FOR CLUES WITH HER FRIEND.
IF SHE DIDN'T FIND ANYTHING, SHE SHOULD BE HOME ALREADY.
TMP TMP
HARUKA? HOW'D IT GO? NO, NOTHING HERE EITHER.
SHAKE SHAKE
OKAY... LET'S TRY AGAIN TOMORROW...

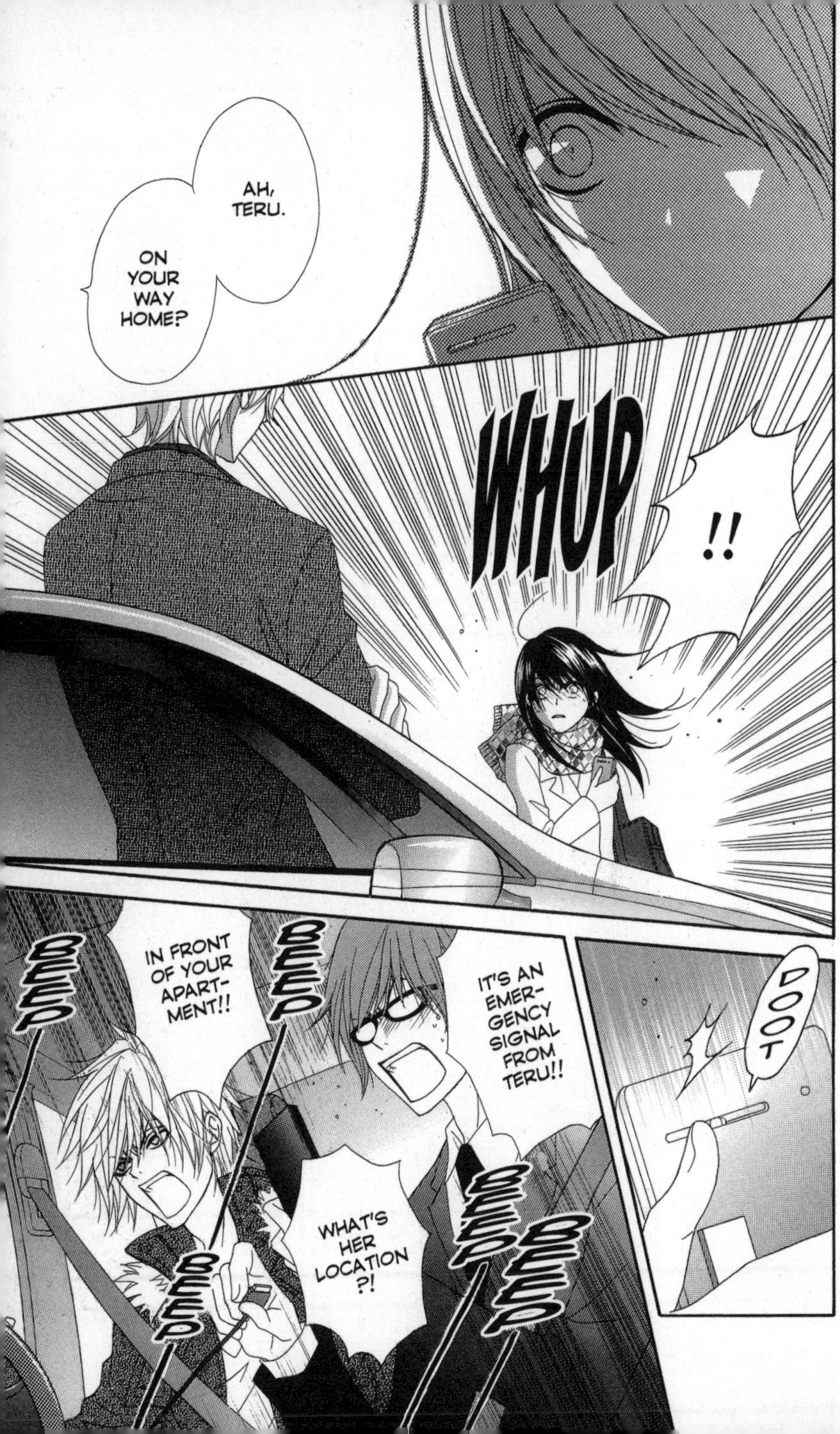
AH, TERU.
ON YOUR WAY HOME?
WHUP
!!
DOOT
IT'S AN EMERGENCY SIGNAL FROM TERU!!
BEEP
IN FRONT OF YOUR APARTMENT!!
BEEP
WHAT'S HER LOCATION?!
BEEP
BEEP
BEEP
BEEP

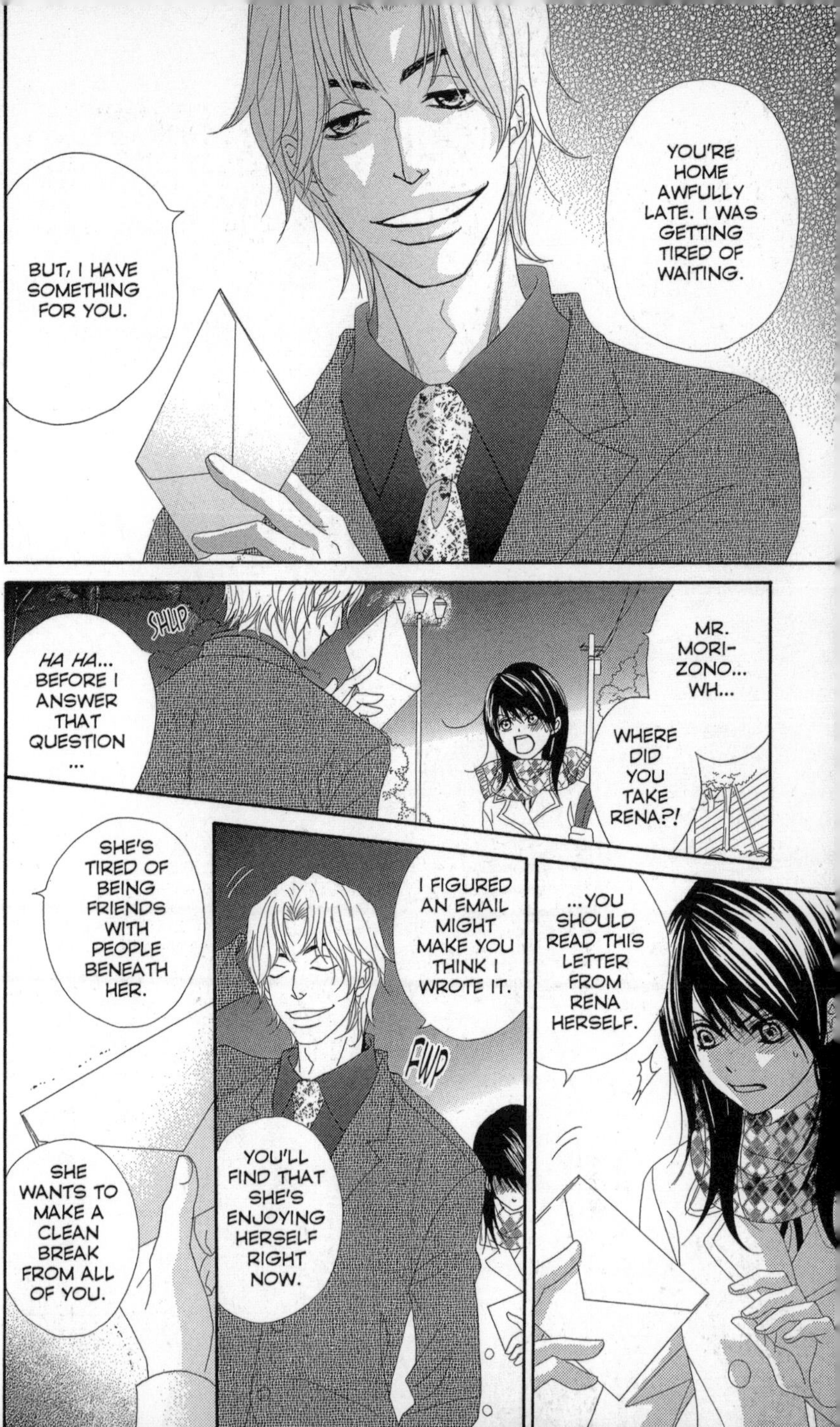
YOU'RE HOME AWFULLY LATE. I WAS GETTING TIRED OF WAITING.
BUT, I HAVE SOMETHING FOR YOU.
MR. MORI-ZONO... WH...
WHERE DID YOU TAKE RENA?!
SHUP
HA HA... BEFORE I ANSWER THAT QUESTION ...
...YOU SHOULD READ THIS LETTER FROM RENA HERSELF.
I FIGURED AN EMAIL MIGHT MAKE YOU THINK I WROTE IT.
FWP
YOU'LL FIND THAT SHE'S ENJOYING HERSELF RIGHT NOW.
SHE'S TIRED OF BEING FRIENDS WITH PEOPLE BENEATH HER.
SHE WANTS TO MAKE A CLEAN BREAK FROM ALL OF YOU.

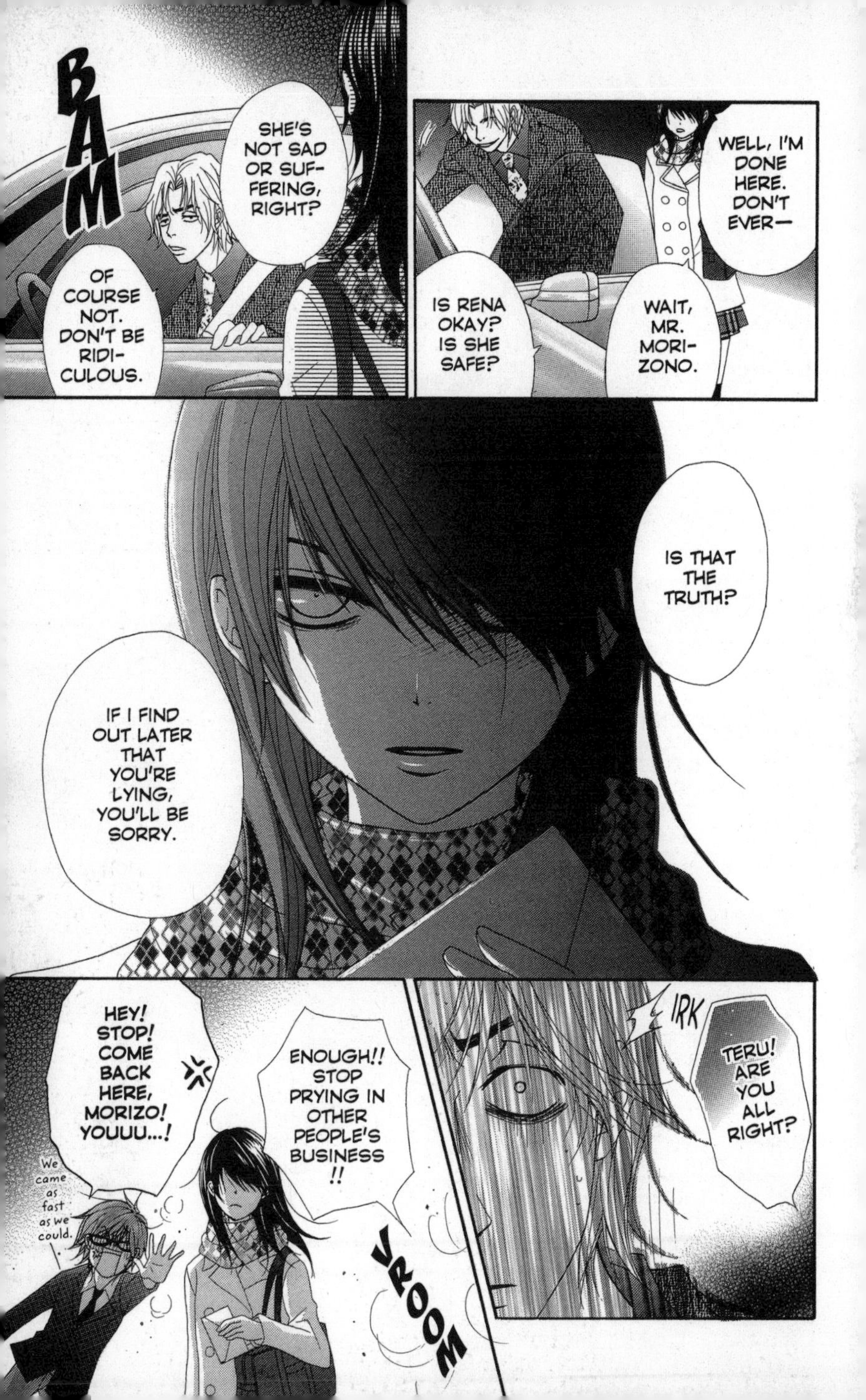
WELL, I'M DONE HERE. DON'T EVER—
WAIT, MR. MORIZONO.
IS RENA OKAY? IS SHE SAFE?
SHE'S NOT SAD OR SUFFERING, RIGHT?
BAM
OF COURSE NOT. DON'T BE RIDICULOUS.
IS THAT THE TRUTH?
IF I FIND OUT LATER THAT YOU'RE LYING, YOU'LL BE SORRY.
IRK
TERU! ARE YOU ALL RIGHT?
ENOUGH!! STOP PRYING IN OTHER PEOPLE'S BUSINESS!!
VROOM
HEY! STOP! COME BACK HERE, MORIZO! YOUUU...!
We came as fast as we could.

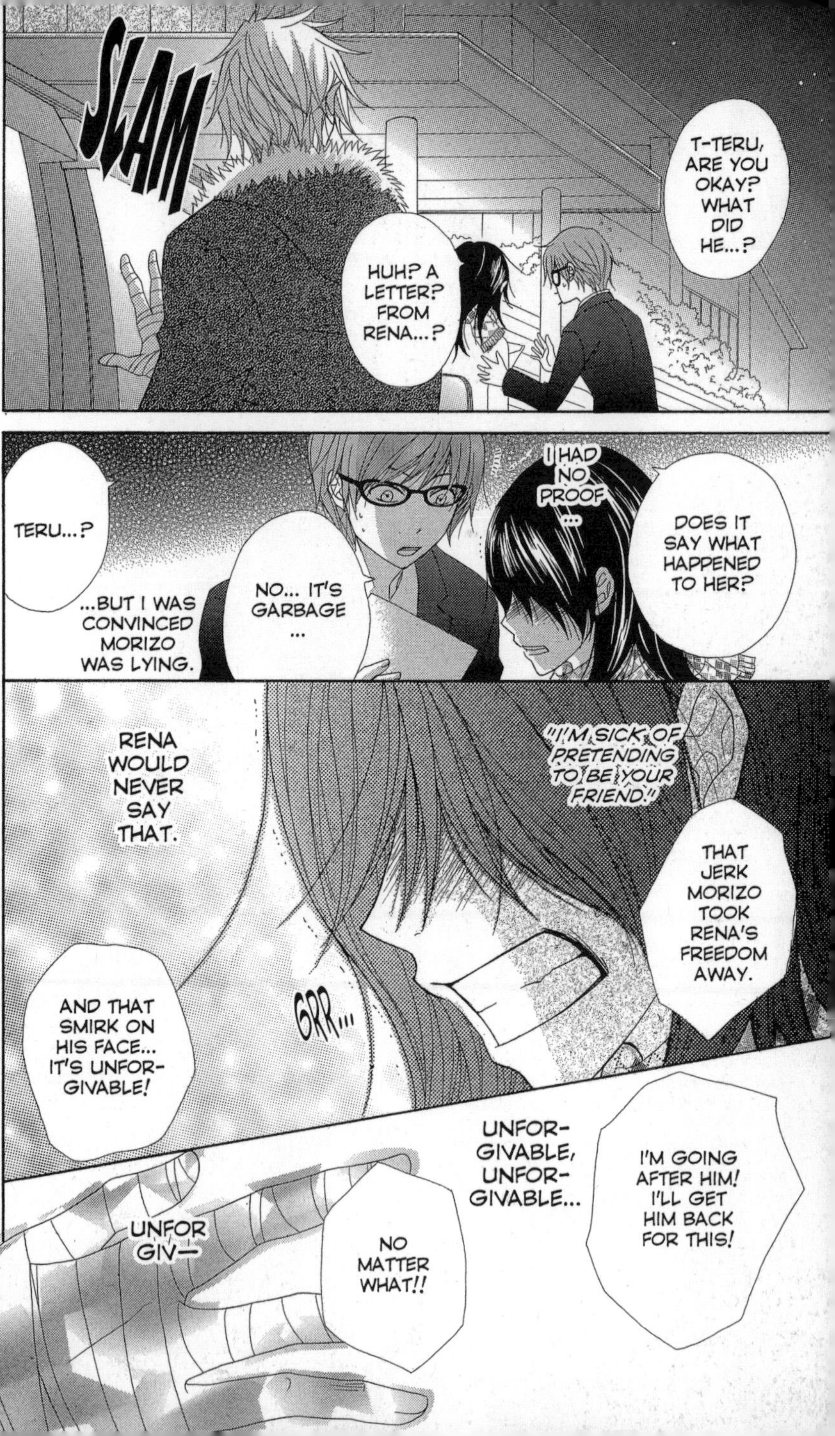
T-TERU, ARE YOU OKAY? WHAT DID HE...?
HUH? A LETTER? FROM RENA...?
SLAM
DOES IT SAY WHAT HAPPENED TO HER?
I HAD NO PROOF...
NO... IT'S GARBAGE...
TERU...?
...BUT I WAS CONVINCED MORIZO WAS LYING.
"I'M SICK OF PRETENDING TO BE YOUR FRIEND."
RENA WOULD NEVER SAY THAT.
THAT JERK MORIZO TOOK RENA'S FREEDOM AWAY.
GRR...
AND THAT SMIRK ON HIS FACE... IT'S UNFOR-GIVABLE!
I'M GOING AFTER HIM! I'LL GET HIM BACK FOR THIS!
UNFOR-GIVABLE, UNFOR-GIVABLE...
NO MATTER WHAT!!
UNFOR GIV—

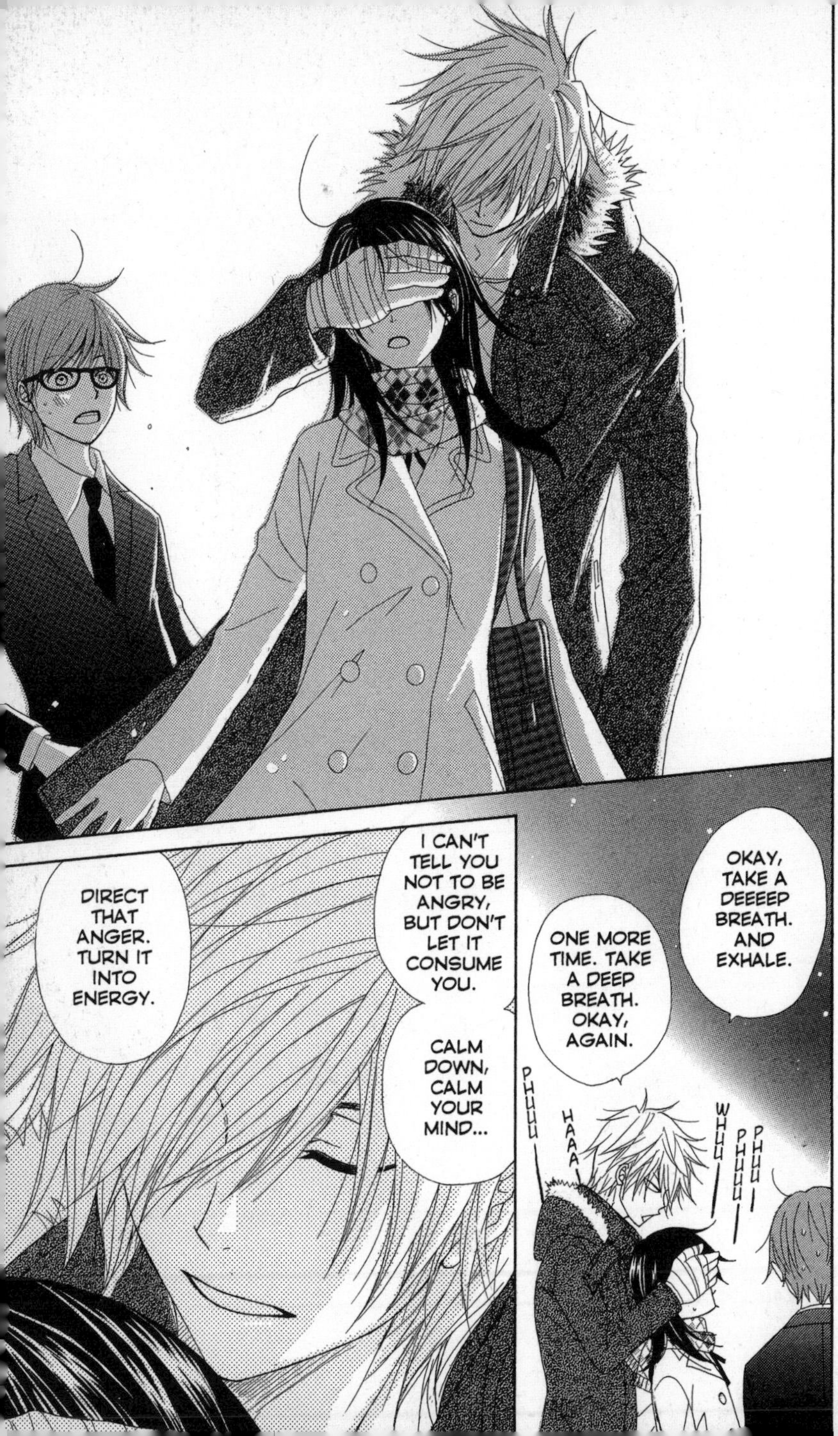
OKAY, TAKE A DEEEEP BREATH. AND EXHALE.
ONE MORE TIME. TAKE A DEEP BREATH. OKAY, AGAIN.
PHUU
PHUUU
WHUU
HAAA
PHUUU
I CAN'T TELL YOU NOT TO BE ANGRY, BUT DON'T LET IT CONSUME YOU.
CALM DOWN, CALM YOUR MIND...
DIRECT THAT ANGER. TURN IT INTO ENERGY.

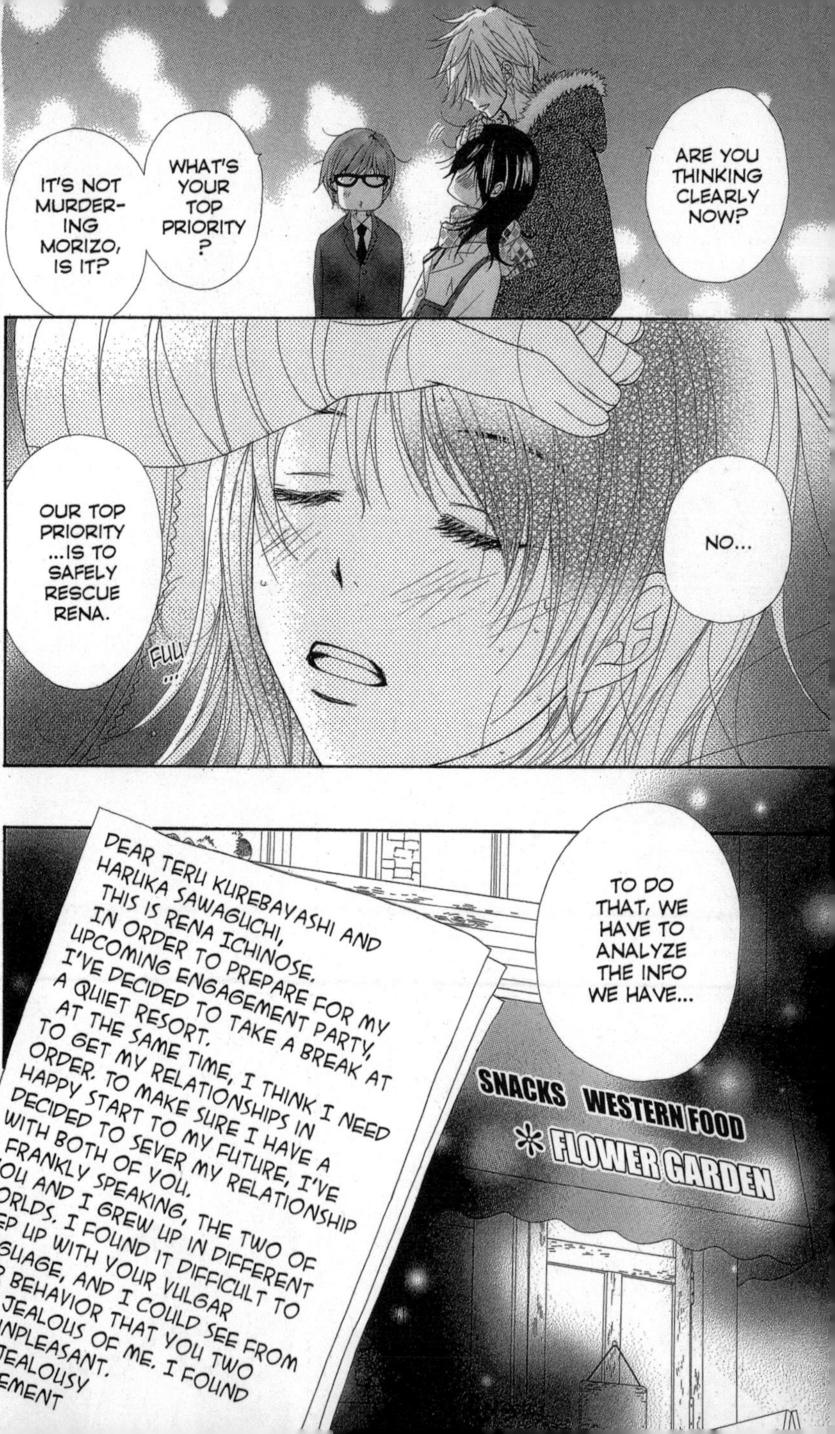
ARE YOU THINKING CLEARLY NOW?
WHAT'S YOUR TOP PRIORITY?
IT'S NOT MURDERING MORIZO, IS IT?
NO...
OUR TOP PRIORITY ...IS TO SAFELY RESCUE RENA.
FUU...
TO DO THAT, WE HAVE TO ANALYZE THE INFO WE HAVE...
SNACKS WESTERN FOOD
FLOWER GARDEN
DEAR TERU KUREBAYASHI AND HARUKA SAWAGUCHI,
THIS IS RENA ICHINOSE.
IN ORDER TO PREPARE FOR MY UPCOMING ENGAGEMENT PARTY, I'VE DECIDED TO TAKE A BREAK AT A QUIET RESORT.
AT THE SAME TIME, I THINK I NEED TO GET MY RELATIONSHIPS IN ORDER. TO MAKE SURE I HAVE A HAPPY START TO MY FUTURE, I'VE DECIDED TO SEVER MY RELATIONSHIP WITH BOTH OF YOU.
FRANKLY SPEAKING, THE TWO OF YOU AND I GREW UP IN DIFFERENT WORLDS. I FOUND IT DIFFICULT TO KEEP UP WITH YOUR VULGAR LANGUAGE, AND I COULD SEE FROM YOUR BEHAVIOR THAT YOU TWO
ERE JEALOUS OF ME. I FOUND
HAT UNPLEASANT.
HAT JEALOUSY
GAGEMENT

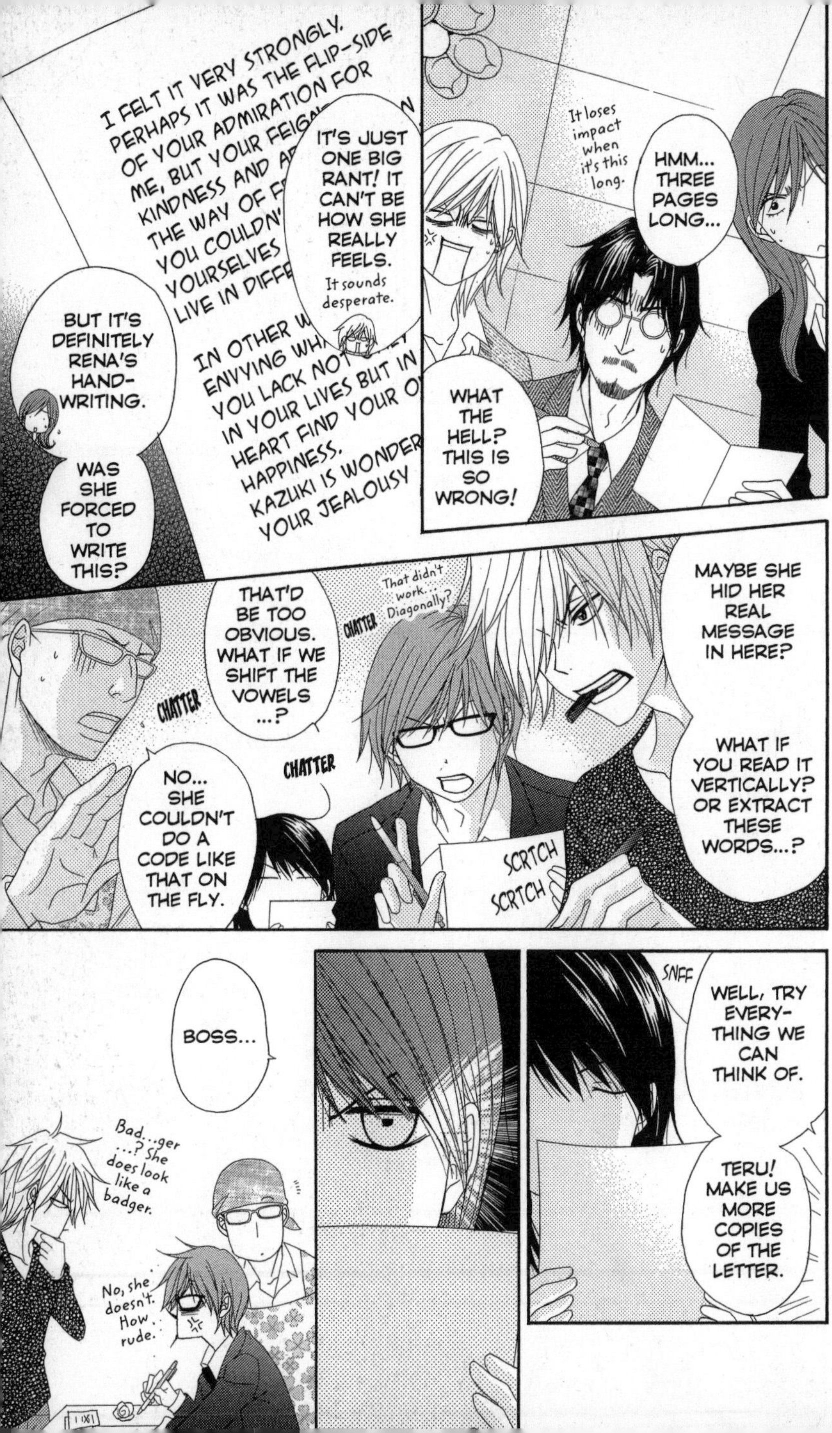
HMM... THREE PAGES LONG...
It loses impact when it's this long.
WHAT THE HELL? THIS IS SO WRONG!
I FELT IT VERY STRONGLY. PERHAPS IT WAS THE FLIP-SIDE OF YOUR ADMIRATION FOR ME, BUT YOUR FEIGN... KINDNESS AND AF... THE WAY OF F... YOU COULDN'... YOURSELVES... LIVE IN DIFFE...
IN OTHER W... ENVYING WH... YOU LACK NOT... IN YOUR LIVES BUT IN... HEART FIND YOUR O... HAPPINESS. KAZUKI IS WONDER... YOUR JEALOUSY
IT'S JUST ONE BIG RANT! IT CAN'T BE HOW SHE REALLY FEELS.
It sounds desperate.
BUT IT'S DEFINITELY RENA'S HAND-WRITING.
WAS SHE FORCED TO WRITE THIS?
MAYBE SHE HID HER REAL MESSAGE IN HERE?
WHAT IF YOU READ IT VERTICALLY? OR EXTRACT THESE WORDS...?
That didn't work... Diagonally?
CHATTER
THAT'D BE TOO OBVIOUS. WHAT IF WE SHIFT THE VOWELS ...?
CHATTER
CHATTER
SCRTCH SCRTCH
NO... SHE COULDN'T DO A CODE LIKE THAT ON THE FLY.
SNFF
WELL, TRY EVERY-THING WE CAN THINK OF.
TERU! MAKE US MORE COPIES OF THE LETTER.
BOSS...
Bad...ger...? She does look like a badger.
No, she doesn't. How rude.

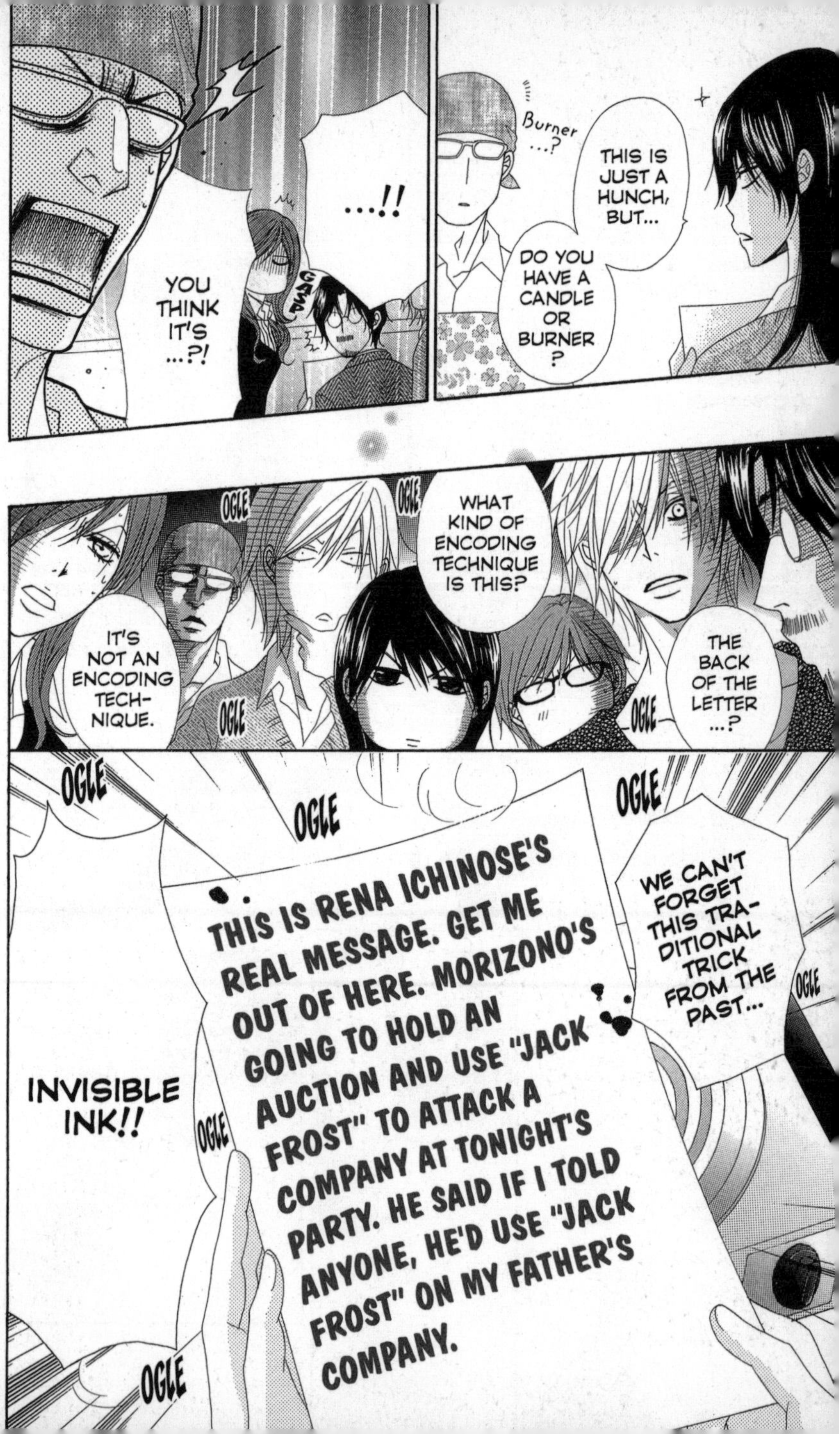
THIS IS JUST A HUNCH, BUT...
Burner ...?
DO YOU HAVE A CANDLE OR BURNER?
...!!
GASP
YOU THINK IT'S ...?!
OGLE
THE BACK OF THE LETTER ...?
OGLE
WHAT KIND OF ENCODING TECHNIQUE IS THIS?
OGLE
IT'S NOT AN ENCODING TECH-NIQUE.
OGLE
OGLE
OGLE
WE CAN'T FORGET THIS TRA-DITIONAL TRICK FROM THE PAST...
OGLE
OGLE
THIS IS RENA ICHINOSE'S REAL MESSAGE. GET ME OUT OF HERE. MORIZONO'S GOING TO HOLD AN AUCTION AND USE "JACK FROST" TO ATTACK A COMPANY AT TONIGHT'S PARTY. HE SAID IF I TOLD ANYONE, HE'D USE "JACK FROST" ON MY FATHER'S COMPANY.
OGLE
INVISIBLE INK!!
OGLE
OGLE

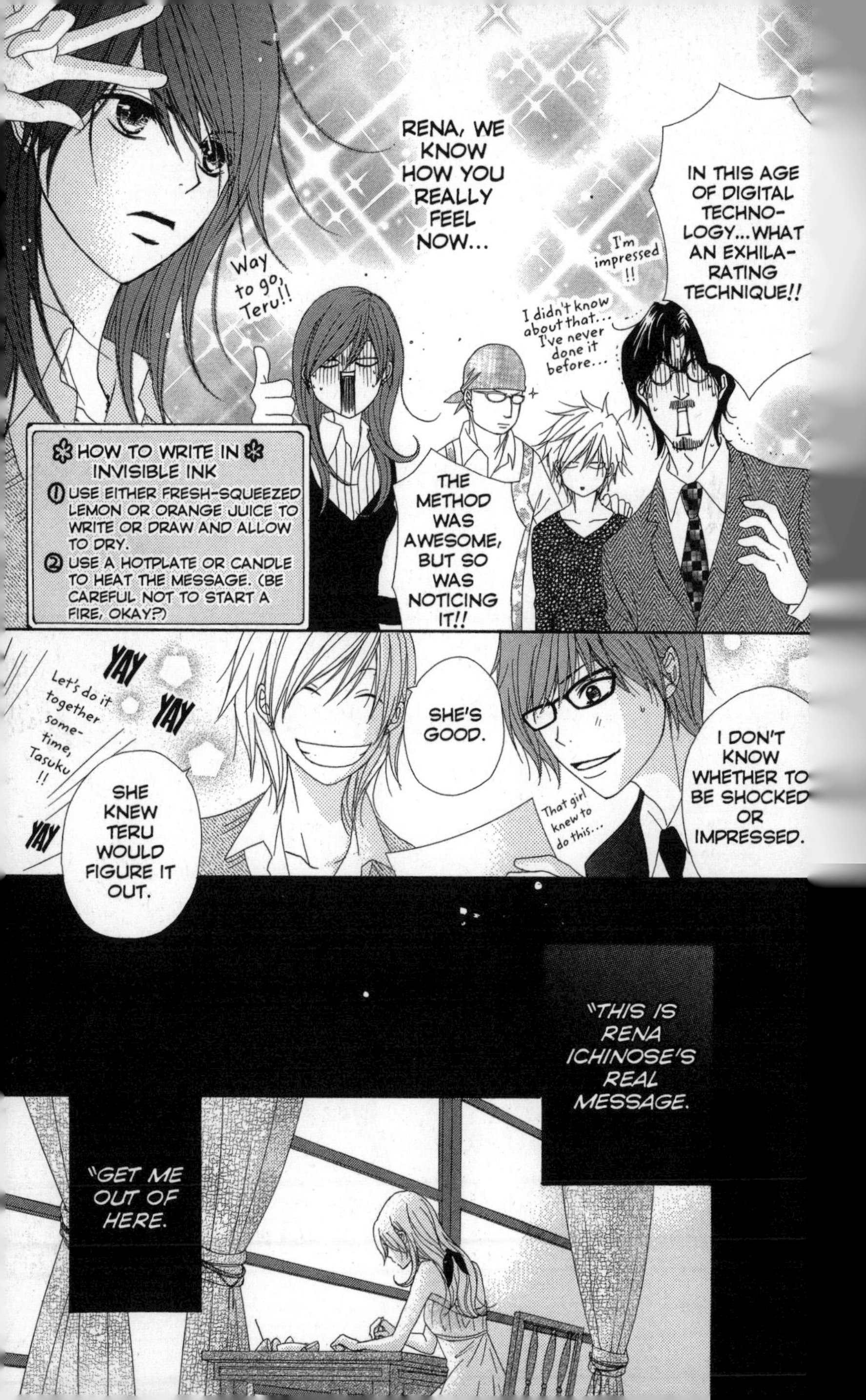
IN THIS AGE OF DIGITAL TECHNOLOGY...WHAT AN EXHILARATING TECHNIQUE!!
I'm impressed!!
I didn't know about that... I've never done it before...
RENA, WE KNOW HOW YOU REALLY FEEL NOW...
Way to go, Teru!!
THE METHOD WAS AWESOME, BUT SO WAS NOTICING IT!!
HOW TO WRITE IN INVISIBLE INK
① USE EITHER FRESH-SQUEEZED LEMON OR ORANGE JUICE TO WRITE OR DRAW AND ALLOW TO DRY.
② USE A HOTPLATE OR CANDLE TO HEAT THE MESSAGE. (BE CAREFUL NOT TO START A FIRE, OKAY?)
I DON'T KNOW WHETHER TO BE SHOCKED OR IMPRESSED.
That girl knew to do this...
SHE'S GOOD.
YAY
YAY
Let's do it together sometime, Tasuku!!
SHE KNEW TERU WOULD FIGURE IT OUT.
YAY
"THIS IS RENA ICHINOSE'S REAL MESSAGE.
"GET ME OUT OF HERE.

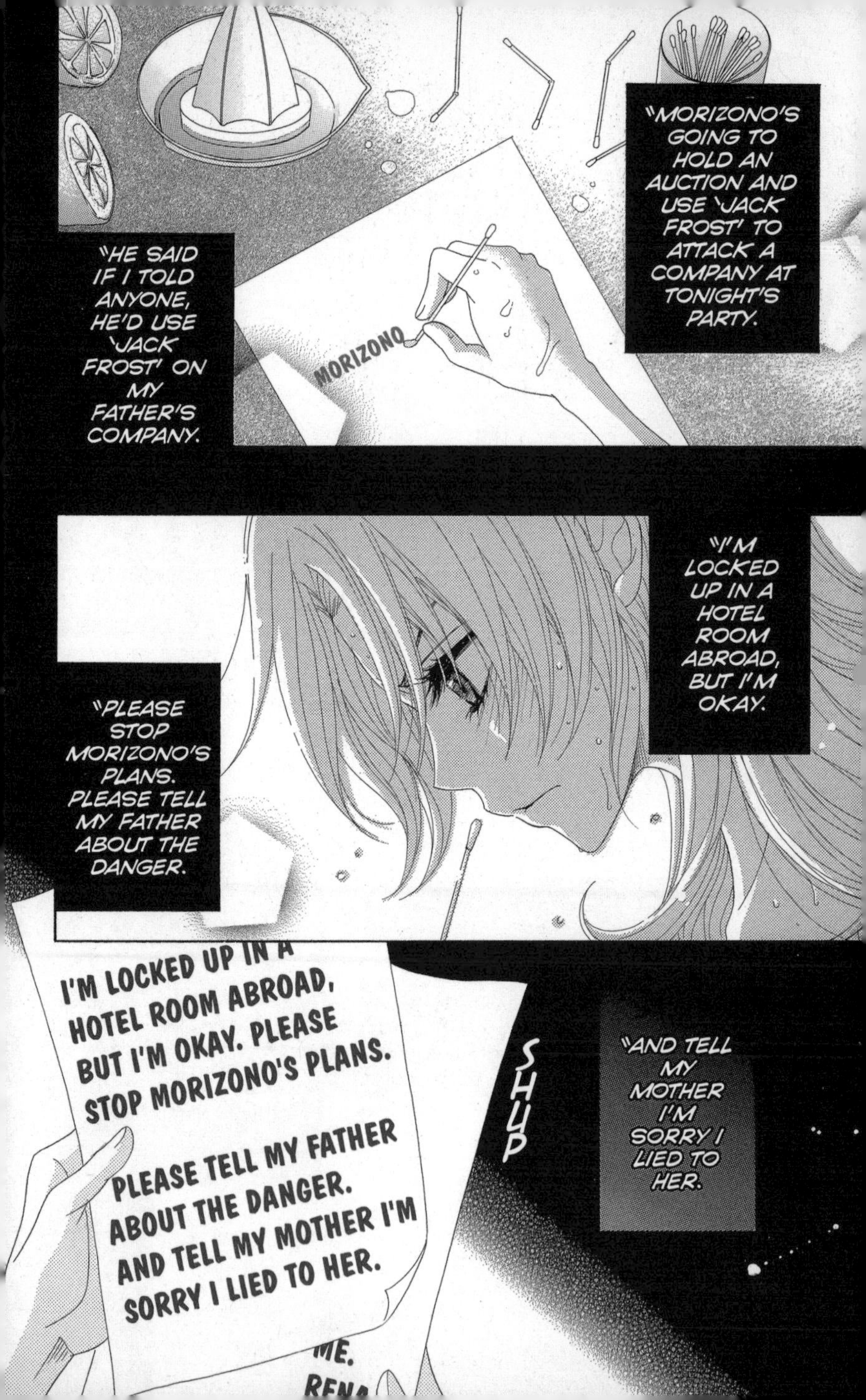
"MORIZONO'S GOING TO HOLD AN AUCTION AND USE 'JACK FROST' TO ATTACK A COMPANY AT TONIGHT'S PARTY.
MORIZONO
"HE SAID IF I TOLD ANYONE, HE'D USE 'JACK FROST' ON MY FATHER'S COMPANY.
"I'M LOCKED UP IN A HOTEL ROOM ABROAD, BUT I'M OKAY.
"PLEASE STOP MORIZONO'S PLANS. PLEASE TELL MY FATHER ABOUT THE DANGER.
"AND TELL MY MOTHER I'M SORRY I LIED TO HER.
SHUP
I'M LOCKED UP IN A HOTEL ROOM ABROAD, BUT I'M OKAY. PLEASE STOP MORIZONO'S PLANS.
PLEASE TELL MY FATHER ABOUT THE DANGER. AND TELL MY MOTHER I'M SORRY I LIED TO HER.
ME.

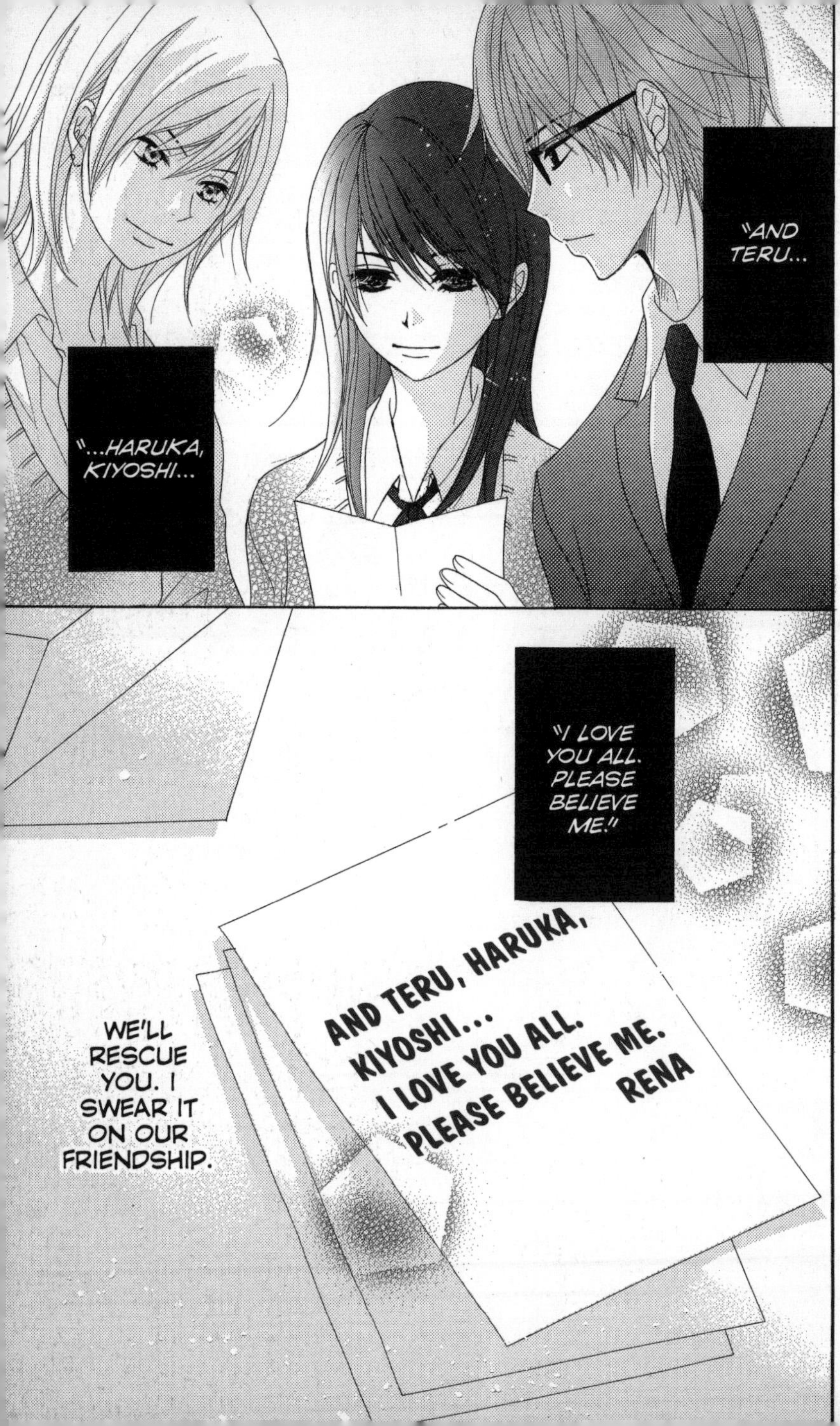
"AND TERU...
"...HARUKA, KIYOSHI...
"I LOVE YOU ALL. PLEASE BELIEVE ME."
AND TERU, HARUKA, KIYOSHI... I LOVE YOU ALL. PLEASE BELIEVE ME. RENA
WE'LL RESCUE YOU. I SWEAR IT ON OUR FRIENDSHIP.

THERE IS A *DENGEKI DAISY* FAN SEGMENT BOLDLY FEATURED IN *BETSUCOMI* THAT IS APTLY TITLED "THE SECRET SCHOOL CUSTODIAN OFFICE♥"! WITH ARBITRARY EYES, WE EXAMINED ALL THE GREAT WORK FEATURED THERE AND PICKED THE "BEST" AMONG THEM THAT WE WANTED TO LEAVE FOR POSTERITY!

THE "BEST OF" FOR VOLUME 11... THE ANNOUNCEMENT OF "THE READERS' '7-7'!!"

THIS FEATURE CELEBRATES THE TOTAL SALES OF 1.3 MILLION VOLUMES OF COMICS THAT WERE SERIALIZED IN THE NOVEMBER 2011 ISSUE OF *BETSUCOMI*. IN RESPONSE TO THE "GOOD" (?) COMMENTS ABOUT KUROSAKI, OUR READERS GOT TOGETHER AND PROVIDED THE "BAD"!!

(GOOD) HANDSOME, SADISTIC KUROSAKI—THE GENIUS HACKER

(BAD)

AUTO-GRAPH WINNER

★ **PEEKS AT TERU'S PANTIES** -WASHAWASHA, MIYAGI PREFECTURE

★ **UNABLE TO DRAW A LIKENESS** -DONATCHO, CHIBA PREFECTURE

★ **JUST NEEDS TIME TO WARM UP TO PEOPLE** -NOTO, AICHI PREFECTURE

★ **NOT GOING BALD LIKE EVERYONE IS HOPING** -SAKINO, YAMAGUCHI PREFECTURE

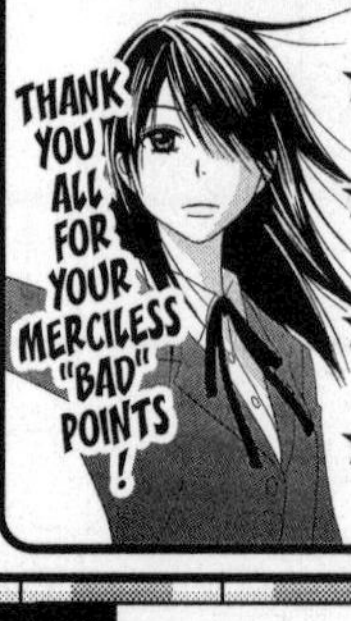
THANK YOU ALL FOR YOUR MERCILESS "BAD" POINTS!

★ **JUST TALKS THAT WAY (HA HA)** -TIARA, NAGASAKI PREFECTURE

★ **MAKES ME WONDER ABOUT THE FUTURE OF BLONDE HAIR** -SAMMY, GIFU PREFECTURE

★ **HAS A LOLITA COMPLEX OVER TERU** -NAN, NIIGATA PREFECTURE

★ **ACTUALLY A MASOCHIST AND A COWARD** -BURNT STRAWBERRY, NIIGATA PREFECTURE

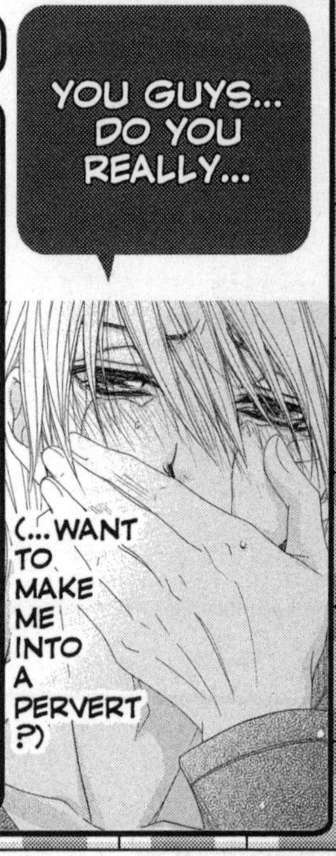
YOU GUYS... DO YOU REALLY...
(...WANT TO MAKE ME INTO A PERVERT?)

JUDGES' COMMENTS

■ FROM AN AUTHOR'S VIEWPOINT, I DON'T WANT TO CONCEDE THAT KUROSAKI IS HANDSOME. HE'S NOT A GENIUS, AND HE'S NOT SADISTIC, EITHER. IN OTHER WORDS, THERE AREN'T ANY "GOOD" POINTS THAT ARE UNIQUELY KUROSAKI. (HEAD JUDGE: KYOUSUKE MOTOMI)

■ KUROSAKI IS SO LOVED, ISN'T HE? AVOIDING OBVIOUS KEY WORDS LIKE "LOLITA COMPLEX," "BALD," AND "COWARD" GAVE OUR WINNER THE EDGE IN SNAGGING THE AUTOGRAPH. CONGRATULATIONS! (JUDGE: DAISY EDITOR)

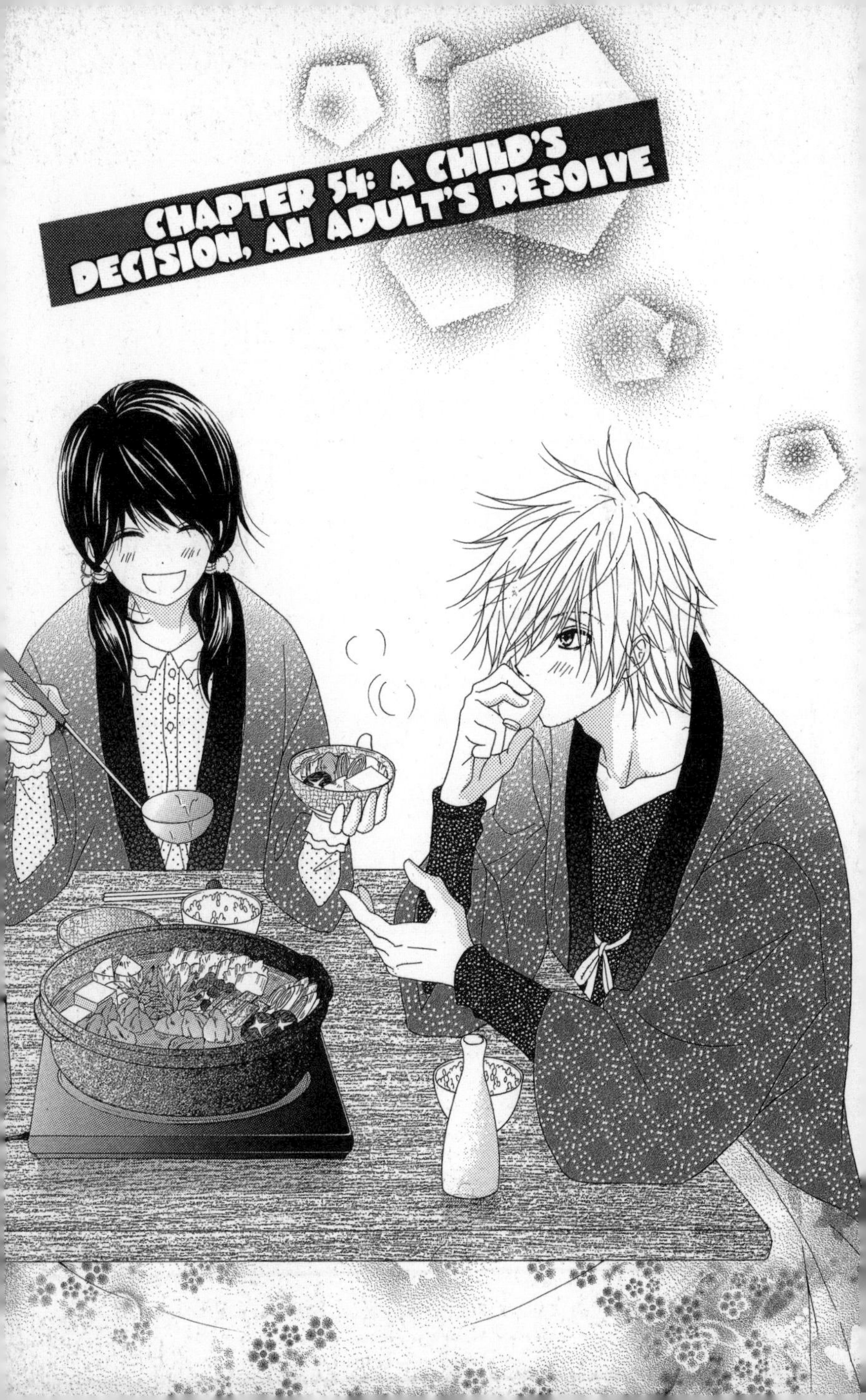
CHAPTER 54: A CHILD'S DECISION, AN ADULT'S RESOLVE

"PLEASE STOP MORIZONO'S PLANS. PLEASE TELL MY FATHER ABOUT THE DANGER."

ENA ICHINOSE'S MESSAGE. GET ME OF HERE. MORIZO- 'S GOING TO HOLD AN AUCTION AND USE "JACK FROST" TO ATTACK A COMPANY AT TONIGHT'S PARTY. ...SAID IF I TOLD ...D USE "JACK A... FATHER'S

AND TERU, HARUKA,

"AND TERU, HARUKA, KIYOSHI... I LOVE YOU ALL. PLEASE BELIEVE ME."

CHILDREN START PLAYING AROUND WITH "INVISIBLE INK" WHEN THEY'RE IN GRADE SCHOOL, SO THE FACT THAT KUROSAKI NEVER DID IT BEFORE HAS NOTHING TO DO WITH HIS UPBRINGING. WHEN I ASKED AROUND, THERE WERE QUITE A FEW PEOPLE WHO HAD NEVER DONE IT BEFORE. (THE AUTHOR HAS, THOUGH.)

WHEN I THINK ABOUT IT NOW, PARENTS WHO LET THEIR CHILDREN DO THIS WOULD PROBABLY BE SCARED.

YOU HAVE TO USE FIRE, AND WHETHER YOU USE LEMONS OR ORANGES, FRUIT ISN'T CHEAP.

IT'S BELIEVED THAT AFTERWARDS, KUROSAKI ACTUALLY HAD BOSS TEACH HIM HOW TO DO IT. AND HE WAS IMPRESSED. I THINK HE STILL LIKES THESE LITTLE EXPERIMENTS.

Hey, who're you writing?

Oh... It's showing. Awesome.

FLAT- CHESTED BUT

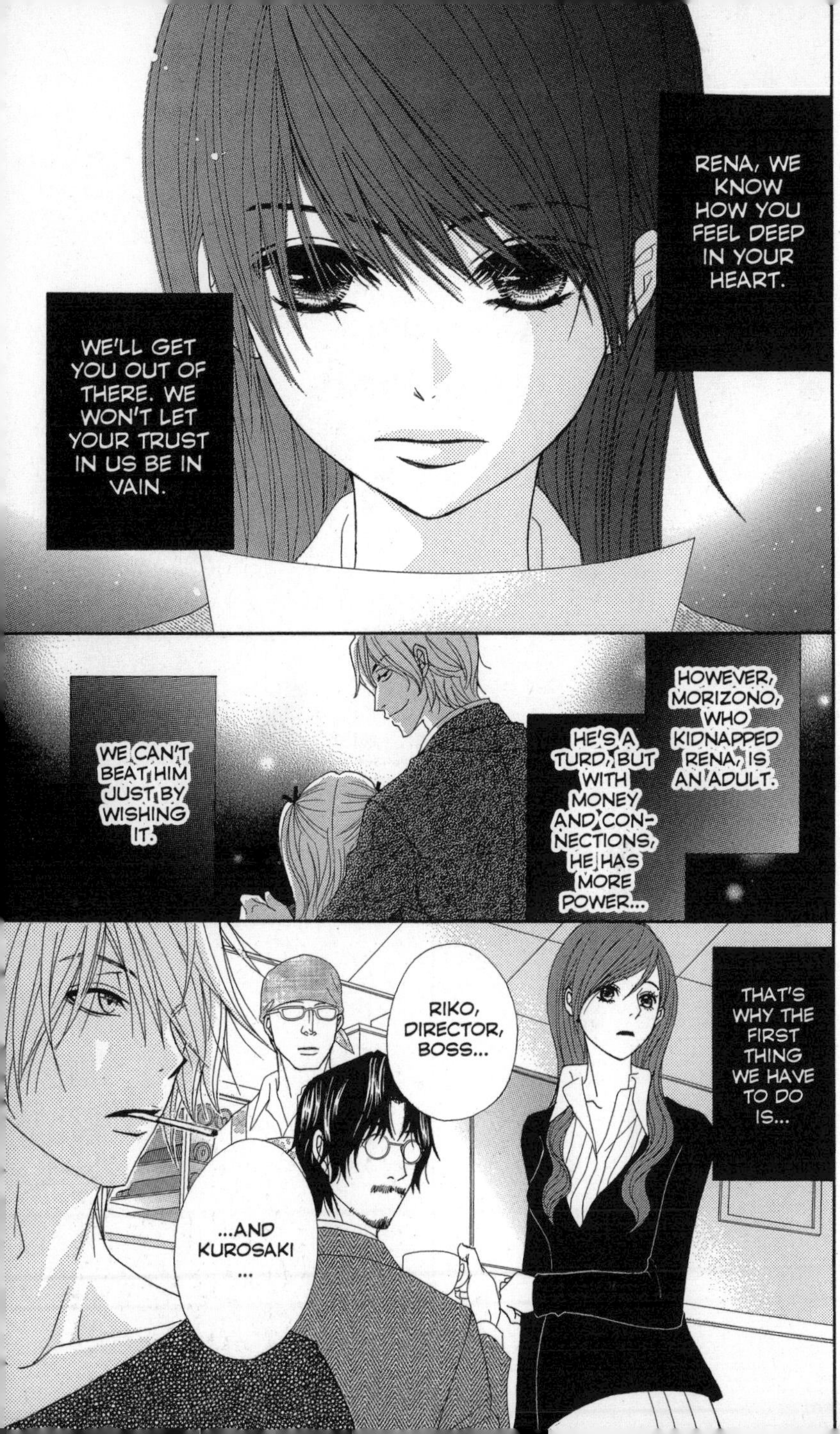
RENA, WE KNOW HOW YOU FEEL DEEP IN YOUR HEART.
WE'LL GET YOU OUT OF THERE. WE WON'T LET YOUR TRUST IN US BE IN VAIN.
HOWEVER, MORIZONO, WHO KIDNAPPED RENA, IS AN ADULT.
HE'S A TURD, BUT WITH MONEY AND CON-NECTIONS, HE HAS MORE POWER...
WE CAN'T BEAT HIM JUST BY WISHING IT.
THAT'S WHY THE FIRST THING WE HAVE TO DO IS...
RIKO, DIRECTOR, BOSS...
...AND KUROSAKI ...

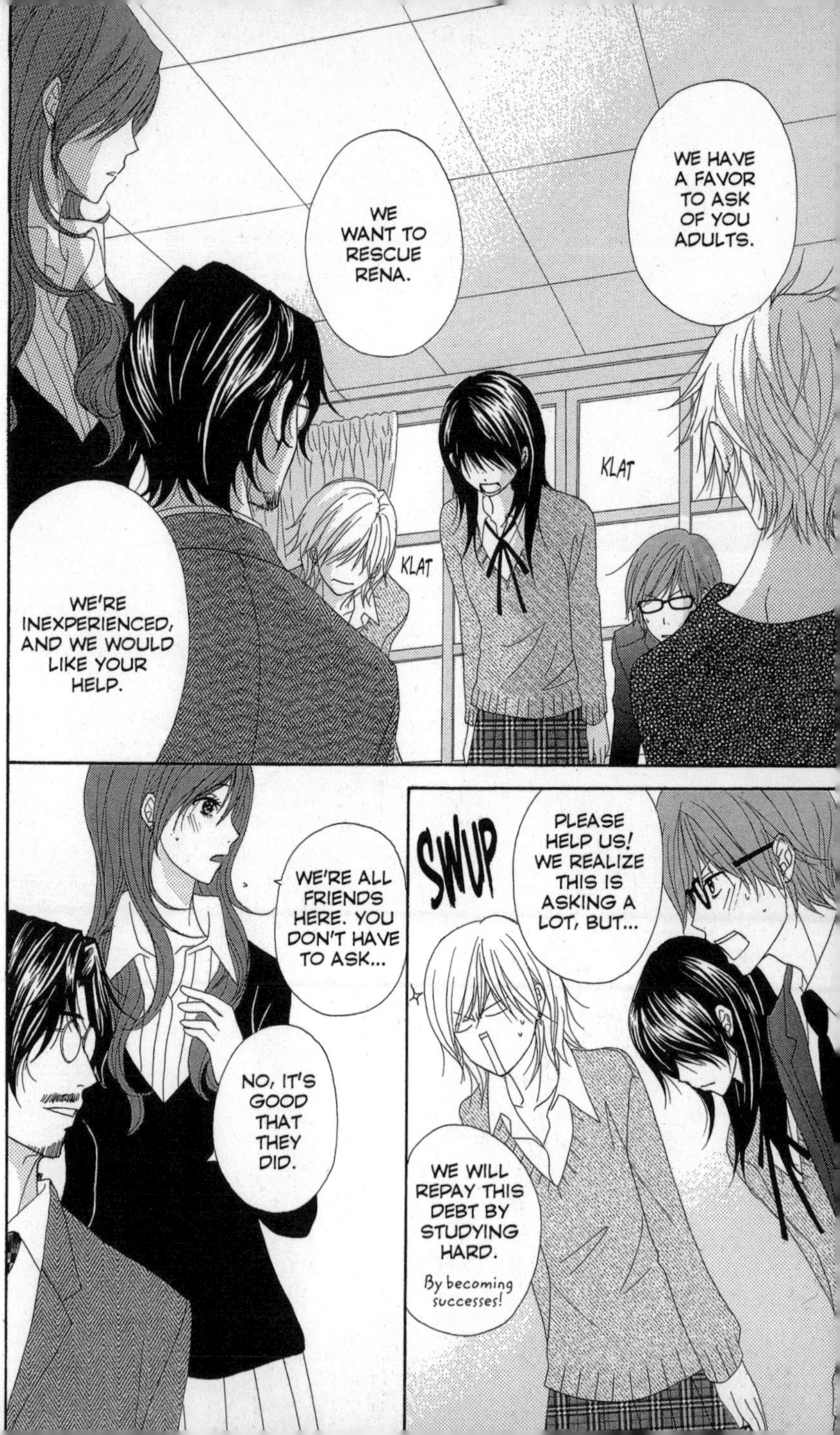
WE HAVE A FAVOR TO ASK OF YOU ADULTS.
WE WANT TO RESCUE RENA.
KLAT
KLAT
WE'RE INEXPERIENCED, AND WE WOULD LIKE YOUR HELP.
PLEASE HELP US! WE REALIZE THIS IS ASKING A LOT, BUT...
SWUP
WE WILL REPAY THIS DEBT BY STUDYING HARD.
By becoming successes!
WE'RE ALL FRIENDS HERE. YOU DON'T HAVE TO ASK...
NO, IT'S GOOD THAT THEY DID.

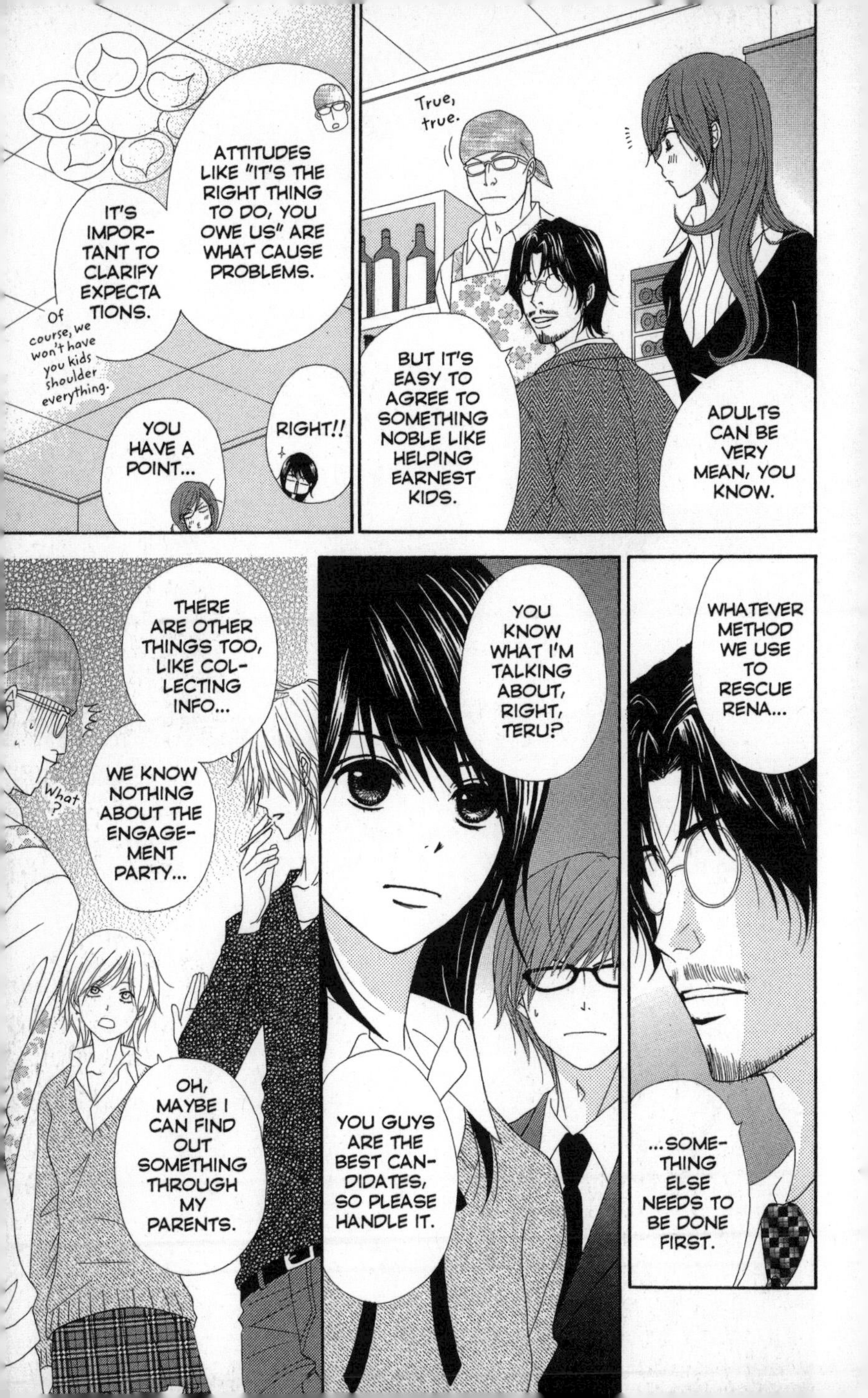
True, true.
ADULTS CAN BE VERY MEAN, YOU KNOW.
BUT IT'S EASY TO AGREE TO SOMETHING NOBLE LIKE HELPING EARNEST KIDS.
ATTITUDES LIKE "IT'S THE RIGHT THING TO DO, YOU OWE US" ARE WHAT CAUSE PROBLEMS.
IT'S IMPOR-TANT TO CLARIFY EXPECTA TIONS.
Of course, we won't have you kids shoulder everything.
RIGHT!!
YOU HAVE A POINT...
WHATEVER METHOD WE USE TO RESCUE RENA...
...SOME-THING ELSE NEEDS TO BE DONE FIRST.
YOU KNOW WHAT I'M TALKING ABOUT, RIGHT, TERU?
YOU GUYS ARE THE BEST CAN-DIDATES, SO PLEASE HANDLE IT.
THERE ARE OTHER THINGS TOO, LIKE COL-LECTING INFO...
What?
WE KNOW NOTHING ABOUT THE ENGAGE-MENT PARTY...
OH, MAYBE I CAN FIND OUT SOMETHING THROUGH MY PARENTS.

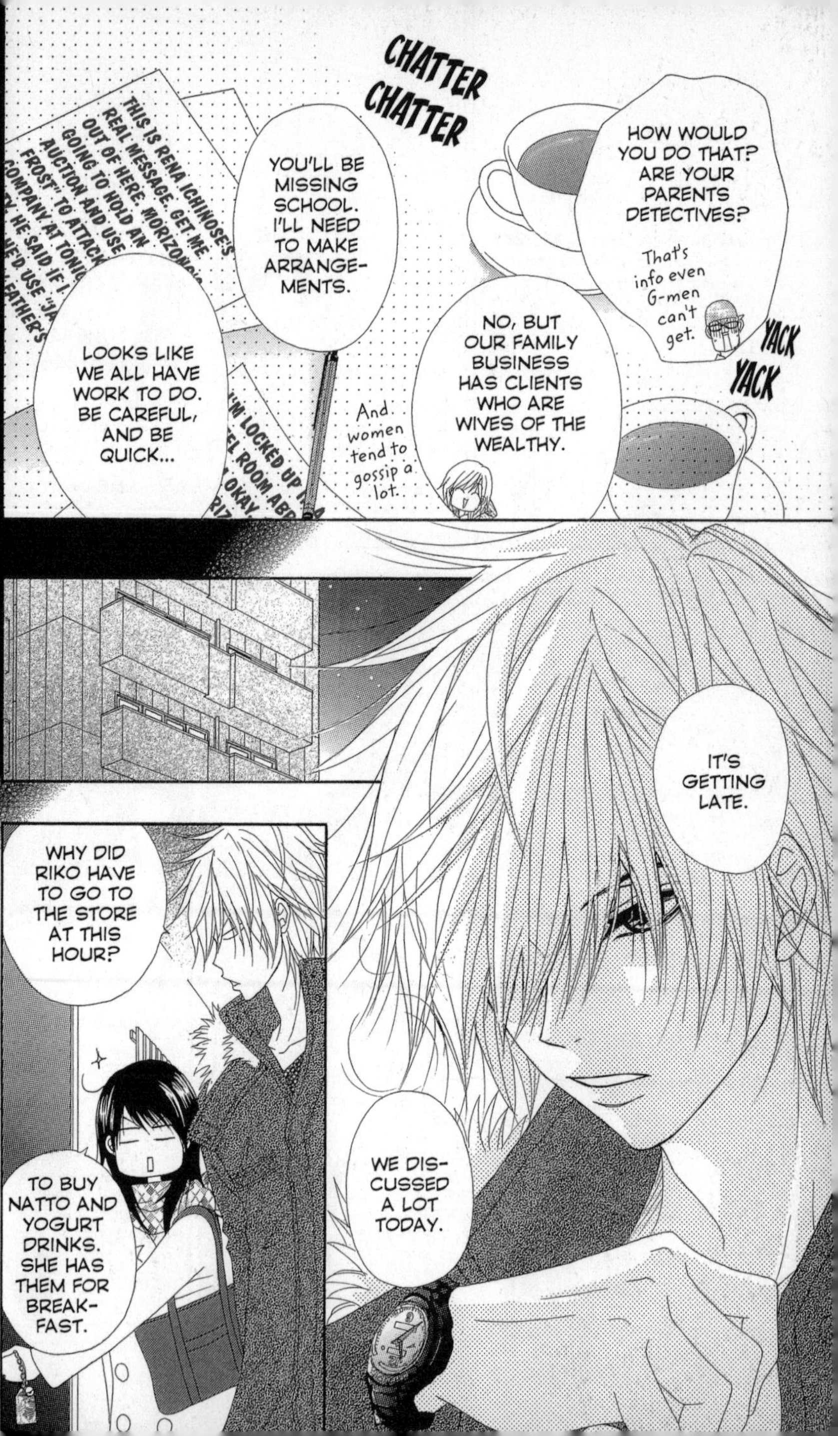
HOW WOULD YOU DO THAT? ARE YOUR PARENTS DETECTIVES?
That's info even G-men can't get.
YACK YACK
NO, BUT OUR FAMILY BUSINESS HAS CLIENTS WHO ARE WIVES OF THE WEALTHY.
And women tend to gossip a lot.
CHATTER CHATTER
YOU'LL BE MISSING SCHOOL. I'LL NEED TO MAKE ARRANGE-MENTS.
LOOKS LIKE WE ALL HAVE WORK TO DO. BE CAREFUL, AND BE QUICK...
IT'S GETTING LATE.
WE DIS-CUSSED A LOT TODAY.
WHY DID RIKO HAVE TO GO TO THE STORE AT THIS HOUR?
TO BUY NATTO AND YOGURT DRINKS. SHE HAS THEM FOR BREAK-FAST.

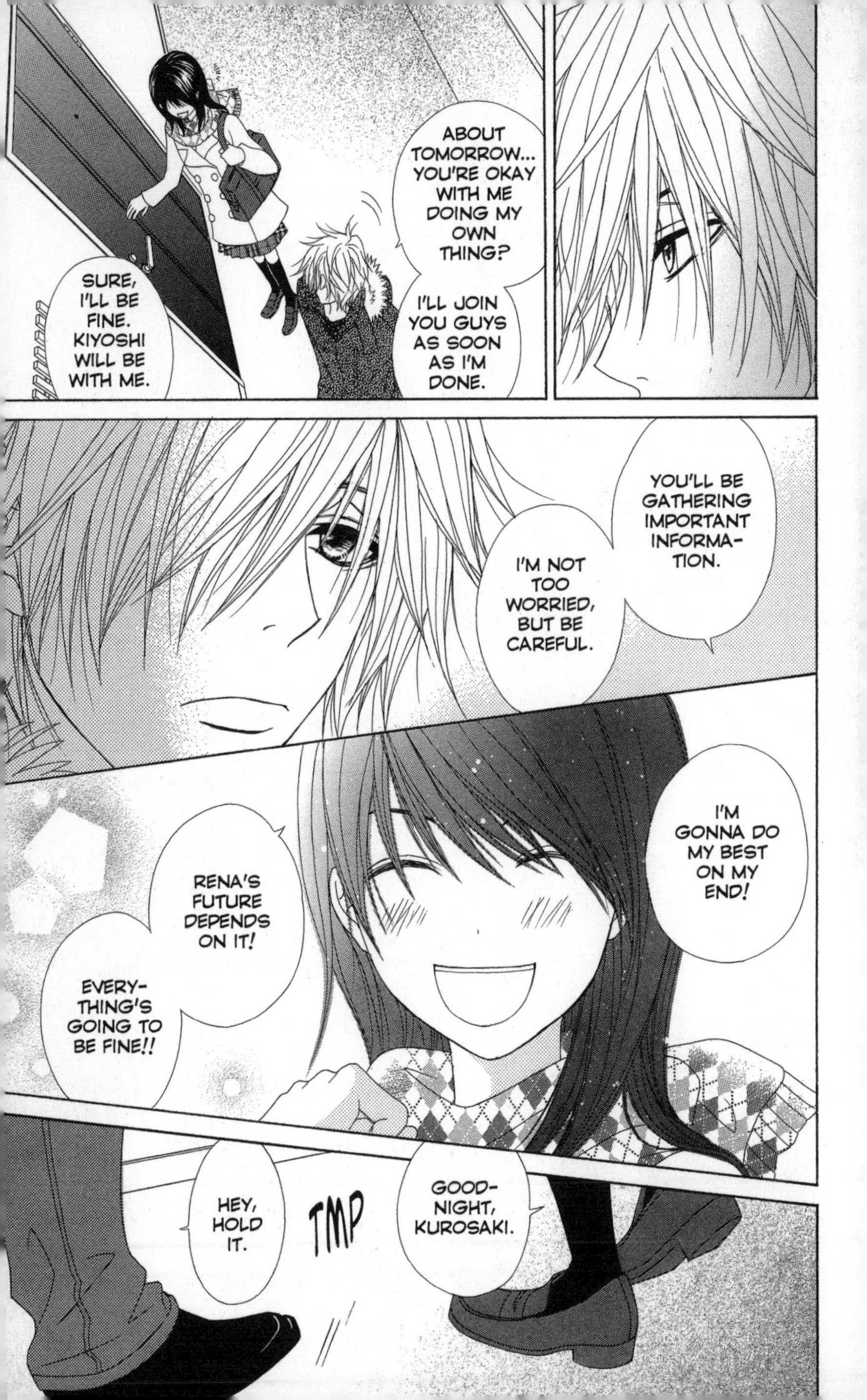
ABOUT TOMORROW... YOU'RE OKAY WITH ME DOING MY OWN THING?
I'LL JOIN YOU GUYS AS SOON AS I'M DONE.
SURE, I'LL BE FINE. KIYOSHI WILL BE WITH ME.
YOU'LL BE GATHERING IMPORTANT INFORMATION.
I'M NOT TOO WORRIED, BUT BE CAREFUL.
I'M GONNA DO MY BEST ON MY END!
RENA'S FUTURE DEPENDS ON IT!
EVERYTHING'S GOING TO BE FINE!!
GOOD-NIGHT, KUROSAKI.
TMP
HEY, HOLD IT.

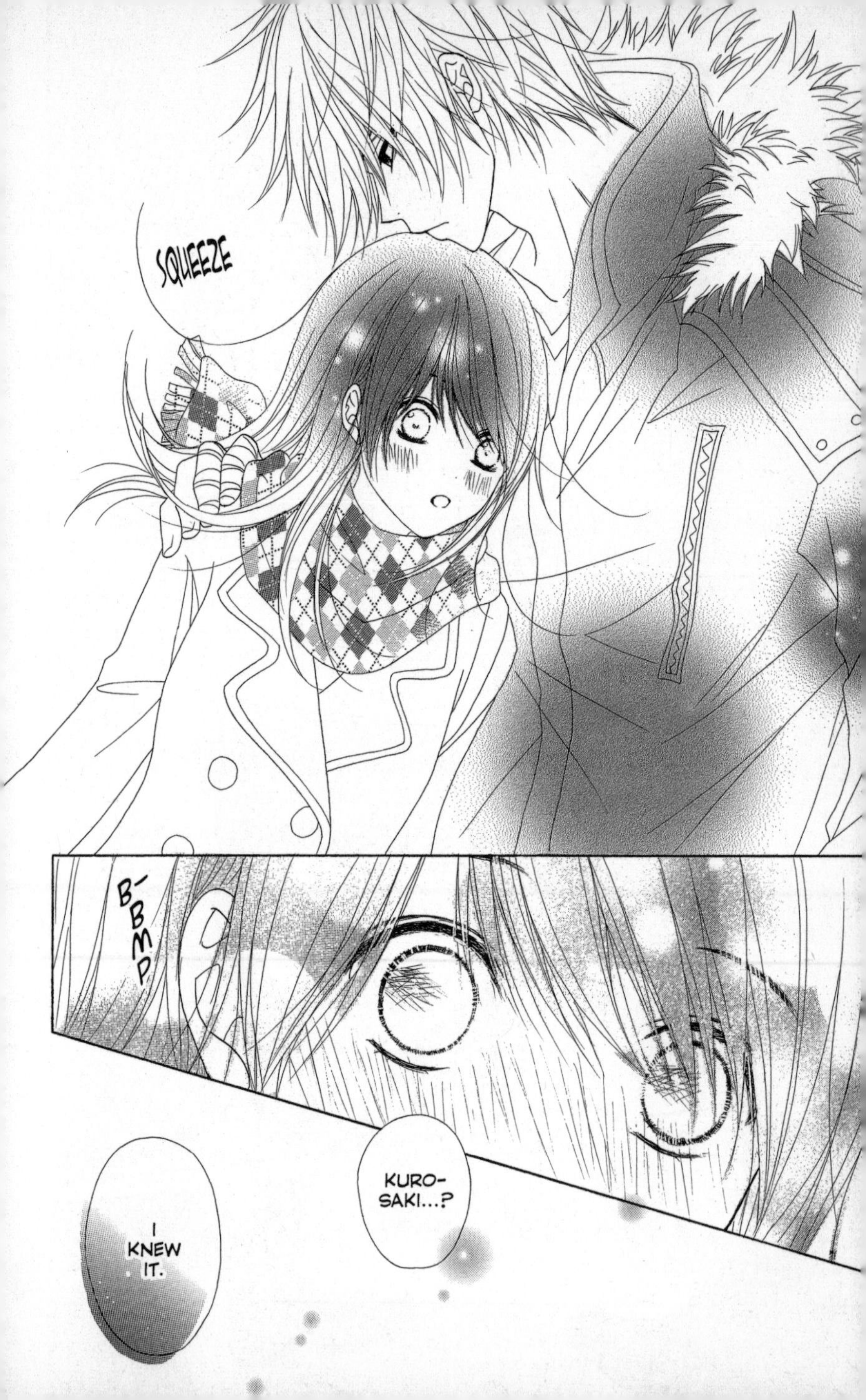
SQUEEZE
B-BMP
KURO-SAKI...?
I KNEW IT.

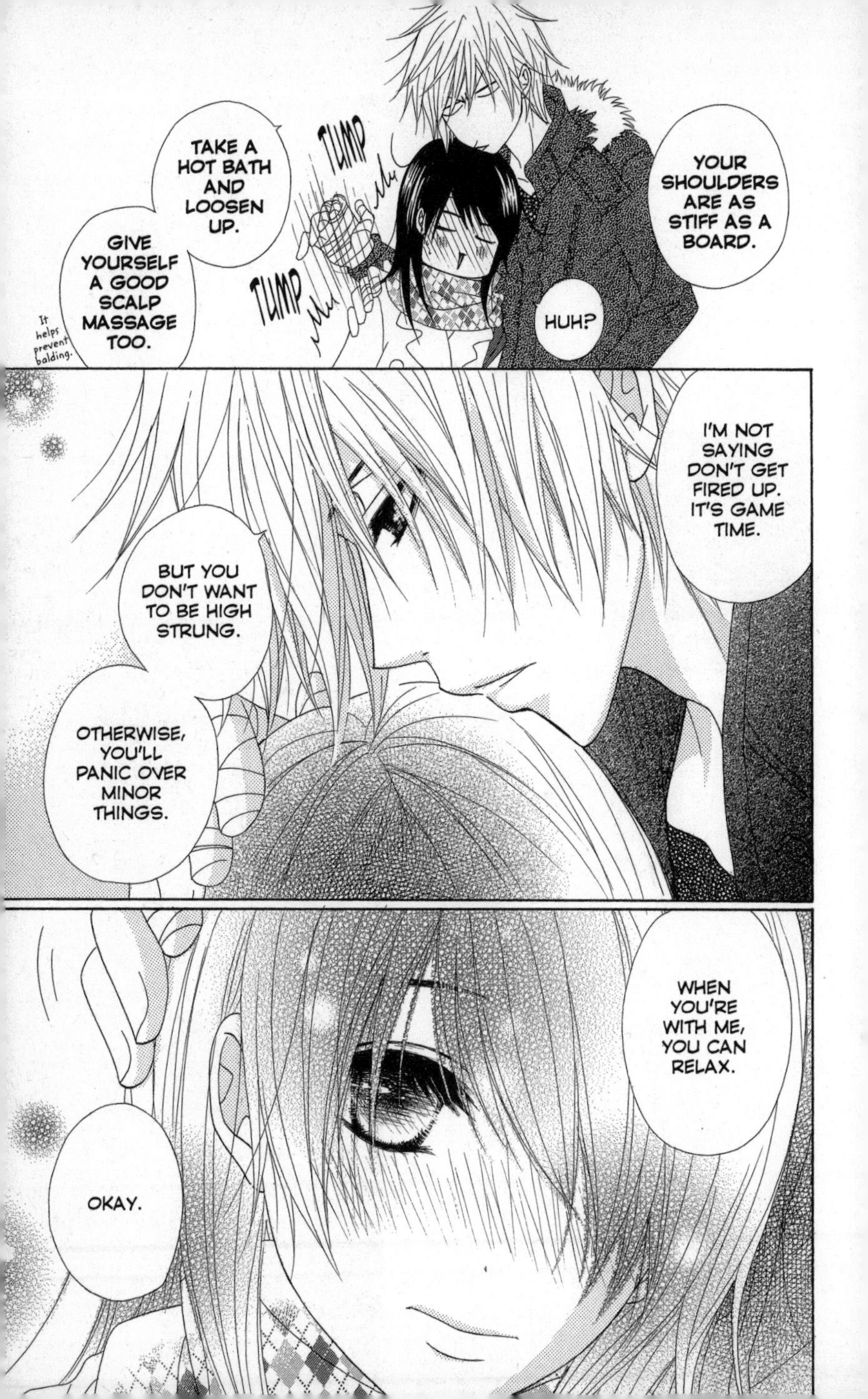
YOUR SHOULDERS ARE AS STIFF AS A BOARD.
HUH?
TUMP
TUMP
TAKE A HOT BATH AND LOOSEN UP.
GIVE YOURSELF A GOOD SCALP MASSAGE TOO.
It helps prevent balding.
I'M NOT SAYING DON'T GET FIRED UP. IT'S GAME TIME.
BUT YOU DON'T WANT TO BE HIGH STRUNG.
OTHERWISE, YOU'LL PANIC OVER MINOR THINGS.
WHEN YOU'RE WITH ME, YOU CAN RELAX.
OKAY.

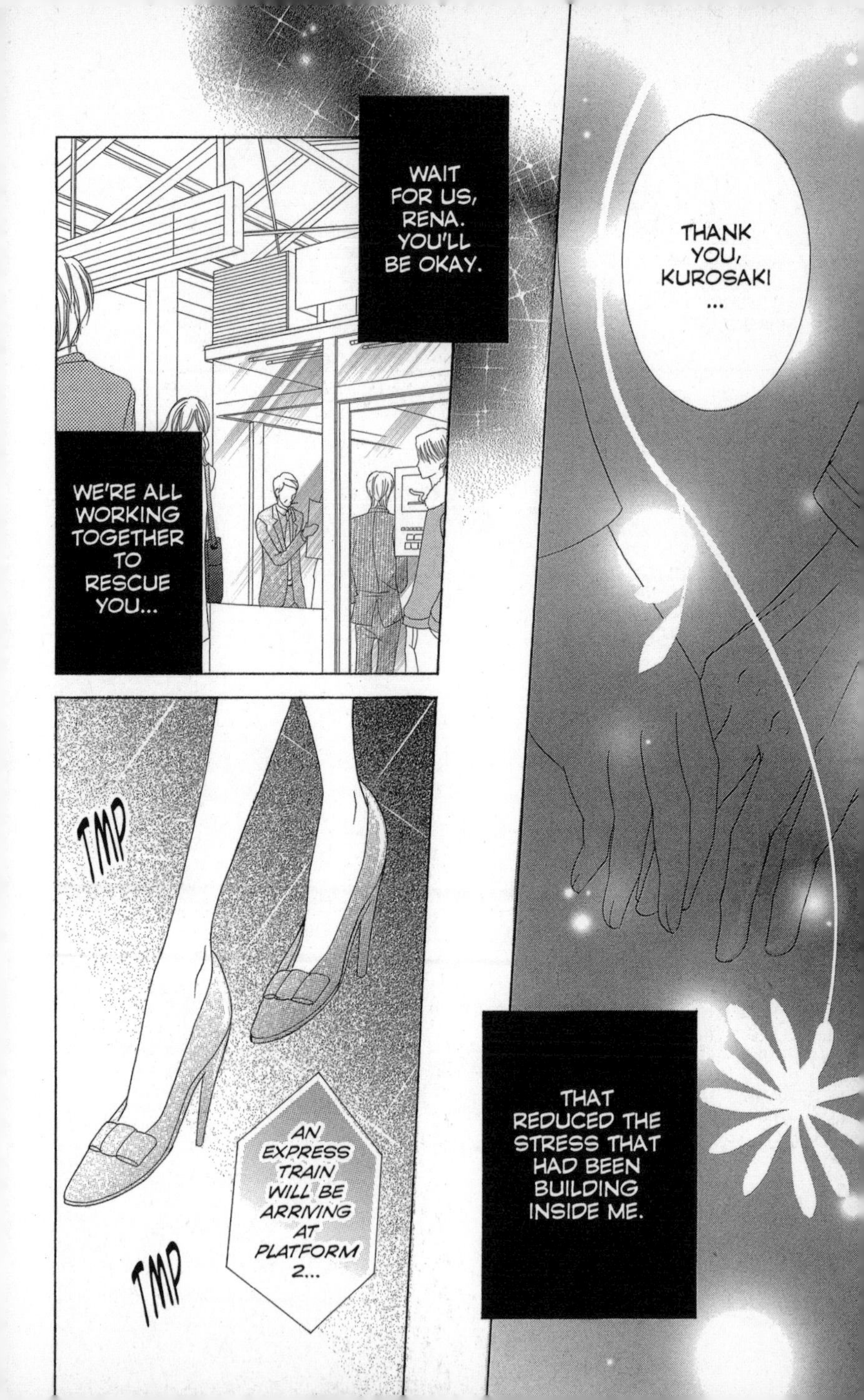
THANK YOU, KUROSAKI ...
THAT REDUCED THE STRESS THAT HAD BEEN BUILDING INSIDE ME.
WAIT FOR US, RENA. YOU'LL BE OKAY.
WE'RE ALL WORKING TOGETHER TO RESCUE YOU...
TMP
AN EXPRESS TRAIN WILL BE ARRIVING AT PLATFORM 2...
TMP

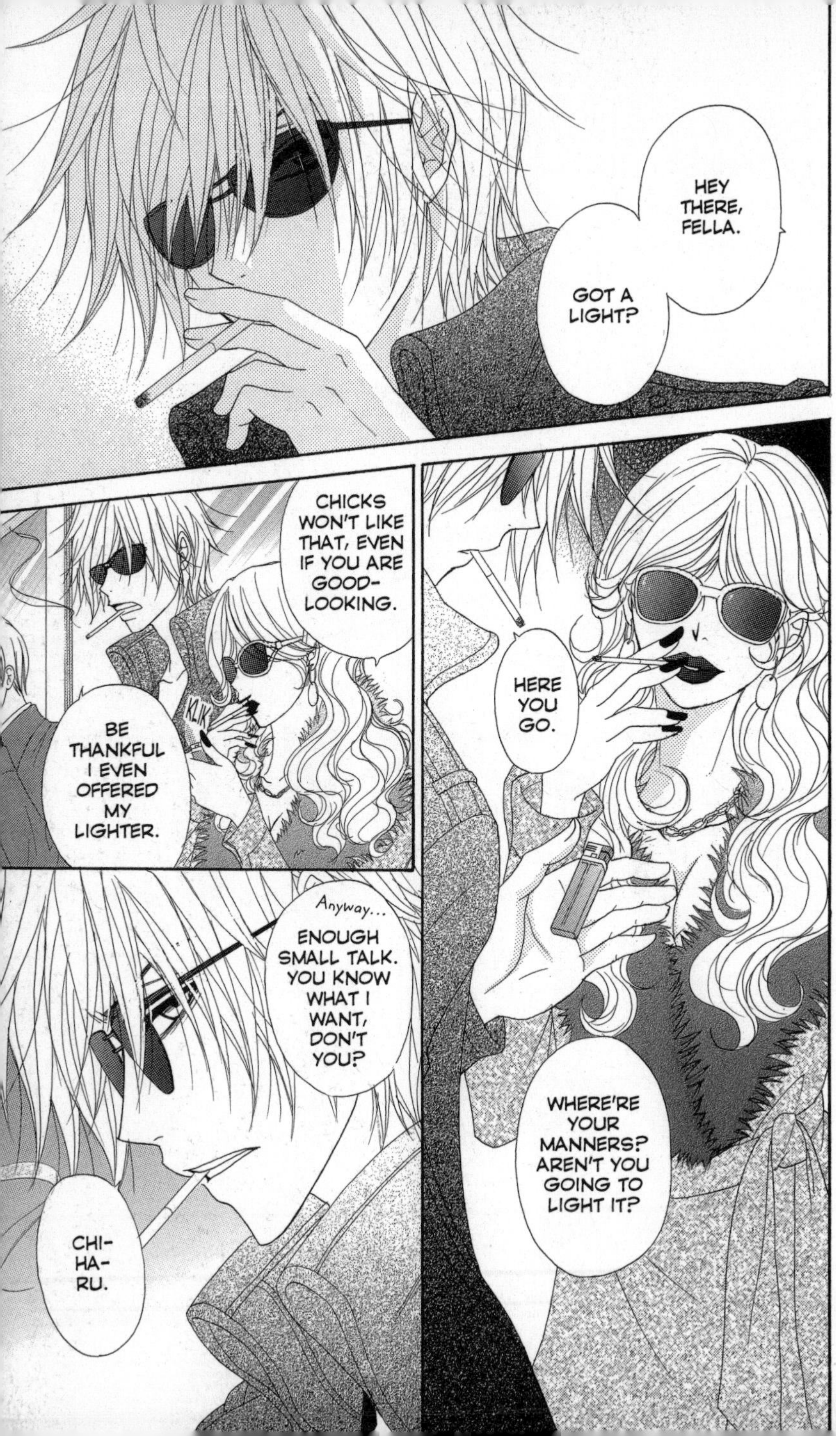
HEY THERE, FELLA.
GOT A LIGHT?
HERE YOU GO.
WHERE'RE YOUR MANNERS? AREN'T YOU GOING TO LIGHT IT?
CHICKS WON'T LIKE THAT, EVEN IF YOU ARE GOOD-LOOKING.
KLIK
BE THANKFUL I EVEN OFFERED MY LIGHTER.
Anyway...
ENOUGH SMALL TALK. YOU KNOW WHAT I WANT, DON'T YOU?
CHI-HA-RU.

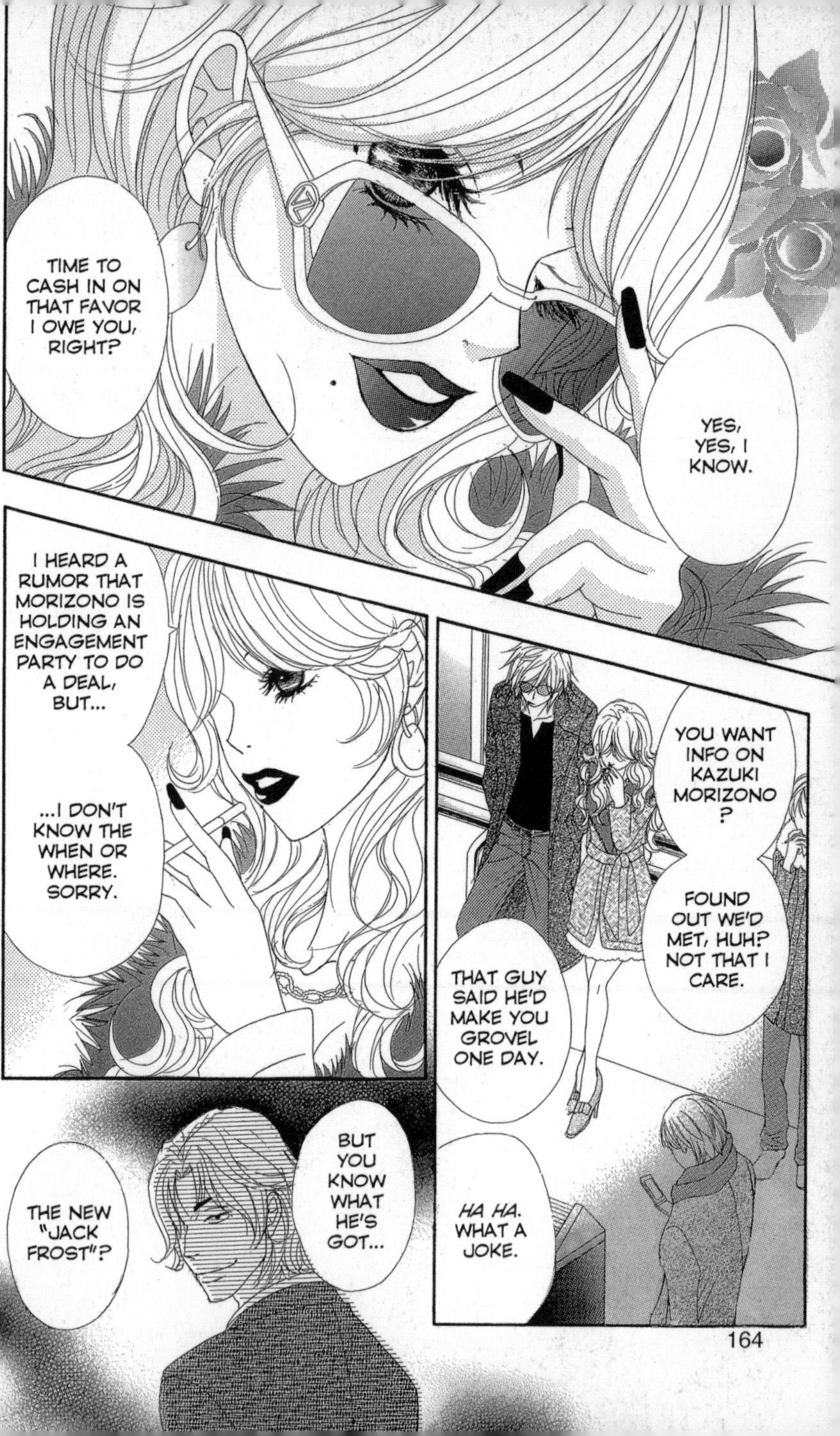
YES, YES, I KNOW.
TIME TO CASH IN ON THAT FAVOR I OWE YOU, RIGHT?
YOU WANT INFO ON KAZUKI MORIZONO?
FOUND OUT WE'D MET, HUH? NOT THAT I CARE.
THAT GUY SAID HE'D MAKE YOU GROVEL ONE DAY.
HA HA. WHAT A JOKE.
I HEARD A RUMOR THAT MORIZONO IS HOLDING AN ENGAGEMENT PARTY TO DO A DEAL, BUT...
...I DON'T KNOW THE WHEN OR WHERE. SORRY.
BUT YOU KNOW WHAT HE'S GOT...
THE NEW "JACK FROST"?

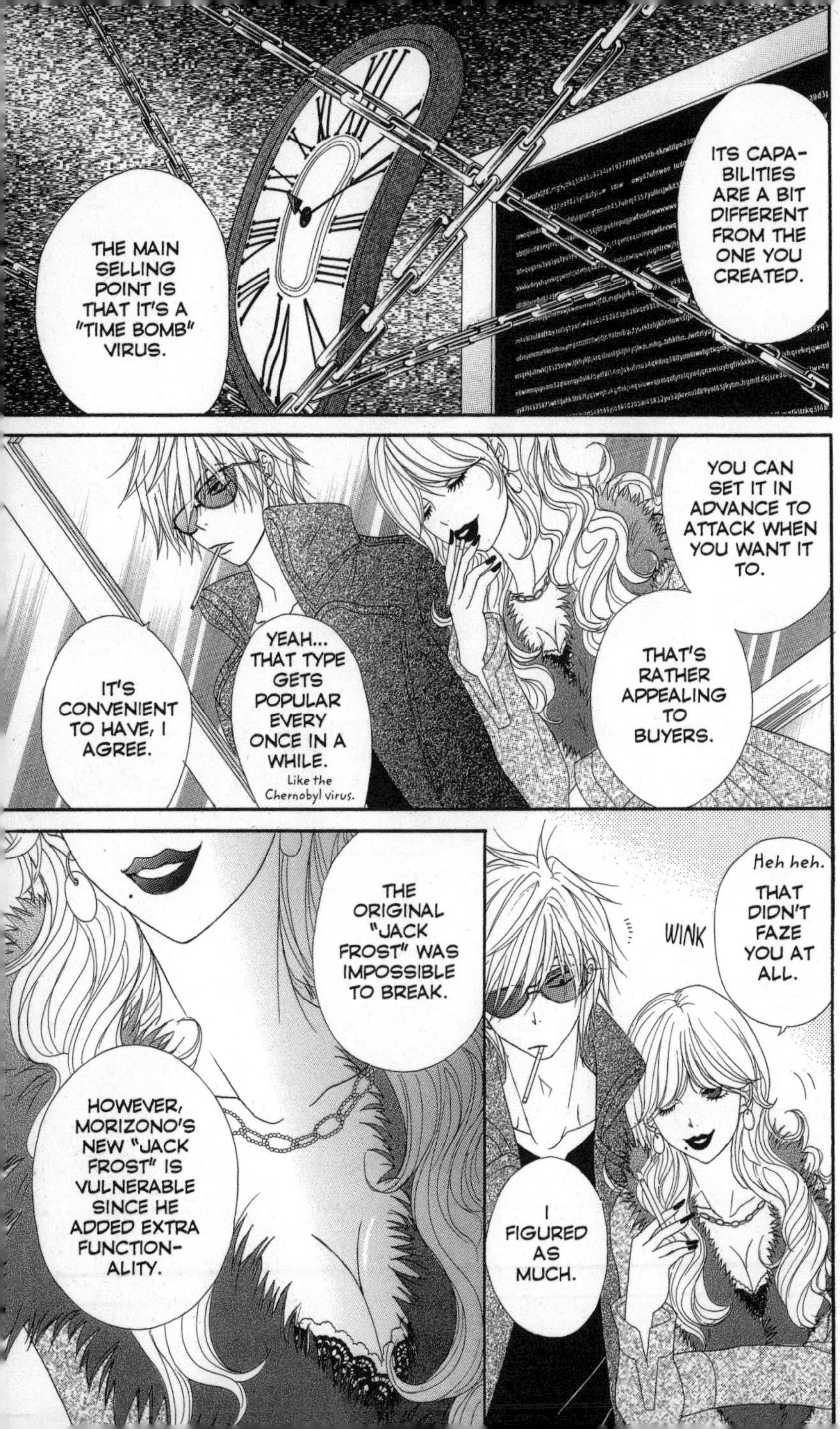
ITS CAPA-BILITIES ARE A BIT DIFFERENT FROM THE ONE YOU CREATED.
THE MAIN SELLING POINT IS THAT IT'S A "TIME BOMB" VIRUS.
YOU CAN SET IT IN ADVANCE TO ATTACK WHEN YOU WANT IT TO.
THAT'S RATHER APPEALING TO BUYERS.
YEAH... THAT TYPE GETS POPULAR EVERY ONCE IN A WHILE.
Like the Chernobyl virus.
IT'S CONVENIENT TO HAVE, I AGREE.
Heh heh.
THAT DIDN'T FAZE YOU AT ALL.
WINK
I FIGURED AS MUCH.
THE ORIGINAL "JACK FROST" WAS IMPOSSIBLE TO BREAK.
HOWEVER, MORIZONO'S NEW "JACK FROST" IS VULNERABLE SINCE HE ADDED EXTRA FUNCTION-ALITY.

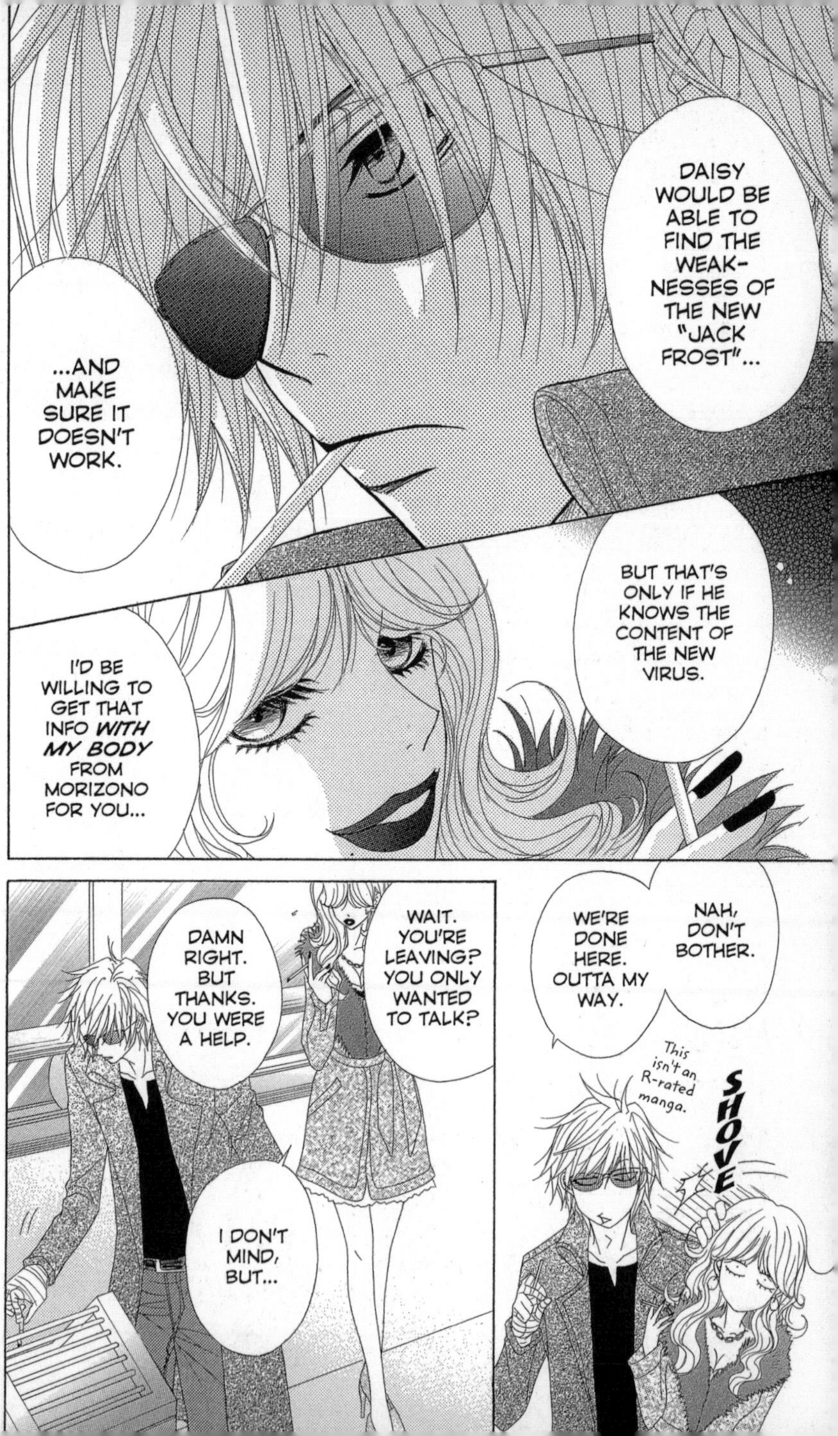
DAISY WOULD BE ABLE TO FIND THE WEAK-NESSES OF THE NEW "JACK FROST"...
...AND MAKE SURE IT DOESN'T WORK.
BUT THAT'S ONLY IF HE KNOWS THE CONTENT OF THE NEW VIRUS.
I'D BE WILLING TO GET THAT INFO *WITH MY BODY* FROM MORIZONO FOR YOU...
NAH, DON'T BOTHER.
WE'RE DONE HERE. OUTTA MY WAY.
This isn't an R-rated manga.
SHOVE
WAIT. YOU'RE LEAVING? YOU ONLY WANTED TO TALK?
DAMN RIGHT. BUT THANKS. YOU WERE A HELP.
I DON'T MIND, BUT...

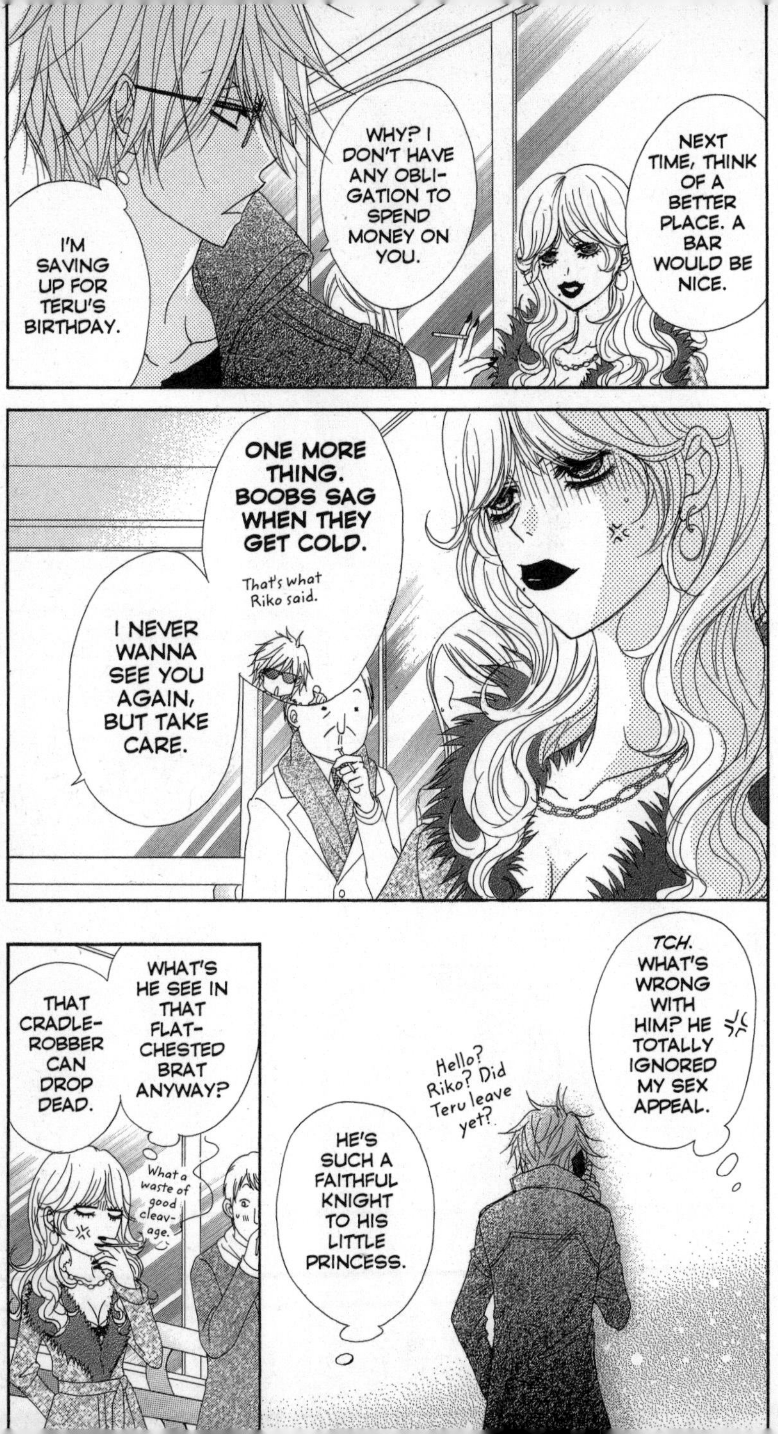
NEXT TIME, THINK OF A BETTER PLACE. A BAR WOULD BE NICE.
WHY? I DON'T HAVE ANY OBLIGATION TO SPEND MONEY ON YOU.
I'M SAVING UP FOR TERU'S BIRTHDAY.
ONE MORE THING. BOOBS SAG WHEN THEY GET COLD.
That's what Riko said.
I NEVER WANNA SEE YOU AGAIN, BUT TAKE CARE.
TCH. WHAT'S WRONG WITH HIM? HE TOTALLY IGNORED MY SEX APPEAL.
Hello? Riko? Did Teru leave yet?
HE'S SUCH A FAITHFUL KNIGHT TO HIS LITTLE PRINCESS.
WHAT'S HE SEE IN THAT FLAT-CHESTED BRAT ANYWAY?
THAT CRADLE-ROBBER CAN DROP DEAD.
What a waste of good cleavage.

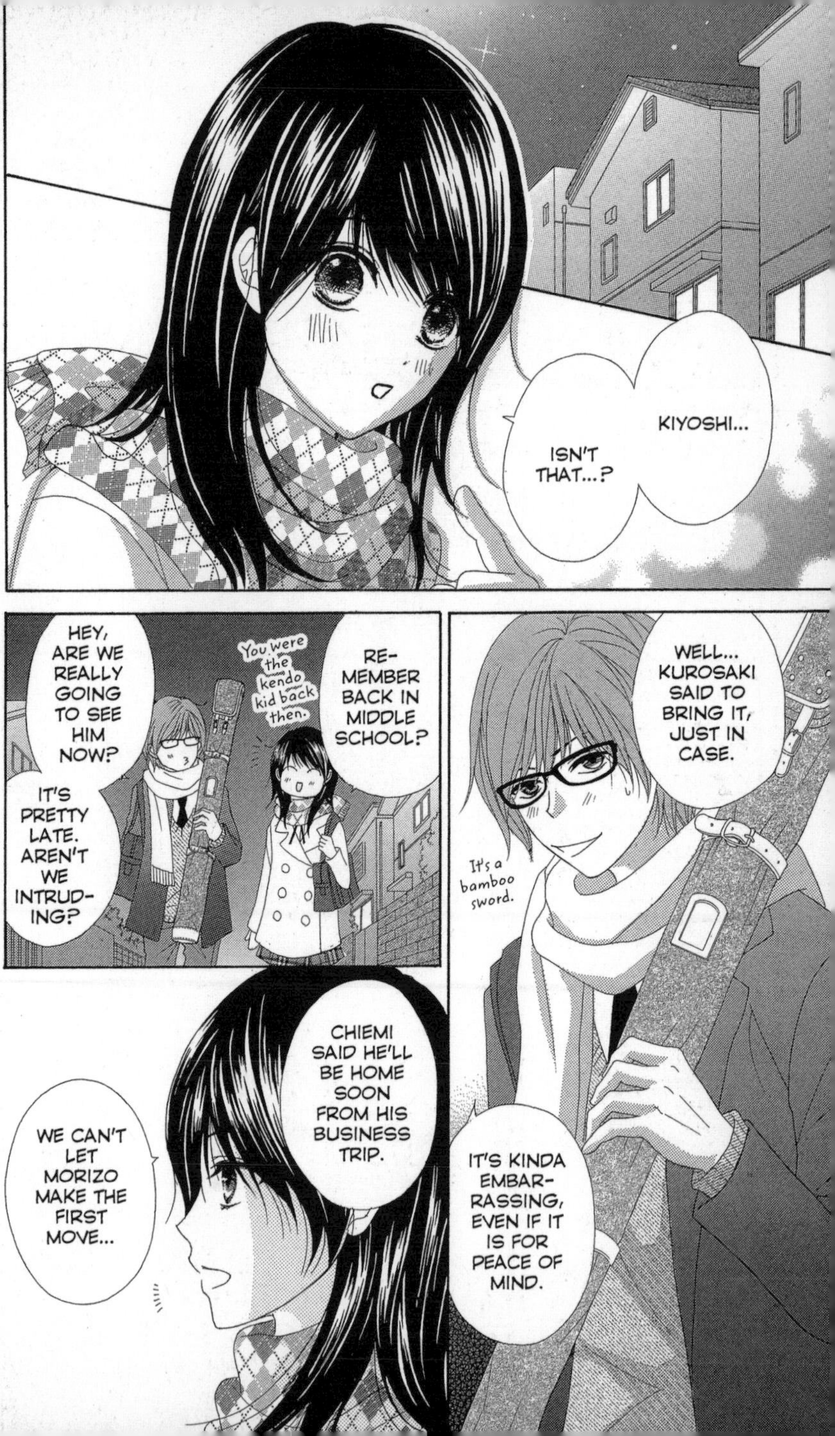
KIYOSHI...
ISN'T THAT...?
WELL... KUROSAKI SAID TO BRING IT, JUST IN CASE.
It's a bamboo sword.
IT'S KINDA EMBARRASSING, EVEN IF IT IS FOR PEACE OF MIND.
RE-MEMBER BACK IN MIDDLE SCHOOL?
You were the kendo kid back then.
HEY, ARE WE REALLY GOING TO SEE HIM NOW?
IT'S PRETTY LATE. AREN'T WE INTRUD-ING?
CHIEMI SAID HE'LL BE HOME SOON FROM HIS BUSINESS TRIP.
WE CAN'T LET MORIZO MAKE THE FIRST MOVE...

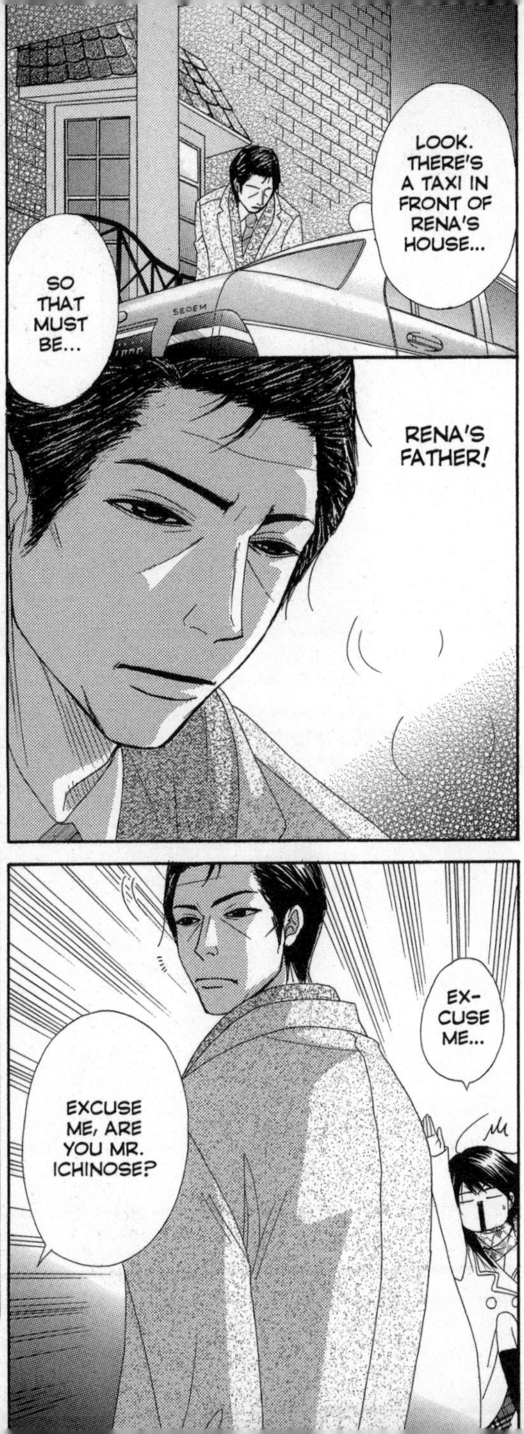
LOOK. THERE'S A TAXI IN FRONT OF RENA'S HOUSE...
SO THAT MUST BE...
RENA'S FATHER!
EX-CUSE ME...
EXCUSE ME, ARE YOU MR. ICHINOSE?

DENGEKI DAISY QUESTION CORNER

BALDLY ASK!!

BONUS

Q. PLEASE TELL ME EACH CHARACTER'S FAVORITE COLOR.
(RINE SAKURAGI, GUNMA PREFECTURE)

MAYBE NOT SO MUCH THEIR FAVORITE COLORS, BUT HERE ARE COLORS THAT SUIT THEM:

LIGHT GREEN OR DARK BLUE SEEM TO MATCH TERU. WITH A NAME LIKE TERU KUREBAYASHI, I SOMETIMES PUT HER IN DEEP CRIMSON-COLORED CLOTHING WHEN I DRAW HER IN COLOR. BUT IT DOESN'T SUIT HER AS WELL AS I THOUGHT... BLACK IS ABSOLUTELY THE BEST MATCH FOR KUROSAKI. AFTER ALL, HE IS "KURO (BLACK) SAKI."

BUT I THINK THE COLOR KUROSAKI ACTUALLY LIKES IS WHITE.

I DON'T DO THE OTHER CHARACTERS MUCH IN COLOR, SO I'M UNCERTAIN WHAT COLORS WOULD MATCH THEM. RIKO PROBABLY IN BROWN OR GREY, AND I THINK SOICHIRO MIGHT LOOK GOOD IN SAXON BLUE.

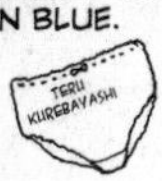
TERU KUREBAYASHI

THE END.

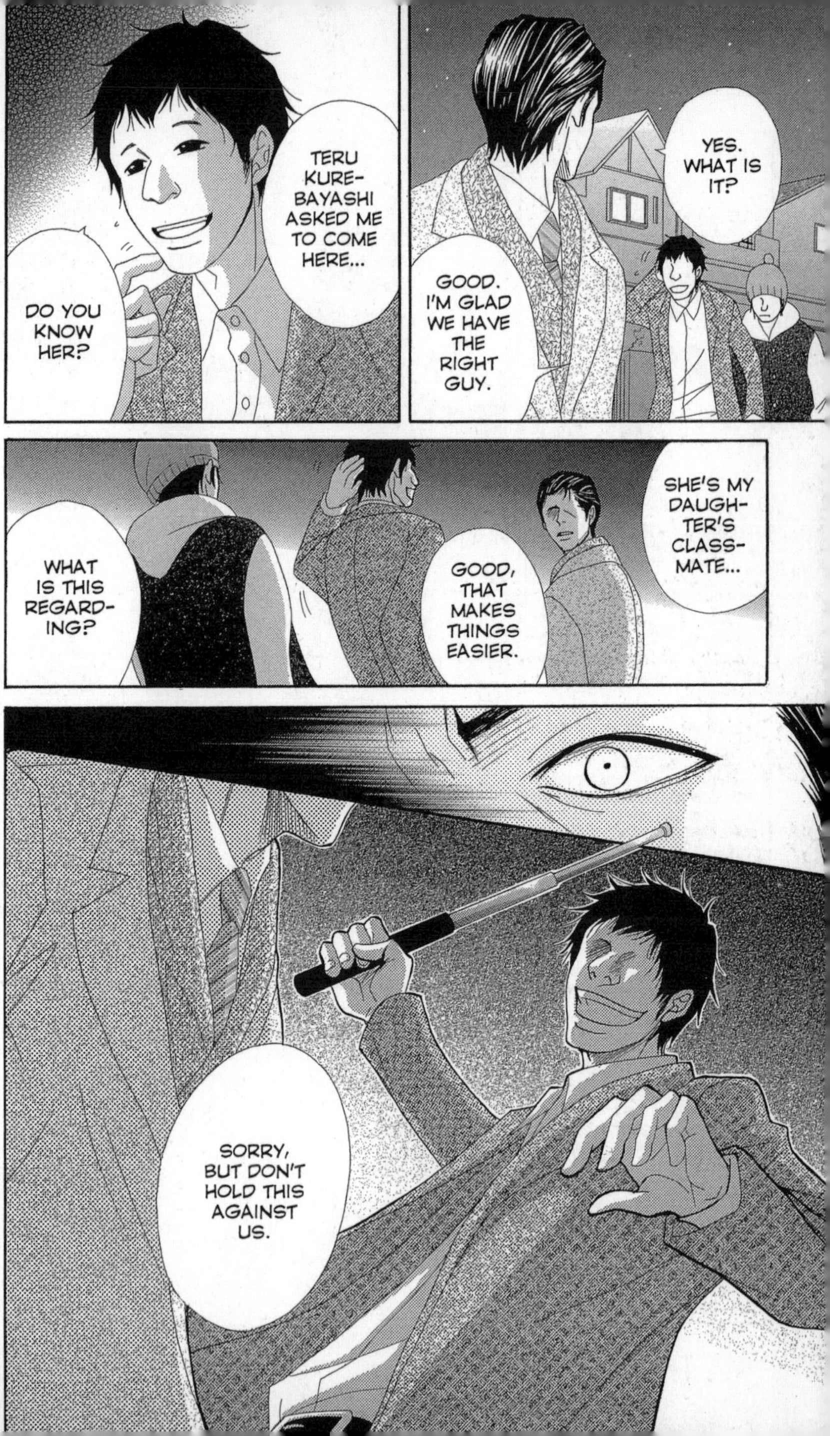
YES. WHAT IS IT?
GOOD. I'M GLAD WE HAVE THE RIGHT GUY.
TERU KURE-BAYASHI ASKED ME TO COME HERE...
DO YOU KNOW HER?
SHE'S MY DAUGH-TER'S CLASS-MATE...
GOOD, THAT MAKES THINGS EASIER.
WHAT IS THIS REGARD-ING?
SORRY, BUT DON'T HOLD THIS AGAINST US.

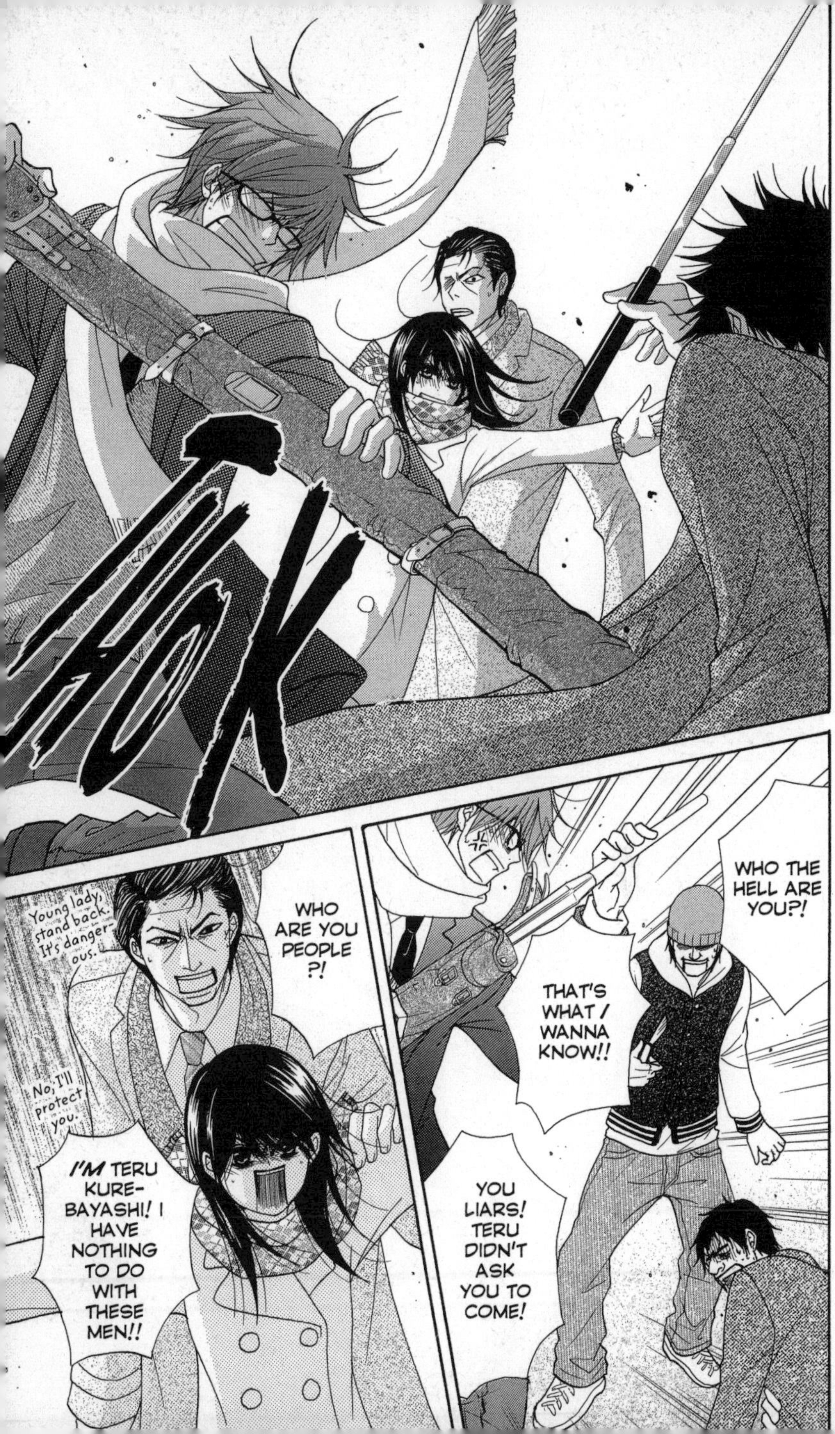
THOK
WHO THE HELL ARE YOU?!
THAT'S WHAT I WANNA KNOW!!
YOU LIARS! TERU DIDN'T ASK YOU TO COME!
WHO ARE YOU PEOPLE?!
Young lady, stand back. It's dangerous.
No, I'll protect you.
I'M TERU KUREBAYASHI! I HAVE NOTHING TO DO WITH THESE MEN!!

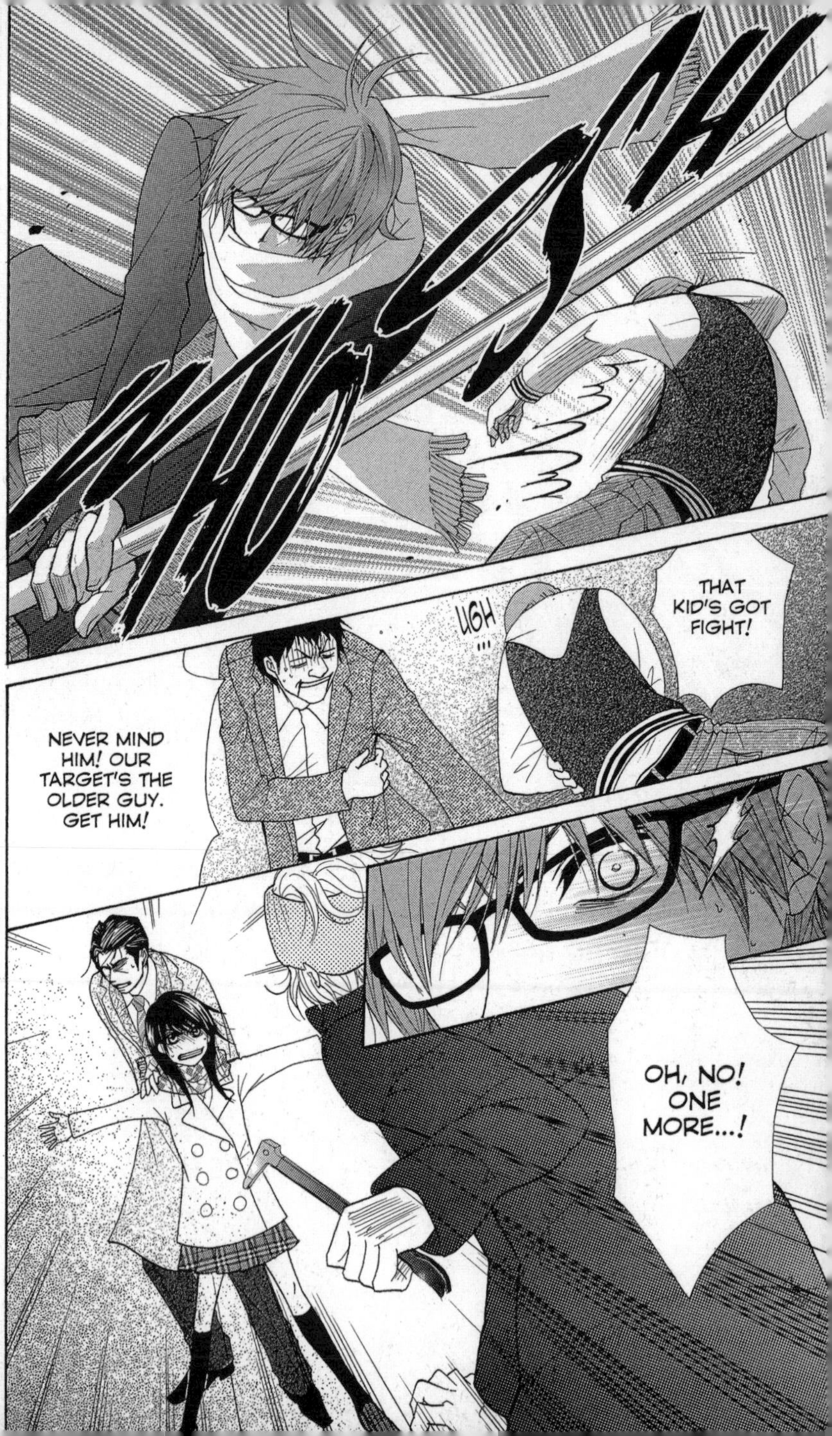
WHOOSH
THAT KID'S GOT FIGHT!
UGH...
NEVER MIND HIM! OUR TARGET'S THE OLDER GUY. GET HIM!
OH, NO! ONE MORE...!

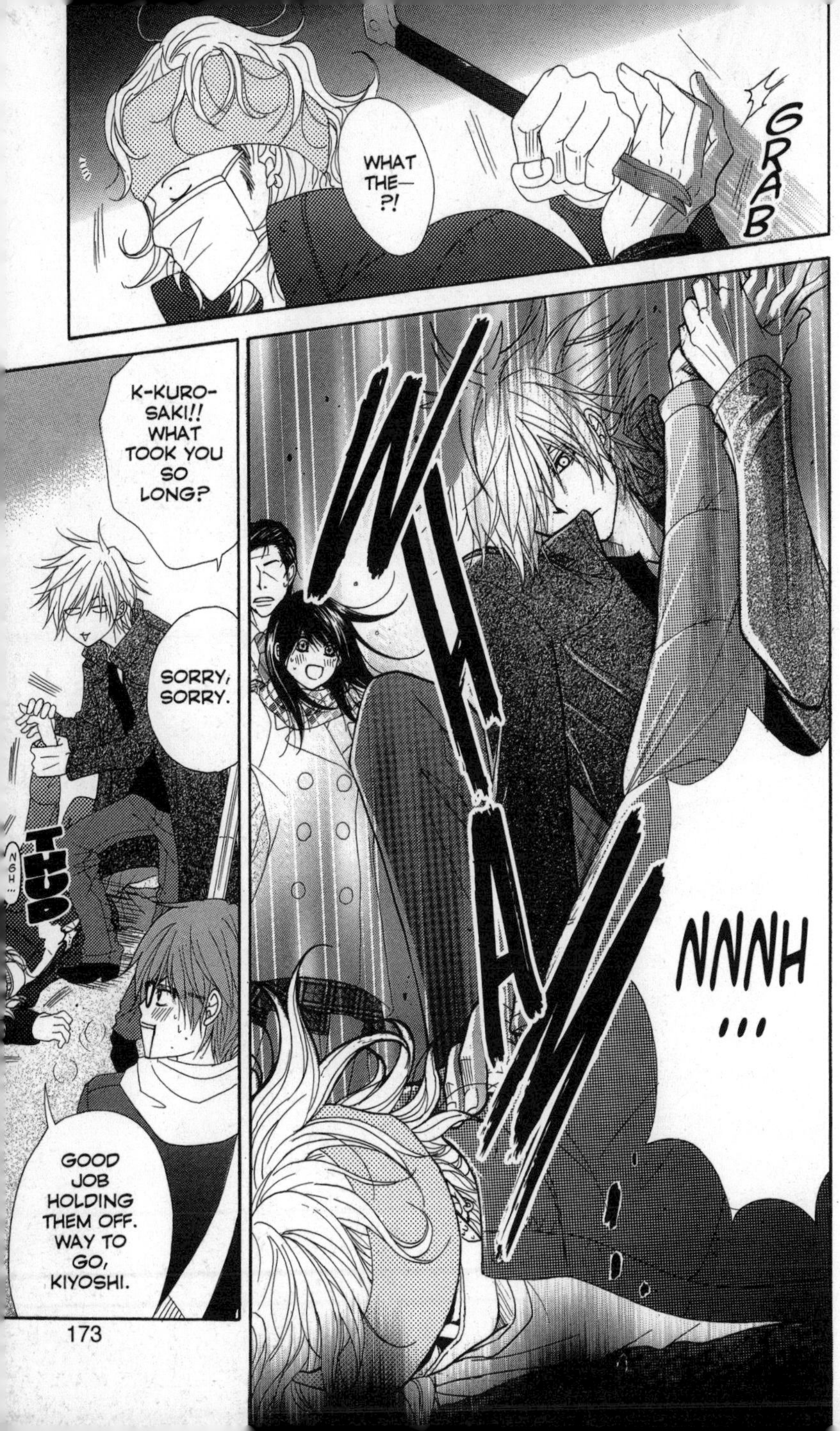
GRAB
WHAT THE—?!
WHAM
NNNH...
K-KUROSAKI!! WHAT TOOK YOU SO LONG?
SORRY, SORRY.
NGH...
THUD
GOOD JOB HOLDING THEM OFF. WAY TO GO, KIYOSHI.

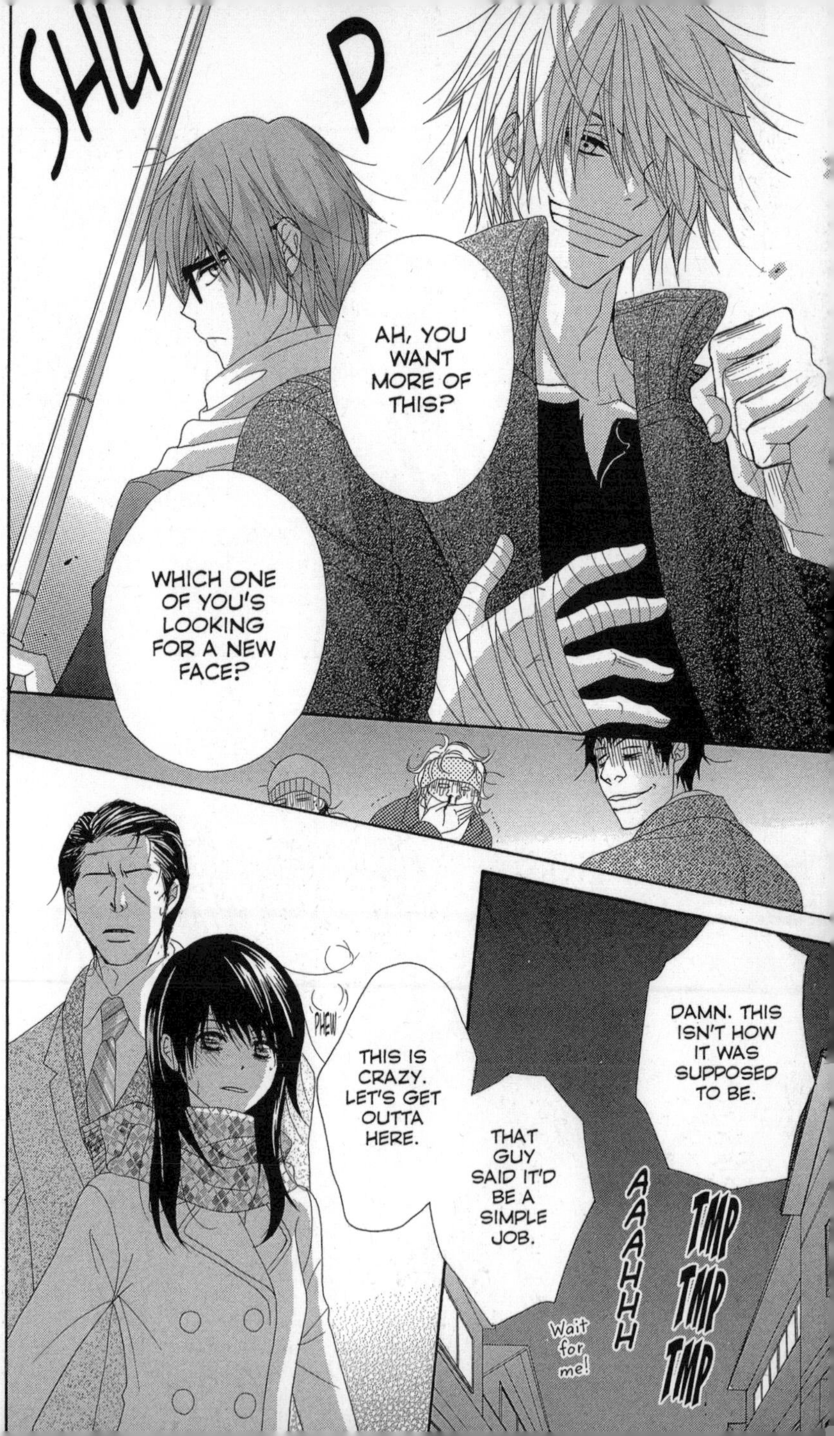
SHUP
AH, YOU WANT MORE OF THIS?
WHICH ONE OF YOU'S LOOKING FOR A NEW FACE?
DAMN. THIS ISN'T HOW IT WAS SUPPOSED TO BE.
THAT GUY SAID IT'D BE A SIMPLE JOB.
TMP TMP TMP
AAAHHH
Wait for me!
PHEW
THIS IS CRAZY. LET'S GET OUTTA HERE.

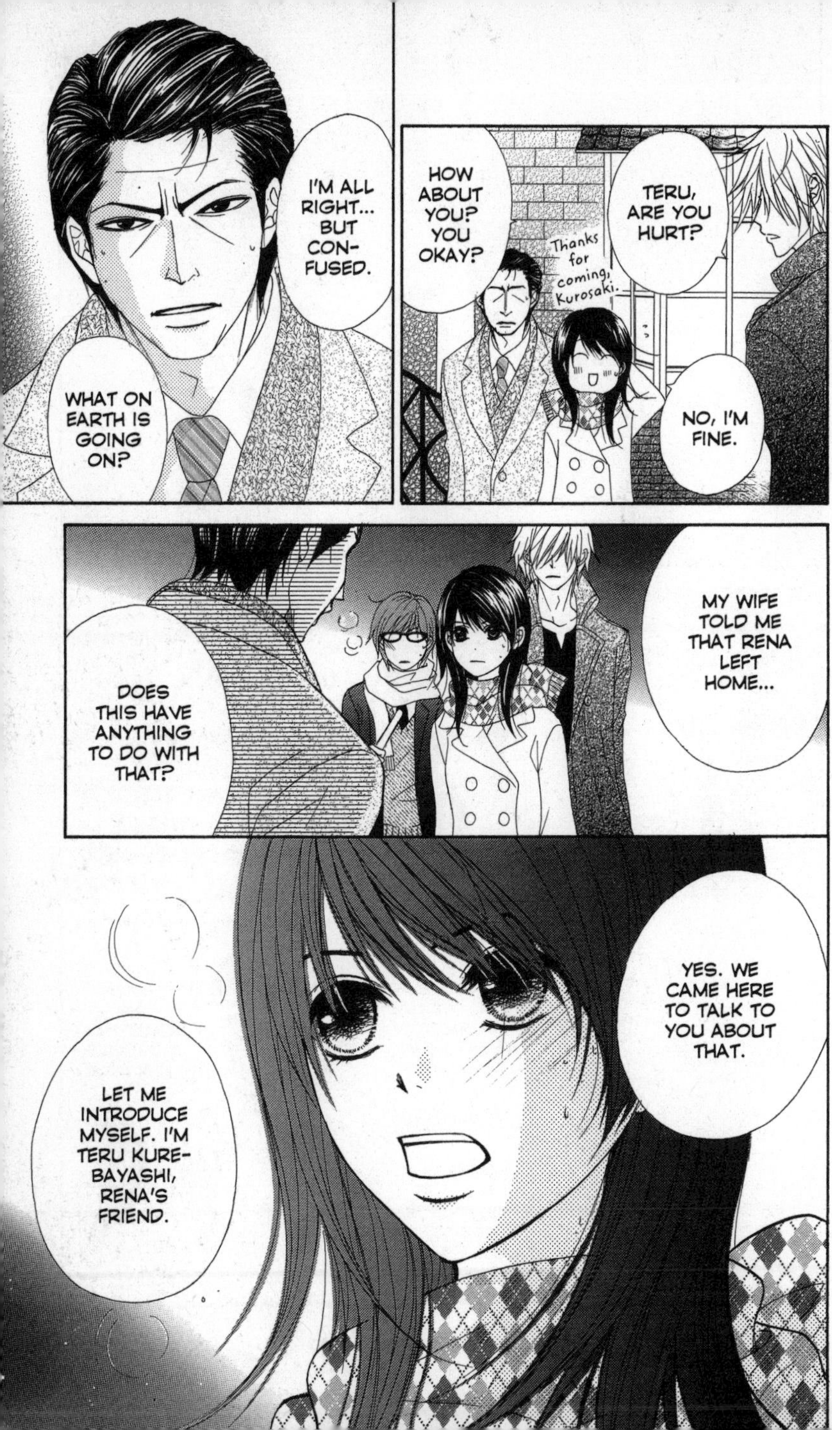
TERU, ARE YOU HURT?
NO, I'M FINE.
HOW ABOUT YOU? YOU OKAY?
Thanks for coming, Kurosaki.
I'M ALL RIGHT... BUT CON-FUSED.
WHAT ON EARTH IS GOING ON?
MY WIFE TOLD ME THAT RENA LEFT HOME...
DOES THIS HAVE ANYTHING TO DO WITH THAT?
YES. WE CAME HERE TO TALK TO YOU ABOUT THAT.
LET ME INTRODUCE MYSELF. I'M TERU KURE-BAYASHI, RENA'S FRIEND.

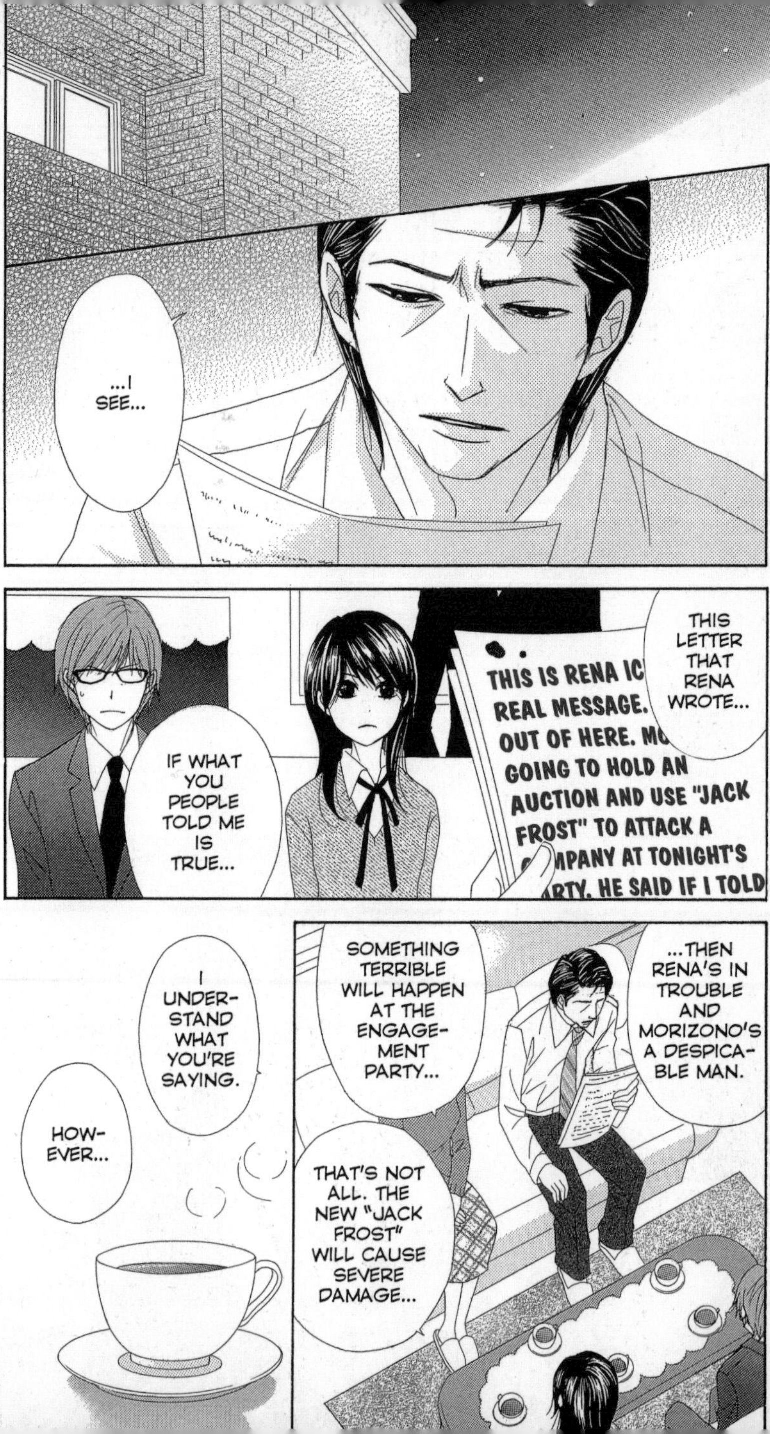
...I SEE...
THIS LETTER THAT RENA WROTE...
THIS IS RENA IC REAL MESSAGE. OUT OF HERE. MO GOING TO HOLD AN AUCTION AND USE "JACK FROST" TO ATTACK A MPANY AT TONIGHT'S RTY. HE SAID IF I TOLD
IF WHAT YOU PEOPLE TOLD ME IS TRUE...
...THEN RENA'S IN TROUBLE AND MORIZONO'S A DESPICABLE MAN.
SOMETHING TERRIBLE WILL HAPPEN AT THE ENGAGEMENT PARTY...
THAT'S NOT ALL. THE NEW "JACK FROST" WILL CAUSE SEVERE DAMAGE...
I UNDERSTAND WHAT YOU'RE SAYING.
HOWEVER...

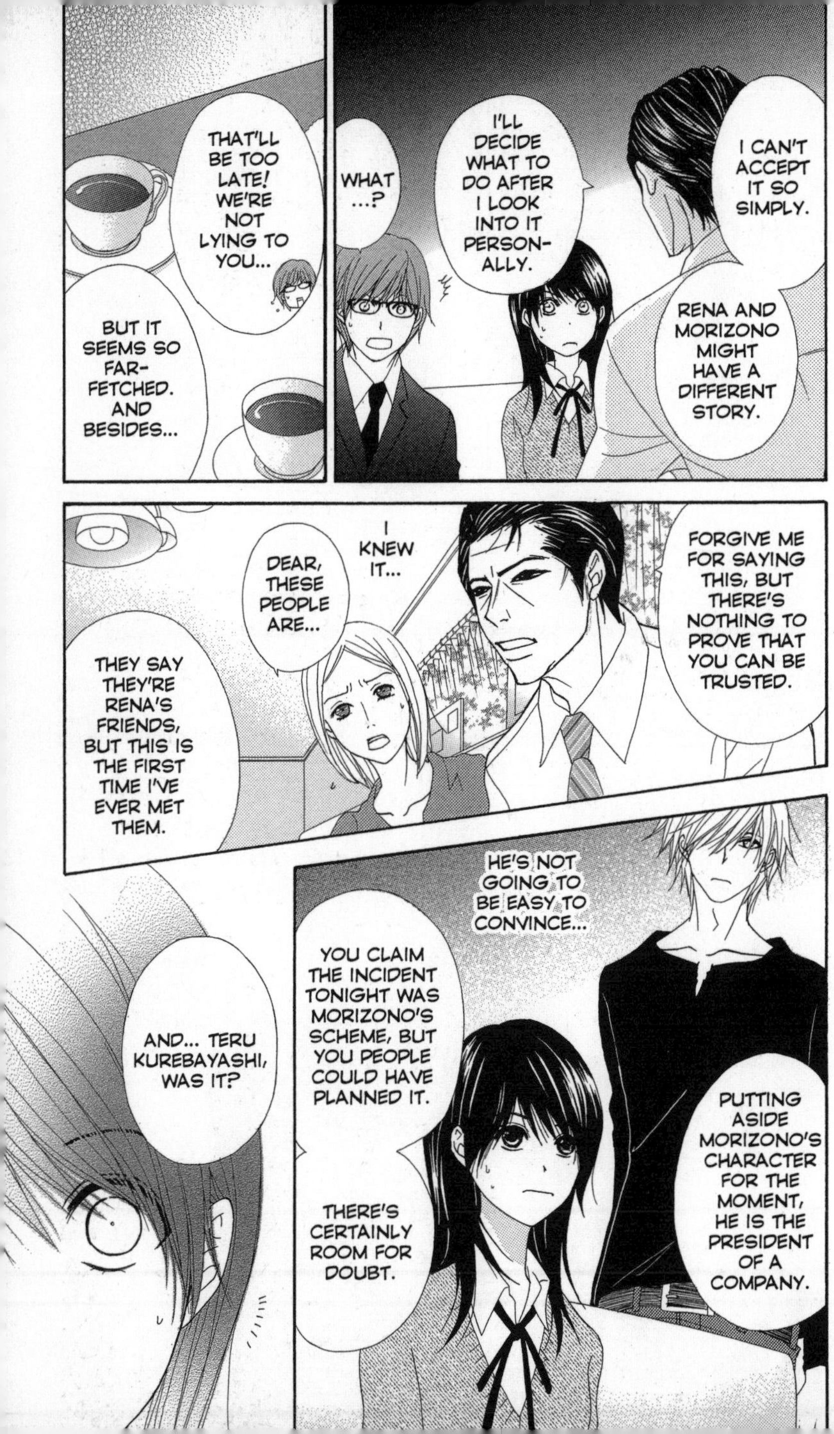
I CAN'T ACCEPT IT SO SIMPLY.
RENA AND MORIZONO MIGHT HAVE A DIFFERENT STORY.
I'LL DECIDE WHAT TO DO AFTER I LOOK INTO IT PERSON-ALLY.
WHAT ...?
THAT'LL BE TOO LATE! WE'RE NOT LYING TO YOU...
BUT IT SEEMS SO FAR-FETCHED. AND BESIDES...
FORGIVE ME FOR SAYING THIS, BUT THERE'S NOTHING TO PROVE THAT YOU CAN BE TRUSTED.
I KNEW IT...
DEAR, THESE PEOPLE ARE...
THEY SAY THEY'RE RENA'S FRIENDS, BUT THIS IS THE FIRST TIME I'VE EVER MET THEM.
HE'S NOT GOING TO BE EASY TO CONVINCE...
PUTTING ASIDE MORIZONO'S CHARACTER FOR THE MOMENT, HE IS THE PRESIDENT OF A COMPANY.
YOU CLAIM THE INCIDENT TONIGHT WAS MORIZONO'S SCHEME, BUT YOU PEOPLE COULD HAVE PLANNED IT.
THERE'S CERTAINLY ROOM FOR DOUBT.
AND... TERU KUREBAYASHI, WAS IT?

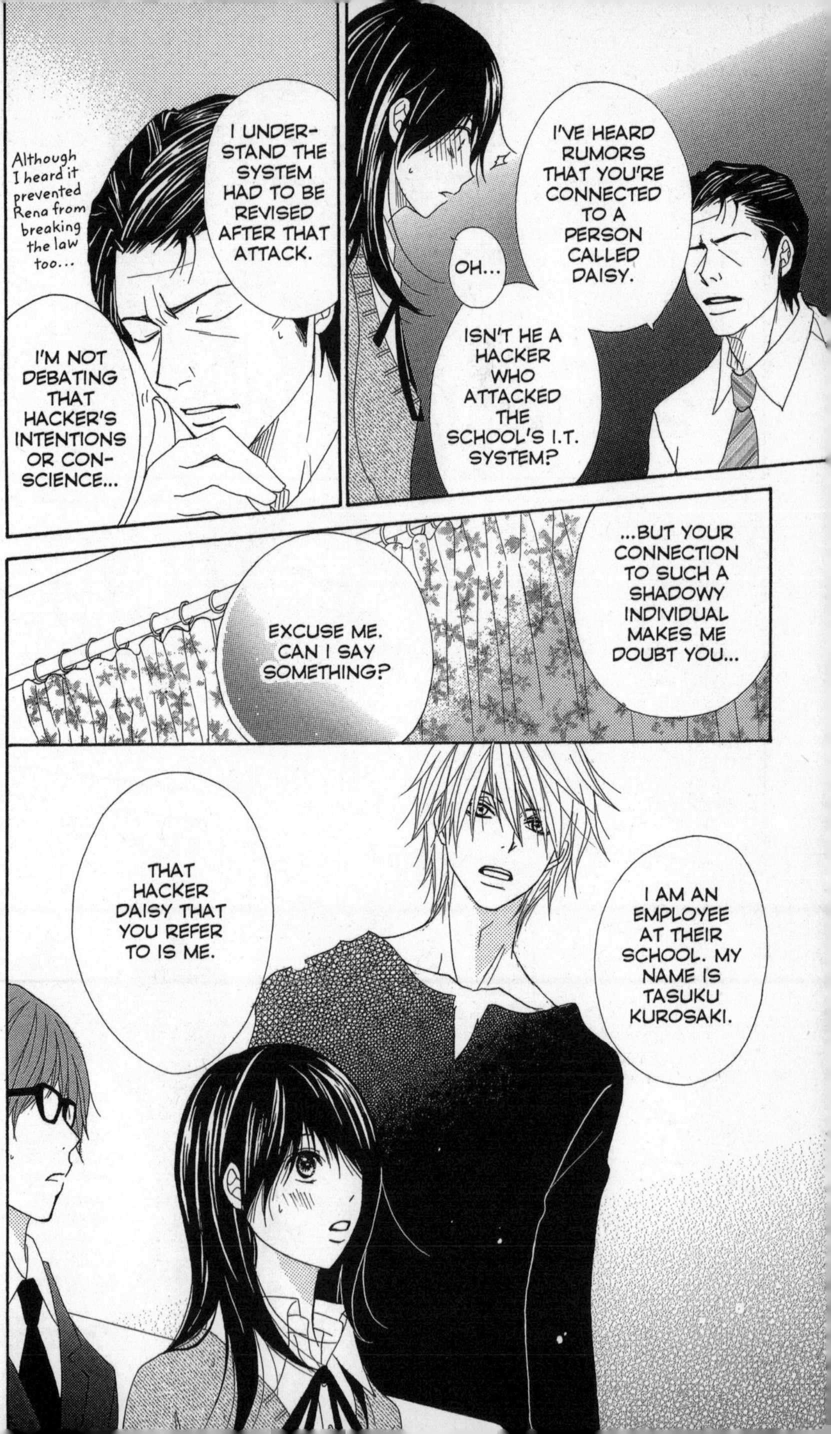
I'VE HEARD RUMORS THAT YOU'RE CONNECTED TO A PERSON CALLED DAISY.
OH...
ISN'T HE A HACKER WHO ATTACKED THE SCHOOL'S I.T. SYSTEM?
I UNDERSTAND THE SYSTEM HAD TO BE REVISED AFTER THAT ATTACK.
Although I heard it prevented Rena from breaking the law too...
I'M NOT DEBATING THAT HACKER'S INTENTIONS OR CONSCIENCE...
...BUT YOUR CONNECTION TO SUCH A SHADOWY INDIVIDUAL MAKES ME DOUBT YOU...
EXCUSE ME. CAN I SAY SOMETHING?
I AM AN EMPLOYEE AT THEIR SCHOOL. MY NAME IS TASUKU KUROSAKI.
THAT HACKER DAISY THAT YOU REFER TO IS ME.

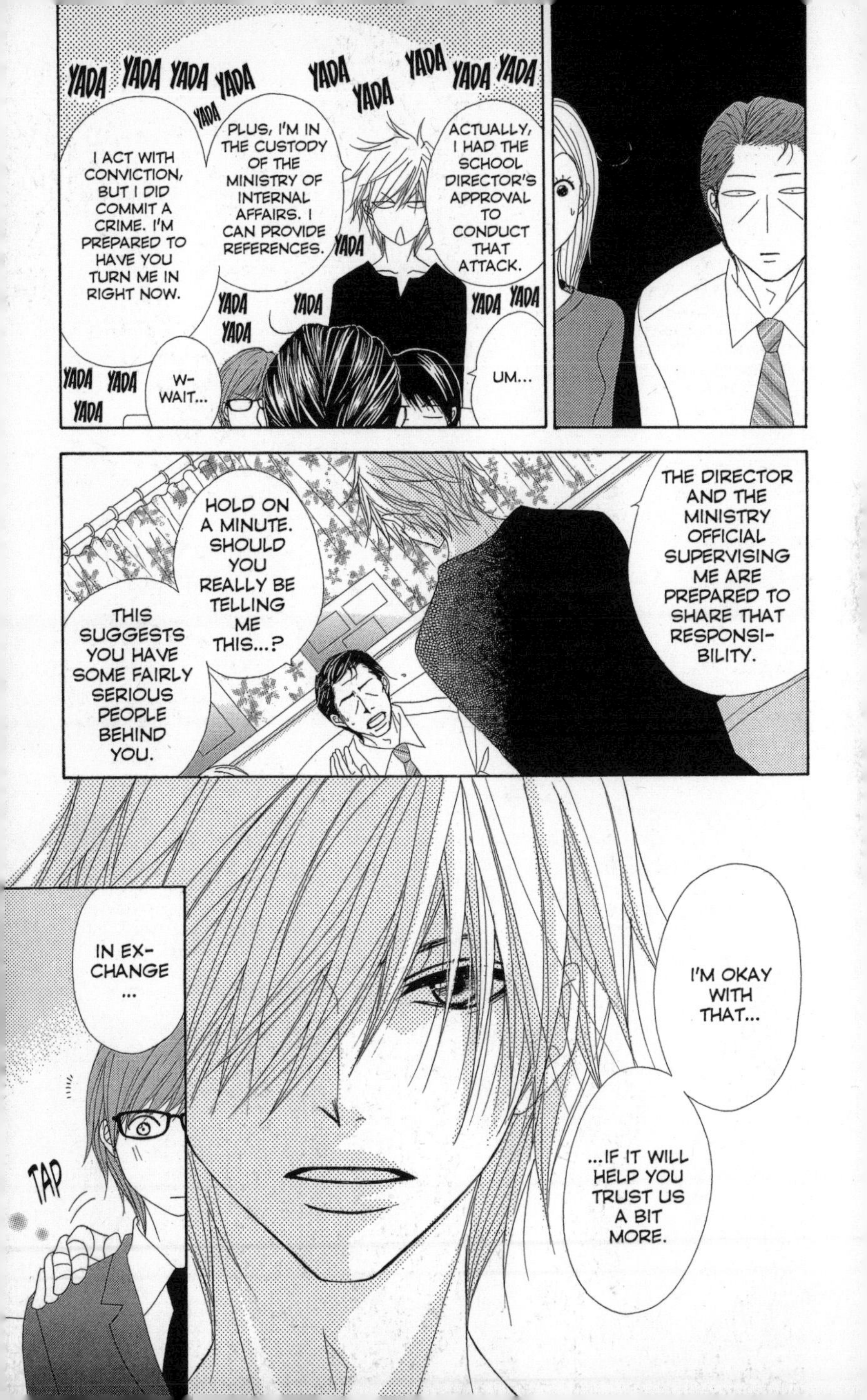
YADA YADA YADA YADA YADA YADA YADA YADA
ACTUALLY, I HAD THE SCHOOL DIRECTOR'S APPROVAL TO CONDUCT THAT ATTACK.
PLUS, I'M IN THE CUSTODY OF THE MINISTRY OF INTERNAL AFFAIRS. I CAN PROVIDE REFERENCES.
YADA YADA YADA
I ACT WITH CONVICTION, BUT I DID COMMIT A CRIME. I'M PREPARED TO HAVE YOU TURN ME IN RIGHT NOW.
YADA YADA YADA YADA YADA
UM...
W-WAIT...
YADA YADA YADA
THE DIRECTOR AND THE MINISTRY OFFICIAL SUPERVISING ME ARE PREPARED TO SHARE THAT RESPONSI-BILITY.
HOLD ON A MINUTE. SHOULD YOU REALLY BE TELLING ME THIS...?
THIS SUGGESTS YOU HAVE SOME FAIRLY SERIOUS PEOPLE BEHIND YOU.
I'M OKAY WITH THAT...
...IF IT WILL HELP YOU TRUST US A BIT MORE.
IN EX-CHANGE ...
TAP

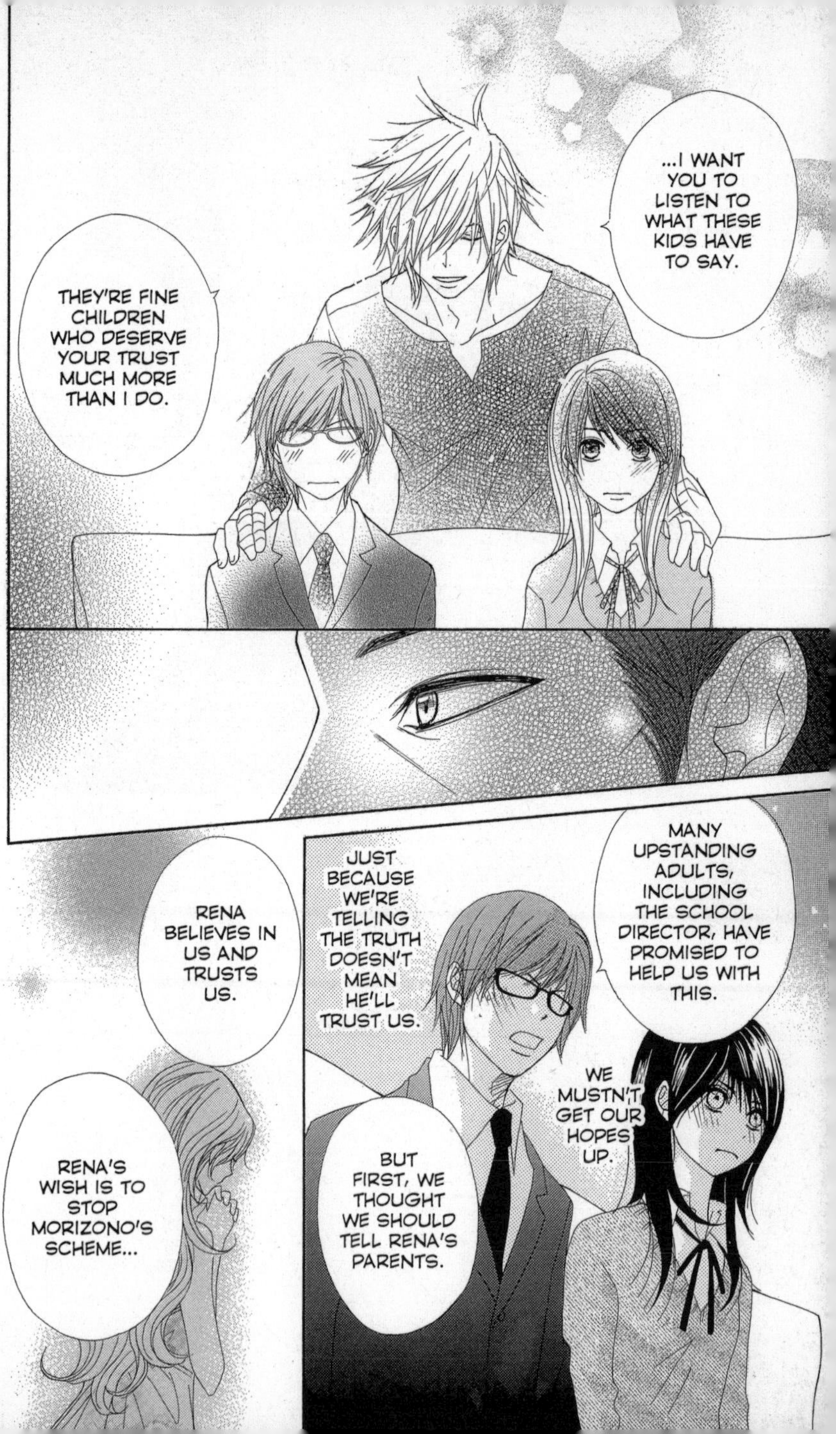
...I WANT YOU TO LISTEN TO WHAT THESE KIDS HAVE TO SAY.
THEY'RE FINE CHILDREN WHO DESERVE YOUR TRUST MUCH MORE THAN I DO.
MANY UPSTANDING ADULTS, INCLUDING THE SCHOOL DIRECTOR, HAVE PROMISED TO HELP US WITH THIS.
JUST BECAUSE WE'RE TELLING THE TRUTH DOESN'T MEAN HE'LL TRUST US.
WE MUSTN'T GET OUR HOPES UP.
BUT FIRST, WE THOUGHT WE SHOULD TELL RENA'S PARENTS.
RENA BELIEVES IN US AND TRUSTS US.
RENA'S WISH IS TO STOP MORIZONO'S SCHEME...

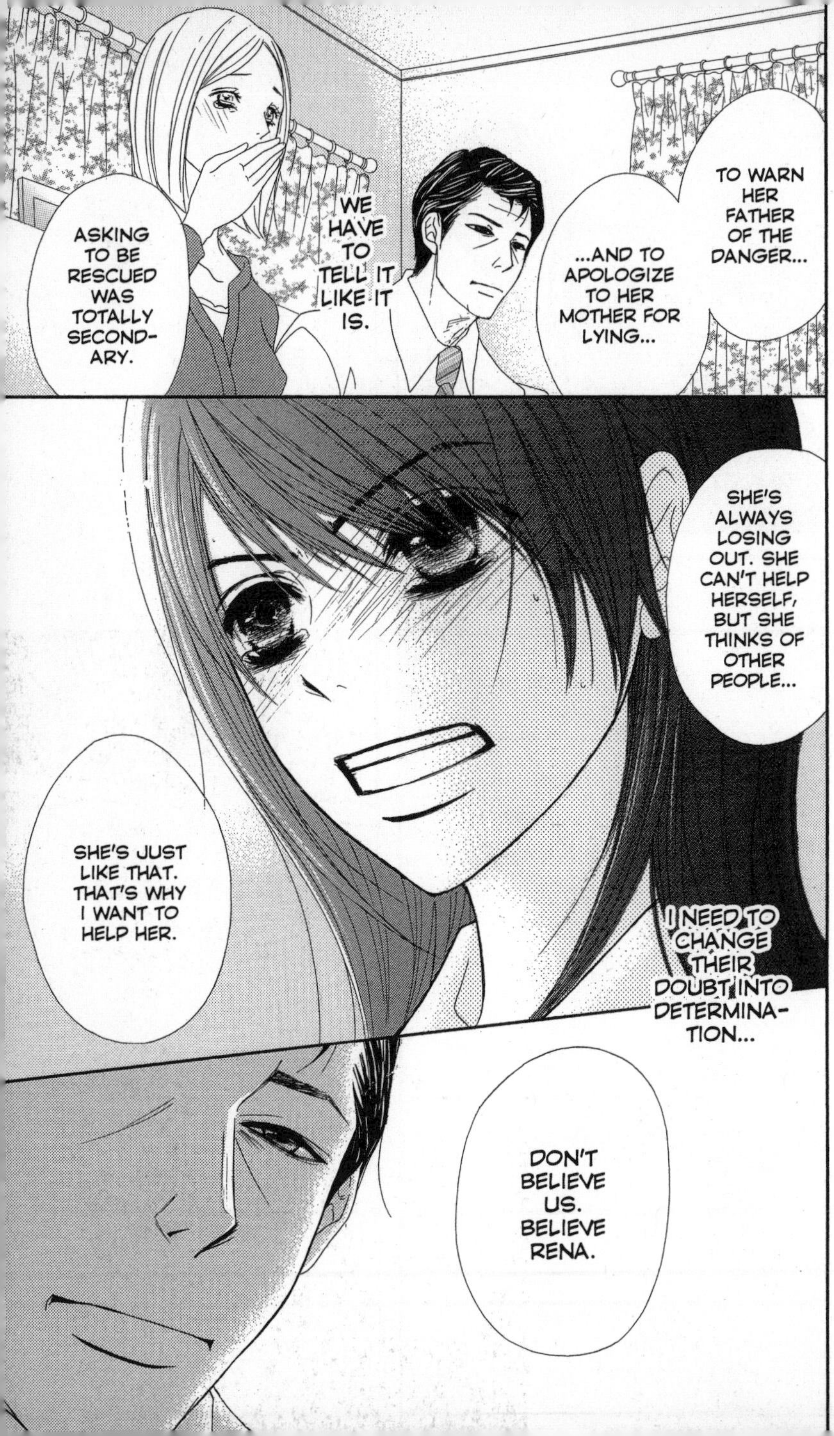

TO WARN HER FATHER OF THE DANGER...
...AND TO APOLOGIZE TO HER MOTHER FOR LYING...
WE HAVE TO TELL IT LIKE IT IS.
ASKING TO BE RESCUED WAS TOTALLY SECOND-ARY.
SHE'S ALWAYS LOSING OUT. SHE CAN'T HELP HERSELF, BUT SHE THINKS OF OTHER PEOPLE...
SHE'S JUST LIKE THAT. THAT'S WHY I WANT TO HELP HER.
I NEED TO CHANGE THEIR DOUBT INTO DETERMINA-TION...
DON'T BELIEVE US. BELIEVE RENA.

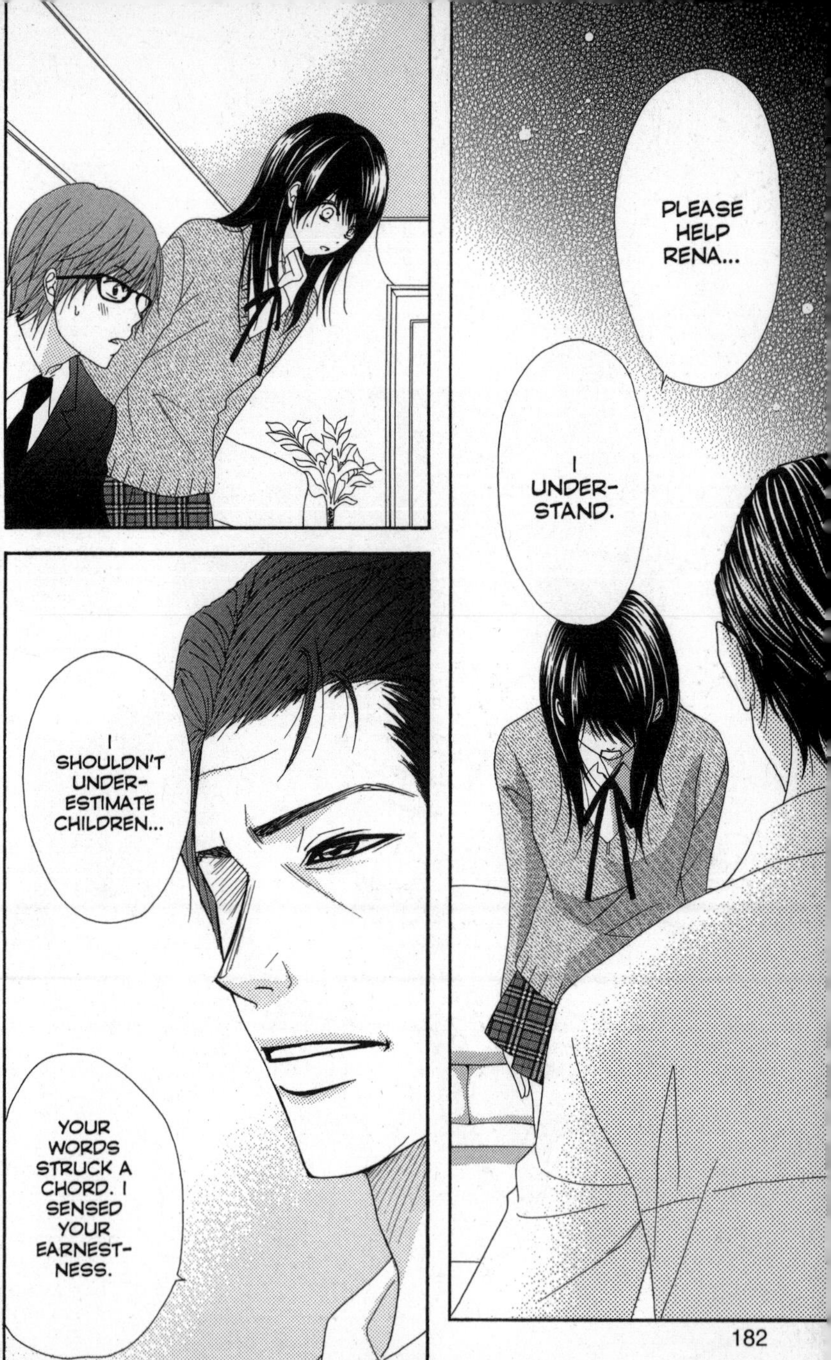
PLEASE HELP RENA...
I UNDER-STAND.
I SHOULDN'T UNDER-ESTIMATE CHILDREN...
YOUR WORDS STRUCK A CHORD. I SENSED YOUR EARNEST-NESS.

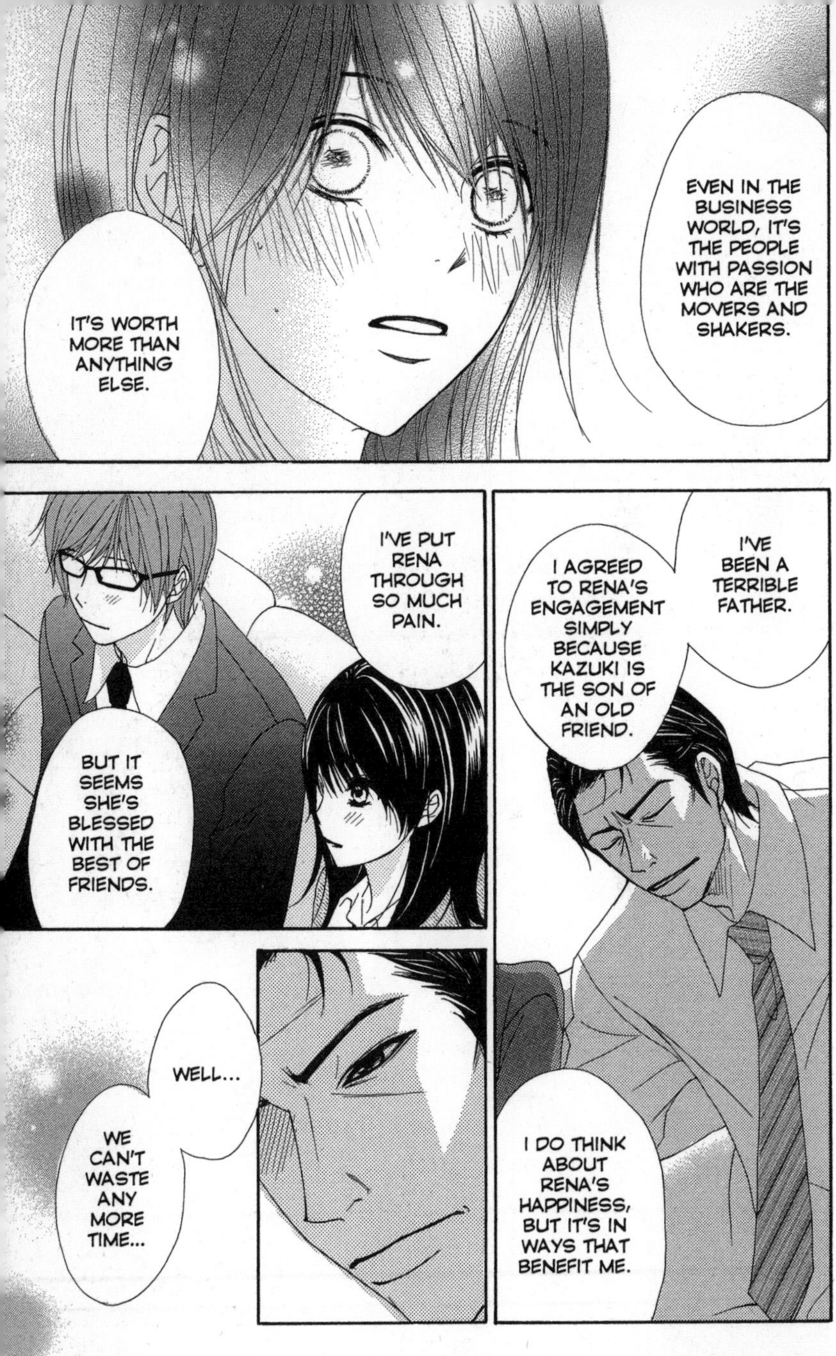
EVEN IN THE BUSINESS WORLD, IT'S THE PEOPLE WITH PASSION WHO ARE THE MOVERS AND SHAKERS.
IT'S WORTH MORE THAN ANYTHING ELSE.
I'VE BEEN A TERRIBLE FATHER.
I AGREED TO RENA'S ENGAGEMENT SIMPLY BECAUSE KAZUKI IS THE SON OF AN OLD FRIEND.
I DO THINK ABOUT RENA'S HAPPINESS, BUT IT'S IN WAYS THAT BENEFIT ME.
I'VE PUT RENA THROUGH SO MUCH PAIN.
BUT IT SEEMS SHE'S BLESSED WITH THE BEST OF FRIENDS.
WELL...
WE CAN'T WASTE ANY MORE TIME...

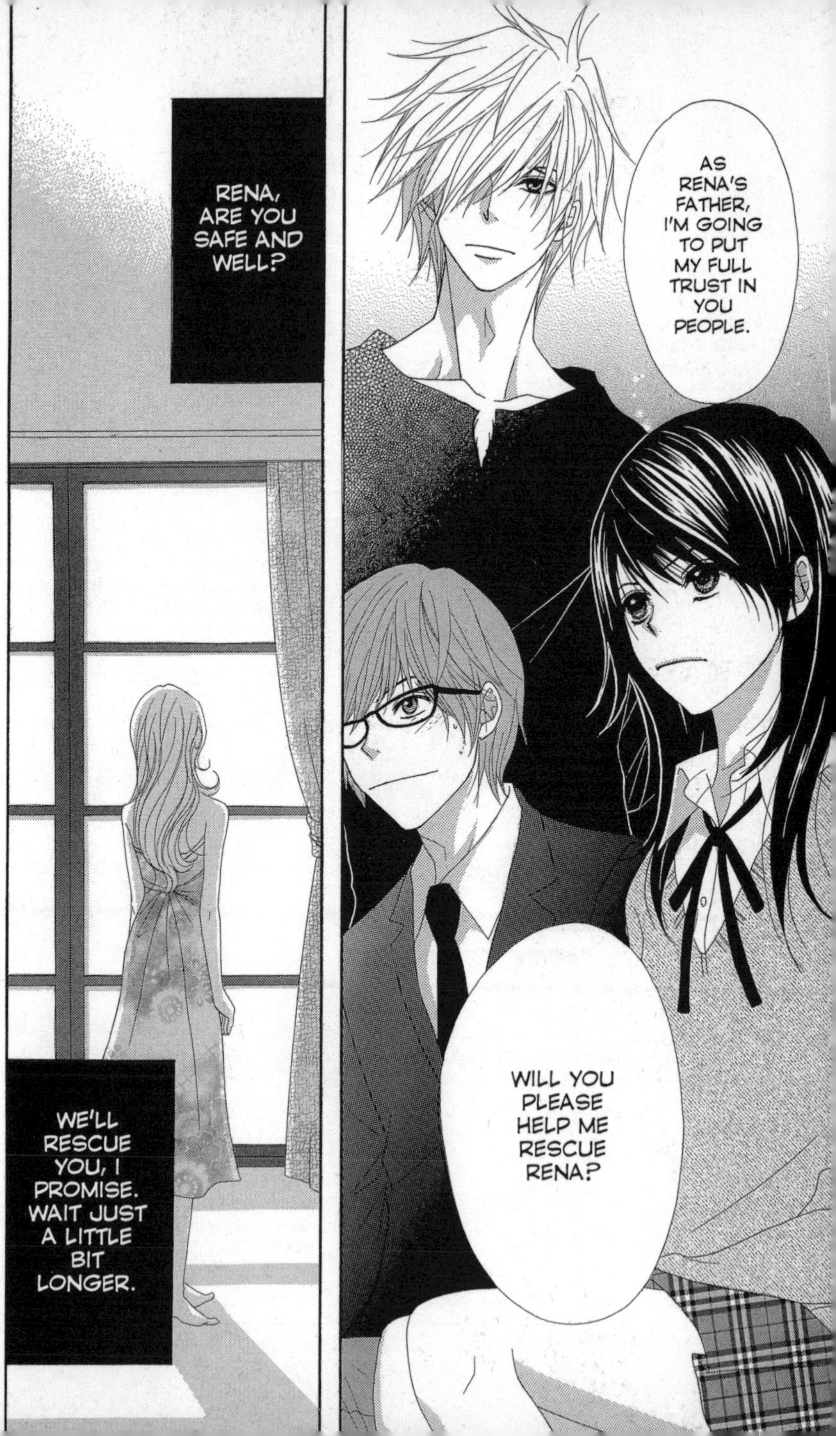
AS RENA'S FATHER, I'M GOING TO PUT MY FULL TRUST IN YOU PEOPLE.
WILL YOU PLEASE HELP ME RESCUE RENA?
RENA, ARE YOU SAFE AND WELL?
WE'LL RESCUE YOU, I PROMISE. WAIT JUST A LITTLE BIT LONGER.

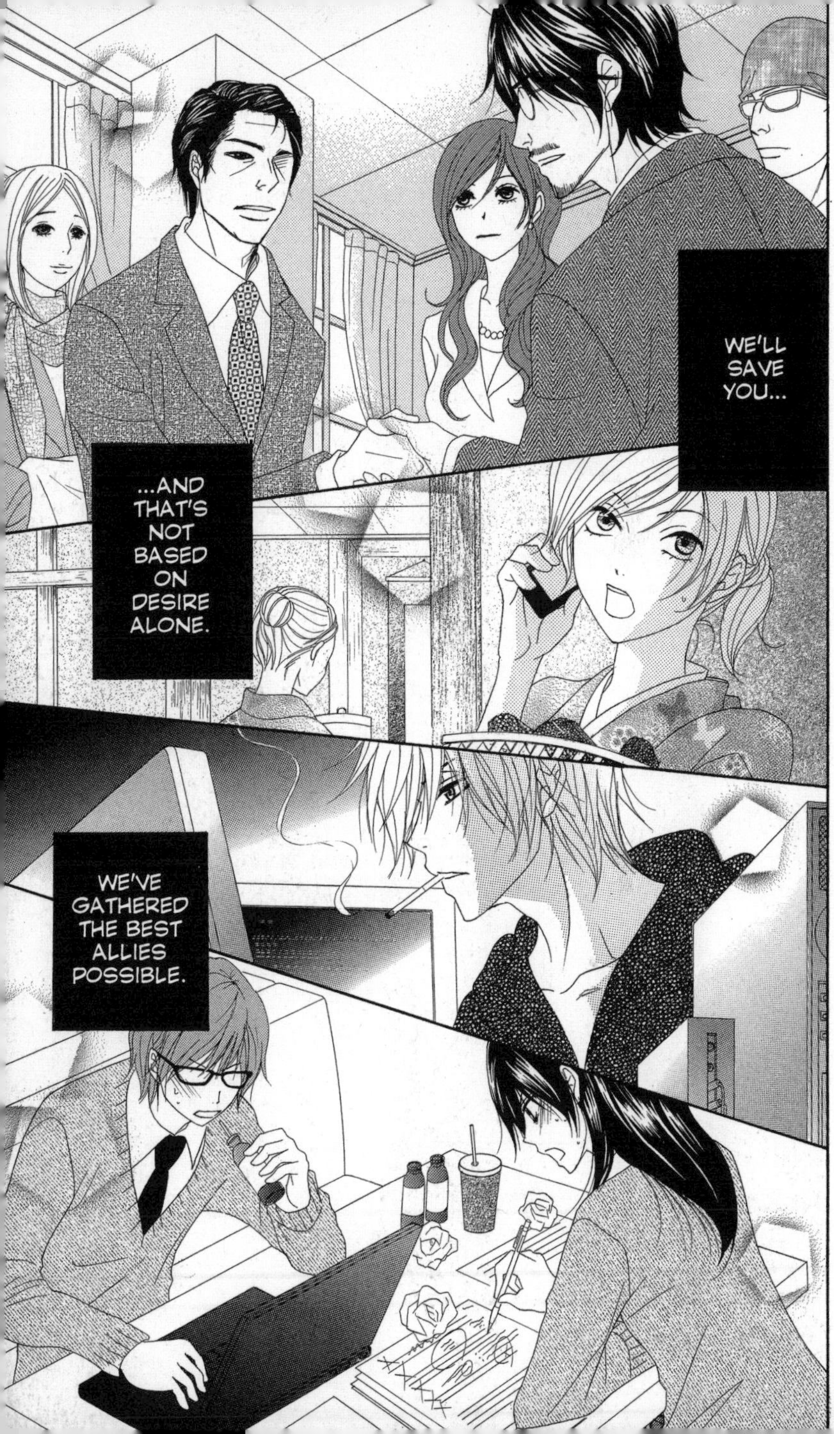
WE'LL SAVE YOU...
...AND THAT'S NOT BASED ON DESIRE ALONE.
WE'VE GATHERED THE BEST ALLIES POSSIBLE.

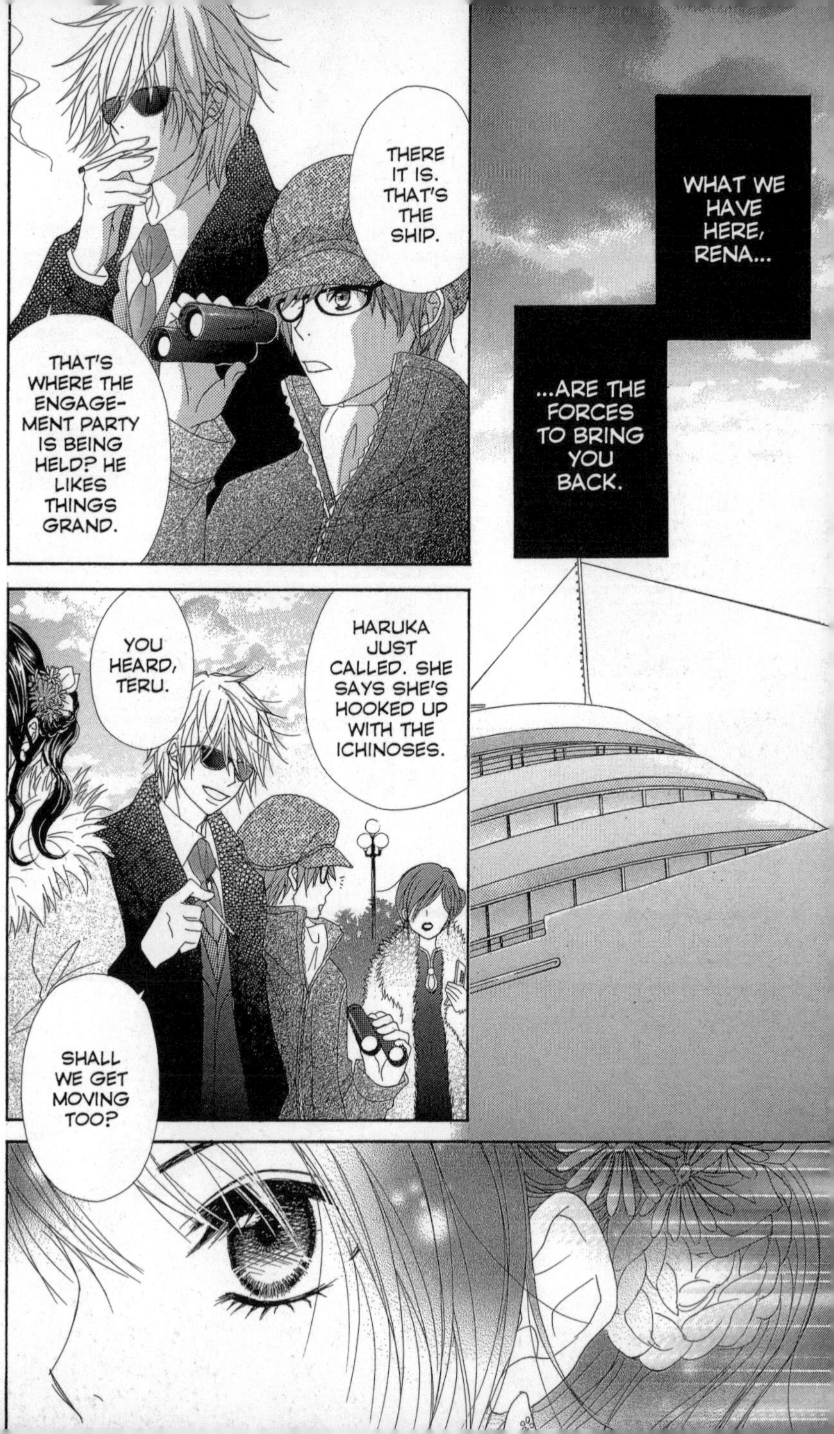
WHAT WE HAVE HERE, RENA...
...ARE THE FORCES TO BRING YOU BACK.
THERE IT IS. THAT'S THE SHIP.
THAT'S WHERE THE ENGAGEMENT PARTY IS BEING HELD? HE LIKES THINGS GRAND.
HARUKA JUST CALLED. SHE SAYS SHE'S HOOKED UP WITH THE ICHINOSES.
YOU HEARD, TERU.
SHALL WE GET MOVING TOO?

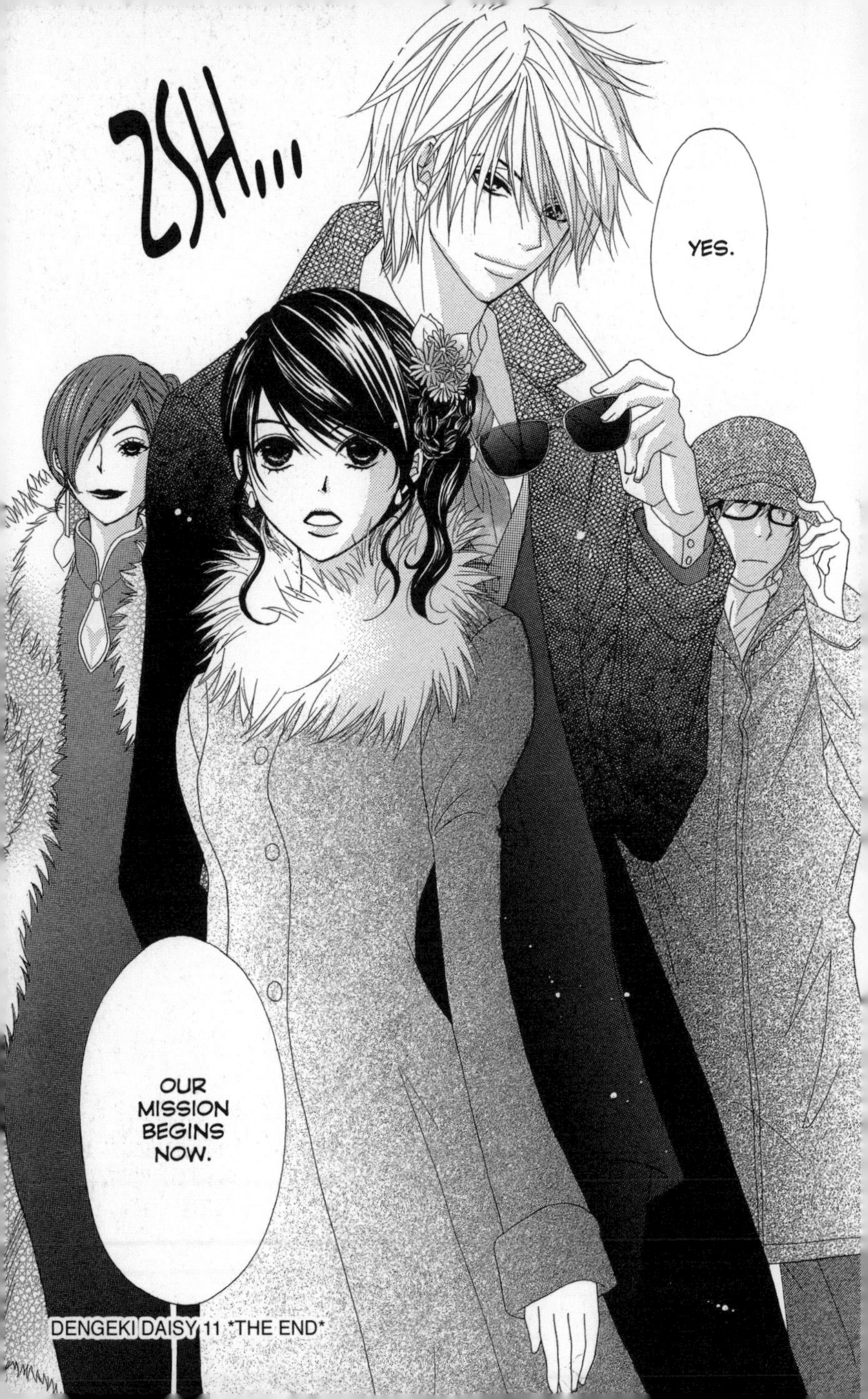
YES.
ZSH...
OUR MISSION BEGINS NOW.
DENGEKI DAISY 11 *THE END*

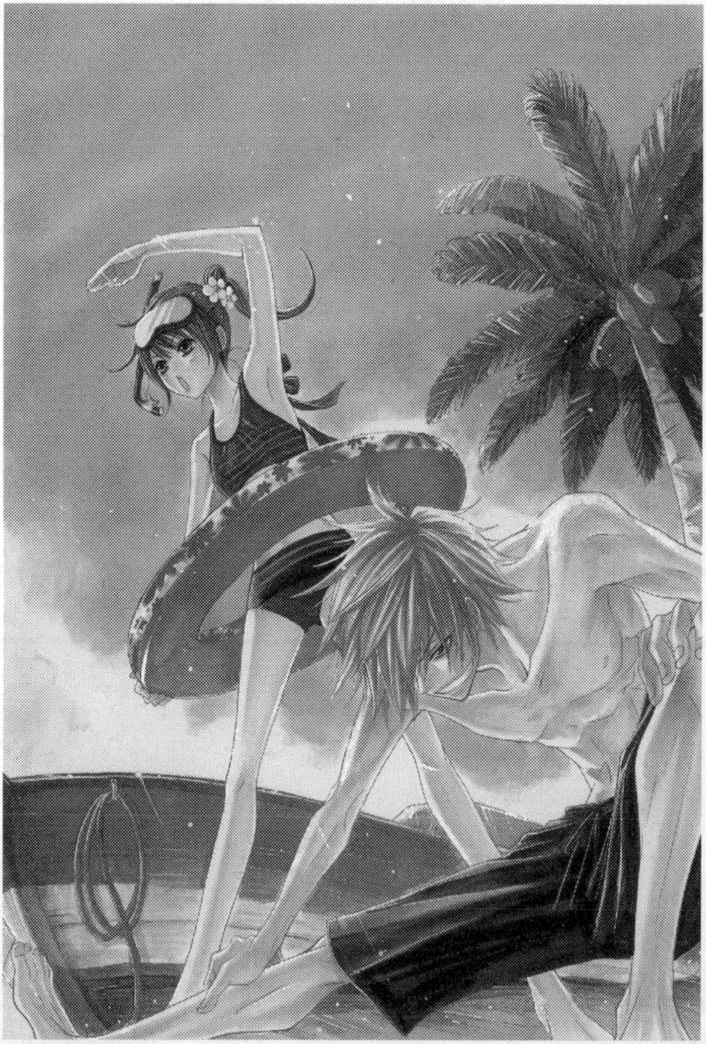

AFTER WORD

Kiyoshi, at the start of volume 1, weren't you standing behind Teru in tears?

Now, now. Adolescent boys have a lot going on.

ER...YES! THAT'S THE END OF *DENGEKI DAISY* 11.

AS I READ IT BACK TO MYSELF, SOME DOUBT CAME UP REGARDING WHO THE MAIN CHARACTER IS. THE REAL MAIN CHARACTER IS THE FLAT-CHESTED GIRL. AND THE HERO IS A SCRUFFY-LOOKING PUNK. THERE WERE A LOT OF PLACES WHERE IT WAS SLOW-GOING WITH SEGMENTS THAT SEEMED PREACHY, BUT NOW, THE PREPARATIONS ARE COMPLETE. STARTING WITH THE NEXT VOLUME, I INTEND TO LET THEM REALLY GO AT IT. RIGHT NOW, THE AUTHOR IS COUGHING UP LOADS OF BLOOD GETTING THE DRAWINGS DONE.

IF YOU DON'T MIND, I'D LIKE YOU TO PICK UP A COPY OF VOLUME 12.

UNTIL WE MEET AGAIN, I WILL BE DOING MY VERY BEST!

KYOUSUKE MOTOMI

DENGEKI DAISY
C/O VIZ MEDIA
P.O. BOX 77010
SAN FRANCISCO, CA
94107

← IF YOU HAVE ANY QUESTIONS, PLEASE SEND THEM HERE. FOR REGULAR FAN MAIL, PLEASE SEND THEM TO THE SAME ADDRESS BUT CHANGE THE ADDRESSEE TO:

KYOUSUKE MOTOMI
C/O DENGEKI DAISY
EDITOR

...AND THAT'S IT. THANK YOU VERY MUCH!!

*Meat

I've been craving meat a lot lately. If I could, I'd eat meat three times a day. What's the matter with me? I'm scared. What if I start howling on nights with a full moon?

-Kyousuke Motomi

Born on August 1, Kyousuke Motomi debuted in *Deluxe Betsucomi* with *Hetakuso Kyupiddo* (No-Good Cupid) in 2002. She is the creator of *Otokomae! Biizu Kurabu* (Handsome! Beads Club), and her latest work, *Dengeki Daisy*, is currently being serialized in *Betsucomi*. Motomi enjoys sleeping, tea ceremonies and reading Haruki Murakami.

DENGEKI DAISY
VOL. 11
Shojo Beat Edition

STORY AND ART BY
KYOUSUKE MOTOMI

© 2007 Kyousuke MOTOMI/Shogakukan
All rights reserved.
Original Japanese edition "DENGEKI DAISY"
published by SHOGAKUKAN Inc.

Translation & Adaptation/JN Productions
Touch-up Art & Lettering/Rina Mapa
Design/Nozomi Akashi
Editor/Amy Yu

Printed in the U.S.A.

Published by VIZ Media, LLC
P.O. Box 77010
San Francisco, CA 94107

10 9 8 7 6 5 4 3 2 1
First printing, January 2013

www.viz.com   www.shojobeat.com

This is the last page.

In keeping with the original Japanese comic format, this book reads from right to left—so action, sound effects, and word balloons are completely reversed. This preserves the orientation of the original artwork—plus, it's fun! Check out the diagram shown here to get the hang of things, and then turn to the other side of the book to get started!